CW01066931

A Rude Awakening
"In Search of the Inner Child"
Copyright © 2013 by Patty Smith

*All rights reserved. This book, or parts thereof, may not be used or
reproduced in any form whatsoever or by any means of electronic or
photocopying, without permission from the copyright holder.*
ISBN-13   978-0615762678
ISBN-10   0615762670

*Registered in Library of Congress
Registration Number TXu 1-854-534
For information contact
pattysmithbooks
pattysmithbooks@yahoo.com*

CONTENTS

CONTENTS

A JOURNEY BACK IN TIME

A Rude Awakening: So where did it all begin

Oh children of the world
What will be?
When all of this eventually
Will be passed along on down
To your children pass you and me.

After father's brutal accident, paralyzed and shamed, he hid away for the next sixty years of his unhappy life. The world in which we lived was surrounded by insanity, the walls padded with misery. Having been placed into the trusted arms of Grandfather, did my warning of silence come on that day I ran out to the backyard to escape his roaming hands and probing fingers? My heart thumping, thumping in fright the entire time I sat and played with my dishes. Then the blinds moved off of the dingy hallway, and I met the piercing eyes of grand papa. *He...was watching me!*

Year after year our unfit life style began to mold me into a copy of daddy's rage, a perfect clone. After years of abnormal living, my roads continued to travel on, collecting pain and abuse, leading to a journey of self-destruction. My own allowances always left me searching for my own inner happiness. My wake up call was in fact a rude awakening, with the suicide death of my husband! Here, all the love and care I gave was not enough. Would he have been stronger if I had given less, would he be alive if I had given more? Every emotion my mind cried out turned into self-blame. These destructive emotions of guilt and fault began to haunt me and were brutally reinforced by my husbands grieving family. Besides being filled with their own pain, they were spilling over with animosity. All their bitter words and accusations were pointing at me; it made me sink down to the ground in shame. I couldn't get their verdict out of my head, that it was my hand, my hand alone that drove him to pull the trigger on the gun that day.

At that time, I only could see things through their pained eyes, like many others I blamed myself for all the feelings, actions and reactions of others. It all began to follow me from behind and the days quickly turned into weeks, slipping into months. It was eating at me, churning its way into uncontrolled anger giving me a real serious attitude. Eventually I was overloaded with guilt and my mind sat pondering, whether I was worthy enough to live or contemptible enough to die. For two grave years, life felt empty and I began living unoccupied inside myself. Often the thought of what would happen to my children if I proved contemptible and did away with myself, only added more repercussions. Living inside the walls of my irrational actions and reactions was pushing me over the edge.

Certainly my children were suffering in their own war to survive. Was it my fault; was I selfish, or just broken down and weak? It was true, that I continued to take them down one unstable road after another. Having felt helpless to control or change what was wrongly touching and affecting our lives, brought my head down in shame.

Where does it begin to end?

A desperate cry for help began to manifest, but it wasn't until haunting nightmares of gunshots began echoing off in my head. It was obvious; I needed someone to talk to, but whom? After calling around, perhaps it was fate. Or perhaps, it was merely destiny in which connected me to a family service. Considering that they were willing to accept me with little cash on hand lifted my spirits.

It was obvious even to them; something was unbalanced in my stress, signaling to them, a warning. Coaching me, they gave me verbal support along with an appointment in just two short days. Before hanging up they informed me I would be counseling with a female social worker. Norma! Yes, that was her simple name. Yet, little did I know when she extended her hand out to me, she would guide me to places, few of us dare to return to. It was a place, a place in which we would tremble at the mere thought of those haunting memories.

Those next two days passed quickly, but not before time again broke my spirit and my insides began to churn from anger. On the day I was to meet up with this Norma person, earlier that day everything as usual had gone wrong. By the time I was on my way, dark clouds began to roll in, setting my mood. In the midst of my misery, it began to pour like cats and dogs. The next thing I knew I was lost on a dead end street and I began wondering if I should bother to show up at all. Oh hell, well lets just say I wanted to forget this whole damn thing and just keep on trucking. But to where, obviously I had reached the end of my road.

Having arrived in a very angry state, when this Norma woman smiled at me, my eyes only met hers briefly. Frustrated, my words rambled on, lacking to take the time for introductions, or to monitor her appearance or disposition. Already feeling on the wrong foot, frustration quickly took over and I began complaining about everything that went wrong that day. In chorus with me, I could hear that familiar little voice inside my head sarcastically sneaking its two cents in, "Hum, what the hell does she think she is going to do? What does she know anyway?"

Walking me down to her assigned room, she kindly asked me to have a seat in the chair across from hers. Restless, my eyes toured around the room, appearing to be filled with modest warmth. With a sigh I took to the seat in silence. Self-conscious and ill at ease, my eyes stayed focused on a box of Kleenex, sitting on a small tabletop. Sitting silent and shuffling my feet, the minutes seemed to drag on. Unprepared, my mouth opened and out from nowhere, my self-concealed secret came rolling off my tongue, revealing how disgraceful I was and not worthy to live. The moment my words slipped out, I was immediately sorry. My first mistake so I thought, because I welcomed no one inside my mind. I didn't need, let alone want anyone to tell me how to feel or how to behave. How in the world I wondered, could this Norma person, possibly understand anything. In spite of all my negative thoughts, she somehow kept her distance, while she managed to keep herself focused. By the end of our first appointment, oddly enough I found myself to be calmer somehow. With no argument I promised to return in a few days.

Days later I did in fact return, only this time, I arrived without the anger. Instead, there was a deep sadness lingering in my heart. But still untrusting, I looked into the concerned eyes of this unfamiliar person, who called herself Norma, still wondering what it was that made her think she could possibly help me. Unfamiliar as she was to me she seemed to know just how far she could push forward, without pressuring or driving me away. In the days that followed, she managed to get a little out of me each time I found myself sitting across from her. After weeks passed, I calmly agreed to begin meeting with her weekly. Our sessions slipped by quickly, although I was always aware of her set clock ticking away to the end of my hour. Silent resentment took over for that clock, stirring up my past emotions. It seemed to me as if the hands on that clock were so much more important, than all these troubles sitting right here with me. In reality, my resentment was merely a shield to cover up the fear of being clocked out. But back then, why wouldn't I be afraid of just being tossed aside as a salad, traded for a tastier dish, after all, it was my track record.

All to soon Norma learned which buttons with one simple push would get me fuming in hysterical anger. My reaction was to cover my pain with this kind of simultaneous anger. These emotional outbursts of mine were definitely out of control, being, I was always ready to play the hard roll. Claiming to be really tough was my protection, which allowed my tears to remain falling into the distance. It wasn't until weeks later, when my inner anger finally began to let go. Replacing that anger were my tears, which were no longer in the distance, but right there in Norma's office. Pulling out countless tissues, I now needed that Kleenex box I had once become so aware of. Norma listened more than she used words and she taught me words more than she showed emotion. As time moved forward, it seemed the more we dug, the deeper she helped me to polish away the tarnish that lay heavy on my bones. After one extensive year, I finally began ridding myself of the heavy guilt stemming from my husband's suicide.

When I wonder where you are and wonder where you were, I wonder if you're like a bird, flying high above the clouds, traveling through Eternity... never reaching Destiny. The choice you made became your own... I hope you found your place of home, with GOD alone... I need to believe you are free within.

...The Rescue...

After moods of time passed, I finally began trusting Norma with my heart and soul. Somehow she had managed to work her way backwards and forwards into my dark life. Through her, I learned the power of the words truth, choice and forgiveness. But during the rough times, often stress and confusion entered into the picture. One occurrence, were the tapes recorded in our sessions. When the tapes were played back to me, all of my own reasoning made no sense. It was hard to believe, that I could not hear so many of my own thoughts or words. If I had not heard these words of conviction with my own ears, I would never believe they came out of my own heart. This left any self-denial unavailable to me. But it was there in Norma's presence, when I learned of all these little people dancing inside my head. Always reminding me, that I was not worthy or deserving enough to receive love. It was during one of my sessions, when my big break came crashing through. The memories still vivid, the shock still lays fresh in my mind. A discovery made from a simple image inside of a mirror. This self-image; face to face, eye to eye looking back at me revealed, this horrible person contained within me.

The Punisher!

The earth-shattering discovery of this horrible person brought out a shocking, emotional outburst of tears. All the buildup of emotional pain she caused, let go, wrenching through my body. Yes, she was the one, one of the many little people of a dissimilar personality, living inside my head. She made sure every happy day was ruined some how some way. She was the one, who whispered the nasty words in my head that I was stupid and deserved all the abuse I received from others. Yes, that horrible, horrible, voice was always lurching through haunting and crucifying me. It was a horrifying voice that accompanied me for a lifetime, ultimately, pushing towards self-destruction! "Why oh why," I had cried out "won't she go away?"

I hated her, yes, the same as she hated me!

Once this inner angry person was discovered, I was able to recognize her conscious abuse and began fighting back. After a period of time, it became easier and easier to tell her to get lost. No doubt, it felt ridiculous telling my inner self to get lost. But remarkably, as absurd as it sounds, as I grew stronger, she grew weaker, until eventually, I became stronger than her. It was only then, that I finally had the courage to take her out on that glorious day. In meditation, my mind set her into a small boat and pushed it out to sea into deep waters. My mind continued to hold the vision, as the boat blew up and sank with pieces left scattered out in the distant waters forever. A sense of freedom sailed its way in. Never again will I ever have to hear that inner echoing voice, feeding and feeding me with destruction.

As areas of my life were getting more stable, I began sharing a giggle or two with Norma. Having learned a lot on this journey, I began to realize she held a special quality inside her quiet shell. Her gifts of patience and understanding moved me forward with a comforting persistence. But my inner child, still remained a dark mystery locked away somewhere, deep down inside me. Often memories would flash in my head of grandfather's deceitful, roaming hands. It went hand in hand, with the vulgar swearing, and all of the holidays that ended in horror and tears. It was only after I confessed of my father's brutal ways, surrounded by violence and cruel name-calling, did I want to identify with her. My inner child! This was the same inner child, who held onto all this aggression, only to pass it down through me, to the next generation, my own children.

But during this time with Norma, many new stumps would crop up, interfering with our progress. It would set me back on my old path, with the same pain creeping its way back in. After my moods were going up and down like a yo-yo, I was left dangling on a string. It was apparent, that I was stuck somewhere on the same twisted road, going nowhere. Being it was interfering with my progress I decided to talk with Norma about her suggestion, of going back to recue my lost inner child. By the time my next appointment had arrived and I was seated in her office, I was anxious to approach her. Norma had already forewarned me that seeking out this child could be a very disturbing and painful journey. Yet she was quick to give me courage, reinforcing, that I was the adult now and that only the memories could be painful. But with a calm smile, she assured me that the healing would be joyous and flourishing. She gave me enough courage to continue and I began pouring out a list of uncertainties, "But how do I find this lost child, who lives where?"

Answering delicately she said, "She lives somewhere deep within you." Confused I asked, "Well, just how do I find her?"

Well, "You must go back to the places where you once lived and left her behind."

By now a wave of hesitation moved in and this whole idea of looking for some inner child, was taking a toll on my patience, "But how do I go back to these places, when they don't exist anymore?"

A gentle understanding smile flashed across Norma's face, "But they do my dear, they exist within you."

The session continued long past the hour this time. Left with a strong determination to go back and find my inner child, I was geared up and ready to begin. According to Norma, by emotionally returning back to the places I had once lived in fear, could trigger pain. But she believed this was the way to discover and come forth with truth. Just the thought of all my hidden secrets and shameful actions and memories, that would have to be uncovered, made my heart hammer in fear. It wasn't until the following session, when Norma began guiding me forward with a gentle hand, "first, you must find a warm and comfortable area, where you feel quiet and safe.

While you are in your comfortable state, you can create a safe and tranquil paradise, enabling you to mentally venture out to begin your search."

Alone in my room with only the shadows of night, with the outline of my familiar sights, just knowing this is my safe place. And all I only needed from me was my own belief, through me. With pictures beside me, and a dream catcher…. helping me to see my dreams in reality. Safe in my mind, this place is mine, with the melodies of meditating songs.

By nurture of oneself, is the nurturing to one's mental health.

For me, my place of warmth and comfort was my very own bedroom, which was filled with healing inspirations throughout my counseling. It was in my room, where my mind experienced peace and where I began to create this Paradise. Let me tell you, it was the most magnificent and beautiful place in the whole world. It had a drawbridge over a deep lake, with no other entry to this paradise island. There was only one lift created on my side of the bridge, giving me the choice whether or not to allow anyone to enter my safe little paradise. It was surrounded with beautiful wild flowers of every color imaginable. Trees stood with large branches filled with clusters of leaves. The fullness of the leaves provided shade, while the sounds of the waterfalls, surrounded me with the warmth of its steam. Occasionally I would hear the sounds of nature calling, adding to my inner peace and comfort. All this peaceful beauty reinforced my goals, to venture out and begin my journey. Whenever I mentally traveled to my paradise, I would struggle to travel to the diverse places I had once lived, mostly to return with no progress. But it was there in my safe paradise after several attempts, it finally happened! At long last, I felt sheltered enough to travel all the way back to the house, where it all began. It was a house that held so many painful, burning memories. It was a house of destruction; it was the house of many moods.

Oh mother dear see here, see here, this story must be told. Our broken hearts our shattered dreams, took us to our destiny.

Uncut… In it's natural state

PASSAGE I

Ashes of Time

As a little child within our souls, we blame ourselves for what's not in our control. Where does it begin? Where does it end? And where does all the guilt fit in? The minds you scarred, the hearts you broke took away all our hope. Our child within lives in our heart, we can't seem to ever part. The memories it holds is somewhere within, I can't even start to begin.
...The need in me is to be free of this elasticity...

I begin my journey at the front of the house. Yes, I remember the house was small, its windows and doors forever shut against the daylight. It is a dark place, but not because it was located in the middle of a poor neighborhood, but because of the evil that once shook under its roof. Be brave and journey with me, step across the cracked sidewalk, separated by patches of weeds. Do not be afraid, for though the door looks abandoned and worn it will not harm you. For it is what's inside that shall connect us, for many of my roads are yours. Let us, find the purpose entwined.

Blowing out a slow long breath, I began walking through the tattered colorless door at the front of the house. Three steps in took me to the bottom of the dark hallway. Looking all the way up, up to the top of the dreaded landing, fear came back at me. Suddenly, interrupting the image, daddy's face flashed before me! His thunderous voice was bellowing out, piercing my senses! My first memory of outraged emotions drifted its way in. Now around the age of two, while sitting high upon the shoulders of my strong, handsome, daddy, he began to walk up those steep steps, with his non-crippled legs. Just a few years shy of the accident that changed our lives forever. As he reaches the top of that landing, he uses his strong hands to lift and set me down. Swiftly, he reached for the doorknob that would lead us through the gray, withered door.

...Uh oh! The door is locked...

Daddy begins furiously shaking the knob on the door! Instantly he began frantically looking for the key under the mat. It was nowhere to be found and his whole body began twisting into a fury and that familiar demonizing look takes over. His handsome face turned into ugly-rage as he begins throwing every object down to the bottom of the steps. In the next moment, the sound of objects crashing could be heard over his angry voice bellowing out. It was all vibrating loudly in my head. During which time, the Witch-like-aunt from below peeked up the steps, before her head darted back out of sight. It was here we lived upstairs from her and her dry-alcoholic husband. They never truly seemed to exist in our lives, other than adding misery to mother's heartache. My father and his sister shared many dreadful traits, one of which was a terrible, uncontrollable temper. Often more than not, it was mother who received the blunt end.

That Witch-like-aunt of mine, and when I say Witch-like, well, I would learn and discover that even the wicked witch of Dorothy's Oz could not compare. Sadly, only one good memory sits clear in my mind and even that memory was stained. Being around the age of four is when mother got word; there had been a terrible accident. All mother let us know, was our daddy was sick. It was all we could understand. It was at this time my Witch-like-aunt purchased brand new coats for my sister and me. It was a brand new coat! I was so excited. It was dark brown with a furry hood; even the sleeves were cuffed in fur. Just as my aunt was placing the coats upon our small frames, she cried out:

"Your Daddy's Never Coming Home Again."

Those words my sister and I understood, and our tears fell until mother rocked us both, after our Witch-like-aunt had left. It was only later in life, when I learned our handsome, strong father had fallen backwards into a manhole that had been carelessly covered over by a drop cloth. As he was painting, he stepped back to observe the house and fell into the open black hole. It was horrible for mother and all of life changed around her young years, just being in her early twenties. She cried endless tears for months, watching, as handsome daddy laid in a coma. His thick wavy chocolate brown hair and closed dark brown eyes sat without any life stirring about. The very same strong arms that had once held mother, now lay lifeless with needles taped down feeding him his nourishment. Being that the accident broke his back and caused serious head injuries, it put him in a coma for months. When father finally did regain consciousness, the doctor broke the awful news that he would never walk again. Even as father lived through this painful ordeal, he never grew to accept, that he would remain paralyzed for the remainder of his life. In his mind, he believed he would walk with his once muscular legs, yes; he would be driven to walk!

My thoughts of these recollections began to slowly drift away, pulling me forward in time with another terrifying memory pushing its way in. It was mother! She was running down the street with tears running down her pretty face. Her cries of fright, terrified my young mind. Being close to the age of five, with mother having disappeared down the street, I hid in the dark stairway, cuddling up, on the corner of the step. Quivering inside and out, I was twisting and turning my fingers in a nervous state, when a wave of panic shook me. It was daddy! He was sitting in his wheelchair, all the way at the top of the dark landing, echoing down my name in full volume. After continuing to ignore him, he bellowed out, "Get up here now."

Frightened I halfway turned around, whimpering out, "No, you hurt my mama."

His voice suddenly became soft and needy, holding his composure, as he sadly began half crying out to me by my pet name, "Beaky nose, don't you love me any more?"

With my own tears running by now, I cried out to him, "No, you hurt my mama, you hurt my mama. I hate you, I hate you!"

Daddy was finished trying to persuade me with his normal short span of patience and affection. He was back to being the angry daddy I knew. His shaking fist, all his uncontrolled swearing, came to a head with a kitchen knife flying down the steps. Jumping up in fear, I began running down the street, as fast as my short little legs would take me calling and calling out, "Mommy…mommy…mommy…where are you?"

Near the end of the street, I found mother and my sister sitting on a neighbor's front porch step. Mothers trembling hands were covering her face, rocking back and forth sobbing, "What do I do, oh what do I do?"

With a blotchy face, my sister was sitting on the step above her with her eyes cast down to the ground. Periodically, she would reach her small hand over; patting mother's slumped over shoulder. Being children, we sat quiet and dazed, while mother cried out all her fears to the neighbor. To us, it seemed like an eternity before mother gained the courage to return home. Only she was leaving us behind, and she was already thanking the neighbor lady for keeping us. Mother never gave us the chance to argue her down. Looking worn and worried, mother put her finger up to her lips, promising she would call for us; once our daddy was not angry. When mother did call for us, and we had returned home, we saw her scrubbing off the mess of dried red ketchup, splattered across the wall. Once mother saw us, she put her finger up to her lips, silencing and motioning us to go to our room. Shaken and frightened, we did as mother signaled, while she turned her tearful face away, continuing to scrub. The next day, we would be shipped over to dear old grandfather's house, until the war at home would pass. His arrival was precise. There he stood silently waiting for us in his blue dungarees, holding out two green apples from his trees. His only expression came from the loud sound of his unclear breathing, coming from deep down in his lungs. My heart began to pound harder than before. But it wouldn't have helped. It was time to leave and grandfather took us each by the hand, as he walked us out that door.

Poor mother, it wasn't what she did that threw daddy into another rage that day. But rather, that she stood guilty, for allowing one of her family members, to dare pass through our gray withered door. Mother definitely had broken all the rules! Those almighty rules of father's, no trespassing, no entering and no interference allowed. Therefore, mother was sentenced to his rage of brutal abuse. After daddy had imprisoned himself inside the house, as far as he was concerned, we were all off limits to society. Being so young when his rules went into force, I never knew life any other way. It became a natural setting for everyone who entered into our world, to be thrown out with casting words. Just like the television repairman who got tossed out in daddy's rage, whom by the way eventually became mother. Mother became the all, the plumber, the painter and even the electrician. It was all arranged under daddy's supervision and management, with his voice bellowing in the background at her.

Although, there is one rare entity from daddy's long list of rules, the acceptance of one particular family member. For some unknown reason, daddy offered this rare authorization for mother's younger sister Aunt Jenny and her quiet husband Uncle Stan to visit. Uncle Stan always brought along his wonderful, calming voice, while aunt Jenny was the gentlest of souls. My Aunt and Uncle were as close to normal as anyone I ever saw anyway. Due to the world we lived in, they were a rarity. In effect, they were not fearful of father, like everyone else was. They just acted as if they did not hear his padded, spiteful words of humor. In spite of his sly secrecy to anyone witnessing his dished out cruelty, I am sure they were able to read between the lines. They even had the courage, to bring along their one-year-old daughter Missy, who was four years, my junior. Little did she know, years later down the road, she would become a very important link on a rough and rugged ride with me, straight through Hell! Poor Missy didn't even know then what was going to hit her.

But it was that earth-shattering day, when mother was running down the street in terror; I learned even mommy's needed to be taken care of. So this is how I learned to express myself, by throwing things! Abusive conditions began to cause me to look over my shoulder, worrying and harboring over mother. It sure didn't take long, to begin to learn to attack back in a verbal, child like manner, whenever daddy hurt mommy, unlike my sister Eileen. My lovely, delicate sister was a year older and stood taller and thinner than I. Her name Eileen matched her beautiful long blond hair and green eyes. As a rule, her eyes seemed to hold vacant, never allowing them to expose any of her emotions. Recalling as early as my memory allows, I never knew or could imagine, what went through her mind during those times of violence. We never talked about our life; we were living as if we both just accepted our own roles within this play. The only similarity that identified both of us, was the fact, that daddy gave us nicknames, including mother. Emphasizing her thinness, daddy nicknamed Eileen, Sucker Stick. One way or another, it always appeared to attack her self-image. Considering I didn't really know what went through her mind, her frown was the only thing that displayed her dislike for that name. Now mother was so very thin, fragile and sensitive, having lived an ongoing traumatic life. She had long dark curly hair, accompanied by a set of soft, brown sad eyes. Those brown eyes she held were the same sad eyes, which learned early in her youth to conceal her fears. Her nickname became Oh, Slalina, or hey you Slalina. Now for myself, I wore blond hair and was just a little one, period. My dark brown eyes stood out, telling all. My nickname became Beaky-nose, especially when I kept my mouth shut and was willing to bear my own pain. Father definitely practiced his ritual of nicknames amongst us, we and the world, were under his verbal attacks. But, because Beaky-nose was the only gift of emotion I could own, I grew to cherish this name, especially when he was the one calling out to me.

These memories all began to fade into the distance and new memories began to flourish, and I was going back to that God forsaken place. After collecting my thoughts, I began once again seeking out the little girl who was once me. After traveling up the steep stairway, I entered through the gray withered door leading into the house, with new memories rising and falling in. Catching me off guard, a strong familiar scent of urine, which had forever lingered in our closed in air, caught my senses. I had forgotten that simple smell! Memories began surrounding me, of my father and all the humiliation in which we were made to live. The amplified bellowing of voices, with the sound of objects shattering, came out from nowhere. A war between Daddy and Grandfather was in full force. My belly began to churn, wanting to push away those deceitful recollections of that period in time. Grand Papa's dirty hands of love and affection! It was after daddy threw the knife at me, that I had to spend vigilant time with him. Good old grandfather would come and pick me up himself, taking me over to his house.

Breathing life into this recollection was arousing the memorized sounds of the disquieting ride to his house. In the midst of the silent atmosphere, were the harmonized beats coming from his turn signal, clicking on and off, in melody to the rhythm of my heart. His posture leaned heavily back into the drivers' seat, while his free hand wrapped tightly over mine. His rough, spotted hand, displayed a finger that was only half remaining. He drove in utter silence until we entered Bird-Town, then, he would release my hand from his. By the time his turn signal took us into his long narrow driveway and the sound of his engine cut off, my heart was skipping beats. After getting out of his car and walking with his assistance, past a large apple tree with its trunk marked with oozing sap, he silently led me into the large, gray house, empty of any presence.

Often I felt a sting of rejection from grandmother, for whenever I arrived, she would disappear. Was she turning her back on this darkness, or simply lacking affection, since I was not her flesh and blood? With grandmother gone, only a silence sat ticking between the walls and us. Only the seconds of the clock could be heard over the sound of his unclear breathing. Near the age of five, upon entering grandfather's dark bedroom for the very first time, a new beginning of unfamiliar fear rushed through. Oh, how I hated his dark bedroom that grew with time, familiar! His dark old chair sat in the corner of his dark and dingy room. And the old, dark purple drape hung straight across the door-less opening, guarding against prying eyes. That vibrating sound of his unclear breathing would intensify, just as that strange dazed look contained inside those deep, dark eyes took over in affection. He held total privacy, while I held total fear learning the silence of the lamb, as he held me upon his lap. That dirty, Grand Papa! He held the hands that found all the places that filled my heart with shame, and this term we call dirt. My Grand Papa, who I loved and trusted, gave me all the silent fear of love and dread.

My first warning of silence came on that day I ran outside to escape him and all of my fear and panic had followed me from behind. As I hesitatingly began playing and fidgeting with my dishes, is when I saw the blinds off the back window slowly move and I met the dark piercing eyes of Grand Papa. …. *He Was Watching Me*...

That was to be my warning, for the next several years to come. Even today, I am torn in which word, stands to be more valuable trust or earned! I lost trust at the age of five, following the word respect, never to feel I earned anything. To lose something as important as trust and respect and to never recapture them back, are lethal to our souls.

As Grandfathers dazed eyes began fading away, I found myself once again back in the house where the misery had all began. My eyes began to travel throughout the house, when I came face to face with the awful room holding countless memories. Here was that room filled with despair, an empty room with only the whispers of misery. That horrible room where all the exercise equipment laid was flashing in my head, reminding me of fathers' drive to walk. One day he will walk again, driving himself mad every single day of his empty, angry life. He was walking, while he was holding on to those shinny steel parallel bars. One-step forward…one step forward. The loud thumping sound from each braced shoe forcefully hit the attached board, accompanied by his unhappy mumbles. Hearing those agonizing sounds of steps, I covered my ears, pushing in silence, till the whispers moved away. It was almost beyond belief how mother, sister, and I grew up through all those years. Everyday, we grew to listen to the sound of each thump from his braced-shoe hitting that board, as if it were a clock, forewarning us how much time we had left till his return.

With twisted thoughts, once again my mind passed through the exercise room resting on a lonely, uninviting looking single bed in the far corner of the room. The bed mother slept upon! Daddy always slept on a mat, which remained in this everlasting, untidy mess, lying in the middle of the living room floor. My thoughts carried me to our small dingy living room. A dark, colorless room it was. The blinds were pulled tightly closed all the way down. The room appears as dark and dingy and as closed off as our lives would continue to remain. In the middle of my thoughts, I shuddered, for there they sat! Fathers set of shinny, silver bar bells, sitting heavy and overbearing alongside his mat. Being they were his means of gaining strength, for he was driven to exercise. Yet, who would think, anyone would gain strength by throwing them at their children! Yet our daddy, through his manipulative nature did walk, all over We, my sister my mother, and me.

Later in life, it wasn't difficult to see into my own mothers' life of abuse she had suffered, which was surrounded by the illnesses that poverty carries. After her own mother was buried on the Eve of Christmas at the age of ten, she was placed into an orphanage. Her life growing up with this old school discipline was surrounded by cruelty, leaving its mark of acceptance upon her. She remained living there, until her father remarried and she lived with her resentful and cruel stepmother. A few years later, she met and fell in love with father. After her marriage, the Church played an important role, seeing mother was committed to their well-known law, never divorce and always obey. Being not much more than a child herself, mother lacked the proper guidance to human rights or choices. Back then; these alternatives were non-existent. This left mother crippled to alter her life or try to save her own children, let alone her self.

So, that desperate need to continue searching for that room, that room containing me, drove me forward with purpose. At this point in time, I had grown to believe it was my inner child, whom held the major key that would allow me to begin to heal. Days fell into weeks of emotionally returning back…back to that house, filled with scandalous dismay. Only to find, upon my return, only my tears returned with me. Norma gave me her support, guiding me patiently with cause. Perhaps it was merely purpose, which gave me the strength and strong determination to continue on with my search. Seeing as I desperately needed to find and untangle this mess of emotions, that was held captive somewhere in my mind by my inner child, gave me additional courage. After having repeatedly returned back to that terrifying house, upon reentering through the gray withered door, an image of me, quickly flashed in my head, recharging my memory.

Out from nowhere, the child's bedroom that was once mine stood out in my head. Boldly looking in, my eyes met a sad room containing no joy or rays of sunlight. The blinds in this room were undeniably closed just as tightly as I had imagined. This colorless room held the same familiarity as the untidy, dark living room. In the midst of emotion, my eyes set upon a plain and simple setting of two beds and a crammed-in dresser. Glancing over to the bed, there on the first bed was the image of my sister Eileen. Oh Eileen, you are so lovely, just as I remember you my sister. But how sad and lonely you are, yes, in a sad and lonely way, she was my only company. My eyes wandered inches away from Eileen, over to the bed once belonging to me. There, sitting upon the edge of the bed,

...She sat...

Shaken, I penetratingly sucked in my breath in sorrow. There she sat silent! All that remained were the emotions of pain and fear that were hiding inside her dormant being. Indisputably, she was a pitiful sight of a sad and lonely child. Her head hung low, while her blond hair was resting around her face. Her small delicate being was reflecting the image of hopelessness. As I began inching my way closer to her, the overwhelming emotions I began to feel were taking me to the plateau of my destination. Sitting down, at the end of what was once my bed, I reached over, cradling her up into my arms. It was so real, as if I was truly there in the flesh and could actually feel the warmth of blood that ran through her body. The frantic need as an adult to ease her pain set in and I began rocking this child's image back and forth. Only the feelings of regret were inside my head, repeating over and over, how sorry I was that I had left her behind.

In some moment of time, I became aware of the sound of loud sobbing somewhere in the distance. It didn't take long to realize, I was weeping to and weeping back from my safe paradise. Weeping and weeping, for this miniature imagine of huge emotion. Oh dear God how she suffered. It took a while before my body was no longer penetrating the pain and for my breathing to return to its normal state. Drained, my mind felt depleted. Oh, but I was so very tired and drifted off into a deep-rooted sleep, lasting for hours.

Upon awaking came a sense of inner peace, surrounding me. It was only then, as an adult looking back at the pure innocence of myself as a child, could I cast out in anger, "How in God's name, is it possible for so many self serving adults to help themselves and devour up a lifetime, by placing their weaknesses and filthy actions, on to the minds and souls of the young and innocent! Oh God, but it hurts so bad, and the pain brought on a wave of continued tears, until a release like I have never known, came to light. Going back, past the old withered door, into the house of darkness and shame, hurt like hell. But Norma was right; the return was joyous and flourishing. After somehow being emotionally tied together with my inner child, a great determination to continue on this journey moved forth. There was still another long, rocky road to begin, demanding truth and forgiveness for all the horror once left behind.

PASSAGE II

Thunder in the Tummy

The Rock is so like, Thunder with the sounds of power within a roar. The lifting of weight in strength fallen… to travel in great length… from the Rock of low earth, to the thunder of great high… from the lands of the Majestic… within of no disguise. Last, came the rains.

An empty vision of nothingness now stands, of the cracked sidewalk, leading up into the dark scary stairway, past the gray withered door that led straight into hell.

Our burning warmth transferred over with us to another house, located just six miles away on a neighborhood street. Past the echoes of children's laughter in the air, were all the curious eyes of the neighbors looking on. Forget those curious eyes looking and looking, for in daddy's eyes they did not exist. But there was one thing he could not deny; this house had a peaceful yard, where a large cherry tree sat, offering its comfort and tranquility for the taking.

But, the hands of time still held no peace. Because an identical exercise room, with the same sounds of the same thumps, of the same forced braced shoe, hitting the same wood board, had moved in with us. Also accompanying us were the same sounds of the same whispers with the same unhappy mumbles. All this misery was packaged, in the very same violent daddy! Right smack in the middle of our new tiny living room floor, once again, laid daddy's disruptive mat! Representing his bed, like a clock keeping time, he would slide down from his chair, onto his mat every single night at the hour of eight p.m. sharp. Our life was ticking to the clock while the blinds remained closed, the walls surrounding us with misery. There was no question about it that the world in which we lived, was filled with insanity.

But mother, no longer would sleep on a small, lonely single bed, which sat in the corner of his exercise room. This time she received the worn down couch in the living room, as her deserving place of rest. But as tired and depleted as mother was, she tried endlessly to mend daddy's cruel moods of destruction, trying to carry the heavy burden of supporting the household. She would have to leave early morning, just as the birds began chirping to go work in a hot factory, while Eileen and I remained with our daddy Joe. It took no time for mothers mind to begin getting bogged down with guilt and fear. Her fear for leaving us alone with him and the guilt for not being there to save us ate away at her daily. When she could take no more, she threw in the towel, quit her job and became daddy's full time verbal punching bag. In spite of her fight to stay home to protect us, with the bills overloading, she had no choice, but to admit defeat.

She took on a carhop job working evenings at a drive-in restaurant just two houses away. Being only a blink away enabled her to breathe more comfortably, in the event she needed to run home for anything! With mother so close, Eileen and I would sit and watch her from our bedroom window, carrying trays of food out to the cars. Even though we thought it was way cool, daddy simple objected. He did not like mother working, he wanted her home to receive and obey his rules and commands.

Wrapped around his controlling commands, were his accidental bowel movements. The control factor was, that daddy often used this to keep mother at his beck and call. Regardless of the normal difficulty father held with this medical matter, he still had his own conniving ways he kept in storage, until he needed them for attack. Whenever mother left and was not home, right when the hour of his clock said so, he would wait! Right at the given moment she walked through the door, he would immediately go into a rage and begin his attack of dumping on her. In a rage, he blamed mother, because she was gone so long, he accidentally messed his pants. So mother was left like always to clean up the crap, while guarding against any foreign objects that might get flung her way. But she was always repaid well with his famous harsh, hateful words, "You stupid, no good blah, blah, blah…when I found you, I found you in the gutter blah, blah, blah…when I met you, you had nothing but holes in your shoes and holes in your underwear and awe~~ if it were not for me, you would be nothing, nothing, nothing!"

He would go on and on, until he was depleted and worn down. As a young child I carried this impression of mother having walked around with her clothes raged out and her toes sticking out from her shoes. But with mother away, there were many days in our lives when we felt extremely sorry for daddy. We would try so hard to take care of him, regardless of the ill treatment this would stir. Daddy would woo you into his web of need, only to chew you up with disrespect. Our bubble burst, when out from nowhere, his temper would flare our way. Becoming confused and afraid, we did whatever we could, until his temper cooled down. Afterward mother took us aside, attempting to soothe over our tears and resolve our uncertainties. With pained eyes, she reminded us that he didn't mean to hurt us and we must try to forgive him, for it was not his fault. In spite of his cruelty we still loved our daddy Joe, besides he was all we had and all that we new. There were the times he would cry for forgiveness to mother. He would cry for all the cruel things he had done, momentarily, feeling our terror from his actions and cursed words. He would be sorry and for a little while, there would be contentment in our home. On these occasions father bloomed, he only held those moments of sweet-blossomed pleasure, for a short time. He would roar with laughter calling out, "Oh Slalina…oh Sucker stick…oh Beaky-nose."

Were we his special babies, or were we his pincushions? It didn't make a difference to me, as long as I could rarely be, his special baby. Although when mother was away, my sister built some kind of imaginary wall to protect herself from daddy's brutal ways. For she always kept herself and her heart, at a distance. To stay into the distance, meant you would not fall into his spell of affection, only left to receive the ending result, pain. The drawback of having received no pain was to receive no care and no love. Looking back Eileen appeared misplaced somehow, as if she didn't blend in. Perhaps, she was just fighting for her life and didn't want to believe she belonged in this life of cruelty and madness. One thing, she was convinced that I was daddy's little everything. In spite of her living in her own protected shell, we had our shared close times as children. It was true, we shared many a giggle and many tears, but we also shared little to the truth of the reality to how we lived. We kept our boundaries away from such talk. Ultimately we remained confused of who was who and what was what, never knowing, what was expected or what was accepted.

Daddy was still undeniably, a creator of his own kind of tornados.

Somehow his ferocious anger could affect all the people who loved and encircled him, us. But still, I carried no true fear to the power nature held. Never did I know or could imagine anything equal to my daddy's rage, that is to say, until a violent storm moved in, greater than daddy himself. It was early evening when the winds began to howl. Bright flashes of lighting intensified the skies, accompanied by strong blowing winds. You could feel the vibrations inside your tummy, as it ripped through the air with a loud boom of thunder. Suddenly hearing this awful earth shattering crash and boom, we ran to the window and tried to peak through the blinds and fogged up the window. With the winds still blowing up a storm, we waited to investigate until the storm calmed down. As quickly as the winds died, with excitement in the air, we dashed out the door one by one. After viewing in horror our large, beautiful, cherry tree that lay lifeless on the ground, our excitement fell, brining us down from our loss. It had stood so tall and protective only moments before, providing us with what little relief and comfort we had against the storm, forever brewing inside our disruptive house. As we were staring down at our fallen beautiful tree in disbelief, the high winds took a turn and immediately turned on us. Running to the porch behind mother for cover, while leaning over the rail, you could see down the street that trees and limbs were down everywhere. Reaching for the door to get back safely into the house, somehow, the door had locked behind us and mother cried out "Oh dear God."

Suddenly it was a downpour and with the winds blowing at us, mother desperately grasped on to the doorknob and began shaking it as frantically as daddy had done on that day so long ago! The night was falling and it was now the hour of eight, daddy's time. Undoubtedly by now, he was heading down onto his mat. As a wave of terrifying chills ran through us, we began to loudly bang nonstop on the door, yelling out over the howling wind, "Let us in. Oh please daddy, daddy, let us in!"

He wasn't answering and no matter how much we yelled and pounded on that door, he continued to ignore us. Standing on the open porch in fear, suddenly I felt small and naked against the storm. This was unlike any storm that daddy had ever released. Fear kept my blood pumping as we continued to franticly pound and yell all at the same time. Finally his voice sailed out, cursing loud enough to pierce the wind and rain, right through the door. His rage followed his silence, followed by nothing. In a panic, I was terrified he would just leave us all out there until a ferocious wind would come down and sweep us all away and I wondered in a child's capacity, if he would be happy that he finally got rid of us forever. After what felt like a lifetime of vibrating thunder and fear, mother got a grip and took the situation into her own hands. We watched as she got down on her hands and knees and literally smashed in the basement window with a round rock. Carefully, she reached her hand in-between broken glass and turned the rusty lock and pushed the wood frame open. As mother crawled into the narrow opening, there sat a vision of our rubber lonely-looking bathtub. In an instant it brought to memory, the colossal tantrum father threw over our porcelain bathtub.

We never did see my Witch-like-aunt's face after we moved from the house with the steep, scary stairway. But father's brother, whose face never existed before in our life, was strangely over that afternoon. Who I will momentarily call, my Uncle Who? Well, that's all it took to lose our tub. He came over trying to make changes in the inadequate space in the bathroom. He was trying to move a wall so father could maneuver his wheel chair in to get to the toilet. Once my uncle's last attempts failed, all hell broke loose. The next thing you knew, tempers began to fly, right out with the good old bathtub. At ears length there were loud, thunderous voices bellowing in the background. Now suddenly, there were two echoes of angry voices, both identical to one another, both trying to drown out the other! All of a sudden, Uncle Who got thrown out along side of a big bundle of debris. It was one big mess, landing everywhere. Right along side of the debris, was a big bag of orange marshmallow candy. All that yummy candy was thrown out the door, right behind my uncle. He had brought them over for my sister and me, bringing a bright sparkle to my eyes. All I could think about was getting my hands on all that candy, scattered in the yard against the debris. Having been hiding and listening from inside daddy's exercise room, it began eating away at me real bad. Especially, since you could see the orange candy in clear vision, right through the gaps of the lifted blinds. I began to think hard, as hard as any child could anyway, how to scheme to sneak outside, to get my hands on that candy.

Tearing all the way up the stairs, I ran as fast as my short legs would take me to our bedrooms. My mission was to search for my sister, in hopes she could help to retrieve it. The moment my eyes found Eileen, her vision stopped me dead in my tracks. Oh, my poor sister's little body was cradled up in the corner of her bed, sobbing and trembling all over. She was so terrified of the odd double echo of angry voices, vibrating throughout the house. She held no care in retrieving the candy. With my persistence, she only curled herself up tighter against her headboard, turning her face away in silence. What a let down, never had I ever seen Eileen so emotional. Never, in fact, I always thought she was just, well, just the opposite of me. She never showed any feeling of rejection or suffering, let alone this outburst of sobbing. Or did she? It was the first and last time anyway, that she ever let me see her sob. Eileen seemed to become more and more of a silent, timid little girl, after the episode with Uncle Who. She began learning to always look over her shoulder in fear, in fact, she became afraid to even voice any opinion or anger. Quite the opposite, I grew up looking over my shoulder believing I was the strong one, ready to throw a blow. Looking over our shoulders today is as normal as looking straight ahead. But it was that day, when both the bathtub and candy were thrown out with Uncle Who, who neither of us ever saw again!

It was the very same day that the cold, damp, creepy basement, moved into play. Throughout the entire time we lived there, that basement is where we had our comforting bath time. This grey rubber bathtub sat on a cold, cement floor. On the ceiling, attached to an old wood beam, a light glared bright, from an uncovered light bulb. Yet there was something good about that rubber bathtub we owned. It became our very own, portable friend and swimming pool. It weighed so little; we could lug it outside ourselves. For me, it was an uncomplicated childlike blessing. Being, it became a way for me to get even with the cruel neighborhood children, for being so mean and driving me away. Whenever I would have to walk to the corner store for bread or milk, the children down the street would spot me watching them. They would be jumping up and down splashing away in their two-foot pool, having the time of their life. Upon seeing me, they would splash the water from their pool over in my direction, yelling and screaming out in glee. "The swimming pool wants you to get out of here; the swimming pool wants you to get out of here."

Stung by their cruel laughter, I drifted away. But after returning home, my rejected heart fantasized the company of my own batch of invisible friends, while we were splashing away. My invisible circle of friends mimicked right along side of me, as we chanted out with glee to the cruel invisible children, watching at the end of our driveway, "The rubber tub wants you to get out of here…the rubber tub wants you to get out of here."

But past the hurt those children often gave, we didn't hold on to any silly fears for our rubber tub. However, that basement did hold a scary, huge black hole in the wall. It was larger than the two of us put together. Both Eileen and I were always afraid to look in the big dark opening. As children, we believed the boogieman was hiding in this scary darkness. Yet there was something safe to be gained here. In spite of all our fear of this opening, the truth was, we were both away from daddy! So we overcame one fear to escape another. But that scary basement allowed us to have some fun, roller-skating, giggling and playing tag and all. We knew it was just a matter of time, till the next clatter of disturbance came roaring down the steps at us. But any happy memories while playing with my sister, that weren't shadowed by daddy's dark energy, are few. In life there were times when I dwelled on whether it is better to have distressed memories, than to have none.

Without question, all of fathers control factors even affected our time we tried to share with mother. So much so, we never even ate together as a family, except on Sunday. Mother always pushed away the issue, saying it was just best this way. Quickly I began to understand more and more, exactly what she meant. In spite of the fact we were very poor and dinners were tightly scraped together, our Sunday festive dinner desert, always turned out to be daddy's fist landing on the table in fury. But in spite of daddy's flying fist, I grew to love Sundays. Indeed, it was not due to the sit down dinner jamboree, but rather, we were out of the house and got to go to church. Every Sunday after mass, we would stop off at the corner drugstore and mother would hand us each ten-cents. Eileen and I were allowed, a two-cent bar of candy. With the remaining change, I always bought a wonderful comic book and would sit in my room reading Little Lulu all day, escaping into the life of the comic book. Despite all of the negativity surrounding our lives, it was a blessing in disguise that we each received our own tiny bedroom, up on the second floor, out of daddy's reach. Mother of course did not occupy one of these rooms, seeing she had to stand at attention for all father's demands. Get me water, get me my newspaper, change the channel, thank God we only had channels three, five, and eight. Oh poor mother, it got so, she eventually became father's personal, homemade remote control.

Anywhere in our house containing steps, was a step away to another safe escape from daddy. Since our possessions were limited, in spite of having little to occupy us, we stayed up in our rooms for hours. Beyond listening to tunes on the am radio, Eileen stayed in her own little world, while I concentrated on my dolls. Oh how I loved the dollies I possessed, especially my "Raggedy Ann." My sister actually never did take to dolls, nor did she try to have anything to do with mine. It left me in disbelief, wondering, without dolls, what was there. But, it was there in my room where I would spank my naughty dolls and yell in their immovable faces. They each received the very same ill treatment that we were experiencing. Some days I would punish them by throwing them into the wide-open, pitch-black attic, in the corner of my room. Not ten minutes later, when I felt lonely and needed them, I would use a flashlight and go retrieve them. After preaching to them how bad and stupid they were, every one of my bruised dolls was right back in bed with me, while I held on to them for dear life.

But daddy had his occasional on again off again soft spurts of neediness and he would call up to us from the bottom of the stairway using our nicknames. Nicknaming everyone he came into contact with from a distance became his most cherished past time. He went as far as cruelly nicknaming all the people on his favorite programs. In-between all father's boredom and his creative angry imagination; he began drawing art in the newspaper. He would add deformed images to the people's photographs, adding in his own editorial feedback. During these times when he was consumed with his cruel drawing and feedback, he would let out loud roars of demented laughter. He seemed to always appear, well proud, as if he were standing tall. Maybe, he wanted to believe he was the editor of our newspaper, for he really got into writing daily graffiti all over it to wound and insult mother. He also took it upon himself to vote himself in and be elected the N.C.T, which stands for, narrator and controller of the television channels. For which his vote stood, the one and only vote, for as long as we remained in his clutches. Being we were allowed to watch, only the programs he had underlined in the newspaper guide, it would be fair to say, the newspaper was controlling our lives. It was when daddy was in his exercise room; mother would switch channels and put on cartoons. In-between the sounds of our laughter and the low volume on the television, we kept an open ear to the background echoes of his braced shoes hitting the board. When the sound of thumps came to a standstill, it told us it was the end of his hour and for us to promptly hush-hush. Often, mother would slip past daddy's rules, just to let us do some enjoyable things, while she always warned us to be quiet.

But on the other side, oh how I loved those cozy cuddling times with daddy. I would lay next to him on his mat, watching his favorite TV show, and come to think of it, Eileen was nowhere to be seen. Poor Eileen, she never went for that on and off kind of affection. Not like me, a love starved child willing to accept love at any cost. Perhaps, she resented it or realistically she didn't know how to weasel her way into daddy's expensive affection. Well for me, that was simple. You simply had to buy it, you bought it; knowing his love portion wouldn't last on a thin dime, and you paid the price, with his on the spot vengeful return. Who knew when his mood of destruction would decide to make your heart bleed and don't you cry! For if your tears turn to hysteria, all then would be left lying in the distance, while he was watching his boob-tube, feeling full and satisfied, with his own successful, triumph.

In the middle of mother's corner-to-corner world, somehow her long silent cry for help got around the church we attended. My poor naive mother was so ashamed and full of guilt and dishonor whenever she went to confession. She believed after carrying a death wish for father, she had sinned bad enough to go to Hell. Years ago, times and attitudes were different. You never heard of a woman leaving her healthy husband, let alone someone paralyzed. You would have been stoned and hung out to dry with ruthless words being cast out to you in judgment. Even the priest reminded her, that no matter what, there was no such thing as divorce in the eyes of the church. A gentle pat on the back, proclaiming this was her cross to bear, was the answer of all answers. Upon urging her to see someone who might be able to help, he took the liberty and gracefully guided a counselor into her direction. Well, when father got word, hell rose up and things got pretty hot for mother. For days, his thunderous disruptive pitch played on and on in the background. In spite of father's fight to instill the fear of God in mother, she somehow managed to stand strong and dodge all of his cruelty. In her strong determination, she began seeing a counselor, dragging me along. Between the toys in the play area and all the extra attention that came my way, I never minded one little bit.

Oh but daddy did. It never failed, right before she was ready to walk out the door; he would deliberately start a war. With a song and dance, he began passing out an earful of knee quivering, heart pounding threats to mother. Before she could turn the knob and get out that door, he'd turn on her. Reinforcing his grave intent that if she dared to walk out that door, all that would be left remaining of him would be his neck, hanging limp from a rope. Mother would leave, but you could perceive her stained face and vacant eyes on the long, silent bus ride there. But upon returning home, father was always still very much alive. In fact his sinister mood had mellowed out and he was back to being the daddy I knew, that is, until the next appointment rolled around. It's needless to say that counseling did not outlast the hotheaded fight from father. Being there wasn't a chance in hell for mother, once again, help remained in the far distance.

Near the age of seven, I was hungry enough to land my very first friend. She hung with her sister at the corner delicatessen, where the colorful gumball machines sat. Her name was Jezebel and she was mentally handicapped, a little girl, less than perfect. Perhaps this made daddy feel better about him self in one-way or another. Jezebel wasn't picture pretty, actually, both her actions and personality were on the clumsy side; bringing attention to her over elevated height, which stood out as if she were misplaced. But she looked just fine to me and I loved playing with my friend, even in spite of the fact, everyone made fun of her. But then, everyone made fun of me. Even while all the children in the neighborhood would constantly make fun of our family, Jezebel never noticed and never received the gift of mentality, as we know. But since all the other children believed I had the crazy daddy, this brought on oodles of laughter. The kids from the neighborhood's biggest thrill came from banging on our door, until daddy's angry voice came roaring out. They would scamper off, screeching at the top of their lungs, as if a boogieman was going to get them. So my only friend Jezebel, in her quiet odd way, was my only company past mother and Eileen. Until, her family moved away, sending Jezebel off to live with her aunt. Missing Jezebel in the days that followed left me feeling pretty blue for as long anyway, as anyone in our house was allowed to dwell on anything, past daddy.

But after having had a taste of friendship, it was a real let down and I believed it was just not in my shuffle. Not like the cards my sister was dealt, because this popularity contest, of how many kids were keen on her, was out of character and unacceptable. In my head, it was totally unfair. Whenever she got to go to the corner for bread or milk, she would sneak out longer. She got fun rides on the handlebars of her friend's bicycles. She even received a beautiful diamond ring from a boy. It didn't matter it was plastic; it was only the sparkle I saw. Making me mad, she would walk a spell with her new friends, with her long blond hair blowing in the wind. They would take turns carrying a black radio in their arms that was blaring out groovy tunes. You heard all their happy voices singing, "an itsy bitsy, teeny weenie, yellow polka dot bikini la, la, la," There was no way that she could hide her secret independence from me, considering, she had to drag me along. It was mother's rule and that was that. So I'd tag from behind and just watch. She was always acting like she was so old, little miss smarty-pants, yelling out at me, "Go away, get lost, you're too young."

Feeling left out, I would stomp off mumbling all the way home, come to think of it, kind of like daddy. Oh, but Eileen had the power to make me so mad, leaving me to cry and wonder, "Why her and not me?"

It was plain and simple; I was overwhelmed in jealousy of her great acceptance. Between my envy and resentment, I threaten to tell all her secrets to daddy, but Eileen was smarter than I. She turned the table, leaving me plenty worried about what it was she was going to tell on me. Maybe it was something I had done while he was in that room, stomping and whispering away. Frightened I backed off, I couldn't take the chance; maybe just maybe, she had some kind of loaded ammunition. There was no question about it, both of us held on to our own fears and insecurities. Living in what one might consider hell, contributed to the darkness we both lived within ourselves. It got so, that neither of us could see the light into each other's doorways, let alone our own. But, there was once a light of hope for Eileen, after she begged to take dancing lessons. After her glow faded, her hope slowly dwindled away. But being there was never money for such foolishness, our dreams became something we did only in our sleep. Consequently, Eileen continued to weep for her loss of a dream, while I missed my one and only friend, Jezebel.

PASSAGE III

Indecent Proposal

The actions of child molesting are the greatest of sin. You need not bother saving your dollars… there will be no buying in. The innocents of child you took with gained control… will live forever grieved, within a heart forever torn

After my short-lived friend Jezebel had disappeared from the picture, daddy began allowing me to venture out door to door. It was right when he got a new hobby! He had sent away for mail order can openers and boot bags, resembling today's backpacks with handles. His proud little Beaky-nose, was about to become a sales girl. All I had to do was smile cute and tell these strangers, "My daddy's crippled in a wheelchair and I'm trying to earn money for food."

My poor mother, she never really had a say in the issues of what father controlled, which of course, was everything. My youth must have done the trick, for my sales quickly began climbing up the ladder. Oh how proud my Daddy-Joe was of my pile of singles. As a reward, Eileen and I got to go out to an occasional Saturday matinee. Oh but how well that nauseating memory of that Saturday afternoon still sits fresh in my mind. On that particular day, my sister and I excitedly scurried off to the show to see a very scary movie. Scary situations were not the only thing we were familiar with, but it was also the only blood circulating excitement we ever knew. We sat in the very last row, plopping down next to each other with both our hands full of buttered popcorn. It could be nothing but a glorious day in our minds. Squirming around in the theater chair, I was fooling around as usual, paying no attention to my surroundings. Out from the corner of my eye, next to me an odd movement caught my attention. There, is where the horrible man sitting next to me, was stroking his penis. Instantly, I could feel myself freeze up, suddenly, I was frozen. When he began making weird sounds, his eyes never rose while the motion of his hand continued to pump. That same familiar fear washed over me, leaving my knees to tremble and my heart to pound. Somewhere in the midst of my fright, his arms reached over and lifted me up and over onto his lap. My reaction of warning moved swiftly in. Silence! "Be silent," my mind cried out and nothing will happen!"

After a period of agonizing silence went by, the man handed me a whole dollar. In a daze while shaking in my skin, I took the dollar out of his hand. With my head hanging low, I could only half whisper my escape. A simple child, yet somehow, I convinced this man I was going to go buy candy with my earned silent dollar. Promising to come right back, he responded back mutely. His head nodded up and down, showing back no emotion, in the mind of a child anyway. He bought the story, with his own dollar! Just one-dollar back then got you two show tickets and all the popcorn you could eat. Tearing out of the show in fear, I took my sister by the hand and began running. She always did claim that I was the quick and clever one. Running side by side, I kept looking behind us every few steps, all the way down the street to the next show. So now, Eileen and I held on to twice the money then we had started out our day with. Well, I told no one, seeing, I was taught silence.

By the time we settled in at the next theater, it was getting late. It was near four-thirty and we should have been well on our way home. Time was the one thing that didn't cross either of our minds and so we stayed for the next feature film. Wow, this movie wasn't anything like "King Kong" or "Return of the Werewolf." It was "The Bad Seed!" Once my mind got lost in the movie, it pushed away my disturbed thoughts of that horrible man at the last theater. The little girl in this movie made that horrible man and his penis, more like child's play, seeing she murdered her victims to obtain her desired possessions. We were both engrossed in the movie and like always, not paying any attention to our surroundings. Sitting quiet in the dark, we both nearly jumped out of our skins, when someone yanked our ponytails. It was Mother! She was hysterical and near tears. She was shaking her fist, kind of like daddy. She was mad all right and marched both of us home, never letting up on her angry lecture of punishment. We were both being grounded, whatever that meant and had to spend the remainder of the night in our rooms. Actually, I felt lucky that she wasn't going to make me kneel in that forsaken corner, with my nose pressed up against that thorny plaster wall.

It was after mother calmed down and we were nearly home, her lecture began to fade away. Her expression became intense, as her thoughts faded elsewhere. Her mood was consumed with the fear, of how she was going to keep daddy out of this one and nervously began maneuvering a game plan. By the time we reached home, mother timidly instructed us to slip in the back way, while she tried to keep daddy occupied. She must have pulled it off, I really didn't know, since I was up in my room all night and never heard heads or tails on the matter. Nor did anyone hear about the horrible man and his penis, not even Eileen! Where was her head, as far as I could see, she was sitting next to me? It was like she wore blinders and had a wall surrounding her, so nothing could reach out to touch her. Nothing was ever mentioned between us for many years, except for the bad seed! That was the day I inherited that troublesome name. Regardless of the uncertainty if it came from Eileen or was self-claimed, it became my justification.

With and through Norma, my inner child and I returned back in time to that theater. Back to that terrifying day, where my silence sat in fear on the lap of that horrible man stroking his penis. Well when it came down to me overseeing the whole picture as the adult and what this Pig, who called himself a man did to my inner child, it sickened me. Being there in adult mind, I saw exactly why he finally handed over his filthy dollar. He was done using me!

In Norma's office, now in angry mind, I began slamming his head into the theater chair over and over and over until he was bloody and crying with shame. The same shame he had inflicted on my innocent young childhood. Quietly leaving Norma's office, I never made it home before loud sobs shook me, taking me to tears of release, leaving me emotionally exhausted. Here all these silent years, in denial, I was proud to believe, I had treated my sister to a show, with my earned dirty dollar.

While continuing to venture out selling boot bags and can openers, the proud new addition of collecting newspapers for old man Sweebish moved forth. Matching his odd personality, he had an old wooden, rickety wagon, he offered to let me use. The air around us was always odd and I did not like the way his bottomless eyes looked over me in his old beaten down garage. His old wooden, lopsided garage, consisted of nothing, but rows and rows of newspapers, piled high towards the ceiling. Right in between all of those stacks of newspapers, hanging on an old crooked wood beam, was a big picture of an exposed full-breasted woman, naked! Only half ignoring the picture, I continued collecting newspapers for him, collecting several coins weekly. With time, I remained timid and never talked more than what was needed to the strange old man, always afraid of what he might have wanted. For that reason, I ignored the familiar sound coming from him. Oh but that awful unforgettable sound of his unclear breathing, reminding me of my dear good old Grand Papa! But with determination, I trucked forward. All that mattered to me was my daddy. My life consisted of nothing, but living and dying to be his tough, strong little girl, while making money to make him real proud. Those were the times when I made him swell with pride and he would show me he loved me, calling me his little Beaky-nose.

This new sense of freedom, even took me to venture out past our street, to a newer location just a few blocks away. One particular summer day, while I was out selling, I knocked upon the door of an odd looking house, with dried out flowerpots scattered here and there. An older guy answered the door, looking as questionable and off balanced as the house. He was around seventeen, old compared to me. He quickly invited me into his home so I could show him my line of dark colored boot bags. After entering through the door, I found myself standing in a dingy living room, with clothing and newspapers scattered around. It took no time at all, to become aware that the inside of his house was very quiet and still. While silently looking around, with no signs of any other life about, he broke the silence. He asked me eagerly, if I wanted to play a game, "Sure, I love games." He left the room and in a few minutes he returned with a deck of cards.

Oh Boy A Card Game!

You could see his excitement, as he promised he would be willing to buy a boot bag as soon as we finished our game. He began to give me the rules of his game; that I was to pick a card and if my card was lower than his, I was to remove a piece of my clothing. But if his card were lower than mine, he would do the same. By the time he finished rattling on, he was getting all tongue-tied in excitement. Young and frightened, I did not know what to do. So…I picked a card. He lost on the first three hands and was unzipping his trousers. Petrified, I wanted to tear out of there; instead my tears began to run. Whining and whimpering, I began warning him of daddy's treacherous ways and how he gets so mad. The threat that my daddy might even try to kill him, if I did not come right home, got his attention. The boy began shuffling his feet looking nervous, as if he were having second thoughts. His next words were accompanied by his uneasy stutters. "No I…I don't want to buy any…any, any stupid boot bag. Besides, I ain't got no money." Inching myself closer to the door, I tore off running, leaving behind my sale. In life, it left in question, why me, was my forehead in-scripted with the words. "Molest me?"

Venturing further out, on another street is when I met this older lady. In my youth, in reality she was not even fifty. Her name was Carmel, Mrs. Whitfield to me. She too, like daddy, was confined to a wheel chair. She had a chubby face with bright red hair, twisted up into a bun. The red bun sat tight on top of her head, pulling attention to her green, cheerless eyes. It was after I had made a few sales calls at her home, when she began inviting me in. Amazingly I was allowed to go. In daddy's eyes, once again, she was less than perfect. She would chatter away to me most of the time as if I were some kind of grown-up. Perhaps, since I never saw anyone else hanging around her house, I was the only one she ever had to converse with. But in many ways, she was like daddy, especially when she would get irritated and begin lashing out, flushed in anger. Her outrage seemed perfectly normal to me in every way. It was easy to just close my ears, whenever she had emotional outbursts, in trade for her company.

From time to time, she would be very generous and buy me little gifts of affection. On one occasion she bought me a beautiful pink little rosary. Sometimes she took the time to sit and pray with me. Other times, she would offer me lunch and in the middle of preparing sandwiches, she'd switch gears lashing out at me again. Often we would share in the times of closeness, from laughter to cuddling moments of warmth. When her hands were tired, frail and calloused from moving the wheels on her chair, I would drive her from room to room…giggling out loud at every corner I triggered with a bump. But it was the times when she would break down and cry that I would want to brush her hair. Often she would release her tight bun, dropping down her long red locks. Each stroke of this magical brush, as I saw it, calmed her and brushed away her tears. Even as a child, I recognized Mrs. Whitfield didn't really hold daddy's true temperament.

Leaving her house early enabled me to take a little detour on my way home. It became a ritual, stopping off at the corner car wash. This is where all the pop bottles laid empty on the ground at the end of every shift, just like clockwork. After collecting every bottle I could carry, I hid the rest behind some bushes till I could return. It was like having money in the bank. After loading up my arms, I would walk to the corner store, turning the bottles into a penny apiece. It was just enough to buy myself two, three-cent double red cherry, popsicles. Other times when I would leave Mrs. Whitfield's house, I would detour to the corner carhop restaurant, going right into the bathroom. There was always some loose change lying around the commode, which had fallen out from the waitresses' metal change holders. Yes, I definitely only saw life full of money opportunities.

Well maybe, just maybe life got better for poor Mrs. Whitfield after she went away. I never did find out where she went, or how she could have disappeared off the face of this earth so fast.

At a standstill, we remained in poverty. Having no luxury of a car, we were our own wheels of transportation. Considering bus fare was not affordable, we walked everywhere. Even though up to now, help never came our way, one day, just like that; we were dealt a lucky hand. Was it by chance, or a sent miracle? Well, we certainly felt blessed. Because suddenly, we began to receive a basket of food on every holiday, while Eileen and I received a hot lunch and a carton of milk everyday at school. Oh but at school, one thing I could always count on, were the degrading voices of laughter. The only problem was, they were all laughing at me and I wasn't having any fun. As a matter of fact, the truth was, I was always crying. You could always count on a disruptive outburst of tears from me, until my teacher was at her wit's end. Frustrated, she would take me by the hand for my weekly drop off to Eileen's classroom. My humble sister, if she was not looking at my tears, she was hearing the brutal laughter from other children. It would not be unfair to say, she became ill at ease and embarrassed every time I was escorted down to her classroom.

Who would think, things could take a turn for the worse. But my humiliation grew larger after I began breaking out with sores all over my hands and around my mouth. Truth was, in the mind of a child, any child, they were ugly. It didn't help that I had to wear a hideous brown salve smeared around my mouth, while a distasteful dressing made of cloth, was wrapped around my hands to keep the salve from oozing. "Leprosy," the voices of my classmates cried out, "look, she has leprosy."

Laughter scored way up the ladder, climbing to a high. It began to penetrate, adding deeper insecurities. Enough shame was left for me to begin hiding in myself. Poor mother, for her, it was an ongoing struggle, just to afford to have the doctor come over. Even after a series of visits and tests, no answers came into view. But after a few stressful years, I came to outgrow the leprosy look, but it was not before my classmate's cruel laughter, was embedded into my head.

Just because I was a crybaby didn't mean my wheels weren't turning. It didn't take many years for my tears to roll away and to put up a shield of protection, anger. It all began to penetrate, that I only stood strong, after abuse made me mad. It placed me into the role of believing; I belonged in a world that was surrounded by cruelty. It was no secret, even to me, that my anger seemed to have the power to stir up all of life around me. It left me convinced, that the only time any acceptance seemed to come my way, was when I was releasing a burst of angry energy.

Sometimes close at hand, was my dear, delicate Uncle Milan. He was my mother's dear brother. From the time I was small, he would fade in and out of the picture of our life. He led a life of heartbreak, being often locked away in an institution, or just wandering homeless. He was guilty for believing, he could hear the voice of God. In those days, you were just diagnosed as crazy. Parallel to the medical opinion of crazy, Uncle Milan was a warm, soft-spoken man. Giving as he was, he would spend the last of his pennies on ice cream for Eileen and me. But even as he only stayed with us sporadically, it had become less and less, being, good old daddy chased him off one way or another. It was out of the blue, when my Uncle bought me an amazing gift, a little parakeet. Oh how I loved that little fellow, he was always excited to see me and would come out of his cage to play. He was mostly blue with tiny black spots marking his neck. It turned out; he was my best and only friend. Being as loud as he was, he ended up with the name Sassy. Seeing Sassy was such an amusing companion, he left me with a sense of fulfillment and some of my troubles began to drift away. But exactly how mother's big brother and his wife managed to maneuver themselves into our house that day, I'll never know. Forbidden as it was, they even brought their three small children. Being perfect and all, they were sent off to my room to keep them out of daddy's mind. Their children were not accepting to maintain our discipline to silence. Soon after, they got out of hand and began to run around. You could see it coming, but it was too late. Overcome with shock, instant illness swept through me. There laid Sassy lying lifeless on the floor, his neck twisted. Uncontrollable sobs instantly shook me. One of the children had stepped on my little Sassy. After escaping under the covers, I never heard the door close behind them as they left.

The next three days of my life were filled with endless tears. After my loud interrupting cries echoed throughout the church, the Principle, Sister Pledge pulled me out from the pew and right into her office. Of course she automatically assumed something was wrong at home again, displaying her normal prudish lips and insensitive manner. In-between sobs, I cried out. "My little friend is dead, dead, he was murdered in cold blood."

After Sister Pledge realized it was only a bird, she blew it off, having no further concern to this silly nonsense. Refusing to leave, I stood there sobbing out. "I want Sister Veronica."

Loving Sister Veronica always understood. Having had a soft heart, she repeatedly wiped away my tears of pain and humiliation. But Sister Pledge ignored my cries and continued to persistently make me feel silly with her innuendo. Fed up by then, she made a sweeping gesture with her hands, brushing me out the door and back to church. Being disgraced inside and out only raised more uncertainty, to why daddy had to go and allow them to come into our forbidden world. Look at what happened when he did, they took away my one and only companion.

Only a few days later, my tears were put on the back burner, because mother was heartbroken! Ashes to ashes, dust to dust, Uncle Milan had passed. It was sometime during the night, when the fire tragically swept away his life. Being on the streets, he found a place to sleep in an old abandoned building, on the poorer side of town. He had built a fire to keep his undernourished body warm. It was during the night when the flames spread, taking him in his sleep. No sooner had I arrived home from school, mother was sobbing on the couch and was consumed in devastation. Poor mother was blaming herself, as she cried out to me with guilt. "Oh, if only someone would have let him stay with them, he would still be alive. I tried really I did, I tried to get your father to understand, oh how I tried."

She filled herself up with fault, even in spite of having fought herself down, while trying to give him a place to rest his head and share our food.

Because daddy knew how much she fought for her brother, in his own remorse, he reminded her of his forbidden rule. You knew, you could count on any special day or holiday being destroyed by his tantrums. Even Father's Day, became logged under the heading of Misery. That horrible sound of his agonizing hysterics, as he held a butcher knife, pointing at his heart. Filled with terror, our hearts pounded and our knees trembled, as he cruelly blamed mother, for everything surrounding our closed in world.

On the eve of Christmas laid the lightly covered snow. Our Christmas tree sat in front of the front door, seeing it still remained off limits to the outside world. Someone unexpected came over that early evening. No one answered, but they persistently continued to loudly knock. Maybe it was just the vibrations that caused the Christmas tree to come tumbling over in the middle of daddy's bellowing. Whatever it was, it was enough to scare off the intruder. Past daddy's rage, Eileen and I were filled with our own kind of excitement. For only minutes anyway, we would be opening our few presents before we scurried off to our rooms, while peace on earth, remained a far cry away. Daddy or father, definitely both his names, held no true intelligence to sensitivity. Did he hate himself? Us? Is that why he was determined to destroy any happiness that came our way? Was he on a mission to set our family off to self- destruct?

By now, many years had passed since that day father fell into the dark manhole; altering our lives forever. Through those years, father controlled us every minute, every single day from the break of dawn, to when the sun went down. During all those years that we felt his anguish from his injury, we not only continued to excuse him from his cruelty, but we continued to love him unconditionally. But it was in Norma's company, with all of her support that I continued on my journey up one road and down another. It was with and through Norma that I began to find all the reasons why I did not love me and had grown up to believe, I was not deserving of any love or any respect.

PASSAGE IV

Unveiling of the Shades

The shades to the windows of our eyes are things that bring all the feeling to our being. To our souls in which our goals are foretold until the day we go, we go without any of our control.

Conclusively after years, the day finally arrived when the courts ruled against the parties held accountable for father's brutal accident. He was awarded money from the state, but the payouts were just pennies on today's dollar. In the beginning, my parents received a small sum. There was enough money to enable them to finally get a car. A superb Nash Rambler! Resting on hand, there was also enough money for father to get mother to put a down payment on a large lot. After he had located it from his nifty newspaper, he came up with the brainstorm to build a house, with him as the subcontractor. He had it all planned out in his head and was looking to his upcoming checks to cover the payments, all he needed was mother's signature and her blood to build it.

Father failed to check out the property for any shortcomings. Was it any wonder, he had also planned this out with no thought what so ever, of how to communicate with the outside world? In his mind, his idea of communicating was to simply, push all mother's buttons. Father began surrounding her with fear. Now holding an air of arrogance about him, he demanded for mother to follow through. After days of his tantrums to get her to set up a time to go and purchase this lot in person, it placed a burden of misery upon her. Once mother began to buckle under all his pressure, daddy moved forth, claiming his victory. So off we went, with mother actually driving our brand new little, "Nash Rambler." Eileen and I were limited to the back seat, but nevertheless, the newness of this adventure, brought on a proud taste of excitement. Mother, on the other hand was terrified. Being a new driver and all, she drove with her knees knocking, as she regulated the newness of the pedals. But it was only the breeze I felt blowing against my face, as we cruised along at twenty-five miles an hour, on a country road. Twenty long miles, heading straight out into our new world. A world surrounded with the radiance of beauty, amongst the deep filtering trees. Sleepiness began to take me, when the car came to a slow stop, stirring my senses.

That twenty-mile trip had taken mother well over an hour to reach her destination. But once we arrived everything was ready for endorsement, and it all took less time than it took to get there. It was a very quick sale, why not; after all, mother was ruled by terrorism to do so. After returning to our closed in world, being father was satisfied with his demands being met, our serenity remained undisturbed and pending. Seeing only days later, when the phone rang, it was terrible news. Mother's tears began to fall as she hung up, whimpering to father that there were major problems sitting on the property. She attempted to get across to him, that the septic system and curb assessments were not included in his price. In mother's next breath, our world caved in and daddy went out of control. Swearing, accusations, it went on and on. Poor mother sat voiceless; twisting her fingers nervously together, her face sitting strained. Daddy was angrily whispering out loud. In-between his harsh swearing and flying fist, I can still hear him clearly, "It's her fault, all her doing, he's done, he's washing his hands clean of this whole thing. She made this mess, now she can lie in it. He was dumping on her and now she was sobbing." My mind cried out to her. "Oh mother, please don't cry, we will help you. But it was too late; her shoulders were already slumped over, now nothing mattered. Father in his rage had depleted her and accordingly, he retired down to his mat. She was alone now; it was all up to her."

With problems rising and falling in mother's path, before long, she began to shake from a bad case of nerves. Struggling to hold on, you could hear all of the shouting and obscenities in the background, coming from uninvolved father. Every time she came home with problems he started in. "You stupid dummy, you stupid dunk off, moron."

But all of these trips to the property also offered us another escape from daddy's restrains. So eager Eileen and I accompanied mother to the sight, while she dealt with ongoing problems. But we'd barely be out of the car before our bets were in place, racing and giggling as we climbed the high mounds of rocks and clay to claim our win. In the distance, you could hear the voices of the builders arguing back at mother. They carried the same familiar gruffness as father, lacking any respect to her judgment, referring back to her as hey lady this and hey lady that. It sure didn't make things any easier to be a woman per say, wearing the pants. Seeing that this in it self was a problem, it was next to impossible to get any of the men on the site to take her seriously. Something pushed mother, because suddenly she got fed up and put the hotheaded builders right in their place. After months with her nerves shot, amazingly, she pulled it off and the house was finally completed. But there was time for mother to take only one deep breath, before father began creating another turbulence in the distance, controlling everything, from the packing to the move.

After all things considered, we moved into the house, with lots of cleanup from the remains of rubbish left behind, while mother faced the anxiety from father's nomination. It was his decision that mother, would learn and take on the cleanup, landscaping and the upkeep of the property. At that time, the inside of the house felt huge, it had four bedrooms that were specifically built to father's commands. He took over the oversized bedroom, with an attached bathroom, which held no bathtub. His untidy mat, now sat right smack in the middle of his own room. But there was one new thing that sat next to his mat, along side of those shinny silver barbells, a clock. Yes, his round silver clock sat ticking away and keeping track of our time. But his room held the same old exercise equipment, same old everything. Only now, his large, half empty room, echoed with each loud thump, from his braced shoe hitting the board. But his on going whispers of mumbles had grown intensely louder, with an eerie silence left behind them.

We sure didn't pay any of that any mind, considering, a whole new world of openness now stood before us. And we owed it all to the fact, that father overlooked details and more details, all to our benefit. Those simple details began to hinder his power, making it impossible for him to control our restrictions. Besides father's blindness to these fine points, fate had it, that the house stood back far enough from civilization that all the tightly closed blinds on the windows, vanished. Instead every room had a pair of long heavy drapes, blending in with mother's choice of bedding. In the living room, father allowed the drapes to be drawn partially open, while the sunlight gallantly streamed its way in, through the oversized picture window. Father also left out the details of enlarging our bedroom doors, making it impossible for him to maneuver his chair in. Forbidding his entry, it left our bedrooms with privacy and easy breathing. Also, for all father's missed details to the ins and outs, we had a stairway, which led out from the basement up to the garage and out to the yard. Our basement ran the entire length and width of the house. Past the empty built in bar and the washer and dryer, it sat as empty and lifeless as a ghost town. That is, for the time being anyway.

Our new surroundings, also offered us a large patio that was attached to the house. And it also had a large cement ramp, specially built to father's specifications, with cursing and flying fist. It sat unused and useless in the summer and in the winter, it turned into a snow-covered hill, giving us a great sled ride. But mother was smart, when she maneuvered father into converting her bedroom, into a small family room for us. She put up a line of mirrors to reflect a larger image to the small room. The room consisted of a built in television, a large picture window covered in heavy plum drapes, with matching pillows on the double sofas. Since the bathroom with the beautiful porcelain tub, was off this room, it gave us even more distance from father. Mother took turns sharing our bedrooms, or sleeping on one of the sofas, just so we could escape out from daddy's control. Whenever father was not in his room exercising, he spent the majority of his unhappy days in the living room. Doing nothing more then editing his newspaper. He took the time every day, to underline which programs in the television guide we were allowed to watch. Seeing that father now slept in his bedroom, we would just sit and wait for the hour of 8 o'clock to pass. Being defiant, right as he began getting down on his mat, we'd just change the channel, sticking out our tongues behind him.

Even though many things stayed the same for us and we still only ate together once a week, due to the same fist landing on the table, we still grew in our surroundings. Oddly enough, even father grew by creating a whole new series of nicknames for our new neighbors. He sat off to the side of the heavy drape, watching. It was as if it was his designated spy area. He sat laughing and amused for hours, making fun of their every day ways. In the middle of all his laughter and bitter comments, I never could figure out what was going thought his head? He was like a puzzle trying to figure out where the pieces of his life fit in. It was mind-boggling and nothing ever pieced together, not even with Norma by my side.

Not long after our move, being less than perfect, my second friend was permitted to move into the picture. She came into view one afternoon as I was running through the open back yards. She was sitting on an old wooden swing, attached to a very large branch with heavy ropes. There were lots of big trees everywhere you looked. They all belonged to this girl that was swinging high and swinging low, while kicking at the leaves hanging on the lower branches. Catching sight of me, she halted her swing to a stop, calling out eagerly with an invitation to play. One simple smile instantly connected us, having similar personalities. After tearing around her woods, we found a dead squirrel amongst the leaves and shared in his burial. Even while she showed off her tomboyish skills, past her petite frame, faded blue jeans and hand me down looking T-shirt, she was pretty enough. Her long pale blond hair and her spunky personality fit her like a glove, just like her name, Wendy. It became apparent; her father was pretty much the same as mine. He was grounded with the same temper and the same grievance, because he could not walk. They just had different names and lived in different houses. He was left bitter, after an explosion while on a job, had blown his legs off. We never spoke about either of our fathers. Our words were spoken through the enormous fits of fury they displayed. Both of us had experienced enough to know, it was only a matter of time, before her father's angry voice came vibrating through the trees. Since we shared the common denominator, fear, we'd run off deeper into the yard, until the distance muffed his petrifying energy. There was no question that I was her one and only friend. Perhaps her father had also angrily driven everyone away from the family. But not me, I felt right at home and would just disregard his disruptive flying temper. But for the duration of time that I was allowed to walk over to her house, came the discovery and thrill, nature brought to my senses. It was then when all the energy from the trees, began to connect with me. It left me feeling whole and good somehow, way deep down to the root of my soul.

Naturally, Wendy wasn't allowed into our home; so, she would just sneak in, tiptoeing past the echoes of father's whispers. We would quietly sneak around, whispering and snickering in free spirit. Most of the time, we ended up hiding in the ghostly basement, disclosing our dark secrets. Having bonded with Wendy, our friendship stayed attached, even after she started having seizures at school. Her seizures only consisted of repeating the very same words over and over, unaware of her actions. While all the children at school feared her illness, I became her caretaker. One way or another, that's what I became for her, after her teacher began pulling me out of class to walk her to the clinic. There is no lying; fear always swept through me, throwing me into a silent panic. Regardless of my yearning to run away, I would stay with her until her seizures passed; always aware that she was just as unaware of whom I was, as the shadows on the wall. But even this panic, couldn't measure up or compare to the silent darkness of being held captive in the filthy hands of Grand Papa, which sat forever brewing in the back of my mind. But in all my distraught, being Wendy's hero in her times of darkness, pushed away his dark face.

What triggered us off to confess to one another? Maybe, it was just the combination, of two young, broken children carrying around a burden of punishment. But at some point, the repulsive actions of both her brother in-law and my Grand Papa were unveiled to each other. In our moments of confessing, after ridding our secrets that had kept us silent, we shared something else, guilt. At first, she would spill over with tears for all the dread and anguish he held her too. But then, it became visible after a few months came to pass; her brother in-law had won his victory, her virginity. She slowly began to change, justifying his actions by showing off her gifts of acceptance. It is now clear in my adult mind. It was simple for him, like taking candy from a baby. He took advantage of her innocents and used her misfortunes to gain her trust. He supplied her with a false sense of affection…adding in the rewards of dime store jewelry to buy her silence. It was unflawed for him and brought to her, starry-eyes.

Then just like that, her false ray of sunshine vanished. It was bound to have happened sooner or later, considering her brother in-law's behavior was habitual. Everything came to a screeching halt, after Wendy's sister, walked in on both of them. It was one big emotional mess, as her sister's poor husband, pointed his innocent finger at Wendy, crying out like a baby with out fault. "She had seduced him!" Even Wendy's mother, who had been informed, reached an unwavering verdict. Well, Wendy stood guilty; no matter what her defense was and no matter what degree her shame rose. At this point it was all her fault. That was that. Actually, nothing about Wendy mattered; all that mattered was that this sick child had violated this defenseless man, now she was labeled as a menace. As far as everyone was concerned, this creepy slimy worm's word was his honor. So without any further dispute, he slid himself right off the hook. His lying deceit added another conviction to Wendy's unstable existence.

Given that her brother in-law was left blameless and poor Wendy was condemned, left me with the creeps. The thought of being released from Grand Papa's hands began hammering at me. Perhaps her conviction gave me the strength, to come forth out from my own silence. That or it simply scared the living hell out of me, fearing, I too would be labeled as trash. It had been weighing on my mind for weeks, all the way up to the day, when Grand Papa came over to our house to visit father. He no sooner arrived, with the unpleasant sound of his breathing, as I scurried off to my room to avoid his wandering touch. Even with my door closed, you could hear their voices echoing back and forth in argument. Planning to change and then split, to go run wild in the woods with Wendy, at some point, I became aware of the stillness in the air. It was never expected and I never heard the sound of the doorknob turn. What raised my eyes was the slow creaking sound of the door, bringing to light the face of my Grand Papa. There he stood. He was watching me! Only this time, it was not through his windowpane, forewarning my silence. Boldly he stood silently, in the doorway of my bedroom, eyeing my underdeveloped breasts. In those next moments, his eyes lingered on mine, and for whatever reason, he began inching backwards out of my sight. In the blink of an eye, Wendy's shame flashed before me and with a sense of hysteria I pulled a T-shirt over my head and darted out the door.

After having arrived at Wendy's, she was no help. She just sat chewing her gum and blowing out bubbles. She continued avoiding the subject of her brother in-law and Grand Papa, while her eyes kept restlessly drifting away. With a shrug of her shoulder, she dropped her head down, claiming she wasn't allowed to play. Getting up out of our Indian style position, I headed back home, wishing hard that he were just dead. Gone forever. But one thing was clear in my mind. I was going to tell! I was going to tell no matter what. The fearful thoughts of breaking my silence haunted me day and night, following me from behind. It wasn't until the following week, when my courage took a stand and then, everything came spilling over into mother's lap. Oh poor mother, having had no idea, she was shocked, shaken and sickened through and through. Ready for a war, she took her rage over to father. She began demanding to know, what he was going to do about his filthy father. Only it was mother, shaking her fist at daddy in a rage. Without even waiting for his response, she began to swear and barred him from our home. She fought herself down, until, she was too small to see, for raging father brought down the house. All then was left, settled, finished! Referring to me, father angrily nodded his head towards me, snarling out to mother. "That fu^#*kin whore, don't tell me, she asked for it, that's right, damn her, she's nothing, but a whore~ that's right, you heard me, a little whore."

While his mouth was angrily raging out at me, a look of hatred clearly sat brewing on his face. The room began to spin, the words whore, whore, whore, were pulsating inside my head. Feeling the blood drain from my face, fear shook me. His cutting words of blame were like a sharp blade, slicing out a piece of my heart. Depleted by his degrading attack, my tears fell as my shame rose, whimpering, "But, but, daddy!" He didn't hear me, but his eyes, held such a strong look of contempt; it backed me away from his chair. In the next moments his arms were furiously swinging at me, running me off and out of his sight. Excruciatingly done, that was that and dear Grand Papa's face? Well, after mother came apart at the seams, he was forbidden to step foot into our home. As for me, I did not see his face for a long, long, time. During the time daddy kept his distance from me, I padded myself in denial with excuse, truly believing, he never meant those harsh accusations. It was easy to fool myself. Seeing that all these years, I was at home with the ongoing degrading names, he called mother. Only now, they had become my names.

Definitely back then, it seemed as if any kind of promising beginnings, were shattered with a dreadful ending. All the dirt and shame had taken its toll, and driven Wendy and me off our road of contentment. Everything began to change. Once our sense of self-worth had dwindled away, our friendship began to turn sour apple. In one of my times of anguish, mother had given me a red ruby locket to cherish. It was very delicate and very cheering. It had its own little gold plated fancy box, lined in white satin. Surprised and happy to see Wendy, as she snuck in that afternoon, I began to display my excitement, as we danced around, admiring the red locket. It was right after my bragging performance, when I looked over to the gold plated box, all I saw was the white satin lining. It stood empty and I cried out, "It's gone, its gone!"

She was looking down over my shoulder at the empty gold box, not saying a word. Both of us suddenly got down on our hands and knees, searching under and over, inside and out. It did not take long for me to begin pleading with her, to tell me where it was. After promising with my fingers crossed not to be angry if she took it, her mean response back, uncrossed my fingers and I demanded that she give it up. After swearing up and down she didn't take it, she began singing our secret club code, out loud, "I cross my heart and hope to die, stick a needle in my eye."

Mumbling bye, she scurried off quicker than I could say, "later." Forgetting not to slam the door, it triggered off daddy's bellowing. In the days ahead, my tears spilled for the red locket that never found its way back to the gold box. After my prayers didn't bring it back, I found myself slowly drifting away from Wendy, into the waves of life.

Many years had passed when I learned Wendy had been shipped off to a permanent hospital dormitory. Due to an increase in her seizures she was forced to remain there, leaving behind her dreams.

Not long after Wendy's friendship faded, a fork in the road led me to become friendly with a girl at school named Jacqueline. In spite of her simplicity, she carried a lot of self-confidence with her. She was so happy and you could never put your finger on what it was that made her so witty. It was after we began walking home together, we discovered she lived off the same dirt path, which led to my house. Being far from flawed, this definitely wasn't the kind of girl to bring home to daddy. Nevertheless, she invited me over and seeing it was easy to sneak off too, I acted right on the spot. The funny thing was, Eileen was already there! Turns out, she was friends with her older sister and it was not the first time she was there. That Eileen! Here while I was running untamed with Wendy, she was up to her popularity thing again. But Eileen and her sister got along really swell. Between all their primping, lipstick and stuff, they were just like two peas in a pod. Seeing this was our first encounter with what society would have considered normal, it left us overwhelmed. Even mother, was willing to cover up for us, making endless excuses to father. For she knew, in his vision of perfection, he would see nothing less than perfect about this loving family.

The most amazing thing was this family did the kinds of things we never knew existed. The two sons and two daughters calmly lived under one roof, with their easygoing mother and father. Their mother's warm heart put us at ease, displaying a bright sense of humor. After an invitation to dinner that was shared with laughter in the air, minus father's fist, left me mystified. Their big comfortable house; had wide-open windows, viewing the largest yard I ever saw. Looking out from the back window, the property was overflowing with colorful flowers, streaming all around. Outside, in wide-range stood every size tree imaginable, apple trees and even trees to climb. With an armload of Jacqueline's dolls, play we did! Every doll had its own complete wardrobe, including a tiny iron, fancy shoes and everything. The way I saw it she had everything in the whole world and I loved it there! Everything that would make any child, believe they were living in a wonderland. There was no doubt, this family was the perfect picture, something that Eileen and I only saw on "Leave it to Beaver." It all began to emotionally captivate me into believing, happy families do indeed exist. So, for a little while, life gave us both a taste of harmony.

That is to say, until, their anguish became immeasurable. It was "Halloween" night and we were all bobbing for apples. It was also the night before Jacqueline's mother was to go into the hospital for minor surgery. It would be a short stay, two days to be exact and everything went as expected. But only hours before she was to arrive home, their world, as they knew it, came to an abrupt end. Unexplained, just like that, she died! She was gone! The horrible sounds of her family's heartbreaking sobs and cries of devastation sent me running back home in fear. Having faced the deaths, of my beloved bird Sassy and my Uncle Milan, a strong feeling of loss and emptiness sat consuming me. Attending the funeral, my uneven emotions followed me there. In reality, my youth held no stability; but still, all of my emotional outbursts were enough to humiliate even me. Somewhere in those dark moments after viewing what was once her lovely face, death became final. All that remained of her was the image of a lifeless statue. Their perfect mother had been taken away. Immobilized to keep my emotions in control, my thoughts began running irrationally with fault and blame. "Maybe it was God, but why would he take her from them. What if, it was my fault and God was punishing me, by taking away their perfect family?"

In my broken down state of mind, a great despair set in, catching my breath, until a loud uncontrolled outburst of sobbing shattered the silence and mourning around me. Every eye was locked on my face watching my uncontrolled outburst. The funeral director quickly reacted and walked me out to a quiet room, leaving me with a gentle pat on my shoulder. After having sat quiet for a spell, I returned back to the others in a calmer state of mind. Recognizing some of the students stricken faces, Eileen's self-conscious face stood out amongst them. She was standing off to the side, while her eyes avoided mine. It was clear; she was too ashamed, to claim me as her sister. With the quiet snickering among the schoolgirls off to the side, who could blame Eileen for withdrawing from me. Shamed, even my shame, shamed me for falling, during their time of need. Their pain and tragic loss of their mother was followed with more loss, only months later. It was the tragic unexpected death of their father, when suddenly he keeled over. Just as sudden as Jacqueline and her siblings had vanished.

PASSAGE V

School House... Rocks

Through my eyes without any real surprise... I find this day with the need of supply to help comply with my everyday ways of rehearsing all my plays... what would change if no one were left to blame, while making my own decisions with no more defensive words...Then would I be ready to play in all of life's natural ways?

Following, Jacqueline's broken heart and my broken dreams, my sorrow got pushed deep into the back of my mind. As I saw it, happy families didn't exist undyingly. Subsequently blocking out my mourning and disappointment, my path took a ten-degree turn, and all to soon, school became my playground of escape. After losing the interest to study, it gave me more time to concentrate on more important things. Especially since mother was too busy, listening to father's cursing accusations about her stupid idea to attend beauty school. It wasn't until after mother fought her way up to a win and began leaving early every morning, my game plan went into force. Finally my chance to do anything I wanted in the whole wide world had arrived. It was all planned out in my head. If I didn't want to go to school, well plain and simple I didn't show up. On those days that I said no to school, I just hid in the house till the coast was clear. Free to do what? Well that was a joke in itself, having neither any friends nor money. Seeing my past ongoing restrictions left me clueless. In lost spirit, I stayed in my room looking for a safe place to hide out. Now with mother away, father was too preoccupied in his own misery to notice my presence right there in the house. You could clearly hear him stomping and cursing her out, all the way from inside my good old closet.

It wasn't so bad actually. If you bear in mind that in-between reading and feeling satisfied with my bagged up lunch, I slept. Being obsessed with living in my magazines, by now all my comic books had been traded in for dramatic, heartbreaking, love stories. They were juicy and addictive, and with the help of a flashlight, I must have read the same stories a zillion times. Any happy endings seemed way too far-fetched and I found myself grumbling under my breath, with daddy's famous interpretation. "Nothing but a bunch of malarkey."

On the days when I decided to turn up at school, trouble began popping up from one place to another. It seemed no matter how hard I tried to walk a straight line; I continually created some kind of commotion, ending in disruptive laughter. This left one very angry teacher, making me the prime example of his punishment. He was a short, balding male teacher, who was intolerant and strong-minded. His well-known method of punishment was handled with one hard swat from his wooden board. He took great pride in this carved piece of art and hung it up in clear view, right next to the blackboard. It was a reminder to our everyday preached discipline. No matter whose turn it was, you would have to stand to the side of his desk and bend over, knowing every eye was intensely on you. As many times as my turn came around, I would stare straight ahead, not releasing one emotion, past silence, knowing the blow from the board was coming. After the wallop hit home, you could feel a hot shiver run up your spine arousing excessive shame, while holding on for dear life to your tears.

But, it was one thing to be part of a majority and another thing to be singled out by Mr. Bomber. He was in charge of detentions and took an instant dislike to me. Being in and out of his class of detentions, he gave me no warning on that day. By the time my eyes rose and I saw his large frame standing over me, his hand came down, walloping me across the face. In that split second, I thought he knocked my head off. It was hard to comprehend his line of attack, having only giggled, as my pencil rolled away on the floor. But the heat that was rising from my face, left more than shame, this time, it aroused pure hatred.

Regardless of their strict discipline measures, my behavior kept leading me in another circle of angry, frustrated teachers and in my mind; this was the way of life. Some of my teachers were convinced; it was nothing more, than a simple case of being a full-blown brat. It's hard to justify such bad behavior; by claiming it was a down right, fight for survival. But in reality, my hunger for companionship was way out of control. Trying to escape out from my life of insanity and loneliness, for a little taste of connection and acceptance, only got me digging myself in deeper.

After signing my own notes, I managed to miss over forty days of school and my grades fell so low, they fell off the report card. It didn't take long for all my detentions to add up high, into the double digits, having to serve them during my lunch hour and after school. Having achieved to receive the highest amount of detentions in the history of my school, it was a job just to keep up with them. It didn't take long however, after having lied my way through it, for everything to blow up in my face. Waiting for me by my classroom door is where I got busted. The principal stood there, accompanied by no one other than the face of mother. Having been marched down to his office, my face stood out hot in fear and I sat defenseless, to their ongoing list of unruly events.

Past the frustrated principle shaking me, the look of utter distress on mother's face made me cringe, inside and out. Considering that the school was aware of our abusive life style, instead of additional detentions, they looked for a solution. One teacher believed, that a good beating was the answer of all answers. Past her suggestion, being placed into a special class was the winning solution. The teachers, who were constantly pulling their hair out, stood in agreement and were more than willing to have me transferred out from their classes. Only once we arrived home, with daddy engrossed in exercising, mother's solution was poles apart. With daddy out of the way, past her tears, mother got out her strap. That old brown, leather strap of hers hurt her, more than it hurt me, considering, my butt was conditioned to take on my teacher's wooden board.

When the very first day of this special class arrived, having met a handful of kids a lot like me left me feeing insecure. Because this program had been designed for problem children living in an abusive environment, there was no getting anything past them. These kids definitely spelled trouble, and being a loner, it came down to do or die. Even the simple set up of this room, didn't look like a real classroom. Other than the teacher having a desk, we were all assigned to tables. It sat four of us at close range, leaving us little choice, than to converse. But the truth was, it didn't take long and within only days I was adjusting very well. So much so, that I began to learn, some of their underhanded tactics, failing to remember the pain on mother's face. Seeing as these kids were advanced and street smart, I figured it was no wonder I got caught, I was green.

Our teacher might have appeared delicate, but she had nerves of steel. She also carried both the strength and warmth to win over the hardest and coldest students. Her patience and her soft name, Miss Ivory, matched the stream of white ribbon falling from her blond ponytail. Her deep blue eyes stood out with confidence and self-control. In one way she was like a tiger, she was fearless as she worked with us daily on our patience and self-worth. She would frequently remind us, attitude was the beginning of everything. So this special class became a little more than just a homespun environment for all of us. It offered us a light of hope, in the midst of the ruckus, during our struggles, to learn the value of being accepted. Miss Ivory, never gave up on us, never looked at yesterday and always moved us forward with encouragement.

But in spite of this class, seeing I was learning from the best of the best, I managed to get caught up in the storm of fighting. Having learned from my tough classmates that fists talk louder, it was daddy that backed me up, after I got sent home for fighting. Only instead of fuming, his excitement rose high as he shook his fist with encouragement hollering out, "Yeah, that's my girl, hit her high, yea, that's right hit him low."

In spite of his proud acceptance to my fighting it was stomach churning somehow. On the tender and soft side of me, my dished out vengeance left a bad taste in my mouth. In my uneasy thoughts, it was mother's tears and compassion that held the power to put down my fist. In spite of her relief for having gotten through to me, her fear that our environment was getting more vicious began to grow. Regardless of all the brutality at home, never again would I raise my hand in anger. Instead I began to breath life into the characteristic that had already been in the making, codependency, caretaking and all of the above. It all began to manifest, when two of the girls in my special class disappeared. Missing was Sweet Sherry, who's spunk was rough as hell and appeared as delicate as a daisy. She had long blond feathered hair and she stood short and tough. Sherry was more comparable and chummy with me, than the other missing girl named Melee. Her mousy brown hair was tapered short around her neck, while her overgrown bangs flopped down into her narrow brown eyes. In essence she was quiet and followed in Sherry's footsteps, every time the going got vicious. While alcohol was definitely the culprit of controlling their environment, it often put them into an abusive situation. Everyone in class knew the girls had vanished and we were asked to be on the look out.

When they showed up a few days later after school, behind a small deli, anxiously waiting on me, a feeling of self-importance ran through me. Feeling all their needs, took over my attention. Sherry's tears ran heavy over her blackened eye and bruised check. She was scared shitless, as she begged me to hide them. They looked just awful, and done in. But with Sherry, you could see it was more than broken bottles forever shattering her personality, which drove her to run this time. As cold and hungry as they appeared, as they continued to beg for help, I melted. Instinctively I knew exactly what had to be done. It was not to turn them in, but rather to save them from their life of abuse. In my childlike blurred vision, it was never looked upon as the blind leading the blind. All I saw was their pain that was now in my hands. In view of that, my heroic mission of rescue pumped into full swing. My thoughts were flashing on and off like a light bulb, sorting out my options. Out from nowhere, the answer flashed before me. It was quite a brainstorm to say the least. After cautiously tiptoeing them down from the outside entrance, down into the ghostly basement, I stuffed them under the built-in bar. Since it still sat useless and empty, it held lots of hiding space, just right for two. A genuine feeling of goodness passed over my soul, as I supplied them with one soft pillow and two brown fuzzy blankets. In their closed in world of escape, I bestowed my entire collection of love story magazines for them to indulge in. Once they were safely tucked in, I believed they were as content as me to be hidden away. Food, they definitely needed food, so, I worked my way out of the house and headed for the nearest corner store. It was a good half-mile away, so I had to literally run to make ample time to beat the clock. It was inevitable, in one short crucial hour of ticking; father would be due to return back to the living room. After arriving at the deli, my heart was pumping from the pressure of having taken in so much risk. Since my pockets were pretty much on empty and seeing I had governed myself to save them from this fury, I slipped the rest of the goods into my pockets. My heart was pumping, pumping in fear. In light of the fact, that I was the only one willing to carry out this act of saving grace, I assumed even God, wouldn't hold this against me. Today my line of reasoning is left without excuse. However being new at this, all I managed to get was one package of Twinkies and a two-cent candy bar. Disappointed I thought to myself, "Shucks."

It shouldn't be hard to believe, only forty-eight hours passed, before mother busted me in the act. It was right after she came face to face with Sherry and Melee. Poor mother was flustered and in a state of disbelief. Darn Sherry and Melee, it was their fault in the first place for coming out of that neat cubbyhole. They just didn't seem to find the same inner peace in hiding, or take advantage of my neat love stories, that they could have.

Their tearful reaction was overwhelming, as they began crying and tattling to mother where they had been hiding and who had put them there. By then, mother's eyes were crossing over to me in anger, while she dialed the number to call their parents. Once they arrived to pick them up, the girls actually seemed relieved to get the hell out of there. A feeling of let down hit my gut when they barely uttered goodbye, let alone, giving me any thanks. Regardless of claiming their need to be saved, my defense went straight down hill. Once again I was grounded and once again, I failed to see the point. Naturally, I should have had a good whipping from mother's leather strap and sent to my room, even if my closet was my castle. Because mother didn't need daddy's two cents, never knowing what price she'd have to pay, it was quietly swept under the rug. It became obvious even to me, that mother was mortified, because I had caused so much grief to their families. But past the guilt mother laid on me, their abusive return home, weighed heavy on me. It weighed just about as much as the fact, that they passed up on reading my precious love stories and left them behind.

Yet you had to wonder, if it was the dark bruises on Sherry's face that held mother's strap back. In lieu of her anger, she only half threatened to use it, having been lost in her own opinion of Sherry and Melee. Child abuse is what it's now looked upon. Once upon a time, our minds were programmed to accept abuse as part of life. Consequently while every one was tied to this belief, everyone returned obediently back to their abusive conditions. But once the heat from the missing girls, cooled off and our class got settled back in, the other kids now looked up to me with a new glitter. Since their parents pointed only to my bad influence, the girls were forbidden to talk to me. Ignoring her parents, Sherry continued to hang out with me everyday after school behind the deli. Seeing she was building her self-esteem through the discovery of boys caught my full attention, and left me to thinking. While her attempts for recognition never went unnoticed, regardless of her height, by the end of day when the school bell rang, it was time to return back home to our shelter of belittlement.

In spite of her abuse, she dressed so cool nearly every boy turned his head. She taught me to wear thick pink lipstick and tease my hair so that it stood five inches off of my head. Being, as my favorite color became black, I looked like a hood. That's what all the tough kids at school were called, hoods. My routine was to rush into the washroom every morning before my first class to reconstruct myself into this character. Believing that this look, was the only cool thing I stood for, kept my hair high and my lipstick and eyeliner on thick. Getting my face washed and my hair back down, before returning home, kept mother clueless. She also had no idea, that on my emotionally off days, I still returned back to my closet. Since she was still attending beauty school, the office was instructed to call whenever I wasn't in attendance. So to simply sign my own notes, would no longer cut it. But after having learned from the best, it was now possible to get past that. Considering that daddy was always exercising, mumbling and never had a clue to when I was roaming around the house, is what made it doable. All I had to do was answer the phone, disguise my voice and then I was home free.

Yet, somewhere in the core of this enlightened class and this hood image I portrayed, still laid a disturbed, overactive mind. It was through all these in and outs, when I began to see that someone else's tears and troubles, could affect and change my life. It was odd at first, for whenever I was in the presence of troubled classmates, I seemed to be able to sense their moods and know just what to do. It was stirring, because it finally gave me a taste of feeling wanted and special in their time of need. Could it have been a gift or simply a curse? With time, it began to move into my life and I began to try to fix others, never applying it to nourish myself. Little did I know or become developed enough to learn, that this trait of unhealthy caretaking, would later hold me captive for years. But it would also leave me with the need to give and that need to give, would grow to be my number one issue. Somewhere in the back of my mind, somehow it psychologically read, without need, who than could love you?"

Years later down the road, two of the students in this class, died through violence.

One girl died.... Strangled, during a violent attack of anger, from someone she was in an unhealthy relationship with.

One girl died...Suicide. Yes, the very same girl named Sherry that I once hid, trying to save her from her abuse. Sad, not everybody in this class lived through the actions of violence, to live life and begin to nurture, heal and grow to adult years.

While mother was away at school, father became obsessed with mail order deals and for a little while it became the highlight of his life. So much so, he actually began cornering Eileen and me to stand and listen to his every word. It was right at the high point of his adventure, with the threat of mother's success staring him in the face, that he abruptly tossed his deals aside. With mother prepared to take her state test, his panic was written all over his moods. Perhaps, he wasn't paying any mind to her drive to finish school, or maybe he just never counted on her to succeed. She had to fight hard to win, just to take her exam. Once mother returned home, she anxiously waited for her results to come by mail. It was only a few weeks later when an envelope addressed to her arrived. With her fingers trembling, she ripped open the seal. After seeing her license attached to the paper with her high, test scores, a proud look of excitement covered her face. She stood beaming at us, as she proudly displayed her cosmetology license high in the air. Mumbling under his breath, father crossly vacated to go exercise. Once he got to his room, you could still hear him mumbling and whispering away. But we were too lost in our own glory, to realize, in all his whispers, he was plotting and planning out mother's life.

Mother's hard earned excitement never even had a chance to come to life. She should have known better than to think she could possibly escape out from the hands of father's confinement. He must have whispered it all out, for he didn't lose any time, when he ruled out mother's notion about working outside our home. Once mother's spirit and strength were broken down and she was back in her proper place, his rule went into full force. Satisfied with his accomplishments, everything surrounding us went back to his way. It might have all continued to go his way, except mother threw him off guard, cornering him with her own plot. Her long days and nights of being confined by his rules backfired! In those hours of devastation, her mind was ticking, way ahead of his clock. Little did he know, that she was absorbed in research to try to learn everything there was about opening a beauty shop down in our ghostly basement. She had the cost factor figured out from start to finish, to the smallest details of decorating. The stairway leading out to the garage, which daddy had overlooked and was a way for us to slip out, became the ideal means for the customers to slip in. It would keep them out of sight and out of daddy's mind. This was her original dream she had planning on working towards. Now with the help of fathers almighty rules, it pushed everything forward. Determined to conquer her dream, there was no stopping her. This time she fought him down tooth and nail and this time, he pulled back and returned to his room, loudly whispering his anger. She held on to her dream and began to embellish the ghostly basement with a new lease on life. She worked nonstop, regardless of father's constant criticism and all of his degrading screaming in the background. He just hated the idea that mother was doing anything besides obeying his rules.

Her motivation was her strength and before you knew it, she proudly tied a yellow bow on her brand new beauty shop. It was a classy shop at that. Mother had definitely outdone herself. She began building a small clientele, after getting a handful of women from our neighborhood to try out her skills. Even with mother only being downstairs, she was still too far from arms reach and father began fuming at the hours she was away. Seeing mother ignored his tantrums, Daddy's wheels began turning the whole time, going around and around in anger. It didn't take him long to wheel his way over to the top of the landing and start in on her whereabouts, the shop. He had just about enough and brought down the house. His loud cursing and profanities traveled down to where mother stood, until, the last frightened customer practically ran out the door. Word quickly got around and how many of her customers returned back, didn't need a count. Mother's shop, now stood empty with everything back to its original state, a ghost town. Mother's dream had been shattered, right along side of her on going efforts, to try to hide this plague we carried. After daddy's profanities became mother's disgrace, she became the talk of the neighborhood all over again.

Father's performance was spectacular. He pulled it off, just as he planned. Only the shattered tears of mother were left spilling over. His destruction didn't make sense, not then, not now. Oh mother's broken heart was bleeding from all the misery daddy had thrown at her. Every ounce of her inner strength had dwindled away. All that was left in her broken spirit was to lay her head down in defeat, dreading what another tomorrow might bring. In the days that followed, mother shared no kind word with father. His head hung down in his shame, for this time, his ruthlessness had backfired. He's sorry today, but tomorrow with mother's forgiveness, everything will go back to his way, thy will be done!

Daddy's allotted time for mother's misery came to an end. But during her anxiety of keeping up with his moods, my new interest in boys began to bloom. Having worked out a handful of short-term boyfriends, my strategy of protection was already worked out in my head. It guaranteed no pain, no rejection and no confinement to silence. With my set of rules an inch thick, none of the boys stayed around long enough to touch my heart, let alone get past a kiss. That was until Timmy, came barreling into my life like there was no tomorrow. Wow, he was one cute, rough looking, Italian boy, with black wavy hair. After he ran right smack into me in the hall, my books went flying. During our awkward moments of picking them up, as I let out a giggle, he let out a low chuckle. As he walked away, he looked back, giving me a once over and flashing me a little grin. Just a few days later in the middle of study hall, someone was annoyingly flinging spitballs at me. Turned out, it was he, the cute Italian stallion. When my eyes met his, it was love at second sight! Every time my eyes rose up shyly, they met his boyish grin and the most captivating eyes I had ever met. It was only a matter of a few hours, when I saw his short stocky frame standing by my locker, monitoring the hall. My heart skipped a beat the moment I realized, he was waiting for me. By the time he offered to walk me home, my shyness had melted away and I gave him warning, it couldn't be to my door. There was no way I would ever sneak him in, not with the smell of urine that forever lingered in our air. But Timmy shrugged it off without question, agreeing to meet me by my locker after his last class. In disbelief that he liked me, my mind sang out, "Goody-goody gumdrops." My cheeks were glowing, as I stirred restlessly in my seat, for the remainder of my class.

When we met as planned, he appeared just as excited and comfortable with me, as I with him. Halfway home, we stopped off on a wooded path, plopping ourselves down under an old maple tree, with its trunk twisted beautifully around with age. As we sat on a weedy sloped hill, looking over a mound of trees, he poured out his heart. Having learned he had just moved here, he proudly claimed he was fourteen and one day soon he would be fighting in the "Golden Gloves." Oh, but the true innocence of his tales and dreams. Well not in this case. He was headed for big trouble with the boys he still hung with from his old school. He excused his bad behavior, pointing out his family's connection to crime, claiming he could handle anything. But his family sounded typical to me, it fit right into the family ties of violence and misery. In spite of the fact he might have scared some of the kids on this side of town off, he only made the blood in my heart boil.

After spilling out most of his guts, he apprehensively admitted to having had another girlfriend that he had left behind. But by his third cigarette, he confessed nervously, she was around my age and carrying his baby. Imagine, a child of twelve having a child. It should have driven me away but it didn't. Instead my heart went out to him, for I understood shame. Besides, he was neat and loved my style of dress, while he was so dreamy as he slipped out of his black leather jacket. After spilling out his secret, in his own state of nervousness, he was unsure of my reaction as he pulled out a fresh pack of cigarettes, packing them down real cool like, pushing one my way. After declining on his offer, I just sat back dreamy eyed watching him blow smoke rings in the air, praying he would just pick me. As we got up to leave, he slipped one arm around me, pulling me close, while with his free hand he slipped a spare cig behind his ear. He stored the rest of the pack, tucking them under his short t-shirt sleeve, revealing his young muscles. With a grin of acceptance, he whispered softly we were one of the same. His lips touched mine briefly, connecting heart to heart, while our fingertips connected blood to blood. Now tied together, he slipped on his jacket and we started back towards home.

Meeting up every chance we had, it didn't take long for us to begin getting into some kind of trouble. By now I was starting to pick up smoking and picked up on where I had left off on cutting school. Since school hours were my only escape from home, those were the hours when I was free to share my time with Timmy. We often went into the beautiful woods to absorb the comfort, nature held for both of us. Other times, we just hung around by the railroad tracks, while we sang along to the sound of Timmy's little black transistor radio. For some good sense, in spite of our pasts we never ventured beyond kissing. Maybe it was the pressure of the baby that was weighing down his thoughts, but we didn't go there and that was just fine with me. Being we were both so overly hungry for just some warmth and genuine comfort, we just found it together. But God knows, he was not only sweet he was never controlling and never belittled me. That was a first and it earned my complete loyalty. In spite of the fact he mellowed out in our quiet time, he appeared to carry the same rough attitude, as he claimed his father preached. His voice may have implied one thing, but his eyes never lied, revealing his worries. Undeniably, the truth read, he was scared shitless. But I didn't see it that way then. At that age in time, I only saw through the young eyes of fresh love.

But you'll never guess whom I saw while roaming with Timmy. It was Eileen herself! She couldn't lie, she was right there in front of my eyes, in that bright shinny red 1957 Chevy convertible. It was her all right and that ponytail of hers was swinging in the breeze as the car peeled away filled with her friends. That Eileen! She was always one step ahead of me when it came to the good stuff. But as far as trouble took us, I always scored the highest rank. Unfortunately, it followed me right up the driveway, while I was sitting in a police cruiser being escorted home. Now I was double busted! Once by the cop's red handed, coming out of the woods with Timmy, only to get busted again after stepping out of the squad car and coming face to face with mother. All I could do was pray that father was still up on his parallel bars walking away. Fortunately for mother, father wasn't around to hear the ruckus going on. You can bet your life, mother didn't have any intentions of informing him, leaving the situation with no interference from him.

Thanks to good planning on my part, no one had known about my well-kept secret regarding Timmy and the classes I was missing. Not mother, not school, not even daddy, but they all sure knew now. Forget daddy for in his unruly mind, it was a contest of strength, but for mother, it was a challenge to the end. Now having to face the music at home it was anything but pretty. By the end of the school day, it wasn't a closed book by any means. Here, my dear sweet mother, called the school to turn me in. Now they knew everything. When morning arrived, it was only to awake and return back to an instant replay of the principal's angry tune all over again. Now that everything had backfired in my face all my lies stood openly with me. Every teacher at school, which had been put through the ringer by me, was thoroughly disgusted! But they didn't issue any more detentions to my long list, this time they shook their heads and suspended me for two whole days.

It could have been a couple of great days off, but with Timmy scolded out of the picture and after having been caught high and dry there was a price to pay. Meanwhile, mother was filled with so much fear of how father was going to react, she got lost in her own defense. Of course, her reaction was quite different from father's ongoing burst of cheer. But I wasn't feeling cheer, not with the fear of losing my love Timmy. Now with mother having been repeatedly deceived, her suspicious eyes now followed my every move. Whereas father, as sure as the morning sun was going to rise, would only hoot out with encouragement. My father, who sat bitter in his chair, didn't know the first thing about me. He believed that all his on going support of my wrongful doings, were molding me into his strong, angry little girl, taking right after him.

After a few rough days, the coast appeared clear and within hours I connected right back with Timmy. But who would believe it! It was sly mother! She had taken it upon herself to track me down. Because there she was, standing guard thirty feet away from the school door I usually slipped out from. Needless to say, as she walked her way towards me, I could see the pure fire in her eyes. Unexpected, she didn't walk me back into the school, but home to face her strap, along side of grounding, pleading and threatening. You name it, she did it and my tearful fight back, claiming my love for Timmy became a no win situation. There was no way I could see myself, without our close connection. Self-absorbed and inwardly refusing to comply with mother, I turned my face away. In the days that followed, nothing mattered. The tables had been turned and I was put back in my proper place. Just like that he was gone! Never having the chance to say goodbye, only left a gap of emptiness without any closure. Truth of it was, it had very little to do with mother and nothing to do with me. When my classmates broke it to me that he was forced to go back to marry his pregnant girlfriend, all of life for me came to a standstill. Even my closet that was once my safe hideaway, no longer held any contentment. My bed and blanket became my escape to cover my head and hide my misery. In my head, my macho Timmy was gone forever, lost in the arms of another.

After the uproar had died down, in spite of mother offering me her compassion to help with my despair, she was guarding me twenty-four seven. Broken hearted and angry, in all my misery, Eileen's whereabouts became my major concern. It was known to me that, she was still sneaking out with some of the most popular kids in school. So with lots of time on my hands, I began to look closely into her life and see exactly what she was into. After reading her diary and snooping through her drawers, I held on to plenty of juicy info. Oh I wanted to tell, really I did, but something was stopping me. Only this time, it wasn't her ongoing claim that she was paving the way for me. Since Timmy was gone it wouldn't have mattered anyway. But it wasn't too late to put an end to all her fun. Especially, since just the day before, I saw her sitting in that shinny convertible again. Only this time the radio wasn't just blaring out loud tunes, instead she was sitting glued next to a dreamy blond boy, in the drivers seat. Oh, but she had the power to make me so mad!

After cornering her, my threats didn't faze her, not even after holding my list of evidence over her head. She was nothing but confident and a lot smarter than most of the cupcakes I had been dealing with. Somewhere along the way she must have learned her own set of conniving ways from father. She knew exactly what buttons to push to keep my mouth shut, as my envy grew greener every day for her independence. In her confidence, there was no doubt, that she carried a genuine beauty about her. She had a beautiful face, beautiful hair and beautiful everything and it never went unnoticed at school, or anywhere for that matter. She seemed to glow, every boy loved her and every girl envied her. My acceptance to the fact she was so exquisite, just was. But Eileen, as she saw it, all the beauty was attached to me. Once again, who was who and what was what, sat forever brewing in disagreement. In this mess of heavy cobwebs, we were both experiencing the exact same confinement and the same brutal life style. Yet being we were driven arms away from ever comforting one another, we never grew to truly understand one another. We were robbed! Yes, we were both robbed of a real childhood and any tranquility to build a strong enough foundation, to give us the strength to emotionally bond.

However, failing to ruin Eileen's fun or put a dent in her independence, defeat set in, pointing my misery back to me. With my heart still carrying a bittersweet torch from the loss of Timmy, I began taking it all out on one person, myself! Missing school came to an end for the most part, sneaking in an occasional miss, with an emotional mood swing. But with my closet finally turning into just that, my grades came back into view, scoring a decent average. All this was great, in the eyes of mother and my teachers, but as for the kids known as the hoods, they no longer held any interest in me. As far as they were concerned, when I lost my cool look, I lost it all. Even the straight-laced kids, remained immobile to acknowledge the new calm side of me. Both sides of their rejection began to take its toll on my emotions. It had all left me feeling misplaced, so suddenly I stood alone. Whatever personality traits good or bad I had managed to develop this far, got shut away and so I just stood on the sidelines looking in, observing! Productively, I had arrived at the point of now living daddy's personality. Following in his footsteps my self-esteem hit bottom and I indulged in my own campaign of hate. Hating my face and hating my whole being for that matter surrounded all of me. Disliking myself to that high degree began to leave me feeling, undeserving. Even mother couldn't get me to take an interest in dressing nicer and she finally threw her arms up in despair. It was just easier for me to wear the same thing than to face the painful ordeal of a mirror. Seeing my reflection staring back at me always made me cringe and only fed me with more inner hate.

But as usual, mother's timing was impeccable. Having been stuck between moods of nothingness, mother threw my life off course. The older we got, the worse father's outbursts were getting, so mother enrolled me in beauty school. Barely thirteen, Eileen was already ahead of me in class by six months. But that sly Eileen pulled it off again, being that she already had her feet planted in the ground. By the time I got there, they too loved or envied her in one way or another and considered me to be, just my sister's little sister. They all thought I was green and began to push buttons that I didn't even know I had. What they interpreted as innocent fun only pushed me deeper into a shell. Compared to their confidence and older years, inside the circle of their click, it put my past conniving ways to win them over, to shame. It was as if I was the center of their amusement and every breath I took, brought out another outburst of amusement. During theory as I struggled to pronounce the muscles my humiliation grew as their laughter filled up the room.

Things only took a turn for the worse, once I got out on the floor. Being I was much too short to reach my customers' heads, their simple remedy of balancing myself on a couple of phonebooks, brought down the place. But when my loyal customer returned with a paper sack filled with her hair, which I had over processed into mush, is what finally did me in. It stripped away every ounce of confidence I might have gained. In my discomfort and shame, I prayed that she would just disappear into the woodwork, out of every eye smirking in. It was getting harder and harder to show up, for their laughter could only be looked upon by me, as failure. In spite of what might have been egging them on, having had no intelligence to sensitivity, their achievements came in harms way. Begging mother not to make me return, did not budge her an inch. Keeping a stiff upper lip, she believed, it was keeping us off the street and out from the clutches of father. Ever since mother had proved she was capable of outsmarting me, all my skills that once pulled the wool over her eyes, still sat useless. This left me defenseless, so I took up wearing skintight pants and still my life remained unpopulated. Little did I know, while everything around me was up in arms, in the making was my future. For out-of-sight, lurking right around the corner, an older boy named Dexter would zoom into my life, taking me to a whole new dimension of existence!

PASSAGE VI

The Hungry Heart

The word of thief you used of me, taking all my hope and charity along with all of my energy... I gave you it all not hearing my own call... continuing to fall.
Till... I heard the words of hope, wisdom and peace and all the things I once believed I could never be. No longer looking back to see... the drops of blood that once made me bleed.

Even with Norma, now by my side, this journey was becoming more complicated and more sorrowful as we sorted through my inventory of shamed memories. With so much time passing bye, flashing doubts began to flourish, if healing really would bring forth a shaft of light. Because at this point, my perplexed mind still believed and insisted there was a dark cloud that sat over my head. And in spite of these discouraging setbacks throughout this journey, remarkably my inner strength had grown, putting its first mark of acceptance on me. With a new foundation set, it allowed me to continue building a stronger sense of self-worth. As we continued moving forward, I found I needed this tool more than ever to develop a stronger sense of inner strength. For now, my flashbacks were growing more intense, while evidently my past tribulations had been growing larger right along with me.

When we first began talking about Dexter, all the build up from the past sat scrambled in my mind. Pausing with hesitation, shame flowed through me and I could not bring myself to start at the beginning, only where the resentment had left off. In my despair, one clustered babbling mess of accusations, surrounded by alcohol, sex, along with all the crying through time, tearfully jumped over to self-thievery. With my resentment kicked off, soaring over to when I never thought twice about handing all my money over to him, while he never thought twice about taking it. But then, I never thought twice about a lot of things that went wrong. Not him, not me, along with all the ways I was unfair to everyone, including myself. With no excuse, I had lived clueless by excusing whose who were self-serving, to just putting it off to need. Even though it was happening right in front of my eyes, it was just safer not to listen to the warnings from my heart.

With all this anger, my attitude turned sour right in the middle of this blubbering session and my beaten down outlook became as such. It didn't matter; no nothing mattered, no matter how much I gave willingly, good-tempered or emotionally traumatized. In my head, it was never enough! Only more lives had been hurt or worse yet, destroyed! Dead silence sat lingering between us, until Norma excused herself offering me a cool drink of water. Having accepted her offer, the quiet echo of water being poured from a pitcher into a glass, brought back a flash of comfort from the flowing sounds. This time out was definitely good and beneficial, easing my unbalanced, rambling thoughts. By the time the water had run its way to my belly, my mood was set back into a calm motion to begin from the very beginning. My mind was locked into thought, as I began to think all the way back to that afternoon, when Eileen undeniably, slipped out of school to sneak over to Sonny's. She wasn't just willing to drag me along, this time she actually invited me and that was a first. A great sense of pride swept over me, that she not only welcomed my company, but she needed me.

All the way to Sonny's, she ran on about this real keen boy she had just recently met. She was all starry eyed and acting as if he was the perfect love of her life. It didn't bother me one little bit this time, knowing there I was with my big sis. Pleased inside and out, my body walked with a proud carefree kind of rhythm, my head held high. Just as we began walking up the driveway nearing the door, Eileen's face was flushed from excitement, giving me a wide-eyed funny face, as she raised her fist up to the door. After only two sets of knocks, Sonny's face came shinning into full view. In today's lingo, he would have been considered a real hotty. He was a stocky Italian boy, who was much older, a calmer version of my Timmy. His face broke out into an instant smile at Eileen's presence, while giving my tight fitting pants a quick once over with disapproval. Following an invitation to step in, it was in the middle of a school day for us, but not for Sonny, seeing he had already graduated a few years past. Sonny's mother didn't even raise the issue to why we were not in school. Surprise! It was apparent this wasn't the first time Eileen had slipped out to go there. That

Eileen, she sure had a lot of secrets hiding up her sleeve these days.

But Sonny's mother wasn't just nice and evenhanded she was also mystical and understanding. From time to time, she wore a knitted black shawl, lightly draped across her rounded shoulders. It matched her black hair with strands of gray, twisted into a thick long braid, generating a sacred image. She came from the old country and with her homeland skills she made the largest, most delicious pasta my mouth had ever tasted. Along with her pasta, that she became known for, she was known to be clairvoyant and read tealeaves. She often used her readings to encourage us to walk straight and not miss school. Perhaps she figured, if we were going to cut school we were safer there than on the streets. But to me, it was nothing more or nothing less than way cool. Now Sonny's father's ways for the most part, were also played out like the old country. As for him, I found myself in what became my normal distrusting mode. Absent in mind, never to truly know him.

Over at Sonny's is where this boy used to hang and where we met for the first time. With a quick introduction, I learned his name was Dexter. He was leaning back against the countertop with his arms folded, when his half crooked smile, instantly took me in. Inside the hour, it became known Sonny and Dexter were best friends and did just about everything together. Coincidence had it, that Dexter and Sonny were thirteen months apart, same as us sisters. Although the similarities stopped there, considering, they were worlds apart from their height to complexion, to their nature and morals. While Dexter took a liking to my tight pants, Sonny threatened to put me over his knee, for wearing skins. Sonny for the most part carried a confident, happy go lucky personality, while Dexter displayed a lack of self-worth, having to walk with a slight limp. Dexter, he wasn't just attractive, he was ripe compared to my young years. Like Sonny, he too had already graduated from high school. He was a real man all right, not at all like the silly ratty boys that had let me down. Once Sonny and Eileen drifted into their own world of conversation, Dexter turned his attention over to me. At first he was rather shy, but as our conversation ran for nearly an hour, he let out a hint of laughter, with surprise at my age. As he remarked how cool he still thought I was, relief for his acceptance, pumped up my heart. There was no doubt in my mind, he was feeling it too and he just had to like me. His on going compliments left me feeling pretty grown up, pretty everything. Everything was in perfect motion, except for the time that was ticking to when Eileen and I had to think about heading on home to beat the clock. But it wasn't before Dexter shyly slipped me his phone number, on the inside of a matchbook cover. There was no question, after only one short hour of shooting the breeze, limp or no limp I liked Dexter a whole lot.

As we headed for home, Eileen and I compared notes and we found that our hearts finally hammered in agreement on something. Wow this was too good to be true and weird all at the same time. Both of us thought they were both breathtaking, while we were both swept off our feet. What could be greater? Both these guys owned their own cars and held decent jobs. Over and above, we would soon learn, they did not only understand, but were willing to turn their heads away from father's unruly behavior.

It was late the following night when I found the courage to dig out Dexter's number, trying nervously to keep the sound of the dialer muffed underneath a blanket. After an hour of whispered conversation, we were both hooked and after a few more meetings at Sonny's we were officially a couple, ring, angora and all. From day one, it felt like nothing but right, since he was willing to share all his disappointments and insecurities with me. Poor Dexter, it had been a crippling eighteen months, since he and Sonny were involved in a terrible motorcycle accident. His voice was cracking as he revealed, not only was he in a body cast from the waist down for months, but out-and-out, his girl had left him. Past feeling his pain, a stab of jealousy passed through me, throwing a list of questions at him about his x girl. But after ruffling Dexter up, I put her out of my mind by reminding myself of the ring he had placed on my finger with love. In my head, I had plenty of reason to be jealous and have self-doubt. Seeing that Dexter was tall, slim and oh so darn, good-looking. His green eyes always had a story to tell, with his desire shinning through. His sandy blond hair fell down wavy into place, flowing into his neatly trimmed sideburns. But for my worries, I reminded myself; at least I was sitting in his blue convertible, with the radio blaring out groovy tunes. Somehow it left me finally feeling equal to Eileen. Only there was something different here and I just couldn't quite put my finger on what it was. Ignoring that uneasy warning coming from my heart, kept me in love. Now with both Eileen and I tied to love, we began drifting in opposite directions, unless we met up at Sonny's.

Getting out of the house past daddy, was becoming more effortless everyday. Whenever he went down on the mat for his afternoon nap, or was up on his braces exercising, it became a built in clock to our freedom.

Even mother on occasion would get out for a cup of coffee and a spoonful of peace. But it's definitely beyond belief how we began to get so much past her, being as smart as she was. Conceivably, she was too tied down to father's constant rebellious behavior, while she endlessly struggled to give us a small taste of normal. Sure she knew when we were out in the early evening. It was right after father went down on his mat at 8 pm sharp. Unquestionably by lying, conning and by disguising her voice, is what got us past him and out for a few hours. She made sure she was at her post, to get his water and meet his called out commands. In mother's heart, Eileen and I knew, she believed we were not only safer with Dexter and Sonny, but we had a far better chance to escape out into the world past father's insanity.

Occasionally after school, Dexter would pick me up and drop me off at beauty school. Saturday nights, once I got out of class, if there was a chance to stay out, they were reserved as ours. Often we took rides to my favorite place, a park where the trees stood tall and the leaves blew free in the wind. Once again, something was different from the relaxing scenery that once purified my spirit. In reality, it speaks for itself. Our dates always ended up at drive-in theaters or the hot spot known as lovers-lane. It didn't take long for my passion of nature to go hand in hand with necking, leading up to petting. Dexter's tender unspotted hands of love and affection, were nothing like the hands that had once kept me a prisoner in silence. This was true love and this kind of love had never felt so, so, well, desirable. It brought out every form of nurturing that was already instilled in me, to the next level. It held the power to control my every need, a need to give, a need to have to give and the need to continue giving.

So with all our love, Dexter took me home to meet his family. It was my first real feast of Thanksgiving. Not knowing what to expect, the anticipation of it all had me squirming. Before we even reached the door, his younger brother and sister came running out in excitement, acting out their joy for the day. Three steps up, took us up into the kitchen where the aroma of the turkey surrounded us. Before there was even a chance for introductions, my eyes caught view of a beautiful long table, crammed with food and scrumptious deserts. But in the midst of all the confusion, his mother let go of a pecan pie. It crashed loudly to the floor and suddenly her tears could be heard. Instantly I felt right at home. Half hysterical, Dexter's mother ran into the living room to finish out her tears, hunched over on a wooden rocker. Just as the Mr. casually nodded over to me, he began sweeping up the splattered pie. By then, the timer went off and everyone gathered around the table to take a seat. At that time, taking the seat next to Dexter's mother, just felt right. Casually smiling over at me, once she dried her last tear, we all joined hands in prayer. It was right after we made the last sign of the cross, when the proper introductions took place. In the heart of their chatter, I sat in silent awe just listening and observing. Before you knew it, dinner was done and everyone pitched in with the dishes. Topping off a perfect dinner, desert was being served in the living room, putting everyone in a laidback mode throughout the football game. The whole picture surrounding this relaxing and calming Thanksgiving Day left me with utter amazement. They certainly could have convinced me, they were the perfect family. But to the assessment of all their perfection, well it never got the chance.

Once all the family members scattered out from the room, I remained in my seat next to Dexter's mother. Still picking at her pie, she leaned back against the couch, giving a hint of slenderness to her long legs, comfortably crossed at the ankles. With a short, simple bubble hairdo, a simple housedress and no trace of make up, she appeared on the simple, timid side. Yet she had warmth about her, which took me in without question. For how young the hours were that I had known her, when she suddenly whispered her fears out to me, disbelief set in. In those next crucial moments, my own acceptance was readily upon her. A mixture of distressing words slipped through her lips, while her eyes glazed over to me with a plea of secrecy. She stuffed me with enough info to fill up a twenty-pound turkey. Here, it wasn't the pie after all that ripped at her heart and made her sob. The pie only pushed what little control she had left of her shattered dreams, right off the edge. Still, feeling bound by her trust, my lips must remain sealed. But understand, through all her sorrow, it was devastating enough that I could almost taste her tears. From that moment, when we touched each other's hearts, it was enough to bond us for all our days, now and forever.

Past Dexter's mother's sorrow, from day one, she continued to treat me as her flesh and blood. It was not so for the Mr., who was becoming more judgmental as each day passed. It was bound to happen sooner or later. Sure enough it took no time, for word got out that Eileen and I came from the roots of a dysfunctional and crazy family. It was the way the Mr.'s eyes danced with suspicious humor, poking fun at father's irrational ways. It corresponded with the way his eyes always stared straight through me, poking around for tidbits of information. It was just less intimidating to stay off to the sidelines observing him, while he was observing me. But after daddy continued to create his on going waves, it was impossible to keep our lifestyle hidden from all his curious questions. Especially now, since Dexter and Sonny began to maneuver their way cautiously into our home. In the beginning, they would sneak in when father was up on his parallel bars or down on his mat. Over time, periodically whenever father caught a glimpse of their shadows, he didn't begin to fume as they crossed over into our fortress. This should have left me fearful, instead it left me with excitement, believing there might be hope for him, for us. Na, it didn't happen! Right after he came face to face with the boys, besides handling it like a real trooper, he fell right into his swing of things. Perhaps he took notice to Dexter's limp, seeing he was quick to nickname Dexter, Chester, from a TV show, because one of the characters walked with a limp. Chester made Dexter stand in the category of less than perfect. Perhaps you could understand Dexter weaseling his way in, but what was wrong with Sonny? Nothing, that's what and it slipped right over all father's almighty rules. It wasn't something I was going to raise from the dead, seeing past Sonny treating me like a kid, he was really pretty cool. Besides he idolized Eileen with starry eyes and in my eyes, he put her on a golden pedestal. It sure didn't take long for daddy to put his acceptance on cornering Dexter and Sonny, with hours of his one-way conversation. All too soon, they began to look both ways before crossing in front of his path, to avoid being cornered. Regardless of their efforts, father still managed to catch up with them at every corner they turned. He was truly in his own glory talking all his deals in his nifty newspaper. His amusement began to escalate, while you sat, he spoke. If you spoke, he never heard. He just rambled on about the headlines, newscasters, quacks, and shysters. In-between gulping for air, he judged the heathens and even the lonely spinsters, as he called them. Now with two new faces in view, father had two more mugs to draw, keeping him temporarily absorbed.

Only a few months later, my glorious balloon popped. All my bliss was shattered followed by endless arguments. In the beginning it was a complete shocker. Possibly in Dexter's mind, he was just looking for an innocent experience. Perhaps he truly didn't have a clue to where this would lead us. But even if he was innocent, his taste buds acquired an appetite, like a hungry dog takes to a juicy cut of T-bone. It was our usual Saturday night date; there would be no drive in theater, not tonight. Tonight was a special treat, since we were invited to his boss's home, to meet his wife and their children. On our way to their place, Dexter was shinning with excitement for his acceptance. We had no sooner arrived and caught view of their backyard, hearing all the laughter and splashing that was going on. Once we came into their five little girls view, they were competing to get our full attention.

We sat by the poolside getting acquainted, when out of the blue, Lilly offered me a beer. The wind was blowing through her long hair, as she grinned over at me, waiting for my response. Wow, it was the first time an adult offered me a real alcoholic beverage of any kind. "Awe- okay, sure," was my simple response back. After guzzling the long neck beer, my nerves laid-back, realizing the question of my age never surfaced. Instead, after they downed a couple of tequila shots, they began to tease me, pointing out my girlish figure and little pint sized breasts. It was true, compared to Lilly, who had what I considered, the largest set of tanned willy-wonkers my eyes had ever laid upon. She wasn't shy she proudly flaunted her breasts in her little bikini top, exposing a clear view of her cleavage. Her ongoing laughter and free spirit set my mind at rest, reassuring me that her teasing was just in fun. Chuckling under his breath, her husband Sly sat voicelessly amused. He was a mechanic and looked the part, as his grease stained hands, brushed back his hair away from his rugged fine-looking face. He flashed his pretty wife another grin, before turning his attention to the children, who were struggling to pull off their lifejackets. By now the sun was already down and the children were shivering and whining up a storm. Lilly immediately began gathering up their things, appearing anxious to get them in for a snack and snuggled in for the night. Excusing herself, she marched them all into the house, while they all waved us a lingering bye-bye.

Sly and Dexter immediately got lost in business, talking car engines and models, until Lilly's voice sailed out the window for Sly to bring the party inside. We no sooner stepped through the door when, Dexter and Sly exited down to the basement, leaving Lilly to keep the conversation rolling between us. She was talkative and chatted nonstop about one thing or another. Basically, they were all surrounded by Sly this and Sly that. He was the love of her life, reminding me of the way my heart still hammered for Dexter. In spite of all her friendly hospitality, as I began to worry over Dexter's whereabouts, it took my attention. Sensing my restlessness, Lilly suggested that we grab a cigarette from the pack and go downstairs to join the boys. Join the boys! That was the biggest understatement of the year. She never warned me nor was I prepared to step into a dark room and come face to face with a full size porno film on the wall. New to my virgin eyes, were several naked bodies all performing in wild sex and gnawing at each other like a pack of hungry wolves! It was my first real introduction to live sex and I just stood there iced up. Sit, someone scolded out, you're blocking our view. With that order, I did what I was always expected to do, obey.

Never would I have thought that we would be at a home theater, with priority front row seating. Another can of beer was passed my way and after watching in disbelief, my awareness to Dexter's arousal came when he placed my hand on his erect organ. In a room of silence, the awkward sound of rapid breathing was all that spoke. In discomfort, I began to guzzle the beer feeling the cold chill of alcohol running down my throat, returning a warm sensation through my body. It didn't take long to feel a buzz and it didn't take long to begin feeling like an adult, from inside a child's mind. My buzz added to a warm feeling of desire flowing through my veins. While at the same time, it looked painful enough, that it sent me into a silent panic, fearing Dexter's next expectations. There was no way I could measure up to those girls taking it all in. But in my naïve young molded mind, it was daddy's voice and only his voice I heard. Could this whore that daddy claimed existed in me have followed me right from Grand Papa's filthy fingers? Suppose it was true and I was that whore that daddy's crucifying words had judged me with, "Once a whore always a whore." Regardless of daddy's convictions, it was a beginning to Dexter's sexual appetite and expectations, leaving me uncomfortable inside my skin. But as porn became a weekend ritual, sex became the number one issue and we began bickering constantly. With all this fighting going on, the pressure of losing him ate at me and I began to hide the fact that I cringed, just hating every night that porn came to light.

Sure it was true, that somehow I had managed to cope in life by building a wall of pretence, only this time it was different. This time, I truly loved this guy. I needed so badly for him to love me back. Becoming weaker with every battle, my stomach churned at the very thought of losing him. But one thing for sure, I made up my mind, nobody but nobody was going to take him away from me, not this time. With that, a desperate need to hold on to him moved forth. In my crippled mind, neither morals nor self-respect played any kind of role in my life. Better said, I never even knew they existed. Our arguments were always the same, activating another reaction of tears, with another list of excuses, begging Dexter not to be hurt. During those times when are relationship was in an uproar, he would gently wipe away my tears. But while comforting me in his arms, it didn't take long for his needs to turn back into another episode of lust.

As we continued going to this couple's house, the pressure of losing Dexter became unbearable. Just the agonizing thoughts of him lusting over someone else, left me crazed with jealousy. Now with everyday filled with the pressure of losing him, I couldn't take another day and surrendered to his hunger. It was a corner gas station, under their lit up sign, where I lost the battle, squashed in the front seat of his blue convertible. Afterward it didn't bring any pleasure or fulfillment, it hurt so I just hated it. Even his moments of tenderness, couldn't make me like it, but it wouldn't have mattered, because he came back at me for seconds. Suddenly, in the midst of all my new excuses, with the ongoing pressures of losing Dexter, it was all put on the back burner. It was daddy! He was very ill and was rushed to the Veterans hospital. It was then, when I began to use daddy's condition in argument to Dexter's needs and expectations. Yes, its true that I was so crippled in mind, that I needed a trumped-up alibi, rather than to just say no. It was enough to win the battle for now, a battle, which sat waiting somewhere between daddy's cries of misery and his return back home. But oh poor daddy, having to be away for weeks from home and his girls, was extremely stressing him out. But in-between our visits to him, our taste buds were watering for more freedom.

With this new taste of freedom, Eileen and I began to argue mother down to allow us to have a party. All our reasoning that this may be our one and only chance was enough to get her to agree. She immediately called on her sister Jenny to help with the chaperoning. Foolishly handing us all their trust on a platter, gave us the total freedom to plan this out with no interference. Eileen invited all her friends from beauty school, while Dexter was the only one who accepted one of my invitations. Nevertheless just our excitement along with a record player and a stack of 45's was all we needed. Not to forget, all of the beer and wine that was hidden and packed down in ice. Feeling free as a bird, I couldn't ask for more. The party had no sooner started when, my one glass of white wine, turned into another, then another. In the blink of an eye, my blood was overflowing with charisma, while my behavior became wild and carefree. It didn't even take an hour to get trashed right alongside of Eileen, who had already passed out cold. Sonny and a few of the guys carried her cautiously up the steps, right past the chaperones. Her long blonde ponytail dangled down, swinging back and forth and all I saw was the beauty she carried. In spite of her condition, alcohol had the power to make me feel desirable without any care to what was really taking place in me. Only this time it was me, who was all over Dexter. Neither my charisma nor my wild and carefree ways could have lasted, after carrying them up the steps with me. With a cigarette dangling out of my mouth, mother was staring at my flushed face in disbelief, as I staggered past her. In a panic she went to look for Eileen and when she found her out cold, end of music, end of party, end of night! At full tilt, once the whispers filled the air, the room suddenly sat empty. Now with mother's stern face silently staring back at me, she pointed to my room and in an inebriated state, I obeyed. But mother's harsh lecture only lasted until father's grumbling from his hospital bed, got the best of her. Like always his demands took priority over our discipline. Only, after having experienced the fulfilling high that wine gave me, as it fed my insecurities with confidence, it followed me from behind and into my life. Wine held enough power, to help me perform at my very best, for what I dreaded the most while sober.

Perhaps all the changes from the wine, along side of daddy's absents, is what got Dexter to think up his new idea. It was early evening, while mother was engaged in another visit with daddy, when Dexter guided me down to our ghostly basement. Holding my hand and his new Polaroid camera, he could hardly wait to load it up. While pulling back in tears with a long list of excuses, his face was falling back at me in disappointment. Quarrelling back with reassurance, he swore that he only wanted his pictures to be of me, beautiful me. But I was so unsure, so everything as I stood chilled and naked in the deserted gloomy basement, while Dexter was engrossed in calling out my next pose. With the round eye of the camera snapping back at me, it felt ugly and degrading. If there was even an ounce of self-respect in me, it was stripped away with each piece of my clothing. It never stopped there; it just never stopped for the length of time, which felt like a lifetime to me. But as Dexter's nude collection continued to grow, my insecurities and low self-esteem grew with them. That simple cynical name Dexter labeled me with, "Little Miss Puratonic," held the power to make me fall right back into formation. Dexter's interest to observe other girls, kept me constantly competing and giving in, while I began retaliating by drilling him about her and her and her.

By the time daddy had arrived back home, it felt safer to deal with his mood of destruction, than Dexter's expectations, which hungrily were coming back at me. But for me, the act of seeking love and acceptance was turning into a sickness. So much so, my ongoing guilt and giving began to set the pattern for our future together. Guilt moved all of me whenever I couldn't give and stayed glued to me whenever I happened to be the receiver. Who knew a plain hamburger squashed between two buns and a piece of cheese could tell the future. It started at a simple carhop diner where Dexter always took me. It was always the same; he was never hungry and never ordered. By the time my food had arrived, his appetite began to stir. And before you knew it, he had devoured more than half my burger. It was never the sharing I minded, just the ongoing idea that I was not worthy enough to deserve the simple cost of a burger. Obviously this was building a pattern, how two could eat as cheaply as one. Most likely, it was my own acceptance that set the mold for our future. "He would eventually eat like a king, while we would eat as cheaply as one."

Between Dexter and home, my life was smoldering at both ends of the stick. Unbalanced as I was, I struggled to hold on to everything before it had a chance to slip away. But no one could have held on tight enough to keep the doors from closing in our faces. It was Saturday morning and when I arrived at the beauty school I came face to face with nothing but the other students. The place looked deserted and had been totally cleared out through the night. All that remained were bits and pieces of all our records scattered around a pile of rubbish. My insides began to stir when my eyes caught sight of the cardboard sign tossed in the middle of the mess, spelling out in large black letters, "Bankrupt!"

Followed by a burst of uncontrolled anger from everyone for what they did, one girl cried out in horror, "Holy Shit!" Within this angry circle of girls, my own reaction got lost in anguish for my own failure. After two long years, with only a few hundred hours left to complete, for the first time in my life, I was so close to achieving something. Now it was gone, but I was not alone! This time, all the girls gathered around the empty room, looked just as paled and grief stricken as me. Now all of our hard work and dreams stood on empty ground. Silence suddenly took the floor. Gone from the air were the sounds of their laughter that once held power over me. Their sounds of laughter were now replaced with the sounds of emptiness. Now crying in their circle with them, it actually felt comforting that I had company this time. It was the very first time that we shared something, something we finally held in common.

As a result hundreds of our hours were never documented, it fell short on our parents' wallets to have to pay another school for those lost hours. Most of us split up, branching out to different locations. Since Eileen had already graduated, mother put all her emphasis on me. She transferred me across town and seeing that it was too far to walk, buses became my transportation. This was perfect as far as I was concerned. Because it gave me time out away from daddy and Dexter's controlling neediness. But again, for the most part, all my concerns past dodging daddy and studying, rested on pleasing Dexter, while he kept a personal log to my every move.

It was a typical day of waiting for the bus to return home from school, when a black rusted out car, began to slowly move past me. When the car began to back up in front of my path, it was then, when I saw him. By the time he casually called out my name, my heart was hammering in excitement. It was Timmy; it was my Timmy in the flesh. Nearly three years had passed since the day he was driven back to his pregnant girlfriend. He looked the same, only older with noticeable laugh lines around his dreamy brown eyes. Leaning towards me, he pushed open the passenger door and he didn't have to ask me once. Without hesitation, there I was, sitting right next to my Timmy. It felt just like old times. With a deep Timmy grin, he reached over and squeezed my hand in delight. It wasn't a surprise when he parked in a deserted wooded area loaded with trees, setting the mood. It did not take long for our familiar comfort zone to set in and we began reminiscing over all our most cherished moments. Occasionally he would blow out a smoke ring in humor, jogging my memory back in the day to his coolness. He was so swell and it almost broke my heart when his face fell, revealing his marriage was on the rocks. Even after he displayed a picture of two of his children, it never sunk in that he was still married to his girl! Living in a flash from the past, I was locked in a time element and only aware of what once was and what was once swept away from me. Being locked into each other's emotions, our conversation drifted into a longing of silence. While his gentle eyes looked deep into mine, they held the same familiar strength that still held the power to melt me down. He was all starry eyed, as he gently bent forward, laying his warm gentle lips on mine. Suddenly I was lost in his arms and a rush of hot desire began to take me. We clung to one another and kissed like we never kissed before. We petted back and forth, in places that had once remained completely off limits to us. Responding back with a strong hunger and readiness, in the midst of our heat wave, Dexter's face flashed before me. Instantly my spell of desire was broken with a wave of guilt. Pulling back halfheartedly, I whimpered for him to stop and to take me back to the bus stop. Flashing me back a stung look, it was hard to read into his emotions, while he gave me nothing back. Instead, he looked away as he started up his car and drove me back to the start of our destination in silence. His lack of resistance left me feeling foolish for half stepping what could have brought us back together. Tense and tongue-tied, he dropped me off at the same bus stop, where we barely uttered goodbye. Not daring to look at his car as he drove off, I stood there wishing the whole time I looked for my bus, that he was never driven away. But regardless of feeling at a loss, with time having gotten away, there was going to be a lot of explaining to do. Of course I lied intensely to mother and Dexter about where and just whom I was with for so long. You can bet on my life, lying I did. Lying about this, lying about that, no matter how much Dexter tried to break my mind down for answers. My heart was actually smiling inside, for having stood strong to my own secret and not allowing him to squeeze it out of me. Better yet, this time it was Dexter who felt the emotions of being violated. There was no doubt in my mind Dexter knew I was lying as sure as the rug was lying on the floor. Smugly I brushed my thoughts of longing for Timmy and the guilt right off as crumbs, far into the future.

At long last my final days at beauty school had arrived. Now with my graduation right around the corner, my excitement was high. Mother got on it and called Columbus to work out the details for the big day, my test. The whole time she was on the phone my heart swelled. Soon I would have my cosmetology license in hand and all my thoughts were lost in my own glory. Only mother's loud argumentative voice is what brought me back down to earth. Something was obviously wrong. The second mother hung up the receiver she turned her attention over to me. Pleading for my understanding, she broke the news with teary eyes. What was this! Really! Really according to state board, I was too young to take my test and it had to wait until my sixteenth birthday! In my angry mind, I yelled and cried my eyes out at mother that the world was nothing but stupid, stupid, stupid. All the tears in the world wouldn't have mattered, there was no fighting it and it would have to be put on hold for several more months. But as sure as spring moved forth with new blossoms, new opportunities for me began to flourish.

It was quite by accident actually, when an opening for further education was offered to me. Wow, a French man, a shop owner at that, offered me his skilled training. It was merely in exchange to be his shampoo girl and sweep up the hair until my test came to light. It all happened so fast I was dizzy with excitement. It was right after he spotted me looking in on his fancy window display. Franz was his first name. His shop, well la de da, is all I could say. When Dexter got the scoop, he responded back to me completely negative. Especially since both Franz's sons were operators there. Sure, they were plenty cute and way over confidant, but seeing they were both living gay lifestyles, they never even looked twice at me. But once I took the job, Dexter was taken back with my decision and began kicking up a storm. It took no time at all for him to begin openly displaying his disapproval for the entire crew. Including the owner who held on to these very dark mysterious eyes. It was all so overwhelming, that this time I ignored Dexter's stressful attitude, putting it off to being intimidated. In fact that was easy to do, considering this snazzy owner disliked Dexter from day one and pointed out all his nerdy flaws. In my eyes, all their critical influence put Dexter in a different light and made all of them stand out as hip-hop stylish. Observing them closely, all too soon it became apparent that they were quite a lively group. Not failing to note, Franz the owner who was fifty something was into young naïve females. Confident as he was, he was always claiming his wisdom, while he always made sure he was in the spotlight. You could say on the outside shell, he was a very handsome man. But inside was another story altogether. Whenever he looked deep down into your soul, his potent eyes opened up a dark side to him. In a strange way, depending on his appetite, he could make you quiver, shiver, or fall madly in love with him. Having been married five times over, his attitude around the shop seemed to reflect the fact he truly believed he was God's gift.

Jody was his favorite girl at the time. Her lovely chubby cupid face stood out among the lot of us, only speaking to her chosen few. It became more than obvious after time she was having a love affair with Franz. Past her shyness and insecurities to compete with the girls that Franz had already encouraged to slim down, it was no secret; she was madly in love. Being so engrossed in every breath he took, it seemed as if she was hypnotized and under his spell. Franz was not bashful to boast, he was doing Jody's young years a favor. He fed her with enough encouragement, to mold her into a thin girl, so she could experience the fun side of life, before it passed her by. In his arrogance, he was always trying to prove that he was righteous in giving her all the confidence; she would ever need to live. It was when word came in, that the big hair show was going to be held, at an exclusive hotel outside of town, when everything changed. Excitement suddenly rose high in the shop. Talk was, it would be one, wild, crazy weekend of fun and more fun with all arranging to go together. In the days ahead, they chatted non-stop, planning out even the smallest of details. Well, almost everyone that is. Being so young, I was absolutely not allowed to go. Not that I was actually asked, but just in case they did invite me, I wanted to be packed and ready! Even Franz was riding on excitement and made the decision to close the shop for the whole weekend for this special event. Before you knew it, the date of the hair show had inched its way up and they were packed, ready and eager to go. Seeing they never did invite me, there was no argument that stood from Dexter or mother. But once they all left, my mind was tormented and filled with resentment and jealousy. Rejection from them set in and I was mad at the whole lot of them.

Once they arrived back, pure relief flowed over me, until their voices carried on nonstop in all their excitement. They all sat around in the back room joking back and forth, exchanging some of their wildest experiences. They almost laughed their heads off, bragging about the bottles of tequila they drank and getting all shit faced. They were so lost in them selves, just because they managed to create enough commotion in the hotel, to almost get thrown out. Stepping it up Franz took the floor with his own masculine attitude. He began to laugh, reminiscing about all his lust and the sexual satisfaction he experienced, with all the hot chicks that had come up to his room. Everybody let out a loud howling roar, all laughing again at once. None of them seemed aware, that I wasn't amused and I wasn't having any fun. Truth of the matter was, I was sitting back sulking in jealousy, because they all had such a spectacular time, after having left me so uncaringly behind. Yet, nobody but nobody noticed, that Jody looked wounded. Both her face and her eyes were holding a very strange, distant eeriness. Perhaps she gave off enough negative energy, because suddenly playtime was over for everybody. By then everybody lost their zest and began moving back their chairs and getting out of their seats, to get back to their stations.

It was only two days later when I was scheduled to return back to the shop and after pulling on the door, it was locked. Noticing that the open sign was turned around, I looked in through the glass window and saw no sign of life. Confused, I wondered why no one had called me, but then, I blew it off with a jealous attitude figuring that they were probably out on another wild adventure. But after three long days had passed and the shop still remained closed, after calling around, it appeared as if everyone had fallen off the face of the earth. Just when I was ready to throw up my arms, I got in touch with one of Jody's chosen friends. Her voice cried out to me in hysteria, trying to get it all out. It was horrible and all too soon it sunk in. Jody was dead! She was dead and all I could do was lay down my head and cry for her. In grief, everyone wished that they had said this or done that, but now it was too late. Whispers were in the air and talk had it, after the owner exposed the details on his sex filled wild weekend, Jody got hysterical and went on a rampage. She was so crazed, the following day she went to Franz's mother's house to confront him. When Jody found he was not at home, she began to argue with his mother. Her emotions went out of control and she shoved her, into a dark closet locking the door behind her. No sooner had Franz arrived home, he heard his mother's muffled voice crying out for help. In disbelief that Jody went off the deep end, they cautiously searched the house for any signs of her. Well they found her, right in the heart of Franz's bedroom. There, hanging at the end of a rope hung young Jody's body…Jody took her own life that day and no matter how hard it was to keep the news hush-hush, her death still left behind waging tongues. Franz, who had claimed he was wise to all of life, was enormously mistaken by demonstrating, how life was passing her by. Poor Jody, after she believed she had lost her own battle, she chose to just pass on life period.

It was difficult to work at the shop without the memories of Jody's death lingering all around us. In spite of the mournful environment, it was only a matter of time, until Franz was back to his old tricks of living in the spotlight. In all his attention, the lack of respect he was breathing in and breathing out, filled me up with a strong resentment. It affected me enough that I started to become indifferent during his haircutting classes and I began pushing the importance of his teachings, off to the sidelines. My attitude must have showed one way or another, because he brought all the disgust I had been putting out there to life. When Franz walked into the break room that day and sat down, not wanting to share the same space with him, after loudly crumpling up my lunch bag, I got up from my chair. Without warning, he leaped up briskly to his feet and came at me from behind. With a yank he pulled me down to the floor. Putting his face in mine, he harshly whispered. "See how easy it is for me to have your ass if I really wanted you. Do you really think you are so much better than me, you stupid little ungrateful bitch?"

A hot rush of fear ran through my blood, silencing me. With a look of satisfaction, he got up and walked out of the room. Left in a paralyzed state of mind, I found myself walking through the shop and right out the door. Never did I return back, nor did anyone ever call me to get the details. Having felt violated, I remained silent about this ruthless man, who used his tricks of wisdom to control and destroy young girls. Glowing with contentment, Dexter won his argument to get me out of there and didn't even have the first clue to how he achieved his victory. After that I pulled the curtain shut tight to my independence and things went back to Dexter's way, while I continued to prove my unconditional love, at any cost.

Now being of age, with my state board test just around the corner, having heard it was tough, I crammed for days on end. With mother's support, after having taken the test, I returned home and waited for the results on pins and needles. Sitting in doubt, when the envelope addressed to me finally arrived, with mother standing over me, I anxiously ripped it open. Mother squealed out in delight, the very second she caught sight of my high passing scores. Now with my manager's cosmetology license in hand, a sense of wholeness washed over all of me. With my head swelled, I began seeking out a job, preferably one that offered me my own station. It was all easier said than done. For all too soon, I came to realize, with no experience or a following under my belt, I had little or next to nothing to offer. Desperation drove me to hit shop after shop. Eventually my fate took a turn and I landed a part time position at a four-station salon. The owner, a beautiful lady who worked out of one station, didn't offer me the world. But what she did offer was a position to start as a shampoo girl and pick up the overflow from the other three operators. It was well, basically a stepping-stone. With my acceptance, the job was mine for the taking. It might have become difficult to compete with four gorgeous operators, but it was the awed look in Dexter's eyes, that left me troubled. But in the real world, who wouldn't notice a stunning redhead or carefree frosted blonde. They were in real tight with the shapely brunette, who bubbled over with personality, who had caught Dexter's eye. Even though I never really felt on their level of beauty or skill, their kindness and wit put me at ease, enough to settle in for now. And with time ticking along side of daddy's clock, the only people holding my interest were the two male figures ruling my every attempt to be me, "Good old Daddy and Dexter himself."

In spite of the times Eileen and I were out and got a taste of normal living, we always had to return back to our unstable world with daddy's swearing in the background. Whereas poor mother, you could say that she did just about anything to hold the fort together. She would hold all those awful names father threw at her, while living his commands, until not just a storm blew its way in, but a full-blown hurricane.

PASSAGE VII

Straight Jacket

There is a man; he sits in a chair never going anywhere...the wheels on the chair you see, kept him from having any company. But with all his hate, he can't even show his face. He lost all his pride within. His life was sad for all he had...never could become that dad...always ruining all we had. As years slipped by, he sometimes cried...wishing he could suddenly die.

No-No not my daddy! I was almost reverting back to a child again, as they placed the straight jacket upon his lean upper body. His eyes cried out with a look of fear, I never saw before.

Those outrageous hours of darkness came crashing down, surrounding our terrified beings on an early evening. Battle, war, thunderous father, he was outraged! His eyes looked protruding, his face twisted in deformity. He was shaking his fist violently at us, yelling so hard I was certain his rage would throw him right out of his wheel chair. Fearing for our lives, mother Eileen and I, were driven down to the basement. With our knees shaking and our hearts pounding, we tore down the steps one by one, as fast as our legs would take us. Now out of father's range, with the protection of the stairway keeping us out of harm, we whispered out our worst fears, to the possible outcome of his behavior. As our eyes met, the mirror likeness in our eyes, were reflecting the same sinking fear, "That our lives were over."

In the midst of this drama, Norma's eyes widened in sheer disbelief. Remaining absorbed, her eyes began to show traces of tears, sharing for the first time in my anguish. Where and how it began, was nothing less than total insanity. It was somewhere in the middle of his mood, when father's rage turned on us. He was convinced we were all in on it, that we were a bunch of conniving conspirators. Sometime during his irrational bellowing, he called the police to turn us all in. He continued throwing us threats, while his ranting and raving seemed to go on for hours. It felt like forever before the police finally arrived and after they got wind of daddy's rage, they immediately came down the stairs to mother. We were so sure this would put an end to daddy's bellowing, being that he never let anyone witness him in action. But he didn't stop and suddenly, he was sitting at the top of the basement stairway, shouting down threats and profanities. Spontaneously somewhere in the middle of his bellowing, his voice would change back and forth into the sound of insane laughter. The officers were intensely observing mother, before resting their eyes back on daddy. In daddy's next breath, the officers moved towards mother and began drilling her with questions. Her head was spinning. She couldn't take anymore and she couldn't think clearly. Even with them there, you could hear father in the background kicking up a storm, he wasn't giving it up and the cops weren't giving in. Calm and collected, one of the officers extended some filled out papers over to mother. With a point of his finger he said, "Sign on the dotted line, right there."

Poor defeated mother, without asking, reading or questioning their intentions like always, did just what she was told. Without a doubt, mother was always so trusting and true. She was certain the police were only there to help calm daddy down. But I couldn't keep their aloofness off my mind, feeling their coldness through and through. My eyes stayed glued to their faces even in my fear, wondering why they showed no signs of care or compassion. Once mother signed her signature, they completely ignored her delayed questions and made a quick phone call. Nerve racking as it was, I still was engrossed in eavesdropping on the two officers comparing their notes. Their low volume of conversing together was muffled, making little to no sense. Probing further, I followed them up the outside stairway leading out to the garage. As they moved down the driveway, away from my ears, it left me in a fog. Lost in the moment, it felt like time was oddly standing still. Bringing me back to the now, an ambulance had pulled into our driveway, followed by another cruiser. Suddenly alarmed, my heart felt like it was pulsating in my throat, while some of the neighbors were already out and looking in. With a bunch of hand gesturing going on, the paramedics followed the officers in through the basement entrance. One of the officers continued to speak in low volume to the paramedics, leading them up the stairs, where by now, daddy had reverted back to a calmer state. Being that we were still uninformed to what was actually taking place, we exchanged a number of frightful glances at each other. Suddenly afraid for daddy mother cried out, "What are you doing, wait, what are you doing?"

With no reply, she shrieked out in alarm. "Please answer me, where are you taking my husband?"

His response was callus "Well lady, you just signed the papers to put your husband into a hospitalized institution."

Poor mother, by now she was gasping for breaths with hysteria, trying to justify her signature, "I didn't know that is what I signed, you didn't tell me."

Her voice rose up louder, quivering as she pleaded, "Oh please, but you didn't tell me, please, I beg you to stop, please do not do this to us, this will kill him."

The officer gave a shrug with his shoulders. "There is nothing I can do; it's now out of my hands. You'll have to take it up with the courts, it's now in their jurisdiction."

In horror, we watched as they placed the straight jacket on daddy's lean upper body. There was no fight, just the look of terror standing out in his eyes as they took him away. It was horrible, we cried clinging on to one another for dear life. We just stood staring out the window, long after the ambulance had moved out of sight. It felt like we were in a dream and that we would just wake up from this nightmare and laugh over the insanity of it all. Only it wasn't. Instead we fell into a state of silence, with words so lost, they felt forbidden somehow. In those next long hours of darkness, it felt as if death had washed over us, leaving us with little to no sleep that night.

It was early the following morning when mother anxiously called daddy's attorney, only to learn it was true that he had been locked up and secured. He gave mother a brief summary of where to visit and to leave all the worrying up to him. He made it all sound, as if it was just a terrible, terrible, misunderstanding. He calmed her down, by reassuring her that before she knew it, daddy would be right back home with us. Once we had the location, without losing a minute in time, we showered, dressed and set out to go see father. After a long drive, the address took us into a deserted area where father was being restrained. Standing outside the overshadowing structure, our hearts were tattered in two. The bars running across all the windows, was the first clue to what we were really up against. We entered into a long narrow hallway, lit up with fluorescent lights, with a loud humming sound following us from behind. The only way into the next door was to ring a doorbell for assistance. After a long few minutes, a thick plate glass window slid open. Once mother gave him all the proper information, we were buzzed in and lead down to a large open area where only tables and chairs made up the room. It was a cold room, lacking comfort and warmth and I pulled my sweater snugly around me. While waiting and waiting in a restless state, still with no sign of father, it was getting harder to fight off our tears. It didn't help that the loud screeching voices, echoing in the air and bouncing off the shallow walls, were spine chilling. It was hard to keep my eyes away from a man sitting two tables away, making perverted faces and yelling out foul names. Everything going on, was very eerie and out of place. In those unsettling moments of time, I was wishing, I was just someone else.

Following what felt like forever, a man wearing a grey uniform, holding on to his poker face, wheeled father down. Oh daddy! Oh but he looked so weathered and beaten down. No sooner had the aid walked off; father's tears began to run. He cried for his misery, calling out to mother by her pet name, "Oh Slalina, please don't leave me in this place to die, let me come home, I'm sorry I'll do anything, I promise I'll be good."

Mother bent over father trying hard to comfort him in-between his long claimed list of being horribly mistreated. Father's huge pride had taken its course. In humiliation, his head hung down, tearfully telling mother they would not even allow him to keep his toiletries in his possession. Mother understood, for these items were not only required, but also crucial to help father relieve himself. By the time father had finished crying out his fears and for all we had witnessed, we became putty in his hands. The more kind words father passed to us using our pet names, the more we softened. Eventually we just melted into his grief. Daddy had made up mother's mind for her and we were in agreement. We wanted our Daddy-Joe back home immediately! Prepared and eager, mother scurried off with a strong sense of determination, with her shadow me, trailing from behind. After stopping off for directions, she headed right for the nurse's station to speak to the head nurse. Just as it came into our view, mother's firm voice came pouring out so loud it echoed in the hollow air. "Hello, hello I am taking my husband home with me right now, hello I need someone here to get him ready. Hello!"

The head nurse on duty came out of the back room and looked up at mother immediately displaying her hardness and her impatience. Just as mother began to ramble on again, the nurse swiftly cut her off, "My dear that is not at all possible, I'm afraid you're going to have to wait till his hearing. That could take up to a month, or maybe more."

Mother argued, she cried and then she was furious, maintaining they could not do this to him. She fought until the nurse gave her another round of reasoning and turned her back to her. Oh but it stood hopeless and no matter how much mother argued, the answer always came back the same. In defeat, we headed straight back to break the earth-shattering news to father. Hugging our father goodbye, in-between his tears was one of the hardest things we ever had to do in our lifetime. In our dismay, a cloud of guilt was hanging over our heads, for leaving him behind in this awful forsaken place.

In the next upcoming weeks, with father away, we visited him as often as possible. He remained as a broken man, with promises on promises, swearing that things would be different. With all his prayers, all he wanted was to come back home and be with his girls. Through all of father's sorrow and misery for being locked away, mother was sweltered with even more heat to get him out. If truth were told, a hint of dread at the same time, lingered through. Because in the days that followed, a strange sense of tranquility had settled its way in. Suddenly, we were exposed to all this unfamiliar inner peace and freedom. It was a beautiful kind of peace, which offered the serenity of feeling safe and content, with allowable laughter. Never having lived life without hostility, we simply did not know what it was like to live without it. Oh, but that pure taste of freedom and peace, made our mouths water for more.

It was during our wonderful environment change and our visits to father, when his hearing date was set. It was a crucial time for mother and she spent hours going over the smallest of details with father's attorney. But with father also having been coached and everything working on his behalf, it was over before you knew it. Daddy made it with flying colors and was granted a following day release to return home to his girls. There was instant relief, but then in the pit of my stomach, was a heavy case of the willies. Pertaining to that agonizing thought of turning back the clock, to that everlasting sound of tick tock, daddy is back, watching his everlasting clock. Perhaps in disbelief, one might wonder, why in the world would we bring him back home with all his violence? But in reality, four short weeks in the world of society, could not possibly have given us enough wisdom or strength to any new growth or change. This was not nearly enough time to absorb the nutrients of knowledge, to know any better. Oh but daddy was so happy when he returned home surrounded by the attention of his affectionate girls. Unbelievably, while surrounded by our loving daddy, there was laughter in the air for three whole solid days. For it only took three short days, for daddy to return back to good old angry daddy again. The institution now lay in the distance as if it never existed, while his cried out promises, were as dust in the wind. It was easy not to dwell on daddy's forgotten promises, because we just settled back in, into what always was.

Time ticked forward into the future and suddenly we had entered into another chapter of our existence. This was the festive year many changes began to move into play. It began when Eileen graduated from high school. Naturally there wasn't any party, in fact come to think of it, not anything. But she did get to go to her senior prom. She looked absolutely beautiful in her long, yellow delicate dress, while Sonny stood proud, shoulder-to-shoulder with her. Also up and coming were her plans already set in motion. Right after graduation she had a date set to marry Sonny. He came from a large Italian family and with tradition, a full-sized wedding, was expected. Somehow, someway, miraculously mother managed to pull the whole thing off, right under father's nose. In all Eileen's glory, I was taken aback after learning Grand Papa was going to have the proud honor of walking her down the aisle. The impact left me nothing but resentful and jealous, seeing she was good enough to receive moral attention from him and I wasn't. My thoughts got carried back to the past, and from the way Grand Papa looked at her, you knew she was as pure to him, as the whites of his eyes. Being he was only allowed to be intermittently around, I knew as far as he was concerned, I was invisible in his eyes. Since that day of reckoning, you could sense his strong bitter resentment, for he remained in his own kind of silence, as far from me as possible. Even mother tried to cushion my resentment by confirming that Grand Papa wanted to walk me down the aisle when my turn came around. With that and time, like everything else, I just accepted what was and moved my heart back to the excitement of being Eileen's chosen Maid of Honor.

On her glorious wedding day, she awoke to clear blue skies with white fluffy clouds. With an abundance of spring flowers and soft music drifting through the air, she became Sonny's new wife. Eileen was breathtaking. Standing next to my beautiful sister in my long, pink striking gown, left me proud to be her little sister. Her white veil sparkled with tiny sequins here and there and was pinned down to her freshly done up hair. Her full veil ran down the entire length of her simple, but elegant dress, detailed in satin and scattered pearls. She wore only touches of makeup, while her peaches and cream complexion glowed from excitement. It was really sad that father couldn't be there to give her away and see her off. He held a stand, refusing to even consider attending the church ceremony or the reception. Naturally, he also kept the house off limits to any company or festive activity. In fact father was rather strange in an unfamiliar silent way that day. What's more, he didn't interject any resentment, nor did he display any kind of signs of the true culprit that had already set the ball rolling…the fear and rage of losing control.

Following Eileen's wedding is when the ship started to sink. It was father he was losing control and began falling to pieces. In a state of panic, he was drowning in his tears, crying out all his fears of losing us. It was easy to love father when he wasn't angry and especially when he was sad. My heart went out to him and I tried with all my might to cheer him. Only the last thing he wanted to hear from me, were the details of my wedding day, that mother had just dropped on him. Even as it still sat months away, he disregarded any talk from me, angrily waving my voice away into the distance. Mother took it with a grain of salt, figuring he still had plenty of time to vent and accept that I was leaving. But little did we suspect that his waving arms and contempt were only days away from eruption! Of course we should have recognized the warnings. But it wouldn't have done any good, for his mood of destruction, was already only inches away from war. One day out of the clear, just like that he exploded and everything surrounding us became a towering inferno of rage.

With each new day, his mumbles became louder and louder, putting the fear of God into us. We would listen in fear, trying to silence our breathing as his insane mumbles intensified to whispers of blame. After weeks into his abuse, feeling drained and robbed of our inner peace mother and I continued to keep our anxiety and fear away from Eileen. We surely didn't want to lay any burdens on her, or dampen any of the happiness she had gained. Only, it wasn't us who let the cat out of the bag that day, but it was daddy himself. It was when Eileen unexpectedly stopped at the house, right in the middle of one of his raging fits. She felt totally deceived by us after we broke down and confessed everything from start to finish. She stared back at us in disbelief. She began to weep, claiming that mother and

I had shut her out and didn't care about her, as much as we cared about each other. After a life of being mislead, Eileen was expressing, exactly what we had been taught, that the giving and receiving of pain, was the gift of love. But like everything else, Eileen quickly got over her injured feeling of rejection and became involved in our war, trying to convince daddy, we would always be his girls.

As the days were building up to my wedding, mother was working on her own strategies, to gain some restraint over father's disruptive behavior. Since we were driven to spending so many hours in the TV room these days, mother knew something had to give. She was smart enough to wait until he had released all his anger and had reverted back to a calmer state, before she began to work on manipulating his moody tantrums. Initially she had gotten his attention, by refreshing his memory about the horrible conditions he would have to endure at the institution, if he started up again. At first it put the fear of God in him and he backed off just long enough, until it all began to penetrate. By the time he came back at her, he had it together and was laughing out in madness, reminding her, he had been proven sane. In her desperation, she gave him the jolt of his life, by resorting to what was once unheard of back in the day, the threat of divorce. It only temporarily put the brakes on to his irrational behavior, seeing, the strength of her threat to divorce him, just wore it self out and lost its power. Not only did it backfire into great anger, but also it gave him the reason he needed, to begin planting his own seeds for his future attack.

My prom and graduation came and went before any excitement could come to life. As far as prom night went, the flowers, the dinner and all the expenses, were a little much for Dexter's wallet. As usual, my acceptance was in its proper place, but deep inside, the emotions of being unworthy were fluttering in my head. But with all the bellowing going on at home, it left me indifferent, with no argument. When I informed the school that I would not be attending commencement, my diploma arrived in the mail leaving me with no regrets. Especially since my excitement was focused on my wedding day, set on the very same date.

My wedding day, was it a true disaster of disaster? Because it was, in the eyes of a bride to be, who awoke to the morning sun clouded over by man made darkness! Before my excitement even had a chance to get off the ground, the hateful sound of father's voice came piercing through. My feet never even got to hit the floor, when mother appeared with her fingertip pressed against her lips, forewarning my silence. Mother's eyes reflected dampness around the corners, as she pleaded in finger talk to hurry along and get showered and ready. Just the night before, one of the girls at the shop did my hair with spiral curls falling softly around my face. Even in my dread, I peeked over to the mirror to see if my curls were in place. Pleased with the reflection looking back at me, daddy's raging voice brought me back to the present. Once again mother held her finger up to her lips, helping me apply the last touches of my makeup. After, she helped me step into my full-length white gown, zipped me in and carefully snapped one hook at a time, attaching my long train. While we whispered amongst ourselves, we agreed, we should keep our lips sealed and not rock the boat. Once mother carefully fastened my long veil in place with her trembling fingers, she stepped back and gave me a loving smile of approval. In spite of the background music, just in case daddy changed his tune, my perfection was of the utmost importance. My mind was set, that once he saw me standing in my shimmering white gown, his anger would just melt away. Reality hit home, when the loud echoes of Grand Papa's angry voice shattered all my fantasies. Here, he had arrived after all, just as planned and joined right into the bellowing. Walking into the room, he and father remained eye-to-eye, face-to-face; both looking like the next world war was about to begin. There I stood like a beautiful princess, waiting to be noticed. Only when Grand Papa mutely turned his hateful face towards me, his bitter eyes displayed his disapproval. As pitiful as it may sound, I continued standing there with the same ridiculous false hope that father would just take notice. Instead, a war broke out in full force! Their loud angry voices carried back and forth, while I was drowning in my tears. Their strong angry current was pulling me down further and further until, I screamed out high above their voices. "Stop it! Stop it, Stop it, oh God why are you doing this to me?"

Everything came to a sudden halt! With Grand Papa knowing in one short hour he was to walk me down the isle, he gave me one last hateful look, before he stormed out the door. Knowing in my heart, he didn't want anything to do with me, it was obvious by his set of unhappy mumbles he was pressured into this. Rejection set in because I was stung and in my shame, fault followed. For all that was holy in me, I swore to God, for as long as he lived, I would never allow my eyes to ever meet his face again. Through all the weeping, if truth were told, I was deeply relieved that dirty Grand Papa would not be the thorn to walk me down the aisle of escape. But even with him gone, father's face continued to stand out red in anger, as he continued on with his tantrum. He was still out of control and my tears sat useless on my face. Now with him holding on to the phone, it only took moments to realize what he was up to. He was dialing the police, to have us both thrown out, gown and all. Worn down, mother gathered up our things and we quickly left, leaving behind daddy's flying fist with the sound of his vulgarity following us out the door.

On the drive to the church, mother allowed me to whimper out my angry accusations, daddy destroyed all that I was. But once we arrived, mother wiped away my tears pleading with me, not to allow him to ruin this day. With my heart tattered in two, makeup smeared, I painted on a smile and met up with Eileen, my Maid of Honor. Once again she stood beautiful in an emerald green dress, while the sun was streaming in, resting on her peaches and cream complexion. Accompanying her was my bride's maid, dressed in a lime green gown, with an emerald green bow across her bustle. She was a good friend of David's, one of Dexter's long-standing friends. Everyone's face stood out in pure excitement, unaware of the morning battle. In the meantime mother had quietly arranged for her brother to walk me down the aisle. Standing off to the back of the church, in a glass room, the vision of Dexter anxiously waiting came into my view. He was standing next to Sonny his Best Man and his usher, David. Dexter was dressed in a sharp white tuxedo, looking handsomely nervous. In those next moments my heart swelled up, ready to move forward, into the arms of this man who loved me unconditionally. Just as the ceremony music began to flourish, one by one, as we slowly began walking down the aisle, I believed my dreams were about to come true. "For better or for worse till death do us part."

Following the ceremony, a decent sized reception took place. Even though we left Daddy far behind, his twisted vision remained to haunt me throughout the evening. But it was mother's hard work and sacrifices that shined, with everything falling into place. After cutting the cake, with our faces smeared, the crowd joined in our laughter. Being literally dragged off to the dance floor, the bridal dance began with me in Dexter's arms, and ended with my lacy apron overflowing with dollar bills. Once the garter and bouquet were tossed out into the singles crowd, as voices cheered us off, my new husband scooped me up in his arms and carried me out the door. That evening we stayed at a cheap motel across town, having planned a little getaway honeymoon for the following day. It was late when we pulled up into the motel's parking lot and while buzzed on alcohol, once our heads hit the pillow, we crashed in each other's arms.

Bright and early the following morning, my eyes met Dexter's sweet face grinning down at me. His eyes twinkled and it fed me a basketful of confidence, that he was so delighted that I was his wife. After an hour of intimacy, we showered and ventured out for our three-day honeymoon in Niagara Falls. We planned on three whole wonderful days, to be free birds and just kick back and have a blast. Only my excitement quickly dwindled away, when I realized that after finally being handed the opportunity to all this freedom, I was afraid of my own shadow. Lacking to enjoy my new independence left me feeling weak and ashamed clearly I had disappointed myself. Being as it was, that my mind was already conditioned to a closed in world, all this new sense of freedom meant nothing. So in my ongoing dreams of flying free, it was a total let down, while all my thoughts were back home, fearing for mother.

So once we returned home, past Dexter's disappointment for my lack of participation, my first concern was mother. Relief took over when she was still standing, touching only on subjects surrounding our honeymoon. It was true that before either of us got married, there was never any concern to what she would be up against. Seeing everything was in a calm state, once we had left, we anxiously headed home to our one bedroom, basement level apartment. Dexter was more than generous, picking out an expensive blue and green couch with two matching his and her chairs. We also agreed, since we were both working, we could spring for a solid oak bedroom set, with a double bed and matching dresser and chest. Since Aunt Jenny had thrown me a bridal shower, we had lots of cotton sheets and some mighty fine gifts. Life had never felt so wonderful, so grand and I thought, "Things just couldn't get any better than this."

Still, this new life felt so weird in my mind. It was so odd, not to have to check out what programs daddy had underlined in his nifty newspaper for us to watch. It was also weird and wonderful at the same time, when handsome Dexter came home to me every night. In my mind, everything had to be perfect. Coffee would be brewing and supper would be ready, followed by a dozen ice-cold beers waiting on him. Oh how proud I was to be his wife. Being married was nothing but fabulous, for five weeks.

Only five short weeks had passed, when these scattered pieces of Dexter's true colors began to filter in and out. Around that time, mother began to display her terror of living under the same roof with father. Given father's rages, were becoming mentally unbearable for her, she consulted with an attorney for his advice. Following a few simple sessions, he advised her to begin divorce proceedings. He began reassuring her, this in itself, would scare the living crap out of him. This attorney was so sure, so confident that this perfect formula would bring father abruptly to his senses. In her panic and trust, mother went ahead and filed. Before mother even had a chance to think out her plan of attack, father got served. It was quick and the timing was impeccable. Out of nowhere, the sheriff showed up, catching daddy out of his room and handing him the papers, got a signature, then he was gone. Now mother stood alone to face father, while he began bursting at the seams, overflowing with hatred and contempt. No negotiating, no pleading and no tears took place, the shit just hit the fan and a new world war was declared. Nothing had gone as her attorney had promised and when father contacted his attorney threatening to take down the house, she panicked. By the time mother contacted her attorney, to inform him of the disaster that was taking place, he took a step back from his original plan. Changing his tune, he was warning her of what she was now up against. In a state of shock, this war had put mother between a rock and a hard place. In view of the fact that he was paralyzed, the ball was now in father's court. Poor mother, if she dared to leave him, she could face charges of abandonment. She would have to stay to grin and bear it, until the divorce was final. With all these obstacles hindering the split, it could take up to several years before it came to court. Even though her safety was at risk and she would be living in constant fear on shaky ground, back then, that was the law.

In time, father's hate began to drive him to breaking all his own rules. Before the fat lady had a chance to sing, father joined forces with, well, well, if it wasn't the voice of our Witch-like-aunt herself, who we hadn't heard from since the days of the steep, dark stairway. Right along side of her, was my uncle with his rights to be heard. Whom, we had not seen or heard from since that day when both he and our bathtub were tossed out, right along side of that orange yummy candy. Both of them were filled with their own convictions toward mother and planned on burning her at the stake. Adding power to all of their allegations, their cruel convictions were backed up by their own dear father...good old Grand Papa himself!

They were quick to judge, pointing to all mother's selfishness, regarding their defenseless brother. They were on their own warpath, claiming to father that mother was useless and should just be dumped. Slowly they were making chopped liver out of her, while they continued to brainwash father. If there was even a chance in hell and mother were to get down on her bended knees and beg him to take her back, as far as his family was concerned, past punishing her, there was no turning back.

But mother always got the scoop whenever his family was plotting against her. In father's misery, every time he had another outburst of rage, he would reveal all his plans of revenge, that he had cooking on the back burner. Referring to her as she, she, she, the more father's family stepped in, the more pumped up he became. This interference was intensifying his vengeance and it all took its toll on mother. She began buckling under and was driven to living in one bedroom to escape the insanity, as father's voice snickered out with madness, that she was to stupid to survive in society and the earth would just swallow her up. Inside mother's confined world, father held enough negative energy to brainwash her to believe, she was doomed and didn't have a chance to survive, outside of his walls. Undeniably father had succeeded and beaten her down once again.

While daddy remained in his corner of his world, mother remained in hers. But during the times Eileen and I went to the house to give mother moral support, daddy always hid behind his locked bedroom door. Even as Eileen cried out to him that she was carrying his first grandbaby, only the silence in the air could be perceived. Catching Eileen off guard, I revealed to her, that we too had a baby in the making and I wondered for a moment if daddy could then turn his back on two!

Continuing to plead with him through the door, Eileen's face suddenly looked confused to his whereabouts. It wasn't as if he were out for the day, I knew he was there all right. You could clearly hear his whispers of mumbles right through the water glass, pressed against my ear to his door. There was an eeriness of energy just sitting around us and still even his soft mumbles had the power to make our knees quiver. It was by chance and unexpected when we finally caught father off guard and out of his room. When he came into our view, his belly lapped over the knot tied waistband of his green army pants. Dear God, but his face was covered with this unrecognizable panic, as he fled to escape us. He was locked into his own brainwashed terror, with each shove he gave to the wheels on his chair, taking him safely back to his corner of his world. Sick at heart, in his irrational behavior, he was sneaking around like we were after him. Here, during the time he and mother were hiding from one another, he had turned himself into the injured victim. Oh daddy, there was no hearing us, but we just couldn't let him go. We were both tranquillized with obsession and feared the deliberation of losing father's love. It was true that we both stood guilty of loving father unconditionally, monitoring his every move.

Daddy wore blinders to the birth of Eileen's newborn son, whom they named after her hubby Sonny. No matter how proud her face stood as she held her baby out to him behind his closed door, he still held the power to rob and dampen her inner spirit and did just that! But following in my sister's footsteps, my own tummy dream come true was expanding into my second trimester. It was understood, that Dexter was counting on my paychecks, after, we touched on my working to the day I delivered and would return back in a few weeks. At the time, his reasoning made all the sense in the world and no argument came back from me. It wasn't until my last month, while frying up a batch of french fries, when my first line of defense moved in. Suddenly the pan was on fire and the flames were high and in a panic I picked up the pot by the scorching handle. In those next moments, the pan slipped out from my grip and the scalding grease poured over my right hand. My screams instantly brought Dexter up on his feet and into the kitchen. Once he got sight of what had happened, fear filled his pale face. In a state of alarm, he frantically began yelling out that he was getting the car.

No sooner had we arrived at the hospital, once they confirmed that the baby was fine, they completely over wrapped my hand, that had first and second degree burns. Being tranquilized and feeling like a mummy with the heavy gauze bandages, this stressful ordeal had drained the life out of me. There was no doubt Dexter had been put through the mill, appearing even more fatigued than me. In fact, he was unusually quiet on the ride home and just listened, as I displayed my concern for all my customers. But once he got it, that I wasn't planning on returning back to work until after the baby was born, a pained look crossed his face. Seeing that Dexter was a loan officer by now, he controlled all the money, including my tips and paycheck's. Being he was so darn dollar smart, he immediately began hitting on just that, our finances. Reaching for my uninjured hand, he gave it a squeeze, reminding me just how tight our budget already was. Before I even got to finish the issue of the pain and difficulty to work with scissors and hair color, he kissed away my defense. Following my track record, my battle was lost to my own guilt for trying to bail out. Prepared to endure the pain from every movement of my instruments, I returned back a few days later, wearing a rubber glove, while I managed to bear it like a real trooper.

Taking into account that I was being a full-fledged martyr, after giving birth, once again, guilt drove me back to work with wobbly knees. And in our excitement, we named our adorable baby, right after Dexter, while his middle name was proudly given to him after my father. In my desperation to reach him, my foolish thoughts led me to use my child as bait to lure him in. Having convinced myself, that my infant's cries were enough to win him over, I held my baby close to his door, calling out to him. When it finally sank in, that I too like Eileen, had lost the battle, my high spirits dwindled, turning into anger. It seemed that I was angry a lot these days, from Dexter's roaming eyes to his ongoing flirtatious ways. It had been intensifying over time and it didn't help when his buddy David, married a very attractive girl named Georgette. In spite of the fact I never fought for any of my own rights, my jealousy and temper suddenly came to life. During the times when he would drop subtle hints of how open his mind really was, it was my tears and denial that kept our marriage alive, blocking out the real culprit to our troubles.

With time passing, into the third year, mother continued to grin and bear her cross, whereas Eileen and I continued to concentrate on building our own families. Before you knew it, I was expecting again and it seemed perfectly natural, when Eileen discovered she was also expecting and following in my footsteps. But it certainly wasn't expected, when word came in that mother's hearing was set and scheduled for only days away. Mother's mood instantly turned to jelly and in a state of frenzy, she called upon her attorney for her next moves. With all his care and loyalty, he had gained her total trust and in her eyes, he simply was her hero. He assured her, due to all her years of being faithful and her dedication to father's care, the outcome would be nothing but fair. Now with the smallest of details worked out, he set her mind at ease and instructed her to take a deep breath and relax. With everything resting comfortably in his hands, mother let out a deep breathe of relief and shyly began planning out her tomorrows. Oh but mother was so cute in herself. Yet she was still frail, knowing her day of freedom would soon be granted and she would be leaving to join society. But as far as father goes, it never really hit home, because his family was still in control of his every move. Right up to the sunny morning of the hearing, which arrived right on scheduled. Oh, but mother looked fresh in her simple cotton dress, with her hair brushed back softly from her eyes. In spite of being worried, she was determined not to sell herself short on getting her fair share. Her attorney was right on top of things, making everything less stressful and complicated for her. Seeing that the courthouse was down the street from his office, he instructed her to just wait there for his arrival. So, we sat in his office waiting and then we waited some more. With so much time having passed, it was taking way to long, bringing mother up in a nervous state to her feet. Pacing, she was in an emotional panic, thinking up one reason or another as to why he hadn't shown. Suddenly the loud ring of the phone took our attention and the receptionist motioned to mother to pick it up. It was her attorney and he was reassuring her that everything was fine, just fine. He portrayed that somehow things got detained and to just relax and sit tight until he got there.

By the time he showed his haggard face, mother was frantic and she had damn good reason. Somehow the wool was pulled over her eyes and just like that, the hearing was over. Father and the whole lot of his family, had won their victory! Her attorney gave a list of weak, lying, excuses to why he never showed his face and exactly what didn't go down. At first, mother was in a state of denial. She whispered back at me with a teary reassurance, that he would never shame her that way. She was so sure, so convinced, that she followed him from behind, into his cluttered office. He passed her another round of his flimsy excuses, until his patience began to wear thin at mother's persistence. Guiding her out of the office gently by her shoulders, he commanded her to go home and get some rest and that he would get back to her.

It didn't take long for mother to hear it through father's demonizing laughter, while the loss was written on mother's face. Seeing that neither mother nor her attorney was present in court, this case was considered a no contest. This resulted in father's being granted the divorce along with the entire house and bank account. The rest of their assets were to be divided amongst them. Oh but mother's attorney, he was a smart cookie all right.

At least to a couple of rookies like us, who were never acquainted with a palm greased in green! After twenty years of ruthless hell, he sold out poor mother as if she were worth nothing and his payoff held no consequences for her. Overwhelmed in defeat, tears of devastation slid down mother's cheeks. In the days ahead, her attorney avoided all her phone calls and letters, turning into nothing. Nothing was the outcome and nothing was left, except for the certified letter, stamped with the date, mother had to vacate from the house. It was only a few short weeks away, poor mother had been raked over the coals and was now being thrown out unprepared, to face a foreign world, having next to nothing. With so much to do, there was little time to waste. As busy as my sister was taking care of this one and that one, it never crossed my mind, that she too was just as much of a caregiver in her own circle of life. Being that we were all caretakers, we put our heads together, to figure out a strategy for mother. Considering her divorce had injured her small amount of creditability, we put miles on our search to help find her an affordable place to live. The fact that she had landed a full time job at a small beauty shop heightened her self-esteem. It also was the key, which helped her get approved for the sale of a row house, on a busy main road. Being that this unit had been on the market for some time and needed work, it was affordable to mother's budget. It was definitely nothing to look at from the inside, the carpeting needed cleaned, the walls were chipping off its loud, yellow paint and mother was discouraged. But in the days that followed, as she weighted out her few options, just the fact that it held three bedrooms and a decent sized yard, was enough to lift up her spirits. Once she started connecting all the dots to her warm creative ideas, she realized it held great potential and was accepting to make it her new home.

With time rapidly moving ahead, in the company of father's demonized bellowing in the background, we began packing up mother's belongings. Pretty much, we were all working around the clock. Time, it seemed as if time, always clocked us in, to when and how, we were allowed to use it. It was no different for us now, having to sneak around the house in a timely manner. As we tried to quietly move and stack up the boxes, away from daddy's ears, my nerves were like a cat on a hot tin roof. Being in my third trimester, due to all the stress and still working, I began cramping, leaving mother and Eileen to finish up. But it was the boys, Sonny and Dexter that gave her additional support, by being available to move all her things to her unit. Inching its way to the day when mother had to vacate, everything was organized and ready to move out. Soon after, the rented truck sat waiting to be filled and in all the commotion, a sad stillness seemed to filter through the air. Neither the vibration of daddy's bellowing, nor the echoes of his laughter could be heard. Even his whispers of mumbles remained dormant. On the last load out, as we pulled out of the driveway the view of a sad and lonely, isolated man, sitting alone off to the side of the window, tore at my heart. This man, who sat without a friend and who was wasting away his life, was my father and I just couldn't stop being compelled to love him. But my sad thoughts and regrets could only be as short lived as father's calmness, sat brewing in his anger. Because once the memories of mother were all that was left, daddy didn't waste a minute in time and called his attorney. Just like that, he disowned Eileen and me and now we stood as mother, no damn good. With our Witch-like-aunt already solid in the picture, even we were aware that she was glowing in what she believed, was her future profit. Little did we know, she was smart and with daddy's new will in her possession, she wasn't letting go, she'd see to it with a tight fisted hand. But one heartbreaking day, daddy's angry words of persecution will be etched into our memory forever.

With mother settled in, before the snow had a chance to fly, an ice storm slid in right along side of my labor. Oh God, it was too early, but even so my baby was born. In his struggle to come into the world, perhaps he thought it would be less stressful, out side of the walls of my womb. When they brought our small baby boy out to us, my heart was filled with gratitude, that he made it, into our arms in perfect health. We named him Brad and once we brought him home, it was obvious he had a bad case of colic, adding pressure to having to return back to work.

Following Brad's birth, you would think that Eileen would have known better, after witnessing father's lack of interest to any of his grandchildren. Even after naming my first-born's middle name after him, father wasn't moved. But when Eileen gave birth to her second son, she proudly announced she had named him after our daddy Joe. She was beaming from head to toe, as she made her way over to his house for the first time, since mother had felt. Her old key still worked and once again, she presented her son to him, through his closed door. It was the same old, same old story. While he never claimed from behind his door that she had been disowned, he still gave her baby no recognition. Obviously, we were both still on the same path, of returning back to our tarnished childhood, determined to win his approval. Like always, he still held the power to rob her of her inner happiness and strength. It's almost ironic, in spite of my ill tempter and Eileen's maintained self-control; we both carried the same identical inner strength to survive in this life.

As for my sister and Sonny, they always took the time and money to share in a combination of activities together. In my own kind of yearning, Eileen reminded me of a wounded captured bird, which was now flying free. Aside from our teenage years, instead of feeling jealous, her sense of freedom inspired me enough, to try and coax Dexter into doing anything. Dexter showed no interest or desire. His on going excuse, always came down to the same thing, the almighty dollar. You would think by now, I would have figured it out. Knock, knock…hello…I still didn't get it. As long as I was married to Dexter, our money would remain glued to the lining of his pockets. He was holding on so tightly to the money, that we always ended up hanging out free minded, at my sister's cute ranch home. Their company seemed to be the healthiest and only thing we did, outside of Dexter's chosen company. It left me with the same familiar longing for life. If I complained, Eileen failed to see into the heart of my troubles. Instead, she only saw the surface of the illusion Dexter portrayed. Instead, it was mother who saw into my heart and into the complications of my marriage. In spite of her struggle to learn the ropes of living in society, she held the determination to learn and often-expressed her worry, concerning my marriage. It was all the subtle hints, like never having a spare coin, down to my bargain barrel wardrobe. During the hours we spent together, all her comments to Dexter's wallet and hungry appetite left me to do my own kind of thinking.

It was also mother's giving soul that brought us the tranquility to put a small down payment on a starter home. It was a small lump of money she had inherited after she had moved on her own. Our new home, was located on a shady side street, populated with plenty of children. It was simply a dream come true, an answer to our prayers. My eyes filled with tears of gratitude and guilt, promising to pay back every penny, as soon as we got on our feet. Still, I didn't get why our money was always tied up and unavailable for any of my needs. Knock-knock. But it was during my suspicious thoughts, when life took a turn in the right direction, leaving behind any doubts that were building. Here, turns out, after Dexter was approved to purchase the car of his dreams, he generously purchased a two door, used Pinto for me. This time, it was my illusion and it felt like I died and went to heaven. No more waiting for busses, no more lugging home heavy groceries with the strings from the ten-pound mesh bag of potatoes, cutting off the circulation to my fingers. These days even my marriage appeared to be sailing perfectly smooth, adding to the perfection, Eileen and I were both expecting for the third time. It wasn't until after she gave birth and gained a darling baby girl, when my envy started to grow. Pink this, pink that, pink streaming ribbons and bows…pink, pink, pink… even her baby's tiny little checks staring back at me, glowed in pink. With my due date only weeks away, my desperate need for a daughter was now being heavily prayed upon. In all my prayers was the promise to always shield and protect the daughter of my dreams.

The days were slipping by so fast and the frosty chill in the air was still hanging around. It was late evening, when I felt my first contraction. Pacing back and forth, once mother arrived, Dexter grabbed my suitcase, signaling me it was time to go. As we headed out the door, I blew mother a silent kiss with my fingers crossed, in hopes for a little girl. Upon our arrival, as my labor quickly progressed, they sent me up to labor and delivery. With some complications of the baby being face down, hours later, with one last push, my baby entered into this world. Worn down and medicated I drifted off, awakening to the feel of Dexter's sweet lips gently on mine. Still groggy, my mind was unclear and before I even had a chance to get worked up with hope, Dexter whispered, nuzzling my face, that we had a beautiful baby girl. Moments later when the nurse walked in with our baby, her pretty little chubby face and double chin, took me to instant tears of glory. She had a pink silk bow, attached to her one and only, long dark curl. Examining her, she was perfect from her curl down to her little toes and as I snuggled her close to my heart, nothing mattered. In the next few days, while surrounded by pink ribbons and bows, with pink balloons floating up on the ceiling, we proudly named our precious baby girl, Mae. After we brought her home to meet the rest of the family, she was a superb baby, eating well and sleeping through the night. But still it didn't make it any easier to return back to work to have to leave my baby girl. But, it was during the times when we were alone and I held her close that I would again promise, to always protect her from pain and abuse. But no matter how strong my mind might have stood to always shelter all my children, I was unaware to any damage; my unbalanced existence could bring forth to them. Ironic, little did I know my unhealthy past would follow me into the future stemming from all my bad choices. Mae, my precious baby girl, never had a chance for a fair shuffle, her cards were just dealt and in many diverse ways, eventually, one day my roads would become hers.

Believing we held the perfect sized family, Dexter's vasectomy was decided. But it was right after Mae was born, when our relationship suddenly took a turn. It was then, when Dexter began to drop subtle hints of wanting to play out his flirtatious ways. Past my tears, responding back with outraged jealousy, led us into hours of arguing. It was all adding up to change, except for the dollar bills, that were still glued to the inside lining of Dexter's pockets, giving him reason not to take me anywhere. Money…money…money…but it was the almighty dollar, which was the ruler of all. It always kept me working and it kept me home. Since all my paychecks were still being signed over to him, in return, he handed me a weekly allowance. After buying all the bare necessities, nothing was ever left. It was getting easier and easier to figure out that Dexter didn't have any problem reaching down into his pockets for his weekly case of beer, nor were his pockets on empty for any of his needs. Without complaint, eventually my acceptance became his expectations. It was that blast from the past only now it became, four could eat as cheaply as one. His weekly sirloin, was served medium, garnished with sautéed mushrooms, whereas our flame-broiled hot dogs, garnished with catsup, was served with a side of cream corn.

These days, it was all staring at me in the face and deep down my gut was telling me the unthinkable, that Dexter had to be hording the cash! Especially, since there was always enough liquor for the company we kept. Dexter's co workers, were real partiers, the chicks, well as beautiful as they were, left me feeling insecure and out of their league. In reality, alcohol played a very important role not only in our marriage, but also in all the games we played. Alcohol, yes it still held the power to lift my ego, stain my senses and slam the door right back in my face. Liquor may have kept me afloat, but once the buzz wore off, my confidence sank with regret, resurfacing in endless tears, crying and crying over spilled milk. Nothing ever came without argument, this life style wasn't my cup of tea, and pleading only took me back to being labeled as a prude. It all left me feeling like dirt and yet in my mind, I believed even dirt was richer than me, for at least it served its useful purpose.

This on-going practice of surrendering all my morals, rights and independence, in trade for kindness and acceptance, was inching its way to additional loss and failure. This trait was becoming just as deadly to my existence, as the need to be needed. Up to now, I had learned absolutely nothing! Not once did I ever comprehend that I was allowing myself to be loved and cared for so unjustly, not to mention the shame, my own behavior brought down on myself.

Past Dexter's wild acquaintances, we continued visiting with Sonny and Eileen on a regular basis. If we weren't playing cards, or cooking on the grill, we sat around tending to our babies. But these goody two shoes, get-togethers, were quite different from the company we began to share with Dexter's buddy David and his new wife Georgette. We drank plenty with them and we played loud, wayward games. Being that Dexter and David were so close, even our children were welcome to tag along over to their house on weekends. We'd all sit around drinking a cold beer, under their good old buckeye tree. Whereas the children, after racing around to collect the most buckeyes, in their thirst guzzled down Georgette's famous ice cold, pink lemonade.

Now good old loyal David, wasn't clever nor a handsome man. He wasn't charming and he wasn't confident, he was just a nice simple guy. Even his awkward frame stood simple, while he frequently tugged at his belt loops, pulling his sagging pants back up into place. His black hair, was kind of hip the way it always stood up spiked, bringing attention to his heavy, black framed glasses. He worked a nine to five grind in a factory. Everything about him from his disposition to his appearance was at odds to Georgette. Standing confident, she was a stunning redhead with a career as a nurse and a very liberated nurse at that! She worked part time for a Dr. James and her only household chores were to take care of the laundry and her kitten, Cuddles. But in spite of our diverse personalities and the fact that she only had to carry a laundry basket for her share of the responsibilities, we hit it off superb and her carefree ways influenced my molded sense of self-esteem. That was easy to do, since I was so hungry for a friend, someone, anyone to share in laughter. And it was that strong need and desire to belong, that kept our relationship rolling, even after her new transformation had transpired.

It was on an evening when we had planned a family cookout, when Georgette came over with a whole new makeover. She must have spent a fortune between her trip to the beauty shop to have her nails done and the low lights put in her hair. Looking her over with a stab of envy, she was pretty in pink. It was definitely her color, showing off every curve that met up with her long, shapely legs. Her long red hair shimmered against her tan face in the moonlight, her lips plump with natural perfection. There was no competing and I kept my eyes glued on her the whole time Dexter was locked into her spell. She knew it and was eating it up. By the time she was dishing out a sexy laugh, Dexter was eagerly eating out of her hand. It was all too much and I sat pouting the whole time, feeling small and betrayed. In a moment of being alone with Georgette, she called me on my mood. There was no shyness in me. With my lip protruding out, I accused her of teasing poor Dexter! Puckering her perfect lips, she threw back her head in dismay. It was all too painful for her, it was injuring her self-esteem and she withdrew from me. She gave me nothing in the days that followed, but a cold shoulder and a quick brush-off. My heart ached for the accusations and anguish that I had caused her and was more than willing to crawl on my hands and knees for forgiveness. With friends so far and in-between, even if I could afford to buy a friendship, they simply just did not exist on any shelf. But Georgette was way cool and blew it all off, before I even had a chance to beg. She won me over, what a pal she turned out to be and wholeheartedly, I began to confide in her, all the ins and outs of my marriage.

PASSAGE VIII

Freedom is Not Free

Through my heart and soul, I sit here with the candle flickering... feeling the loss of my life control. From my heart I wish you would have known all the things that bring love to spring and all the things that songs relate our life to be... and for me not to have to say... trust is a word that has to be earned.

It's amazing how faces, attitudes and appetites, could change in a year. It went hand in hand, with Dexter's new sense of feeling free and liberated. Day by day, he was getting bolder to expound on his desires, becoming a mover and shaker. Exactly what made Dexter decide to free his soul and confess? He didn't get caught, so why spill your guts and rip out my heart? Oh God, how long had I been sleeping? Here my dearest friend, beautiful, sexy, irresistible Georgette, was trying to steal away my husband. It shook me hard enough, to wake me out of my foolish bliss. My mind was locked into a crazed picture of his lips on hers, his hands roaming her perfect breasts. My mental image saw it all. Oh God, their naked bodies were locked together, while at the peak of their ecstasy, their hungry moans were thrashing inside my head. A strong bolt of jealousy emerged and I got locked into hating her, just as much as I hated me, and all this hate spilled over to Dexter. It didn't move him and he wasn't buying into my tears, tantrums or any of my accusations. Remaining together, he reached into the refrigerator drawer for a chilled long neck, bitching out loud with excuse, "It just happened, she teased me that's all, it's over. "

So, according to poor Dexter, he was the tormented victim here. After his claim of innocence, he put an abrupt end to any further discussion and turned me off. Hysterical, I tore out of there and took my rage over to Georgette's to have a show down. She wasn't expecting me. She had no idea Dexter had spilled the beans. Her face turned pale and she couldn't put it into words, becoming a stuttering idiot. The mark of guilt read clear across her face, yet she continued to fight her defense, dropping down her laundry basket and claiming her innocence. Oh, but she was so mortified from the judgment I had set upon her. She started to stomp away, while her long red hair breezed through the air, trying to get in the last word. Her image sickened me; it was so typical and so distasteful that I wanted to throw her arrogance back in her face. Before I got a chance to challenge her lies, she yelled for me to just get out, slamming the glass door behind me.

By the time I arrived back home, my shoulders were slumped over like mother's once were, in her long ago defeat. As I sat starring at a candle flickering, I felt beaten down, with self-blame oozing in and out of my thoughts. In the company of this latest misery, a pain sat gnawing at my heart, I couldn't sleep and I couldn't eat. In the days that followed, I cried hard inside myself, until my shattered trust, was only a cry away from going off in jealousy. In the weeks that followed, my vengeful mood grew strong and I wanted to strike back with revenge. Only, there wasn't time for retaliation, because by the time poor naïve David had been informed of the affair, it was a day too late and three months after the making. But, I never should have told. Now she was gone! All that was left of Georgette, was a pink envelope sealed with a kiss and the fragrance of her sweet perfume lingering in the air. In a state of madness, David came running over with the pink envelope in his trembling hands. There were bristles of his once spiked up hair, now falling over his forehead and he looked terrible, just terrible. Suddenly, poor Dexter was his cry pillow and in his broken down state of mind, he handed the envelope over to him. Hey wait a second. David seemed to have forgotten all the details about Dexter and his wife, I had readily reported to him. Yet, Dexter lost no time taking out the crumpled letter from the envelope. While he began smoothing out the crinkles, his eyes were cast down just long enough, for his face to come back up flushed.

"Dear David.

You can keep the world in which we lived and everything in it! The love that Dr. James and I share is everything we never had and he is everything you can never be. Well, this is goodbye.

P.S. Please take good care of Cuddles for me.

Georgette."

Who would have ever thought in a million years, that Georgette would pack up her clothes and take her whole new look and shack up with the Doc! Here, she didn't want Dexter after all! Suddenly feeling stupid in Norma's presence my tears turned to untamed laughter. Norma's face was soberly locked on mine and responded, "And how did that make you feel dear?"

Remembering quite well, past a moment of relief, a lump of resentment and betrayal had swelled up in my throat, because our friendship had been nothing but a lie. Having felt double-wounded, the only way I seemed to be able to lick my wounds were from my thoughts of evening up the score with Dexter. Only all my thoughts were all wasted energy, because I was to busy worrying about his next moves. Inside my hysteria, for what I put myself through with all the shameful snooping and panic attacks, was simply a waste of self-indulgence. It was all bringing me down, devouring my self-respect. It was once only a weekend worry, but now it could be anytime, anywhere. The outcome from this affair only seemed to reassure Dexter, that no matter what he did, he was free from having to pay consequences. But if truth were told, there was going to be a price to pay, and an almighty price at that! Because all my misery began to set me back in time. Not only did the same self-hate as a child return, but also anytime Dexter's eyes began to wander, I began playing out daddy's tantrums, throwing an army of accusations at him. Locked in this misery, I believed I was the only one on the planet, who allowed them self to be treated so shabby and unappreciated. The truth was, what I was willing to alter was absolutely nothing and I was convinced, Dexter would suddenly wake up out of his hunger and realize our love, was everything he ever longed for.

Once Georgette had moved out of the picture, it was always Eileen who I called concerning Dexter's tight fist and infidelity. Even as she had never witnessed his infidelity, or took any real notice to his tight fist, she took on the role, of becoming my caretaker. During our phone conversations she was more than willing to give me her ear, trying to mend my every thing. But whenever we got together outside the walls of our home, our frame of minds sat in a difference of opinion. We usually met up for coffee at Eileen's favorite hamburger hangout. After piling into a booth surrounded by our boys, sitting on the table in their own baby seats, were our gurgling baby girls, dressed in shades of pink. With the boys content munching on fries, Eileen and I always started out lightheartedly until our conversation shifted to the past, awakening both of our tainted images. Suddenly we were competing and it jumped from husbands, to finances, landing back to good old daddy himself. Suddenly in argument, we both said a lot of wounding words, but after Eileen lashed out, that all my stories were wild and far-fetched, my temper rose and both being quick to the draw, we were in another war. It seemed, no matter how hard we tried to connect, the past and all its unresolved issues, kept an invisible wall between us. With all our tattered emotions and unbalanced facts, we were living inside a shaded truth. And it was inside all this shaded truth, when the mystery letter came in the mail, addressed to me.

Immediately recognizing the handwriting, my mind was racing a mile a minute. Trembling, my hands tore away at the envelope in disbelief, there was no doubt in my mind, just whom it came from. It was from daddy! Overwhelmed in excitement, I couldn't read his desperate words fast enough. "Oh poor daddy. Here, it seems my Witch-like-aunt had been mistreating him and now he was done with her for good. He was alone now and he was begging to see me. Oh God, he needed me."

In all my excitement, my heart was doing flip-flops, tucking this one into secrecy, out of Eileen's reach. Guilt ran up my spine, but with the fear that she might get furious and mess everything up, I just couldn't take any chances of blowing this opportunity. My sneaky thoughts were pulling at me, but then daddy's face stood out and I though. "Oh hell, I'll just tell her later."

Without losing a minute in time, once the children were fed, dressed, and snuggled in the car, we were well on our way.

By the time we were pulling up into daddy's long driveway, the boys were as excited as any two and four year olds could be, to see their long lost Grandpa. Stepping out of the car, I gathered up Mae in my arms and instructed the boys to follow me from behind. While gazing around and taking in all the familiar sights, I walked along with the children across the sidewalk, past the big picture window, leading up the steps, right to the door. All of a sudden in a heated sweat, my enthusiasm was replaced with flashes of past memories. Now I stood petrified and with hesitation, I gave three calm knocks. Nothing was happening and I quietly shushed the boys, and rested my ear up to the door. Listening as quiet as a mouse, a sense of eeriness began to fill my gut. With the children getting restless, my hand slowly moved down to the doorknob, giving it a quiet slow turn. It was open! By now, all my courage had drained and I felt out of place and spooked inside and out. This was daddy's time to be off his parallel bars, and in front of the picture window and buried in his newspaper. My mind got carried away, imagining that it was too late and he was lying or sitting dead in his chair. Working myself into a panic, I frantically turned the knob once again, giving the door a firm push and stuck my head all the way in, yelling out loudly.

"Daddy... daddy are you there? It's me, Beaky Nose."

All that came back at me was a gruff "huh."

That was enough for me, and the children and I worked our way into the living room. There he was, just off to the side of the heavy drapes! He was sitting knees bent, cluttered in newspapers. Never looking up at any of us, he stayed absorbed in his nifty newspaper, gabbing on and on, about all his neat deals. Loudly clearing my throat, after pushing my children up in his face, it silenced his rambling. At last, I had gotten his attention. He looked up sheepish, as if he had awoke from twilight, locking his eyes on us. Nodding over from me to my children, he half smiled from the corner of his mouth and silently absorbed the moment. Except it was only for the moment because, something triggered him off. In his next breaths, he brushed off the children and was ranting through the days of yesterday nonstop. It was as if I had never been gone. Inside his head, he was emotionally in the same place, as where he had left off years ago. The situation was hopeless, it was no use he wasn't hearing me. Through it all, I reverted to silence, while my eyes rested on the open rooms, filled of nothingness. By the time the hour had ticked away, I already had the scoop on my Witch-like-aunt's lies and conniving ways. But it was mother's name that made my skin begin to crawl, because by now, daddy had started up on her. The time had come and he wanted me to choose. He wasn't taking no for an answer. He began cursing her and cursing me with pressure and I couldn't do it. The room was spinning and the energy of hatred was bouncing off the walls. My temper, his temper, they were one and the same. While shouting in defense for mother, he was bellowing back at me to get out. So we did. With ill feelings, as injured as he left me, I left the inside door open, so he would have to wheel over to close out the world himself.

On the way home the kids were crying from anxiety and I was silently crying right along with them. To ease their tears I stopped off at Mickey D's and got the children a burger and fries, from a pocketful of change. And for myself, I lapsed into deep absorption, believing the world was filled with nothing but deceit and cruelty. In my last attempt to nurture myself, I convinced myself that daddy still loved me and began soothing myself out loud, "Maybe tomorrow, yes definitely by this time tomorrow, he will be sure to call."

The children's loud giggling, broke my concentration. Content and entertaining themselves, they seemed to have forgotten about the howling episode. Lost in thoughts about daddy during all those hours, it was only then, when I became aware of how late it had gotten.

By the time I walked in, Dexter was home, having only worked a short day. He already had attitude, because dinner didn't reach the table on time. It only created another ruckus, leaving me on edge the whole time I was spilling my guts to Eileen, who was on the other end of the phone. The second the sticky news, concerning daddy was out, she was madder than a disturbed hornet. Perhaps, I should have kept my mouth shut, but I didn't! She was accusing me of being deceitful and cruel and began blaming me for ruining her chances to see him. God, she wasn't hearing a word I said, kind of like daddy. Now, she was throwing a massive temper tantrum kind of like me. Oh God. Then the phone went dead, but it wasn't over yet by any means. Not until she called back three more times to get her piece in…only to hang up after I began throwing up her faults, kind of like her. Dear God, every emotion we owned good bad or otherwise was all tangled together in a mass of madness.

The whole evening my anger was smoldering and by the time my head hit the pillow I was mad as hell at the whole damned world. Mad about Eileen, mad about daddy and mad at Dexter, for anything and everything, he ever said or did. Tossing and turning all my emotions turned on myself. Believing I was not worthy enough to be loved and cared for, I began to dwell on all Dexter's fantasies and all the lies he had fed me. It left me wondering why there was never any happiness or contentment among us and why my misery never came to an end. In my mind, an escape out of this life, could only be achieved through death…

But Daddy, in the days ahead he never called. He lied when he wrote to say he needed me…there was no truth in him. Thus far, everything I had experienced with the outside world, was telling me that maybe, daddy had the right idea after all. My corner of the world was filled of lies and more lies. All this deceit was piling up and I wanted to crawl into bed and pull the covers tight over my head. Whoever came up with the bright idea, retiring to bed with tears and depression will bring back sympathy and remorse? For me, it never worked, let alone solved any of my problems. It only brought me wasted time, generating another dose of retaliation. Throughout our relationship, I know now, there were all the things I could have done differently, starting with me. But I didn't know any of that then, not even after finally reaching a point of no return.

In a nutshell, my marriage, well hell what could I say. He was wrong, I was wrong and the whole damned marriage was doomed from day one. When is enough…enough? Evidently I was a glutton for punishment and willing to swallow another portion of Dexter's hand fed crap. Little did I know, when the howling strong winds blew in a treacherous blizzard that March day, it would literally hit home. It was late afternoon, a day of working at the shop and due to the weather, everyone packed it up and called it a day. Getting home was another problem altogether. No sooner had I pulled onto the main road, traffic was slipping and sliding past a three-car pileup. Before I even reached the bottom of the steep hill, I knew I was in trouble. Sure as hell, losing control, my car went into a spinout, and landed knee-deep in a snow bank. In spite of being shaken up, it had to be my lucky day. There not ten feet away was a telephone booth. After digging through my purse, I held on to several dimes and stepped out of the car. Heading for the phone, my short legs struggled through the deep snow and I pulled with all my might to slide the glass door open to get inside the booth. Dropping in the dime, with ice-cold fingers, three rings then four, five, six, what the, where was he? My first inkling that perhaps, he was out hunting for me, dissolved as quickly as it emerged. It was getting worse out and my pile of dimes was dwindling away. Damning the phone, no coins were being returned as I continued trying to call. With two coins left in my hand, sounding out of breath, he finally answered. Oh, he was fine claiming he was just busy with the children. But by the time he got half the story out of me, he was out of patience. Sounding infuriated, his high-pitched irritated voice came back at me, "Don't you realize, what you're asking me for here? It is damn hazardous out there. Look, with having to pack up the kids and all, it's less than a mile. Come on, you'll make it home before I could even attempt to get there."

He didn't even wait for an argument back, when the phone went dead. Perhaps the storm had taken us to disconnection. Yes that had to be it. Come on, Dexter wasn't a beast. In my heart, I knew if he even thought it was dangerous, he would never have left me out there. Feeling despair at that point, there was nothing to do but work my way back to the car. Oh but the gusting winds were picking up and my heart was hammering in fear. Trying to get the courage to move forward, I sat just long enough to warm up my fingers and chilled bones. While stepping back out of my car, the temperature was dropping fast and the stiff cold air, hit me in the face. Burr, it was so bitter cold, ice was beginning to form over the accumulated snow on the sidewalks. With each step up the long hill, my foot cracked through the thin ice, sinking down into the snow. The pace seemed long and endless. With frozen hair and numb fingers, I was so relieved to see home sweet home come into vision.

That is to say, until disbelief met me, after walking through the door. There, relaxing on the couch with his legs stretched out, with a drink in his hand, was Dexter himself. He wasn't alone! He was with some hefty, male character and they were chatting away non-stop. Instantly I was taken aback, with bitter second thoughts that the click that had taken us to disconnection, was sure as hell, Dexter's doing. Holding on to that notion, he wasn't taking any notice to me. He wasn't worried. He was too busy having a grand old time, without so much as a care in the world. Oh but I was so mad, there were flames in my eyes. Never having seen this fair complexioned, rosy-faced character before, he already rubbed me the wrong way and I wondered, "Who in the hell he was anyway?" Breaking the ice, one chilling "Hello" fell sarcastically out of my mouth. This chap, who I will call the Character, just sat there looking up at me, with his greenish eyes. His half assed grin showed no more concern than Dexter, even after I bitingly underlined, "Ya know…I could have froze to death out there."

Instead Dexter took his concerns of the weather over to this Character, offering him the comfort of our home for the night. Upon his acceptance, Dexter got up to refresh their drinks. "Great, just great! Now this anal fiber was stuck here in my face all night, to just sit around and drink up our money."

Oh…man I was screaming inside myself and marched off to go warm up and prepare dinner. After throwing a casserole together and putting it in the oven, I yelled down to the basement play area to fetch the children up for their baths. As far as I was concerned, this was going to be an early night…and early it was. Because once dinner was served and the kids were tucked in for the night, the time was seven-eleven. It was definitely a ridiculous hour for us to go to bed. But regardless, wanting no part of their alcohol charade, I retired to my room, mumbling goodnight sarcastically under my breath. Popping open one of my love story magazines, after sipping on a can of cold pop, my mind began to clear. By the time I was lost in my forth adventure, time had melted away and my eyes grew heavy and I drifted off to sleep.

It was the chill in the air that woke me to the sound of voices in the room. In a drowsy state of mind, I became aware that the blankets were twisted off and my nightshirt had risen up high enough, that my naked breasts were sitting perked and exposed. Their whispers began to come through, piercing the silence of the still night. With my eyes shut tight…thump…thump…the sound of my heart, thumping to the sound of their whispers. All too soon, I understood the bartering that crossed between them. Oh my God, he was checking out my goods, to see if they were worthy enough for a trade. Mortified, I couldn't stand it. I wanted to cover my ears and push their voices away from my burning heart. Oh Dear God, he wanted to trade me for a different taste. In a sandy state of mind I felt like the grains in an hourglass, waiting to be released before their whispers finally trailed away. Once they were gone, there was no reason to pull the blanket back over me. Dexter had already seen to that, right after he finished putting me on display. It appeared from their on going whispers, that this bargaining had been discussed earlier between them, over cocktails. Dear Jesus, what was happening to me, to us? The answer my heart was telling me was just too much to bear. My tears started to run, reminiscing back to all the yesterdays and feelings of daddy's misery and the shame of being branded as a whore for Grand Papa's violations. Locked into this twisted sentence, I curled myself up, regressing back into the image of a little girl. It was so typical in times of ill treatment, to revert back into the past and this time was no different.

When morning arrived, my mind had never slept. But it was sometime during the night and the morning sun, when my attitude and determination emerged to get his motive out of him, by putting on a false everything. By the time my feet hit the floor, my worst fears and tattered emotions were hidden behind my painted face, as I cornered Dexter revealing what I had overheard in my pretence of sleep. In spite of all my mixed emotions, another part of me was holding on to a flute of hope. Or maybe, it was really the fear that my heart would surly melt down in his absence if he left. While waiting for his response, I was holding my breath that he would be filled with regret for his degrading falsified actions. Covering my emotional breakdown, by displaying a drummed up phony attitude of acceptance, threw him off guard. A flash of eagerness filled his face and without even a stutter, he boldly owned up to his actions. In his excitement, he didn't just want me to have sex with this Character, but he eagerly expressed the thrill and desire of wanting to watch. It had all backfired on me! In a moment's moment, my false face and attitude shattered, bringing me back to reality. Feeling ill and full on insult and rejection, my angry face and temperament, were out in the open, displaying all its true colors. Face to face, we began loudly whispering back and forth in argument. It quickly turned ugly and everything got thrown back in his face, including the cold glass of water, clenched between my trembling fingers. Winded, he stepped back and then he lost it with me. He wasn't willing to lose to another one of my tantrums. Red-faced, his voice rose high, mocking, "Come on, come on, your such a damn prude, you spoil everything, why do you always have to act like such a little Miss Puritonic all the time?"

He was staring down at me. I could feel it down to my bones, as his disgust for me ran the entire length of his face. Gasping for air, my guts were churning and my knees were as soft as warmed butter. Something in his own anger, took him to pacing the floor and mumbling under his breath. Prude was the only word in a series of words, which could be openly heard. Prude, did he say prude, why that bastard. One dark streak of fury ran through me and my mind was devoured up with hate. It was hard to believe, the Character was still sitting around waiting and waiting for what? Dexter had pushed me hard enough, that I began expounding on revenge and getting even, mumbling under my own breath, "He'll be sorry, I'll fix him… yes I'll fix him real good."

It was my spiteful attitude that took me over to Dexter's side. He failed to take notice of the true meaning of my mood or to my pale drained face. It was my unexpected come back, that brought his anger down and his attention back over to me. "Hey Dex, sure, hell okay, I'll sleep with him, if that's what you really want, it's no problem, go on, go on I said, go tell him."

Eager to give the Character the verdict, Dexter did just that. Being the boys were playing at the neighbor's and Mae was down for a nap, it was time. Once I joined them, this so called Character made me sick. He not only looked like a leach hanging around to suck the blood out of me, but he carried the same half assed grin, as the night before. It was all up to me now and my spiteful energy was slowly having a meltdown. Dear God we were playing with fire! But somewhere in my mind, I believed that once we were walking into the bedroom, Dexter would come running after me, and beg me for forgiveness. Only, he never did! Forget hurt; that was no longer an emotion found in my vocabulary. Slamming the door shut was unexpected. It was not part of the deal and that wasn't nearly enough. In my own kind of rage, with every bit of strength I had in me, I somehow pushed the dresser with my legs and all my might, in front of the door. With twisted thoughts, a bitter laugh emerged, whispering inside myself, "Now Mr. Dexter can't come in to watch, well that aught-a fix him."

By now, the Character was giving subtle hints to his annoyance with our performance, remaining in a restless state. Anxious to get started, after wetting his lips, he ran his fingers through his sandy hair, just watching as I removed all but my panties. By this time, Dexter was angrily pounding on the door and his persistent voice came through the door with a fury. "Hey, let me in, what the hell do you think you're doing in there? Damn you. Let me the hell in!"

What the hell did he think I was doing? His selfish persistence to obtain his fantasy, gave me back the courage to seek out my revenge. Once I had crawled up into our bed and laid myself down across the spread, beads of perspiration were forming over my lips. When the Character's hungry mouth came down on mine, his full lips were wet and heavy, grabbing right for my panties. Being self-absorbed he never took notice to my silent tears. In only minutes, his organ thrust forward penetrating and wounding the last of my self-respect. It was quick and dry and after three last, loud grunts, it was over. Without so much as a word, he got up and stepped back into his trousers, pulling them up and securing them with his loud speckled belt. Well, the cat must have gotten his tongue for sure, since he had no simple words for me. Me, who he had just pounced on, with no care and no respect, well what did I expect? Oh God, I felt like the same whore, daddy referred to me as being. Oh daddy, why, oh why, don't you love me? Love…what did love have to do with my own inflicted pain, which I myself had chosen, out of hateful revenge.

Disgust for this Character sat brewing, right next to the hate for Dexter, still standing outside the door. Knowing I had belittled myself, my head hung in disgrace. It was too late to turn back now, for it was done! No sooner was the path to the doorway clear and the door open, Dexter's red face met mine. It appeared all puffed up, displaying patches of his uneven emotions. His green eyes were filled with heated resentment, but still, I speculated to myself, "If it was from his deceived anger, or perhaps, it was from his, too late now, sudden regrets and tears." Who knew, since I was too busy getting even, on the other side of the door with his fantasy! But this whole affair must have worn him down, because he wasn't fast enough to stop the bathroom door from slamming in his face. Moments of heavy silence followed from behind the door, then the sound of his footsteps could be heard, as he walked off. The faucet was running loud, with a blast of hot water streaming out, while I embraced my knees, just rocking, my mind lost in a daze. When the water reached its full level, after heavily soaping up a washcloth, I profoundly began scrubbing and scrubbing away my dishonor.

This Character, it was obvious that once I frigidly entered back into the room, it put a chill in the air making him uncomfortable. This time the cat had gotten my tongue and I had no simple words for him. Him, who by now, was squirming and stretching out his neck, trying to loosen his stiff collar, without looking like a cat on a hot tin roof. Some tomcat he was. He couldn't wait to get the hell out of there and stood up to leave, tugging at his collar the whole time he rambled over his awes, "Hey look awe, my girl is waiting for me at the house, awe, I better get a move on, hey guys, later."

No sooner had he walked out the door, I sizzled out hatefully to Dexter, "Hey later what?"

Fueled up and ready to argue, he let all my nasty comments roll off my tongue and over his head, before he spoke. Past angrily giving voice to his injured feelings of betrayal, he refused to argue, keeping his composure. Beaten in the end, my own battle was lost, producing no fulfillment or gains. All my uncontrolled anger and spite managed to accomplish, was to nourish my misery. In the next quiet hour that followed, the only words that passed between us were the threats that I was finished with him forever. His unshaved sheepish face looked over at me, locking his green eyes, on mine. It was apparent he was probing me with doubtfulness and wanted to call my bluff. Once he looked away, all I could figure was that he figured, this was just another one of my many fits. Observing him back, for any signs of remorse, as he grabbed on to a long neck beer, oh but he was so damn smug. So arrogant in his chair, his chair, just drinking his long neck, taking it for granted, there would be no consequences. My fury was on the rise and I wanted to strike back and hurt him below the belt. With the lowest of dignity, I did the next best thing and walked over to him and spit in his face. Now, we were one of the same, both abusive and unrefined mates. That evening, after taking the couch for the night, my thoughts were lost in my fantasy of being free and happy. Whether I meant it or was even strong enough to carry out my threats, in reality, the fear to be on my own with the children scared off all my strength. Hell, it took no time at all to figure out, making threats was one thing, but it was another, to hold on to the strength and courage to follow through. One excuse after another filled my head. In the days and weeks that followed, life just fell back into its everyday routine. In spite of my troubled mind, my heart stayed glued on love and hope. Still, no matter how foolish it was, I just couldn't let go and eventually, it backfired in my face.

There wasn't even time to recover from my own allowed injuries, when salt was poured over my open wounds, bringing our infected marriage to a head. The day started out sunny, but they say, when it rains it pours. Just when you think you buried the past, things have a way of resurfacing and coming back around to haunt you. Like I said, it was sunny that day and with the sun beating down on us, after raking the lawn, the children helped to bag up the leaves. It wasn't long after, when the mailman worked his way over to us. Smiling as he handed me the mail, he commented about the beautiful day. He was gibbering away, but my thoughts were locked on the pink envelope he had delivered, addressed to me. It had more than captured my interest and curiosity and I quickly waved him off, anxious to get inside. Observing the letter, while I was getting the children's crackers and filling their glasses with juice, it had my full attention. The envelope didn't have any return address, but oh how well I remembered! It was the exact size and shade of pink, as the crumpled envelope David had come running over with, the day his wife ran off. It was eerie, it was unsettling, but somehow, I just knew it was from her, Georgette!

Her long red hair and pretty face came into my thoughts and moving past her betrayal, a wave of loneliness for her company washed over me.

Only the pink envelope, I didn't hastily tear at it, instead I used Dexter's long silver letter opener, being sure not to rip what was inside. Smaller than the envelope, it slipped out. It was a cute postcard signed to a friend, the rest wasn't pretty and it fell from my fingertips to the floor. Stunned with confusion and humiliation, being unreachable, there was no way to lash out and accuse her of trying to get even. This absurd notion she tipped me off with, couldn't possible be true, but immediately, I dialed David. Since their split, he came around from time to time and I was counting on him for truth. On the third ring, when he answered, relief set in. Perhaps he had enough time on his hands, to dwell on his own bitterness, because before I even finished crying out my fears, he spilled his guts. Falling over his words he came clean, confessing, he's been carrying several nude pictures of me in his wallet, for something like years. As remorseful and guilty as he claimed he felt, he began pointing the guilty finger back over at Dexter. Numb in disbelief, sickened and nauseated, silence filled the line until I realized the dial tone was buzzing. My skin began to crawl, dear God, here Georgette was telling me the truth.

Due to my own allowances, by now, Dexter's prime collection told the story in black and white, no ifs ands or buts. Flashes of the revealing poses ran through my head and the thought of them being passed around, made my gut begin to churn with nausea. It left me with a great fear of who else might be viewing my naked exposed body. It was nothing but true, that I had been working through our marriage with nothing but rocks in my head and again my allowances became my own shame and disgrace.

Shaking inside and out, as my trembling fingers dialed Dexter's office, I couldn't imagine just how he was going to talk his way out of this one. Again, his attractive secretary Maria gave me the same, uppity response, "He's with a client and I'll see to it, he gets the message."

In my frame of mind, this time, it rubbed me the wrong way and I began scornfully imitating her abruptness. Banging down the receiver in a state of fury, my mind began madly running over my argument, which was waiting on him. Pacing and waiting on him to call, in my uneasy rambling thoughts, I began imagining the worst. Suddenly my head was full and my blood was boiling. Still, an hour later, with no call back from Dexter, my mood was building up to destruction. It was revenge of the nudie cuties, and after a decade too late, I was determined to reclaim my rights. With Mae napping on the couch and the boys dozing off to their cartoons, in his top drawer, the cardboard box sat overflowing, with my nude pictures.

Helping myself to the entire box, I planned to destroy every single picture and every thing that they stood for, including Dexter's pride and joy. In a bottled up rage, a tin can of charcoal fluid and a box of stick matches, I headed to the rear of the yard, straight for the barbecue pit. After gathering some fallen kindling from our old apple tree, I grabbed on to a big handful of pictures, dropping them into the pit. After empting half the can of fluid, it only took one strike of the match. The flames were shooting hot and heavy, sending back a blast of heat. After throwing in the whole cardboard box packed with pictures, I kissed off the pile of black negatives, before tossing them into the flames. Instantly they generated a heavy black smoke polluting the air with its filth. It sat lingering above my head for a spell and while lost in its glory, satisfaction passed through me. Following my high, suddenly the reality of what I had done to years of Dexter's pride and joy, clicked and registered.

By the time the air cleared and I returned into the house, once the children were up, I put on a pot of coffee and just waited! Pacing, smoking and keeping a close lookout for Dexter's arrival, kept my blood pumping. The minute he walked in, anxious to have it out, I followed him into our bedroom. Pointing to the open drawer, immediately he took notice and intensely looked over at me. Before he could even open his mouth, my cunning comments describing the bonfire, tipped him off. In his own disbelief, he began lashing out at me. His face was covered in hate; his eyes were bulged with resentment. The pink envelope, David's wallet, the past, the present, it was all being thrown in his face. It wasn't until after he yelled that he was through with me, when I tried my hardest to take a swing at him. It was no use, I was to short…he was too tall. But on the next effort to shove him, his hand swung towards me, slapping me across the face. Stunned and holding the side of my face, while even as the blow restrained my hysteria, I began backing up. It had all taken its toll. Staring at the walls in defeat, silent tears washed down my face. This was not at all like Dexter to throw a fit…that was my job. It was only his hungry sexual appetite and his need to exploit me that left a burning void in my heart. Suddenly I feared that I had pushed him too far and I ran into our bedroom. Throwing myself into bed, I sobbed into my pillow. "He doesn't love me, oh God, he was suppose to love me until I died."

Lost in pity after a good cry, dwelling on the past, exhausted, I crawled out of the bed and called down to the children, believing they had been safe from all the bickering going on. In my underdeveloped growth, this tinted image would have been blamed on all my injured senses, rather than an unhealthy past. Blinded, who thinks of things like heat registers or thin walls, through battle and war? By the time it came to light, it was a day to late and a lifetime to long.

Once the nightmare of the nude pictures and my shame relating to the Character faded into the woodwork, things only appeared to go back to normal…at least in Dexter's eyes. This time, something in me, deep down in the root of my soul, died. Over the weeks, as my tears fell, nourishing and cleansing my spirit, my heart began to bloom with strength and all of me began to change. In my mind, everything was different, starting with my job at the shop. With Dexter's hungry appetite always stirring around the girls, it was no longer working. Just like that, after years of building a following, I gave notice and quit. With the exception of my combs and scissors I put all my supplies in a cardboard box and buried them up in the dark attic. Out of sight, out of mind and while still having to maintain an income, I took to the streets, job seeking. Yet who would believe it, after only two days and no experience I landed a server position at a three star restaurant. It was a real break, with plenty of opportunity to make money. The real bonus was, that Dexter couldn't track any of my tips, as long as I was willing to lie. Faithfully, lie, connive and stash I did, all for my secret future, in which as yet, I had no clue. In my mind, no matter what the cost, I wanted to be free.

But while working nights, the children slept and a whole new world opened for me. This strange surrounding was different from anything I had ever experienced. Independent and self-supporting, describes the majority of people working on my shift. Silke, she was my inspiration, never letting me give up. Being experienced, she held a second job in a club, working as a bunny girl. She didn't bend, unlike the rest of us and preached, " Stay true to your self." With all this excitement going on in my head, I began to stay secret inside my thoughts, while Dexter grew more and more unsure of me. In time, after pulling further and further away from his interference and needs, I left him in body, spirit and in mind. All the deceitfulness and complications that began to buildup, was never planned out in my head, at least not consciously. But it was just easer to do things my way, all wrong, with a list of hard-core consequences waiting to be had.

PASSAGE IX

DECEIT

How much longer until it begins to storm again, blowing away the last of the pieces left scattered among the winds… blowing away the last of my trust and hope, to any of our lasting tomorrows…blowing, blowing… for gone are they in trade…

Having solved nothing, not for one little minute did I believe that the outside world could ever hurt me the way daddy or Dexter had. Sitting and facing Norma in this chapter of my life, all my lies, deceit and sins sat waiting to be uncovered and revealed. Having hurt myself, and everyone close to me, I began withdrawing. My life, it was true, I was now living it in a bubble, going nowhere and hiding inside myself. Yes, hiding from that awful fear of coming face to face with the naked truth. Oh God. I was choking on the painful memories and devastation, recalling all the harsh judgment that had once been cast on me. Oh how long I wanted to make it right only…it was all too much and Norma put her pen and pad down to rest. Our session was over! Dread followed me from her office, eating away at my spirit. Many, many days, slipped away before I returned back to see Norma. But this time the fight to move forward without resistance, was somehow, soundly instilled in me.

Once his handsome face popped into my head, tears of mixed emotions ran down my face. Awe yes, beautiful young and witty Jessie. On that day when he walked over to me in the waitress station, his deep blue eyes twinkled, enhancing his sweet smile. From the moment my eyes met his, I melted in his gaze, turning my knees to jello. Fair skinned, his chocolate brown hair, fit him to a tee and one cluster of his wavy hair, fell casually over his forehead. He was a real looker and had a genuine laugh that made everyone around him smile. He sure got my full attention and a wave of disappointment set in, when throughout the evening, I didn't catch another glimpse of him. It wasn't until the end of the shift, when fate met us head on and we collided at the door, knocking me off my feet. His laughter was all I heard, but as he lowered his hand to help me up, he was looking down into my eyes, melting every ounce of me. Gazing back up at him, he was just the right height, just the right everything and for a moment, a wave of hot desire shot through me. Giving me a cute and mischievous boyish grin, in breathless anticipation, he said " Well hi beautiful, care to have some coffee, tea, or milk with me?"

Holding back a scream of excitement, instead, only a shy "Sure, why not," escaped from my mouth.

Jessie knew just the place. It was a twenty-four hour dive, right around the corner. It turns out he hung out there many nights, before he got his wheels. Starting with a cup of coffee, with two cubes of sugar for him, a lighthearted chuckle of having family troubles set us both at ease. That was all it took and we began to confide in one another. Depending on the friction at home, he was content to live in and out of his coupe, until he got his own place. Gently rubbing his finger, around and over my wedding ring, a shot of disappointment crossed over his face. All at once, reality nipped at me and the thought and excitement of getting to know him better, slipped away. Still, he was extremely easy to talk with and it felt like we had known each other for a lifetime and a half. Beyond having a charming personality and tender heart, his morals he respectfully claimed, were high. Bringing understanding to the table, after laundering my soiled marital status to him in tears, he heartily agreed that my anger and sweet revenge was more than justified, not to say, he was partial to me.

But regardless of how things could have or should have gone, five hours later into the morning, our connection had a mind all of its own. As our discussion deepened, we ordered a piece of apple pie, topped with a jumbo scoop of vanilla ice cream. When Jessie generously spoon-fed me more than half of the serving, it was the most giving, intimate time anyone had ever shared with me. After that evening we were simply crazy about each other, stealing every minute we could to sneak away and be together. During the hours we sat by the pond, with the frog's croaking, his eyes shined deep into mine. We shared our food, our thoughts and our past tears. Up to now, past being unfaithful to my whereabouts, our friendship was uncomplicated and purely plutonic. He definitely looked up to me as being wiser, being a number of years older than he. He was willing as I, to share in his past failures and regrets, stemming from his own rocky roads and hardships. In the company of Jessie's needy ways, was my own needy appetite that began to stir and my role as a caretaker began to kick in. For the first time in my life, I felt so needed, so cherished and so padded from the rest of the world. In our determination to hang together, nothing could alter the platonic closeness we shared, except for ourselves!

It was all bound to happen sooner or later. Hell, even a fool would have seen it coming. Our longing, our needs, they had been building stronger everyday, into a hot passion of desire. Then one day we couldn't take it any more and just like that, we headed out into the country, with green fields and wide-open spaces. Stepping out of the car, a heavy burst of wind, blew through our hair, taking our breath away. Holding my hand securely in his, as we walked the dirt path to the door, we were showered in colorful leaves, falling all around us. It was a small cottage that we had arranged to use for the day, nothing fancy, but the old stone fireplace set the mood. Once we gathered up some kindling and an armload of mixed wood, as Jessie knelt down on one knee to strike the match, he grinned mischievously at me. Smiling to myself everything was perfect! Snuggling into the soft music, my blood began to boil at the closeness of his breath. But I needn't go on, the next thing I knew I was sipping a glass of white wine, as we watched the flames crackle in the dim romantic light. The comforting aroma of burning embers filled the room, smothering away the last tinges of guilt that were pulling at me. Surrounded by his sweet presence, his lips gently met mine, our hearts pounding, blending into one. Jessie took all of me vibrantly and sweet, both of us feeding on every hungry emotion that was running through our bodies. We tumbled in each other's arms, bonding in love and infidelity, like paper to glue. Worn down and lying damp in the tangled sheets, Jessie smiled at me, as he gently brushed back the blond strands of hair from my eyes. With a sigh of contentment, he reached over to the nightstand, taking out a cigarette from his pack and lighting it with his Zippo lighter. Letting out a long slow exhale he tenderly put it up to my lips. By the time we finished sharing those last moments, a feeling of dread to face the music, came over us. It was definitely time to go! Right before leaving, Jessie reached down into his pocket, for a tip. Pulling out a few crumpled up bills, with a confident wink, he casually tossed them on the dresser. Returning back a smile, we walked out arm in arm.

On the ride back, it was already dark; time had gotten away from us. Surely this time, there was going to be a price to pay, but in spite of the reality staring us in the face, we stayed lost in our own sweet world. Once he dropped me by my car, on the way home, the thoughts of our ecstasy, among the sadness of parting, ate up my brain space. It left me completely unprepared to face Dexter. Not two steps in; there he was, waiting right by the door. Quite honestly, he looked terrible and having been drained of his patience and composer, he let me have it full blast. He had thrown me off guard and with no lies in hand; he had the best of me. After giving him one flimsy excuse after another, he began throwing accusations at me. He had me on a string and was yo-yoing me up and down and toying with my mind. That night, with lots in my head, as he carried on, I took the couch, keeping my lips buttoned.

The following morning, when Dexter confronted me again with his fury, Jessie was introduced as my platonic friend. He never got the solid truth; it went from one extreme fabrication to another. Staying strong in denial to his accusations, having been as naïve and gullible as I was in our marriage, Dexter fell into my lies. Now that the tables were turned, I was standing too arrogant for my own good. In my head, it was never about my own deception but rather, Dexter's earned consequences. But it was never the same after that. I was lying and sneaking in at all hours. Regardless of how reckless and complicated our love affair had become, Jessie lit up my life. Every morning his face was the first image I saw and last, as I drifted off to sleep. Hiding in love and bliss, even Eileen was fed up with me, after handing her a big fat bowl of bull. Wary and skeptical to every story I fed her, all her lectures and words of warning, slipped from my mind.

In our lack of care and in our boldness, it became impossible to keep our affair a secret from everyone, including Jessie's mother. She got wind of it and in her eyes, it was unacceptable and she had no plans of sitting quiet. In spite of their differences, Jessie had a strong connection with her and no matter how much she expressed her disproval for me, in Jessie's eyes she could do no wrong. She argued with him, between his troubles and the fact that I was married and older, we were headed for failure. Jessie always described his mother as beautiful and ravishing. Perhaps it was the image of perfection she always carried, no matter what her mood portrayed. Her control, shapely body and pretty face, stood out to me as flawless. When she first tried to reason with me, I claimed our relationship was purely platonic, unlike Dexter she refused to buy into my crap. In her life, her long list of hardships remained private, but it never drowned out the fact that she had become wise through it all. In defeat of not making headway with me, she became angry, trying to shock me out of his life by warning me, "When things get rough, he'll crumble, he'll run, you'll see."

What was she saying? Jessie would never do that, not Jessie, not to me, not us. But still it left its mark of uncertainty upon me. It left me thinking, about a few of Jessie's actions and reactions, which reflected back to his untidy past. But those uneasy thoughts were quickly brushed away, after our lies came back and hit us where we laid our heads. Once Jessie was told to take his clothes and get out, he was back to living in his coupe. Just the thought that he was alone and sleeping in his cold car, sent shivers up my spine. It all began to eat at me and the need to save him and the need to fix everything began to generate. Before long, it got the best of me and I put all these needs into action.

Still working at the restaurant I had continued to stash every dollar possible and it had quickly added up. It was safely hidden away from Dexter's reach, under the floorboards, inside the dark attic. Still it made no sense, that I wouldn't spend one penny for any of my own needs, but was more than willing to put a nice dent into my stash for Jessie. His funds didn't stretch nearly enough to get his own place, but together, it began to fall into perfect place. Having hit numerous garage sales, from the drapes to the candles flickering in every room, proved, that the rickety place only needed a woman's touch. Willing ready and able, I never stopped to come up for air, adding in this and that and before you knew it, he was settled in all comfy and cozy. It was a new beginning of openness and freedom for us. Sometimes we'd cuddle for hours, planning out our future, while truth and consequences sat only a cry away.

Now with all the sloppy clues I left trailing behind, it didn't take much time for Dexter to catch on to all my lies. It was right around the time when he began to do his own kind of investigating and put two and two together. Then, just like that, the whole truth was out. It was finished…. he wasn't buying into any more of my cock-and-bull story. But in disbelief, suddenly Dexter claimed he wanted me and no one else and in his panic, he began to try to win back my love. Regardless of his desperate efforts, it was too late. All I saw was this dark shadow of Dexter and the bright love I held for Jessie. Of course deep inside I felt like a rat, and you can bet your life I was in too deep, over my head and drowning. Forget seeing clear to the intensity of cruelty I was dishing out. Poor Dexter, by now he was beaten down. In my heart, I knew my sweet revenge, was becoming scratchy inside my soul, even with the justification, he drew first blood. But it wasn't about any of that any more. It was about the love I had with

Jessie, the need to be with him and the courage and strength I didn't have to do things morally right. Exactly how much longer did I think I could go on, burning both ends of the candle before the flames caught up to me? But now, I could no longer figure out who was the one getting hurt and who was the one that was dishing out the pain. But even now, if I could make things right, it was too late. A fork in the road had driven me to pure hysteria. Now, there was no exit, nowhere to hide and nowhere to run.

It couldn't be…it can't be true. I couldn't think and sat staring at the walls dazed, wondering how I got here. Emotionally my mind crossed back through time, reminiscing my past. There was nobody to blame, but myself. In those hands of time, nothing was clear in my mind, nor was I aware of Norma's voice, until she reached over and gently patted my hand, bringing her image back into my focus. Choking back the tears that sat unsettled for years, a burst of guilt came streaming through. Reacting back as if Norma were my judge and jury, I tearfully began to defend myself, repeating that I just couldn't lose my children. Norma let me cry out my emotions, before she reached for a piece of Kleenex to wipe away the beads of perspiration, forming above her upper lip. With a subtle move she eased herself back into the chair, while my thoughts began to drift back, when all my prayers seemed hopeless and unanswered.

It was in the midst of our love affair, when suddenly my world got turned upside down. In a state of alarm, after having frantically watched the calendar for days on end, my appointment was already penciled in. On the morning of my blood test, Mae and Brad took to my mood, taking turns crying for one thing or another. By the time we were on our way, we were late. Praying that they were behind schedule, after being greeted by a friendly smile, with a sigh I signed in. Settling nervously back into the chair, while waiting for my name to be called, the children sat content snacking on "Cheerios." There wasn't even time to think, when my name was called. Quickly responding, it was quick, a couple of questions and a tube of blood, with instructions to call back for the results in forty-eight hours. While gathering up the children, I thought to myself, "God, forty-eight hours, by then I'll be a mental case."

In the next long agonizing hours, I could only plead with God for a second chance at life, praying that it wasn't so. Pacing only gave me more time to speculate and I bit down my nails until they bled. Sleep only came after my mind shut down and my eyelids grew too heavy to hold open. It was right around the time when the sound of the chirping birds told me, the children would soon be up. Finally time had inched its way up to forty-seven hours and once my mind was prepared to call, I dug out Popsicles from the freezer to quiet the children. Right at the very second my hand reached up for the receiver, Dexter's loud voice came up from behind, "Hey, what are all these toys doing lying out here, like this?"

My mind cringed. "Oh no, what in the hell was he doing home at this hour?" My heart skipped a beat as he began to complain that he had left work due to a bellyache. With no coffee brewing and no supper started, I resentfully thought. "Great, just great, he's got a little bellyache, oh, damn him. Just damn him!"

With my irritation climbing, when he called out to me twice, without giving me a chance to answer, my voice rose out in sarcasm, "What?"

Mumbling under his breath, in his own irritation as he began to pick up the toys himself, I mumbled back, "Fine."

By now with the anger that he was home, having replaced the fear for the outcome of my results, Dexter was well tuned into my sour mood. With a change of mood, he was willing to pass on the coffee, offering to take a beer instead. Realizing that I hadn't made it to the store either, only added pressure to my plate. Entering into the living room, he was already reclined comfortably back in his chair, when I broke the news he was out of beer. Beating him to the draw, I threw out a handful of excuses to why I couldn't run to the store right then. His face fell into a frown, getting out of his chair and slippers and stepped back into his brown penny loafers. With a loud grumble and a bang of the door, he was gone. Without losing another minute, with my heart pounding, my tender fingertips, dialed the number. By the third ring, a female answered, "Hello, Litton Laboratory, can I help you?"

"Yes, hello my test. I'm calling to get the results."

"Name please?"

Now attached to a name, she put me on hold. When she returned, she began to read my chart. Getting impatient, my mind cried in frustration, knowing Dexter had to be on his way back by then. "Come on come on already, God, just spit it out."

Interrupting my mad thoughts, "Okay now, let's see, yes, it's a definite positive."

Fear ran through my veins, as I pleaded back, "Could you please check again, you know, just to be sure."

Following a brief pause, "Okay, yes it's a definite positive."

Oh God, there was no denying it. I was going to have Jessie's baby! Oh my God, what have I done? Now an innocent life that never asked to be born into my disgrace, was growing in me. Filled with anguish, I was wishing the earth would swallow me up. But somehow I got through the motions and the coffee got brewed and frozen potpies was the name of dinner. As soon as the kids were down for the night, for some reason Dexter was lost in his own thoughts and with my head pounding, my mind shut down. In spite of running mentally away from the reality of this baby, the night came with plenty of tossing and turning. Seeing that Dexter had a vasectomy, there were no lies that could get me out of this. The fear of losing my children on the grounds of infidelity, left me believing, I was doomed. How many times can you sit over a cup of coffee staring into space, while every decent solution seems out of reach? My emotions were pumped and I began reacting like a lioness, fighting to protect her young. My mind sat untamed, searching for something short of a miracle to keep my baby. Since there was no honesty in me, nothing was getting solved. With a head full of irrational answers, I came up with what I believed, was the only key solution to unlock me from this mental madness. Jessie must never know! It would destroy him, me, us and the fear that he would find out, drove me further away from reality. In a state of alarm, emotionally I waved the flag surrendering, for in my head nothing mattered. With my thoughts twisted around to saving my baby and keeping my children, I began literally crawling to Dexter. While promising my affair was over, there was no mentioning of a little something here, the baby. Unexpected, Dexter appeared relieved and content, that I was finally back home in mind and spirit where I belonged. Seeing we didn't really know how to communicate, we didn't. Robotically as Dexter took me in his arms, my mind cried out, knowing tomorrow I had to say goodbye to my Jessie.

With the sunrise, tomorrow did come and with the day, dread washed over me. Telling Dexter my affair was over was one thing, but facing Jessie was another. Of course he reacted, it hit him hard and he pulled back as if I had slapped him and he laid his face down in his hands. He wasn't listening to anything that I frantically was trying to justify. Once his face came up for air, he didn't even try to reason with me. He just sat traumatized, staring at me in disbelief, with a look of pure resentment. Oh but his tears held the power to move all of me. Getting lost in emotions, I wanted to forget this crazy lunacy and be back in his arms, only the tiny image of the baby held me back. Since Dexter now had me backed into a corner, our time was limited. He was timely awaiting my return. It was his test, to see if I would stay true to my word. There was no doubt in my mind, if I was even a minute late, it would be guns and roses for us. With that fear, I headed right out the door, leaving Jessie behind, to believe it was about me going back home to mend my broken marriage. Looking tearfully back, one last time, life felt over.

Only hours later, filled with regret, my strength began to break down with second thoughts and after trying desperately to reach him, it was too late. Here, his mother's prediction proved to be true after all, he was gone. My tears ran long and heavy, crying out, "Oh God, maybe if he knew the truth about our baby, he never would have left me."

With Jessie gone, there was no place emotionally to go, except forward. In the days that followed, Dexter was on cloud nine. For the first time in our marriage, he was displaying a more loving kind of care and generosity. Here, it only took revenge and another man to get him to take a stand, that he only wanted me for his very own. In fact, his generosity was coming straight from his wallet and it almost bowled me over. In spite of the painful void that sat in my soul for Jessie, I figured perhaps with time, Dexter's pure sweetness could have lured me back in. It only took two short days for this all to surface. It's unbelievable, how just two short days of foolish and irrational behavior, can destroy everything in its path. It started with a nice ride out in the country with Dexter. A pang of guilt tugged at me, while thinking that the ride would do us good. In fact it did, for after only a mile on the road, the breeze and view of the scattered trees, cleared my mind. My spirits were on the rise, forgetting the pressures that had been eating me alive. Obviously when Dexter pulled up the gravel drive, next to the model homes, he already had this day planned out in his head. Jumping out of the car, he looked rather carefree, almost like the confident Dexter, I once knew and loved. As he held his hand out to the guy standing in front of the model homes, they chatted for a spell, before Dexter waved me out of the car. It seemed, after doing business with this classy high roller named Joey Gaza; he offered Dexter a deal of a lifetime. It was a beautiful, new brick bi-level home! Sitting on a wooded lot, oh it was nice all right! But, it did carry one little drawback. It was miles and miles away from my familiar territory and comfort zone. Just that unfamiliar thought, terrified me. Regardless of my uncertainties, Dexter argued me down, while the means to keep my baby flashed before me. Surrounded by the pure scent of nature, as it lingered through the air, just the temptation would have swayed even a fool and I was that fool. Blinded by the light, believing this was the answer of all answers I attached my name to the papers. On the drive back, with the children chattering away, an odd sense of stillness suddenly sat between us. It was as if something had changed, perhaps it was reality.

It wasn't until morning when my eyes suddenly opened and the realism of what I had done hit home. This awful truth left me squirming in my skin, the baby, the house and Jessie. Oh Jessie, just the very thought of not having him in my life, was too much to bear. In a given moment of inner peace, I swore to God I'd fix everything somehow, someway. Filled with this strange unfamiliar feeling of inner peace, besides feeling weird, it was strong enough to stay with me. Between tending to the children, I ignored that silly sanctimonious feeling gnawing at me and as I began to conjure up a way to try to get out of this mess, this inner peace thing faded away. Once evening had arrived and Dexter was home and relaxing back in his chair, my plan of attack went into action. Holding on tight to my nerve, while he was drinking his second long neck beer, I cornered him in his chair. Hysterically throwing all the reasons we needed to get out of this deal at him; only made him suspicious of my motives and he came back at me insisting it was a done deal. Fighting back, it was all getting under my skin and with our tempers flying, Dexter shouted, "Stop it will you please, please, just stop it already."

Looking over at Dexter, he appeared worn out. I had not realized, just how much my love affair had affected his wellbeing. It was all beginning to show one way or another and it was hard to tell if it was pain or fury that was written on his face. Suddenly he got up out of his chair to get a tranquillizer from the medicine chest. He had been taking them ever since he had learned the truth about my affair with Jessie. Pacing back and forth, by the time he returned back into the room, I was going to blast him with another round. Only something strange stopped me in my tracks. It was his eyes appearing glazed, as I stared into them. Composed, he avoided eye contact with me and slumped down into his chair. Willing to talk calmly with me, I bit my tongue from further argument. Dexter ran through the deal as the loan officer he was. Skillfully, he failed to mention anything about the three-day cancellation period. Instead, he informed me it was going to cost a lot of money. Not how much, just a whole lot of money. Where was my head? Most likely not on the intellect side, because when

Dexter gave me the verdict, I sat in agreement. Desperate, anything to get things rolling and get the hell out of this mess sounded promising. Since Dexter was a financial brain, I assumed, he knew how to get us out from under this deal. He proved me right, uttering with impatience, "Alright, alright already, I'll check in the morning to see how much it's all going to cost us."

To my surprise on the following evening, Dexter dropped the news, money and more money; it was going to cost us. Obviously he didn't have it, or did he? Because, it was ironic that it was just about the same amount of cash that I had stashed under the attic floorboards. He must have read my mind, because he interrupted me uttering out, "Hey, I sure as hell don't have it, unless, you got it."

Awkwardness filled the room and a light bulb was flashing on and off in my head. Untrusting…he had me rattled. Restlessly I began shuffling my feet, contemplating whether or not to spill the beans. His eyes stayed glued to my face, as if he were searching as to whether or not I had any loose dollars hanging around. Perhaps it was just my imagination. Or perhaps, it was my guilt creeping in for holding out on the greater part of my tips. But green around the edges, it had never entered my mind that he might actually already be on to my secret stash. At this point, my mind began to irrationally race in fear. "God, there's no way he could possible know. But suppose he smelled a rat and became suspicious, or heard me digging around in the attic." My blood was draining, yet I remained on my guard keeping my lip zipped shut. Then he softly began to reassure me, that we surly didn't have it, but, if we did, he'd take a buy out for me. His genuine smile, his concern, it all went hand in hand. Just like magic it worked! Not only did he soften me up and mellow me out, but he also won me over. Falling right into his tightfisted trap everything came pouring out longwinded. Once I confessed to having hundreds of dollars hidden under the attic floorboards, it was too late. There could be no turning back now. Heading up the steps to retrieve the money, while casually looking back, I caught sight of what appeared to be a faint smile, crossing over his lips. Although, with his emotions all tangled and in an uproar, it could have merely been a sign of his own relief. Of course, that had to be it, because by the time I returned with the money in my hand, the air between us was much calmer. Even better yet, after he eagerly removed all the cash off my hands. Gradually, his mood shifted and that was that. Sitting preoccupied in his own thoughts, after ignoring several of my efforts to talk about the deal, he finally looked my way with his brow creased, "Okay, okay I said, I'll see what I can do about it tomorrow."

His change of attitude rubbed me the wrong way, seeing he had already confiscated all my money. Feeling hateful inside myself, my inner anger went off the wall. "What the hell did he mean he'd try, why in the hell did I let him finagle me out of my money? Why that lying bastard!" Joining him in his silence, he was holding the upper hand and once again, he was toying one way or another with my emotions. That night, while Dexter was holding my stash, it must have gotten the best of me and followed me into my dreams. In comic relief, the crispy bills had grown feet and were laughing as they ran off into the distance. But regardless of my nightmare, when Dexter returned home from work the following day, he gave me his word it was a done deal. So with a quick snap of his finger, the pressure of the house deal disappeared, just about as fast as my money had vanished out from my hand. Having put my nightmare to rest, relief flowed and that night I slept like a baby, as my pregnancy grew with each breath I took.

The days fell into each other, with things falling right back to where we had started…nowhere. It seemed the whole incident of Jessie and the money had both fallen off the face of the earth. The only difference was, that I began to realize that everything for us would always go back to the beginning. Nothing changed here, not him, not me. Only now, I was broke since my stash and secret future were blown away by my own obtuse foolishness. Kind of like Joey Gaza's story, that abruptly came to an end. When Joey's picture appeared on the front page of the paper, it stirred up angry memories of the house, taking us into another argument. In Dexter's shocking disbelief concerning Joey's death and dishonor, he felt betrayed by Joey, mumbling something about not knowing whom you could trust these days. He was looking right at me when he said it and I'd be a liar if I said I didn't know exactly whom he was referring to. But as far as Joey, the paper was associating his brutal death to the mafia and a bomb that had been planted in his car. But the only thing I knew of this man called Joey, was his face and name and that he was the culprit, who had all my money, or did he!" Now with that suspicion floating in my head, all my frustration to the whereabouts of my cash began to eat at me real bad. These bitter thoughts of having no money, with no hope to a brighter future, took me to a new dimension of wanting to even the score. In the days that followed, with still no word from Jessie, my poise began to descend, while Dexter's mood of satisfaction was on the rise. He didn't seem to take notice to my lack of response or interest to his efforts to continue where we had left off. My heart was miles away with Jessie. By now three unbearable weeks had passed and lack of sleep began to show in my face. Then Saturday came, it was morning and the sun was streaming it. Lost in the misery surrounding me, it took my attention over to our shelves and my lack of dusting these days. Pushing away the guilt for my lack of care, my heart returned to Jessie and I relinquished self-judgment. But that night at the hour of midnight, right after the sound of the bells on the clock finished chiming, the ringing of the phone took over. It was Jessie! Oh my God it was Jessie! Before I even had a chance to cry and beg for forgiveness, his loud voice came through out of breath, "Baby it's me Jessie. Baby listen I love you, I'm not letting you go. Oh God, it has been hell without you."

"Who's that?" It was Dexter standing sheepishly over me, insisting on knowing who was calling me at this hour. Moving the phone from my ear, I whispered, "Awe, it's nothing, really go on, go on back to bed."

Dexter didn't buy into my crap, giving me back a distasteful look of annoyance. Persistent, he wasn't budging and he plopped himself down onto the kitchen chair, lighting up a butt. Staring intensely at me slowly blowing out smoke and eavesdropping, he was restlessly taping his foot. Avoiding eye contact with him, by the time I hung up, sweat was rolling down my belly. There was definitely going to be some explaining to do here. But then, after gazing over at Dexter's pained face, a flash of my money and all his wrong doings pushed my guilt and deceit, into my own corner of justification. In my mind, it was never about Jessie or me doing right or wrong, but rather what had been wrongly done to me by Dexter. Seeing clear I wasn't! Even as Dexter was making an effort to mend our broken relationship, it was too late. I wanted out so bad every brain cell in my mind was searching for a chocolate covered way out. So what was stopping me? In any case, living in a world surrounded by deceit, left me gutless and lost, scrambling in my own web of lies and misery. Ironically, through these obstacles, there was also this unhealthy inner characteristic of mine, the caregiver, which led me to believe and fear that if I owned up to my love for Jessie, it would just kill poor Dexter.

But after Jessie's call, it was a bright new glorious day. Just knowing in only hours I would be with him, my heart was on cloud nine and I dusted away. Rejoicing inside, I walked the children to the park and afterwards they were holding on to their own, double dipped, chocolate ice cream cones. Less than twenty-four hours later, once I managed to get out of the house, Jessie and I eagerly met over at his place. Oh how we missed one another and hugged like there was no tomorrow and kissed like it was only yesterday. We couldn't keep our hands off each another and after we cried and shared our tears, it felt like we were never apart. Only one hour after uniting, we clung together with our hearts full of new promises for a future together. Lost in his love, even with this enormous weight of the baby tugging at my conscience, my lips remained sealed. We had gone back to the beginning, exactly where we had left off. In view of the fact that Dexter didn't have to guess, he just knew, sure as hell, Jessie was back in the picture and this time it was guns and roses.

PASSAGE X

Blood Red

Was I not worthy enough? For I became unworthy to become worthy enough to give any and all that I stood for away... While all that I was, was not all that I could have been, if only I would have listened to the whistle of warning from the fallen wind.

Obviously the blind was leading the blind as far as Jessie and I were concerned. But who was leading Dexter and his tantrums, heading straight for hell? By now Dexter was more than angry and depressed, he was flat out deflated. He had been pushed to the limit and now he was sitting on the edge. It was happening more and more these days and it was always after the sun went down and after the children were asleep. By then, with several beers and a tranquilizer under his belt to calm his jagged nerves, it would start. He'd had enough of this Jessie thing and the liquor and tranquillizers gave him just the right edge to fight back with persecution, into the early hours of the morning. No matter how close to the brink he appeared, I remained emotionally in my own world. Especially since his tantrums compared to mine, were a walk in the park and as I saw it, like daddy, it was all nothing but a bluff.

Only this walk in the park was about to change. It couldn't have taken much that night, a tone, an attitude or any kind of anything for that matter. Whatever it was; was just enough to push him over the edge. Undeniably, Dexter had been toyed with repeatedly to the limit, but now, the table was turned and he was emotionally pushing all my buttons. Feeling locked to my chair, my eyes met his and there he sat, watching me, watch him. But nothing could have mattered in those next few hours to come, because by then, he was holding me in a state of fear. He sat voiceless and pale faced, his eyes standing out detached, griping two bottles, one in each hand. Recognizably, he was holding onto his tranquilizers and a bottle of his uppers. With his eyes cast down, soft-spoken, his suicide threats began to soar. Falling into silence, it appeared as if he was already tranquilized, giving me a dose of unspoken threats, by dropping some of the tablets out of both pill bottles, into each palm. He just sat staring straight ahead, as if he were possessed, bringing the hairs on my arms to stand up. Intently he would look at the pills, than back at me, as if he were contemplating his death wish. Watching in disbelief, he took one, then two, it was all taking me back in time, right back home with daddy. My knees began to quiver and the silence of the lamb moved its way in, afraid to challenge his ground.

Falling into fear, tough I wasn't. In reality to my past, my shield of defense by playing the hard role was over. Once the shit hit the fan, it proved me to be, not a hard-hitter after all. My heart was pounding, it was hard to think, hard to catch my breath. Oh God, my head felt like it was going to blow off. His eyes stood out unreadable, what the hell was he thinking in the midst of this madness. He was emotionally beating me black and blue. In my prayers, I prayed he was only bluffing and would go to bed just like daddy, when it was over, it would be over. Not so, the sinister night continued to drag on. Suddenly infuriated at my rag doll image and lack of response, he broke out in an angry rage. Determined to punish me, he began to insult and color me with blame. Remaining mute to every cruel word he threw my way, the argument remained one sided. Still, nothing was cooling things down and perhaps to get control and ruffle me out of my silence, he felt pushed to act upon something more forceful and he did just that. With his face twisting into madness he began swallowing handfuls of pills, washing them down with his beer. Seeing that both bottles of pills now sat empty, my hands began to tremble in alarm, taking me to pure hysteria. In a state of panic, fearing that the pills would penetrate into his bloodstream, I began screaming for him to throw up to rid him self of the pills, before they killed him. Dexter's face was filled with fright and in his own state of panic, he ran into the bathroom to purge.

Restlessly pacing the floor, it seemed to take forever before Dexter returned with his face drained of color, mumbling he had eliminated the pills. Relief set in that he was okay and the agony of the night was finally over. As he said he was going to bed, I let out a long breath. As defeated as Dexter's image portrayed, with his shoulders slumped, feeling like I had been to hell and back, kept my heart cold. Worn down and locked in my own misery, exhausted, I dropped down to the couch, staring up at the white shadowed ceiling. Snuggling deeper into my heavy robe, my mind got lost in deep judgment. Still in my mid twenties, with all my deceit and bad choices brewing above my head, my life was a shambles and the only one accountable was myself. Dwelling on my miserable past and the now, somewhere between our bleak future and heavy worries, I drifted off into an uneasy sleep.

Suddenly my eyes opened, drenched in sweat, my heart was rapidly beating out of my chest. My mind flashed, bringing to light the pills and the quarrelling that had gone on. Confused to how long I had been asleep, in relation to the morning sunrise, it had to be three hours at most. Past the sound of my breathing, the house was sitting in an eerie state. There was no reason to believe anything was wrong, but somehow I knew. Groggy, I pulled myself up until my feet found the floor. Heartfelt, this spine chilling eeriness began to run with my imagination and I began to creep my way towards our bedroom. Standing at the doorway, my head moved forward to peek in. Oh dear God, the worst of my fears was staring me in the face. The uppers were showing their destruction. Dexter was sitting up, no; he was down, no he was up. Oh God, his eyes rolling, never focusing, never aware. Desperately trying to bring him around, I shook him violently, hollering. "Dexter, Dexter wake up, Dexter come on, please Dexter, oh God, please don't do this."

It was too late, he was out of it, oh, but I was traumatized and began praying and begging God at the same time to help me. But it was no use, Dexter couldn't see me, he couldn't hear me, and God wasn't listening. In shock, I ran into the living room and began pacing back and forth, aware of every deadly moment ticking by. Oh God, what do I do, oh dear God, what do I do?"

Anyone in their right mind, would have dashed immediately to the phone and called for an ambulance. Instead my mind froze and I slumped down whitewashed into the chair. Staring out in misery, my mind was flashing over our problems and all our disgrace and humiliation, was left trailing from behind. Overflowing in anguish and self-pity, all of life felt hopeless and I began to sob out, "No, there is no such thing as a stupid splendid rainbow of contentment, not ever, not for me!"

Having lost that dream, my heart began crying buckets and my mind began running like a racehorse. Consumed with the panic that Dexter was going to die, I dreaded the blame, the scandal and the shame, which I had allowed myself to be a part of. With my belly on the rise, when everybody took notice, their response, judgment and their verdict, terrified me. Win or lose, I was surely damned and began hyperventilating. Frantically, it brought me up to my feet, trying to think things out with some sound control. Only I couldn't think at all. It was all distorting my thinking. It all had gotten the best of me and I began to lose sight of reality. Unthinkable? Unacceptable? Just the thought of do-or-die covered my body in sweat. Running my hands through my damp hair, my fears linked to solution and salvation. "Oh~Oh God" my mind whispered out loud, "Oh" In those next dense moments, crawling back under the covers and pulling the blankets over my head until it was over, appeared to be the sound way out. Squirming inside my skin those insane sinful thoughts quickly got the best of me. Miraculously, by some means, my madness delivered me back to earth on sane ground. Given that, murder for sure, it would have been. Sickened through and through, oh God, had I gone round the bend, only to meet up with satin himself. No, no, truly I didn't want him to die; I just wanted him to let me live, live without this thing called shame. With time ticking by to the count of five minutes, a high wave of shame came over me, while poor Dexter's life sat pending. With my belly muddled up, I felt a need to vomit. Instead, I leaped to my feet and ran to the phone, leaving my gut to fend for itself. Fumbling to dial the emergency number, my weary body leaned heavily against the wall for support. Within moments, the guy who answered barely got out his name, before my voice cut him off, pleading and weeping with justification. "You, you, must help me, oh please hurry, he's going to die, he's going to die I tell you, please hurry, it wasn't my fault. I swear to God I tried to stop him."

He cut me off, advising me to calm down and give him the name and address of the victim. Victim, did he say victim, what did he mean victim? His terminology rattled heavy inside my head, instantly putting me on the defense. In the middle of giving him the requested information, long winded, I worked in my own justification of not having made anyone a victim. It was useless; he wasn't interested in any of my reasoning. Regardless of pointing the blame at Dexter, it still left me feeling like a naughty child. Hanging up the receiver, they were on their way and I ran into the bedroom to Dexter, where he was now laying quiet. When I saw his peaceful face, a flash of memory to the days of wine and roses, when our love was once fresh, took me to more tears. Desperately I began to shake and pled with him at the same time, to awake from this madness. "Oh Dexter please don't die, please wake up, I'm sorry, I love you...Oh

God, please let him live and I swear, I'll be a good and perfect wife."

Even after swearing to God to be all that I had been preached, it was no use. All the shaking and promises in the world, wouldn't wake him. By the time the paramedics had arrived, I was ready to spill my guts and sell my soul so I would not to be blamed for this. It wouldn't have mattered; they weren't interested in neither my tears nor my version, abruptly ending my defense by requesting any pills, Dexter may have taken. As they were moving their way into the bedroom, I began to work myself into a sweat. "The bottles, the bottles, they wanted the bottles, oh God, where the hell are the bottles?"

Not knowing what Dexter had done with the empty bottles, I began ransacking every drawer and wastebasket in the house. With time running out, the top shelf in his closet was my last hope. Standing on my tiptoes, my fingertips managed to grasp what felt like two pill bottles. Letting out a sigh of relief, there they were, triggering flashes of the drama. Extending my clammy hand out to the paramedic, as he took both empty bottles he flashed me an intense look, as if he was waiting for me to say something. In my head, it was as if maybe he thought, that there was something more to this story than what was meeting the eye. In-between the fear and the paramedics main focus on Dexter, it left me with guilt for my part and in self-judgment, the bad seed ran through my head. Rushing Dexter out on a stretcher, as efficient as they were, within minutes, with screaming sirens blaring, they were off and speeding away into the distance.

Moments of nothingness stood alone with me and in a blank state, I suddenly realized I needed to find someone to mind the children. Breaking down to mother, in-between sobs and partially filling her in on the agony of the night, she agreed to come to the rescue. Gazing out the window, while waiting for her car to come into view, the dread of her seeing the full picture of the mess we had created, left me determined to candy coat the story. She must not have lost a minute in time to get over and remained out of breath as we gathered up the children and all their things. Even as she only received pieces of my reasoning, her devastation for the outcome of our marriage, put her into a nervous state. She rambled on endlessly, never noticing that I was a hundred miles away from hearing her. Lost in a daze, suddenly I realized both Jessie and the baby had been overlooked and excluded from my faithful promises to God. Sick at heart, it put my good intentions in a different light. Just the lonely image of not being with Jessie again, but then, interrupting my thoughts, Dexter's face flashed before my eyes, bringing me back to earth. With Dexter's life sitting in a critical state, waving mother off couldn't come fast enough.

All the way to the hospital, my foot stayed glued to the pedal, while the dying image of Dexter pumped up my blood. Rushing into the emergency doors, no one was present at the desk, arousing the must to find Dexter. Impulsively I darted right through a pair of double doors, leading down a hall. In only a matter of five steps, a doctor wearing a white jacket with a stethoscope around his neck spotted me. Walking towards me, contrary to my size, he was a big man and if his voice had been gruff, he would have emotionally bowled me over. Once he got it out of me, that I was Dexter's wife, he lightened up for barging in and informed me they were pumping his stomach. By the time he got to the part that they were doing all that they could, my imagination took it from there. It was all too much, all the buildup of guilt, stress and more. In the midst of the quiet atmosphere, my tears started and my emotions let go, "He's going to die isn't he, oh God, he's going die and it's my fault."

Rubbing his head, he looked bushed; suggesting I go have a seat in the lobby until they called for me. Sobbing and wiping away at my tears, a trip to the restroom and the cold water splashing against my face, restored what little good sense I owned. It was definitely going to be a long and stressful wait, even with the cafeteria at my rescue, having purchased a hot cup of coffee and a sweet Danish roll to fill my need to eat.

But one thing for sure, during my intense waiting, I wouldn't be alone. Coming from around the corner, walking briskly towards me and looking disoriented, were both Dexter's parents. Oh dear God, I had completely forgotten about them, adding additional discredit to my shame. It had to be mother who called them, seeing their faces, revealed their alarm. Without a second to get any composure, we were face-to-face and emotion-to-emotion. When Dexter's mother began to whisper out her fears, my face stood red. Opening my mouth with reason, nothing came out, except that Dexter had somehow gone crackers. But the angry response on Dexter's father's face said it all; he didn't like my absurd answer. Demanding to know how this could happen, he kept digging for any rational reason. Not having any better come back, I broke down weeping insisting again, that Dexter had just gone crackers. This time, my offensive answer pushed him over to Dexter's corner of defense and he began to claim, someone or something, had to have pushed him over the edge. Seeing that there wasn't any other someone around, it felt like a sure bet, that it had to be me he was pointing his finger at. Emotions were getting hot and heavy and while we all took a seat in the unoccupied chairs, he hastily withdrew from me. Dexter's mother, in her frightened state, her pain was filtering in and out of her quiet shell. Wanting to comfort her, after locking my eyes on her pained face, my heart could only pull back in guilt, for having added to her grief. Her temperament was not the same as the Mr. because once a thick silence filtered in, his eyes darkened deeper, becoming unrecognizable. Sinking deeper and deeper inside myself, even with this silent thing going on, you could perceive the resentment and blame that was sweeping across his face. It was obvious that he appointed himself judge and jury and in his eyes, I stood guilty as sin. It was as if I could hear him silently blaring out, guillotine give her the guillotine! Squirming in my skin there was nowhere in me to sink any deeper.

With the sound of this silence thing, still going on, it was hard to think clear. Somewhere past the clock ticking and ticking into the night and the uncomfortable visits to the vending machine, the doctor finally walked in pronouncing Dexter, "Out of the woods."

Quickly getting out of our seats, my mind began rambling in thanks to God, reinstating my sworn promise, to be the perfect wife. Once we were informed we were allowed to see Dexter, we were given directions to his room and for the first time in hours, my breathing came with ease. Being allowed only a short visit, we all rode the elevator up to the third floor, while Dexter's mother only, talked with me. No sooner did we walk in the room, the nurse on duty reminded us to keep our visit short. Nervous and eager to be alone with Dexter to clear the air and to begin our fresh new start as I had promised, was a letdown. He looked strung out in his own world, barely taking any notice to me. Looking like death warmth over, he looked weak, struggling to keep his eyes open. Between still feeling knee deep in crap with Dexter's father and utterly washed out, we were ready to call it a night. Kissing on Dexter, his lack of care or response began to put my promises at risk. Slipping on my pink sweater on the way out, Dexter's mother gave me a needy hug, showing signs of her own exhaustion, while the Mr. by now, was far out of sight. In the wide-open fresh air, I took in a long deep breath and was relieved it was over. Getting in my car, the sun hit me square in the eyes, squinting, my mind shut down and I headed for home.

Barely in the door, the phone was loudly ringing, it was mother and she was filled with question after question concerning Dexter's condition.

Claiming she wasn't able to get a wink of sleep; she demanded to know, what the hell was going on with us. Still not wanting to expound on the truth, a heavy weight of weakness fell over me. It didn't take much before my tears were all she heard. Easing back, she let me slide off the hook, maintaining we would resolve this issue later. Buzzing, the phone sat dead in my hand. Oh but all of me was so tired, so very, very, tired. Time was getting away from me, oh how badly I needed to think and sort through the mess I had made of my life. Falling into sleep, my last thoughts drifted with me, that maybe tomorrow would be a better day."

Only a better day to look at our problems never came. The following afternoon Dexter was already being discharged. Seeing that the incident was recorded as misuse of his medications, as I pulled up to the door, he was ready and waiting in a wheelchair. It should have been a moment of love and recognition, a moment of gratitude to God for being alive. Instead his mood was filled with resentment and self-pity. He was very bitter that he was spared and had to go to hell and back because of me. It all left me full on resentment for all his hand fed hours of misery and in a moment of fury we glared at one another in pure hate. Driving the rest of the way home in total silence, my mind wasn't.

It didn't take any time, two days at most and everything was a mess. Nothing changed, not him not me. This was nothing like I had fantasized in my head. Completely convinced, that I had done everything to make our marriage work, like daddy, that was that. Looking to his side of things, the way I read it, Dexter was firmly holding on to his own set of ideas and rules, on how things were going to be run. It just wasn't instilled in him to give and it wasn't instilled in me any longer to give in and become the person he needed me to be. In theory, way down deep to the root of my soul, the past of Georgette, the pictures, the cheating, his lies, my lies, all our scandalous memories, wouldn't die. With nothing laid to rest, my mind was full of regret for putting Jessie and the baby on the back burner, while Dexter was trying to die. What the hell was I thinking, having made all those empty promises to God? It's plain to see, I was only going to bury myself, with my yearning choice to see Jessie, while more lies were growing around my baby. Now for which it stands, my promises turned to dust and were scattered amongst the winds. They now stood with no value to anyone, not me, not Dexter, not even to God. It had all caught up to me, and it was time to finally face up to my lies and pay my consequences. Spinning out of control, my own war was about to begin, with the outside world now standing as the enemy.

Time suddenly turned critical; all to soon, my belly would be poking out revealing my sins. The vicious circle of consequences that were facing me ate away at my sanity around the clock. Still with no one to turn too, my strength was beginning to buckle. Past mother, Eileen was still my only friend. But while taken in with my drama, more times than not, she was suspicious of my tales, believing that they were larger than life. These days, she was even more fed up with my stories about Dexter and my ongoing tears and began avoiding my calls altogether. Insecure and afraid to dump on her with another botched up tearjerker about my baby, she was put on the well-known back burner, until I could figure things out.

Meanwhile, the endless sheep counting, ran it's sleepless coarse into morning, carrying its own alarm and despair throughout the day. Reality was knocking at my door. Turning back the hands of time, back then, the availability of an abortion was hush-hush, unless you had a connection. Consciously, the thought of an abortion was never an option for me, but unconsciously, it had to be streaming somewhere inside my head. That's where the brilliant idea, that a simple D and C, was the ultimate solution and the best answer of all answers. My mind got locked into believing this was my simple solution, giving me enough strength to sleep peacefully that night, without the sheep.

It took nothing more than a cry of emergency, to get penciled in with my regular gynecologist for the following day. It was one of those waiting room visits, where my mind ran, plotting out rhyme and reason, praying not to be looked down upon. Unprepared my name was called, taking me into one of the rooms empty headed. Unrehearsed to answer my doctor's questions, quite frankly, none of it mattered. Once the examination was complete, judging by the written prescription for vitamins and estimated due date, he carried on as if he had not heard a word I said. Interrupting him with my reasons, from the baby having a different father, to giving me a D and C, it registered. Once he got it, that my intensions were not to keep the baby, a cold distance fell between us. Gazing through me with a strong energy of disproval, intimidated, I began defending the mess I had got myself into. His frown deepened with every flimsy excuse that I threw at him, until I surrendered with tears. It was then; he calmly gave me my options, which offered no resolution. Crumbling I began begging, "Please, but you don't understand, if you don't help me with a D and C, I will lose my children."

It had gone from bad to worse, he was no longer seeing me, somewhere in all my begging, he had turned his face away and was staring out the window. Even as I couldn't judge his expressionless face, his firm voice intensified, cutting me, "No, giving you a D and C is out of the question. That would be murder and I will have nothing to do with murdering your unborn child."

It was a knife to the heart; wounded, the room was spinning with the echoes of murder-murder-murder, sending chills through me. Being a cry away from losing my children, even my discredit couldn't stop the fight in me. Compelled to get through to him, it was a wonder he heard my faint plea, for the name of a clinic willing to do an abortion. Trembling, that dreaded word had finally slipped off my tongue. The realization of having been in my own denial, hit me in the face. It was my own rude awakening and it took my head down in shame. At that moment, something must have moved him, for he turned his face into my view again, displaying a glimpse of sadness. One moment he was composed, the next, he abruptly scurried out from the room, closing the door behind him. Left hanging to wonder if he would return, it was only a minute at most, when he walked back in with a white piece of folded paper and set it down next to me. Coolly pushing the paper towards me, neither our hands nor our eyes came in contact, as he spoke out with a quiet sense of defeat, "Here, here is the name of a clinic that would perform such a thing."

He quickly exited the room, leaving behind a strong sense of anger indicating, I had invaded his morals. Getting back into my clothes, guilt and more guilt leached onto me like a bloodsucker. But obviously, it was not enough guilt, for when I left his office behind, I was still holding onto that white piece of paper. Holding onto it for dear life in the palm of my hand, as I let out a sigh of relief, a heavy burden was lifted off me.

With the children at the neighbors, after gathering them up, there was just enough time to start dinner, push the button on the coffee maker and make sure Dexter's long necks were chilling. After dinner, my thoughts were a million miles away while I went through the motions of getting the children off to bed. Turning my attention over to Dexter, he was already kicked back in his chair and barely responded back when I mentioned I was going to bed. Ever since that gruesome night, we barely talked, while something in him had changed. Pushing any worries of him away, past Jessie, the white piece of paper holding my solution was ransacking my brain and I buried myself deep under the blankets. Not able to sleep, nothing was planned out in my head and my mind searched for a way to hold onto my baby, knowing either or was doomed. The same agonizing thoughts of losing three children to save one, or lose one, to save three, went around and around in my head and pounded at my heart. All those hours during the night that came to pass, felt like time without end. My mind ran over the same options and I knew the same inevitable solution, was a one-way trip to destruction. Thinking like a caged animal, I was ready to draw blood to free myself. My flesh was beginning to crawl and I couldn't get a grip. Evil forces were overpowering and stealing what moral sense I had left. It had all come down to one dying solution, "The baby couldn't stay."

Up before the alarm buzzed, at the start of the day, even my hot mug of coffee offered no comfort. Staring at the phone staring back at me, took no time for me to weaken. Going into my room, hidden securely under my mattress, was the folded paper with my way out. Slowly looking back over my shoulder, it felt as if someone was watching me, feeling eerie, my imagination got the best of me. Spooked, I lifted up the corner of the mattress, grabbed the paper and fled for the kitchen. My fingers fumbled with the first few numbers, then momentarily pulled back in hesitation. But the sinking thought of do or be, forever doomed, triggered enough courage to finish dialing. On the third ring, her voice came through the receiver. Muted in instant fear, my first reaction was to hang up; instead, my tongue came untied and began spilling out my guts. Discarding all my justification, she wanted to verify that I was still in my first trimester, before setting up an appointment. Her instructions sounded simple, until she began disclosing the cost of the procedures, one awake and one under anesthesia. My head began to spin and after mumbling the cheapest way would be fine, it was set for only a few days away. Hanging up, it finally sunk in, cost, what cost, with all this stuff going on, money never entered into my head. Feeling like a moron, hell, I didn't have any money, since I had passed it all over to Dexter. Being that it was half the cost to stay awake, I would be lucky if I could scrape up enough just to have it done. Banking on my prayers, that by some miracle, the money would just show up, was shamed out of my head. Time was not standing still; it was ticking away faster than I could think, leaving only a tinted image of hope. Dear mother was the one and only hopeful answer within my reach. In my heart, I knew, she must never know the truth, for it would surely destroy all we had and just that thought, held the power to take my breath away.

Desperately needing this cash, with the children tripping under my feet, I swallowed my resistance and what pride I had left to tap on her door. She took one look at me and by the look on her face; it was obvious, she figured it was trouble again. Poor mother, her ongoing worries regarding me, never seemed to end. Today would be no different. On that particular day, she looked fearful. Perhaps it was something she read in my face; all the same, her dread became my burden. But with mother being who she was, she opened her arms and let us in. Immediately, she turned her attention to the children, offering cookies and milk for the taking. With mouthfuls of chewing and slurping going on, I tensely sat on edge and waited until they ran off to play. As mother's kind face sat across from me, mouthfuls of reasons for needing some cash casually dropped into our conversation. Believing we were having marital problems again, she had worked herself up and now, my concerns were resting on calming her down. It was crucial to pull her from the truth and by the time I had finished penciling it all in she appeared calmer, but only half convinced. Still sitting with questions, my face stood out red and I gave her back no answers and no admissions. But she knew something was up, she always knew, giving me back that look of hers. Once she got up out of her chair, she went to her white ceramic cookie jar, where she kept her hidden stash. Feeling like a slimy snake, I had to borrow nearly as much as she had saved. Grateful wasn't the word for it, being it was just about enough if I stayed awake. Yet I couldn't bring myself to ask for one more cent and could have thrown up for having been so damn needy and effective, with all my penciled in lies. Noticing that the time had gotten away, we hugged long and hard before I stepped out the door. But it was not before I caught a glimpse of mother's sad and tearful brown eyes.

Driving home, watching the clock was not getting me there any faster and my guilt for having lied to mother, left me unhinged. By the time we were pulling into the driveway, it was nearly nightfall. Struggling to open the door with Mae asleep in my arms, the boys squeezed past me, creating a ruckus as they tore up the stairs to their room. Just as I was setting Mae down on the couch, the stressful memories of that horrid night came back to life. Looking over to Dexter, seeing he looked annoyed, I gave him a handful of excuses about the time and shot out to the kitchen. Having been so late, he must have pushed the start button on the coffee maker himself. While in the oven cooking, was my prepared casserole with Dexter's favorite cuts of beef. Being well over baked, it resembled a big dish of dried out hash. All through dinner there were no happy faces, just a lot of crunching going on with a grumble here and there. Perhaps during dinner, Dexter thought that some kind of bug was eating at me, because he not only kept to himself, but also any comments he may have had tinkering around in his head. Considering his traumatized death wish was only days young; maybe he was just worn down. Even more unlike him, he retired to his bed an hour earlier than his schedule read. Relieved, there was more time to think, the entire evening turned out to be a washout. Seeing as my mind was running over every option to get more cash, that hateful inner voice of mine came at me and like always, left me believing I deserved to be awake and endure the pain. That angry inner voice of mine back then, never quit, it was my lost inner child all along, viciously rebelling, with self-hate.

But the hours were creeping forward and now the time was readily upon me. Breaking down in tears and confessing to Eileen I was carrying Jessie's baby, was followed with a drill of questions and more. Dropping everything, Eileen showed up ready and able to provide me with her comfort and care, insisting on going with me. Refusing to take no for an answer, it wasn't hard to break me down. When push came to shove, she was completely devoted to my problems, emotionally throwing her whole heart into them. She was for sure a figure of mother's giving temperament, and definitely holding on to the same disposition of co-dependency and self-punishment as me. In all my tears and lack of control, Eileen moved up to the front line and with her plans in order, the dreaded day was facing us. All those strong moving memories brought me back to the now and suddenly Norma's face stood out, intensely lost in the moment from my loud outburst of tears. Handing me a tissue and a cup of cold water, while feeling the coolness go down my throat, Norma settled back into her chair, crossing her legs, giving me a moment to continue…

My memories began to slip back in time; when Eileen and I rode the train that day in utter silence, even after having to get a transfer to get to the other side of town. In those hours of my need, I felt so grateful and indebted to my sister, that once again, she was willing to pay her price to be my caretaker. Here, we had gone through three pregnancies side by side giving birth, only now, there would be no new existence. During the ride, the sounds of the clanging from the metal wheels hitting the tracks and the steady movement, took me into my own world. Daydreaming into it, my own reflection was facing me from the window, fading in and out with the rays of sunlight rapidly passing me by. It was putting me into a trance, taking me deeper into myself. Failures, all my continuing failures were running through my head, when I caught this glimpse of Eileen's perfect reflection. Eileen, with her perfect image, appeared so damn composed, so flawless and everything I couldn't be. Those everlasting failures flashing in my head, brought a current of self-pity and resentment, only to point the blame on the bad shuffle of cards, in which I had been dealt. Out of the blue, darkness filled the train as it sped through the long dark tunnel, bringing me back to earth. Once the red flashing sidelights came into view, the train cut its speed and people began getting up out of their seats. By the time the train came to a loud screeching stop, I had emotionally beaten myself down. Letting go of the metal pole, we stepped off, heading into the direction Eileen's homemade map was pointing us to. Side by side as we walked, Eileen reassured me from time to time, we were heading in the right direction. She was cleverly right, for it was only a few more blocks, when the building was clearly in our view. Only the sidewalk in front of the building, was occupied with a number of protesters, holding onto their painted signs with red letters spelling out, "Murder."

That word murder once again shook me, this time, panic shot through my veins and the uneasiness of illness churned in my gut. Not Eileen, somehow she appeared composed and stood her ground, as she worked us to the door. Past the comments of sin and murder, once we were safely inside, their scary protest slowly began to fad from my mind. Still shaken, after being handed some forms attached to a clipboard at the desk, Eileen aided me with answers, until my unsteady signature took it to completion. Setting it on the desk, the receptionist gave me back a faint smile, pointing us into the direction of my assigned room. Walking down the hall, a lump was settling in my throat and it was impossible to stop my tears from running. Okay, so what did I expect, seeing all my own actions and lies had brought me here.

The room was small, with half the chairs already occupied, leaving Eileen and I sitting cattycorner from one another. Sitting in the stillness of the room, an uncomfortable energy sat hovering in the air. During one point, Eileen looked over to me crossing her eyes, giving me some weird perplexed look. Encouragement? Pity? What? Her look was hard to read and I crinkled my nose back at her. With a quick wave of her hand, she let it go and buried herself in a glamour magazine. Time was ticking by slow and it was obvious in our wait, there was going to be plenty of time to do nothing. Looking past Eileen and into the other women's faces, they all looked stressed in one way or another. No matter what any of our hidden motives might have been, we all knew exactly why we were there. Off to the far corner, a girl barely appearing to be more than a child herself, led me to wonder what could have possible happened to bring her here, beside the adult sitting with her. It was all getting to me; reality had set in and I could no longer look into the face of anyone. That infectious belief, that the bad seed had once grown in me; was cluttering my head with scary thoughts. It began to fill me with panic, drawing the sweat out of me. Oh God, I wanted to get up and run, I wanted this to be a bad dream I could wake up from and escape. But when they suddenly called my name, it brought me back down to earth. Once they took me from Eileen, after hours of testing and counseling, it was my turn to walk through that door.

This middle-aged assistant, said her name was Claire and that she would be by my side throughout the procedure. Past her faint smile, she remained in a calm state, getting me to where I needed to be. Walking me into the surgical room, a large metal table with metal stirrups caught my eye. In my frame of mind, it appeared to be staring at me, whispering out my name as if it had been waiting for my arrival. With the help of the assistant, I stepped up on the stool and laid my body down on the cold table. Even with the liner underneath me, the table still felt cold to my flesh, adding chills to my body, nude from the waist down. Everyone around me was moving to fast and I was conscious that every emotion I harbored, was being invaded and exposed. Overloaded in anxiety, a sense of aloneness passed over me. It was all too much and I began shaking so much my teeth began to rattle. The piercing sting of the needle pushed way up deep inside me generated excruciating pain. While reaching out to God, all my merciful words got lost in my moans and cries, "It hurts, oh God, but it hurts…I cannot move…oh but you never told me it would hurt like this."

Ignoring my outburst, as the assistant patted my arm, numbness took over quieting my cries, but I wanted to cover my ears to block out the roaring sounds of the vacuum that filled the room, sucking the life out from me. Stuck somewhere within the loud vibrating sounds, a tiny image of my unborn baby flashed before me. A boy? A girl? I would never know. Emotionally, it put me in a fragile frame of mind and the empty void put me in a state of need and I began to whimper out. Abruptly the loud roaring sounds of the vacuum stopped, bringing their voices back to life. Dazed, it was over, it was really over and yet my heart felt neither relief nor peace. Moaning out, this time as the assistant patted my arm she assured me everything went fine and my pain would quickly drift away. Promptly working together, they transferred me over to a ward, occupied with several other patients. But as intense as the pain was when I arrived, it was just as she said, for the most part, it drifted within an hour. It only left me with a case of mild cramping and fatigue, but in the end a mood of depression began to move its way in. In just thirty minutes of additional observation, it was over and I was reunited with my sister.

She had waited around with worry for hours without so much as a complaint. But her drawn face showed an eager mask of concern, yet I just could not bring myself to talk about it. Knowing there was no turning back left too much shame, too much everything. Even the tense train ride home, seemed longer than the ride there. Eileen must have sensed my downturn, for she kept to herself, for the entire ride. By the time we stepped off the train and got into her car, she seemed to be carrying a heavy mood of her own. Even with the guilt that Eileen's mood had passed over from me, my mouth stayed shut. Past the stillness in the car, the voice on the radio turned on low bass, began to make my eyelids feel heavy. Fighting to keep my eyes that were glued out the window open, the forecast was calling for sunshine, yet all I wanted was to bury myself in darkness. By the time the house finally came into view, all I wanted was to be left alone to lick my wounds. Following a hug, Eileen drove off quickly into the distance. Staring around the room, the house was quiet and lifeless. Suddenly I realized just how weeks tired all of me was. Relieved that Eileen had maneuvered mother into keeping the children overnight, gave me time to rest in solitude. Feeling depleted, I crawled into bed, curling myself up into a fetal position, nuzzling deep into myself. When Jessie's image came to life in my head, I could only respond in a whisper, "Jessie oh Jessie, no you must never know."

In my prayers, I prayed I would just die. In the next hours to come, I found myself staring out the window at the blue April 1st sky, feeling guilt and sorrow, for what should have been a day of relief. By the time I had the emotional strength to drag myself out of bed, if I was lucky, there was just enough time to get Dexter's dinner started and his coffee brewing. While the whole time, I was dreading to face another tomorrow.

Time was not able to mend or repair the damage, which had been done. Following the blood shed of my baby and the countless hours that Dexter was so close to death, every morning when my feet hit the floor, the day became a burden. A dark cloud of blame sat over my head and the days fell into emptiness, falling into weeks of nothingness. Regardless of the fear of being alone, out in the world of society, I threw in the towel and filed for a no fault divorce. Naturally, I carried an enormous tower of guilt for all the lying and cheating I had dished out. But even so, the cheating that I allowed to be done to me was of my own doing, having believed, I was unworthy. Persecuting myself, I became my own judge and jury and allowed the guilt from the past and present, to rule the bartering between us. For everything Dexter gained, I gave into, another loss. After all was said and done, believing I was not worthy to bear another child, I returned back to my doctor. Being so young didn't interfere, seeing my doctor who had given me the number of the clinic, was in favor. So my childbearing years came to an end.

Facing myself, it turned out, the answer was always there, in the reflection of one's self, my own. Putting a face on all my lies and deceit was life changing. It was too late to turn back the clock to the, woulda-coulda-shoulda's. But it wasn't too late, to try to change my tomorrows. Having learned through Norma, all about my inner child, she opened my eyes to one thing. That being said, after living a lifetime with inner hate and the need to be needed, with the fight to fill that need, my angry inner child wasn't leaving anytime soon. Unfortunately, at that time, still never having learned the importance of self-respect, self-love, or self-deserving, all these unhealthy traits still lived on in me, proving Norma nothing but right, hindering all my earnest attempts to make a new life.

PASSAGE XI

Dungarees and apple trees

Release this kiss dear grand papa, as you can see, there is no more of you and me. I'll say something sweet and you can dwell in your own heat for the feeling of yourself in which only you believe. And we will see what you will be at the very end... when we meet again in eternity.

Dexter stayed on at the house while our divorce sat pending. Looking in, it didn't take long to get the drift that Jessie wasn't going anywhere, and that our ties were growing stronger everyday. It all began to leave him with a mouthful of bittersweet resentment and more. His hurt, his pain, I can't lie, it was eating me up alive. But the financial deal pending between us was the deal of a lifetime for him and a whiplash for me in the years to come. But once we got word that the divorce was final, Dexter moved out as planned with his angry heart tattered in two. Now that he was all settled in, my life per say, was my own. Even as my ingredients were on the short side, after checking off my need to do list, next to the list of babysitters, everything was in perfect order, giving me a boost of new confidence. Relaxed and feeling in control, my hot mug of coffee never tasted so good.

In the short days that followed, I was so sure handling things would be a piece of cake. Only there wasn't even time to let my hair down and feel the breeze of freedom. Here, less than a week, my confidence began to unravel. When I arrived home from work that evening and found the kids still up and the babysitter's face all flushed, a spark of anger emerged. It had been a long night of demanding customers and I just wanted to rest my achy feet. Handing the sitter some cash, along with attitude for the children still being up, her eyes widened in fear. Struggling to hold back her tears, she broke down claiming she didn't have anything to do with the refrigerator and furnace not working. Provoked and trying to make sense of her outburst, brushing past her, burr she was right, it was definitely chilly in the house. Making my way to the refrigerator, I threw another comment her way, for not calling me. Opening the refrigerator door, the warm air hit me in the face. It was obvious it had gone off hours before she got there. Feeling guilty for snapping, I wanted to apologize, only she was gone. Glancing out of the window, I caught a glimpse of her in the spotlight, hightailing it down the driveway. Judging by the way she fled, I should have got it, she had no plans of returning back.

But right then, my mind was preoccupied with the refrigerator and the thermostat that would not kick on. Judging by the looks of things, we were in trouble. The majority of our food was ruined, except for the few things that could be saved, if they were cooked right away. Small chance of that, with the time being what it was. Even the frozen bread dough had risen and was ready for baking. While the whole time I greased the pan and put the dough in the oven, my mind was racing over our loss. Barely making enough on my own I was already penny pinching and this unexpected ordeal, left me in a bad way. It brought to my mind the agreed amount of child support Dexter would be providing and being it was pretty darn low, wouldn't put a dent in this mess. Here I had only had the responsibility of running the household for less than a week and already I managed to lose our food supply and heat. With all the tension in the air, the boys' faces were covered in fear and began wearing me down for attention. Really, who could blame them, they were cold and hungry and my list of fears seemed to be able to convince even the youngest of minds, I was sinking fast. But once the children heard they were allowed to camp out in the living room and wear their sleepers they were running off in excitement to get their blankets. Once they were snuggled in, my mind drifted, praying they would soon fall off to sleep.

With my back to the wall, even with these problems facing me, the truth was, I couldn't bring myself to call Jessie, let alone Eileen or mother. Besides, Eileen was still in shock over my divorce and had just gotten the juicy scoop from Dexter, all about Jessie. Lets just say she was trying to digest it and was convinced I went off the deep end. So my guard was up, and I wouldn't take the chance to call anyone. The worry of proving to be a failure again, gave me the strength to lower my pride and pick up the phone to call Dexter. Half asleep, it took him a moment to clear his voice and to realize who the heck was calling so late. Before I even had a chance to plead for help, the boys started bickering, setting Mae off. Now with her bellowing in the background, it was so loud, it was hard to hear anything. But I still got the drift that he was not happy to hear from me. Of course he knew damn well, Jessie was still around visiting me in his fortress, where he had once laid his head. Dexter's attitude came at me, he was clearly uninterested and tired and filled with resentment. He was not bending and offered nothing, past having one of his friends come over, to take a look at the refrigerator. Claiming he was low on cash, he said that was the best he could do. Right before the dial tone hit me in the ear, he had pretty much summed it up, that since I was so damn smart, I should just handle it myself. This time, he was on fair ground and judging by his tone of satisfaction, he knew it too.

Once the children were asleep, I made a big cup of coco to help calm my nerves and I headed out the door. Knowing the children had enough traumas for one day, I was careful not to let the door slam behind me. Burr but it was definitely dark and chilly. It was a good thing I had put on a big, hooded sweatshirt, one that Dexter had left behind. Regardless of the chill in the air, I journeyed over to my preferred corner of the yard, under the old apple tree, surrounded by falls leftover leaves. This little corner of my world had become my favorite place to think things over. Overburdened with worry I sat on the edge of my seat, just thinking. It all began to sink in and penetrate, our food and heat were burnt toast. My insides were churning like a cup of spoiled milk and a streak of bitter resentment ran up my spine for my lousy luck and Dexter's neglect to help. Seeing he had helped himself to all my generosity to get him-self settled into his place, only added more aggravation to my bleak mood. Feeling emotionally numb, even the cool air wasn't moving me back inside. Snuggling back into the glider, I set my cup of hot coco down on the brick retaining wall and laid my face in my hands, whispering out words of desperation. Half out of my mind I began to beg God for an answer, any answer at all. It was somewhere in the peak of my misery, when a strange feeling of inner peace got me to stare up at the sky, it appeared mystical in some way. Momentarily lost in this vision, no answers came, but this miraculous image went over my head and I began to whisper out, "What do you want from me, Oh God, why are you doing this to me, why God why? "

It felt like hours since I had sat down with my cup of coco and the open skies appeared normal again. It felt like God just wasn't there, so I turned my back on him. Rubbing my tired eyes, it was cold, it was late and I was defeated. Returning back into the house, I took the bread out of the oven to cool, then wrapped it and climbed into bed pulling the covers over my head. Drifting off, I wondered if God was doing this to me because of the pain and grief I always left trailing from behind. But morning did come quick, with the sun brightly shinning. It wasn't the only thing shinning, for the answer to my prayer, sat sparkling on my finger. Breathing a sigh of relief, my wedding rings surely, should bring in enough cash to fix the furnace. Before I even finished my first cup of coffee, my excitement to call on Sonny, got me up and moving. By now he owned his own heating and cooling business and was doing well. Perhaps he would be willing to fix the furnace, in trade for my rings. Within only a few hours, he got back to me and agreed to come by. Perhaps I should have mentioned then, that I intended on using my rings as payment, only I didn't, fearing he might say no.

Once we finished our phone conversation, since it was past breakfast, I threw together some peanut butter and jelly sandwiches on fresh bread, and waited on Sonny. Just as I held my rings up to the sunlight, second thoughts began to gnaw at me. Staring intensely at their sparkle, they were definitely the most expensive gift anyone had ever given me. But while arguing with myself that the diamonds couldn't keep us warm, someone was banging on the door, throwing my debate off course. It was Dexter's friend and standing right behind him, was good old Sonny. With so much going on, I was pointing to the refrigerator one minute and walking down to the basement the next. Having left Sonny behind to tend to the furnace, after running back up the stairs, Dexter's friend was already vacuuming the dusty coils on the refrigerator. Believe it or not, that's all it took and when he turned the knob, it kicked on with a loud force. It was amazing and then he was gone. As I waited for Sonny to come up and give me the verdict, I was admiring my rings, fearing he might not accept them in trade. In a restless state, by the time he came up the steps he also brought the bad news with him, the motor was toast.

Smiling at me to help nurture the blow, he claimed since I was Eileen's little sister, he would do the installation free and all I needed to pay for were the materials. He was already giving me the deal of a lifetime but before I could open my mouth he read it in my face, I didn't have it. Quick to reach out, I handed him my rings, while running my sentences together, trying to sell him on the deal. Looking dumbfounded at me, my face must have tipped him off to just how desperate I was. Intensely examining the rings with one eye shut, it must have registered that this could also be a deal for him. Because suddenly his face lit up with that crooked smile of his, mentioning Eileen's birthday was right around the corner. With the rings now tucked in his shirt pocket, as he left, he promised to have the new furnace up and running the following day.

At any rate, after he had installed the new furnace, disappointment was written all over his face. He broke it to me that my main diamond was flawed, shortchanging him on his materials. Passing on getting another appraisal, he agreed halfheartedly to allow me to pay the difference over the next few months. Once he left, between feeling grateful, I felt deceived that even my sparkling diamond had been flawed all along. By the time Jessie swung by the house, now problem free, as we sat down to share a pot of homemade chicken soup, with fresh hot bread, we laughed over the day.

Living on my own was more difficult than I had ever imagined. Jessie pitched in here and there, even while his bank account sat on zero. Frustrated with his job and wanting more, he was always out putting in applications for sales positions he found in the paper. With no luck, Jessie continued looking for a better job than pumping gas, while our love grew deep rooted. Sweet wonderful Jessie, was definitely on top of the world and wasn't afraid to express his love and devotion. It felt so right and for the very first time in my life I was walking straight and making an honest woman out of myself. In spite of Jessie's strong yearning desires to bunk up together; vowing it would be now and forever, he reluctantly left every night, fighting me all the way. Despite his disappointment, it left me feeling decent somehow and a little self-respect grew in me everyday.

But then, it was a real let down, a stab in the heart, to learn that the neighbors wagging tongues, were having a field day gossiping during their coffee jamboree. In spite of my goody two shoes life style, obviously they had been chatting about Dexter and me and chatting about Jessie and me. The cat would never have gotten out of the bag, if I hadn't walked outside that afternoon, having taken a cup of coffee outside myself. Sitting under the apple tree, the sun was shinning and the birds were chirping. Suddenly overhearing their loud laughter and caddy remarks, I couldn't imagine just whom they were taking about so awfully and hatefully. It took less than a minute to realize it was I that they were condemning and making fun of.

Instant tears filled my eyes, their comments were reminding me of the whore daddy referred to me as. With my face flaming I crept back into the house before they could spot me. Once I escaped inside, after pouring myself another cup of coffee, with trembling fingers I lit a cigarette. Their unkind words and awful names, they referred to me as, put all of my earned self-respect, back on zero. By the time Jessie had arrived, after eyeing all the crushed out cigarettes in the ashtray and my tear stained face, he knew something was brewing. Dropping it on him that their horrible gossip was condemning our relationship and labeling me as a cheap tramp, he remained calm. Crying, I even confessed that everyone around there, only talked about me instead of, to me. In-between blowing my nose and on going tears, he pulled me close to him, discarding any seriousness to their awful name-calling. Pulling roughly out of his arms I felt stung and angry at his reaction. It appeared as if it wasn't serious to him, since he obviously wasn't the one that was being called the whore of the neighborhood. Jessie wasn't moving into my mood and pulled me back to him, hugging and kissing me down. Of course, his dazzling laughter and persistence won me over in no time. Still loaded down with anger, I began to vent, "You know, it would serve those stuck up snobs right if you never went home. Hell, since we're number one on their gossip list, maybe you should just move in, it would give them more to talk about."

It was a long-winded release, enough so, that it calmed me down. At first my mean comments were getting quite a rise out of Jessie and his eyes twinkled. But suddenly a serious frown crossed over his face and he crushed out his cigarette, slightly trembling. Reaching for me, he kissed the tip of my nose, reassuring me that he loved me no matter what. Then, just like that, he darted out the door and was gone. It was like he had vanished into thin air and had left me standing there, with uncertainty. Thinking that this was one of his silly pranks and he would probably bring back ice cream so we could lick our troubles away, set my mind to rest. But after hours had passed and the sun was starting to go down, panic began devouring me up. In desperation, after calling his house time and again, with no response, I began to restlessly pace, imagining the worst. It left me believing that he was so upset, that this was his way of sneaking out to escape from all the gossip. The fear of him being finished with me forever, left me in a state of alarm, "Oh God, what if his mother was right?"

Interrupting my absurd imagination, the sound of music blasting from our driveway filled the room. Nearly breaking my neck to get out the door, it was Jessie, my sweet Jessie. Smiling from ear to ear, he was sitting in his open convertible, with the back seat piled high with all his belongings. Just knowing he had returned back safely, with a sigh of relief, I laughed when I saw him in spite of myself. It didn't take much to figure out where his head was. Obviously while I was venting, my outburst gave him the stamp of approval to move in with us. In his mind, this was a dream come true and he jumped at the opportunity. When his eyes met mine, he was flashing me the widest smile, I had ever seen, making him even more handsome. Turning off the motor, he stepped out of his car, leaving the radio on, whistling to the tune. As he walked towards me in a carefree manner, a burst of wind blew through his hair, putting him in the spotlight. Jessie was on top of the world and I didn't have the heart to break it to him that I was only venting. Instead, as he placed a sweet kiss on my lips, my heart melted into his. Whistling to another tune, he walked back to his car and turned his radio up to full volume. He began to laugh and shake his booty to the beat of the music with every armload he carried in. It was hard not to be amused, he was so damn cute, making me think just how much easier things could be and so, I gave in right there. Taking in a breath of satisfaction, yes, it would definitely give the neighbors some brand new gossip to add to their coffee, stirring right into their long list of hearsay.

Right from day one, Jessie was great and there was nothing but love in the air. Once I got his old place cleaned up and discarded all the things he had left behind, he proudly picked up his security deposit. As we began settling in, no matter what, his carefree ways and handsome grin, always won me over. Adding to our perfect life, after months of applying from one end of town to the other, Jessie finally got his first break to begin his new career. It offered great potential for growth, with the opportunity to make beaucoup bucks. Jessie jumped at the chance and eagerly took the position as a salesman. Not only did all of life change, but also as proud as he was, he began to take on a different personality. Being filled with ambition, it grew non-stop, driving him forward with obsession. He loved it when he was recognized for all his skills and wanted to climb-climb-climb, that big ladder of success. During which time, grow he did, right along side of his pride. Having top sales week after week, soon after, he became number one in his store, month after month. It kept his co-workers on their toes and green with envy, while it fed him endless confidence and drive.

It felt like the world finally opened its arms to me. Suddenly lost in this wealth of pure love, the need to give back, multiplied and my traits of caretaking rapidly intensified. To me, it was all about love, devotion and the need to be needed. While long extensive hours became a must for him, support of his job came easy for me and I began throwing myself into all his needs. My dedication began to fit in perfect with Jessie's strong need to succeed and his needs eventually became my greatest triumphs. There is no dismissing the fact, I was wrong for continuing to wear myself down, fixing everything that went wrong. Becoming Jessie's caretaker achieved nothing, other than to hold me captive to this sick trait. Because the more he needed me, the more I did, the more I did, the more it made me believe I was worth loving. Simply said, there was no price too high to pay for love. Despite the consequences, I didn't perceive any of that, truth was; I was living with the ongoing struggle to strive for perfection.

In the days and weeks that were slipping by, with our love still on the rise, we were living in total bliss. Everything was picture perfect from the romantic dinners to our lovemaking. Things were going smoothly; nothing could have ruffled our feathers. Not even Dexter's angry comments; that were on the rise. It got so bad, even his weekly visits with the children began to dwindle away. Eventually his support check was the only thing that arrived; otherwise, you would have thought he fell off the face of the earth. Like everything else, I tried to fix the children's injured feelings of rejection, with Jessie's love and acceptance. Between all the amusement parks and the fun filled holidays, we shared in a day-by-day closeness. Then out from the dark, a blast from the past was knocking at my door. Oh God, the last thing I wanted to do was bring Jessie anywhere near my shady past. I figured my past was my past, but that wasn't the case, for good old daddy called, to drop the shocking news! "Dear old Grand Papa was dead."

Yes, dear old Grand Papa was dead he was dead! My feelings for him were never really dealt with, other than the hatred that was still attached to me. Lost in all the abusive and shameful memories from the past, I felt this strong need to convey my feelings to him personally. Just him and I, one on one, it did not matter if he was cold dead or buried. Although one might be quick to utter, that I only became bold and fearless to converse my attack, with a silent corpse. Perhaps it seems meaningless, like running water over the dam. But for me, my mind was determined and geared up to go. In the back of my head, the excitement of seeing daddy again was on the rise. It was my hopeful thoughts of reuniting with him, which gave me the courage to walk through those doors. Once I arrived, everyone was gathered around the casket and no one seemed to be paying me any mind. Searching from one end of the room to the other, he was nowhere to be seen. A wave of disappointment settled in and I sniffled inside myself. "Oh daddy why aren't you here?"

In disbelief that he would not even show his face at his father's funeral, I continued to scope out every possible corner. Drawing in my breath with a sudden jolt, suddenly I was gazing into the shallow eyes of my step-grandmother. Sinking fast, my feet felt like they were stuck in quicksand, locking my face on hers. Once she looked into my eyes, she showed no more care than in my youngster years. Standing weak against her lingering stare, I couldn't stop my mind from wondering about the abuse she had suffered. She definitely carried her own misfortune of shame from all the ill treatment that grandfather had inflicted on her. Being that I had once overheard some gossip, that gruesome hearsay was enough for me. It was less intimidating and painful for me to harbor on her shame, rather than my own. It mentally allowed me to push away my shame with Grand Papa, whom I believed was already standing in judgment. Yet, the thought of her shame was enough to free me from the quicksand beneath my feet. Now standing with my feet on solid ground, compassion for her set in and I wanted to reach my hand out to her. But she looked so frail, so shriveled in thought, I found myself withdrawing for my part. But her eyes remained vacant as she turned her attention the other way. Uncomfortable, I felt out of place and looked for something to turn my attention to. It was strange that everyone around me appeared as a stranger, yet at the same time, they appeared to be gawking at me. One long shiver ran up my spine. Ignoring my paranoid observations, I reminded myself I was only there for Daddy and dear old Grand Papa.

Walking over to where Grand Papa laid his head, I felt aware of every eye following me from behind. Were the silent daggers of their judgment nothing but my imagination, because it felt as real as hell? Someone had to have been talking here! Could it have been my Witch-like-aunt, standing off to the corner with a bottomless stare of disapproval? None of it had time to matter! Grand Papa, there he laid lifeless, stiff as a stone. His presence was taking me back in time. No longer did he hold any power over me, no longer could he hurt me with his lashing tongue. Those awful memories of his spotted hands and the sounds of his heavy breathing, would never reach me again. Lost in the stillness of that memory a gust of relief ran through my blood. He was dead, he was dead, he was dead and I was glad! Looking intensely at his wrinkled face, all the inner buildup of pain and sadness for his lack of love and deception, began rising to the surface and it filled me with pure hatred and I whispered. "You, dear old Grand Papa, I will never, never forgive you, I hate you, I hate you, I will always hate you!"

At last, those words of revenge were spoken. A wave of relief and satisfaction passed through me and I walked out those doors with my head held up high, only looking back twice, still with the hope of seeing father. In the days that followed, my words of revenge held no power, for they were not my fate. It seems after he passed on, my dreams started to become a part of my life. Being still young in spiritual growth, I had not yet reached a level of any true acceptance. This was merely a beginning that never kicked into full force, until much later, when I learned that not only did I heal through sleep, but grew as well. Call it what you may, because it appeared as if all the tarnish that passed through my day, the nights would polish away. At this time in my life, this level of spirituality was very perplexing for me. Let's just call it a form of hallucinating, since I have no answer for such magnificent images.

But dear sweet old Grand Papa on this particular night was not my hallucination, my dream, nor my nightmare. As I began to fall into a strange twilight of sleep, I began to make out a dark image of a circle rotating. At some point it stopped and was left lingering in the midst of a nameless place. It was then, when this powerful voice traveled out to me in question.

"Can you forgive all those who have hurt you?"

Taken in, my mind began to focus on this image set in this time element and I could mentally hear myself answering yes to every face and wrongful action, slipping into my heart and vision. In the strange drops of time that followed, I met the perplexed eyes of Grand Papa, freezing my mind in its path. Feeling forced to feel, my head felt like it was pried open and my mind cried. "No, I can never forgive him, never, for my hate and calloused heart will live on forever."

My heart continued to weep until a wave of warm energy washed over me and I began to float deep into the eyes and down to the soul of Grand Papa. In those split seconds, I could feel all his emotions passing through his spirit. His shame and remorse had left his soul unable to rest. In spite of fighting to hold on to my hate, somehow inside this strong energy, I found the inner strength to surrender and give the impossible, forgiveness. The very second I gave forgiveness a sense of peace came flowing through me. Within moments the circle began rotating again and the power of the voice called out and this time, my own fear was upon me.

"Can you ask forgiveness, of all those in which you have hurt?"

And the image of the circle brought before me, all the faces of the people I had injured and had crippled with all my words and actions of unkindness. Cringing, shame washed over me for all the anguish and pain I had callously inflicted onto others. Inside my shame and remorse, I could only sob and beg the taunting faces, for their forgiveness. Exhausted and starting to fall back into sleep, the image of the circle began to rotate again and the voice again, called on me.

"Now can you give forgiveness onto yourself?"

In those next grains of time, I forgave myself for the first time in these short-lived chapters of my life. Then peaceful undisturbed, beautiful sleep followed. In all my forgiveness and peace…I slept like a baby unaware of my future, which was already headed in the wrong direction, which would bring to life, all the sinful secrets we shelter.

Plenty of forgiveness was at hand, but only days later it was all pushed away when the crude voice of our Witch-like-aunt came barreling through the receiver. Well, well, what a grand surprise to hear from her, being a stranger and all, past the painful droppings of wickedness she left behind. There was definitely a lot of anger and resentment brewing, as to her true motives. But once her cold voice broke the news, there wasn't time for bitter thoughts. Oh my God, it was daddy and he was in critical condition. Remaining cold to my emotions, she informed me, he was calling out for me. Me, he wanted me! Immediately my heart moistened and swelled up with love and gratitude, in view of the fact, he wanted me and no one else. Interrupting my thoughts, suddenly her voice was filled with criticism, claiming I was not deserving enough, to see him. "Damn her, just damn her," I thought. While she continued displaying her disapproval, my mind began to drift back in time, to when she would drag me with her to the butcher shop for red meat. The sound of her shinny backless high heels, hitting the sidewalk, click-click-click. Click-click-click, against the dry pavement, stopping at each worn down curb, while she roughly tugged at my hand. Abruptly she brought me back to earth with her deadly warning, "He's on his death bed you know, he's not expected to live through the night."

Without another word she hung up on me and the receiver went dead. Oh daddy! Twisted thoughts of remorse and guilt tugged at my heart the entire time I scrambled to get the kids off to the sitter. With a note left for Jessie sitting on the table, stamped with a kiss, I locked the door as we left. Time was ticking and the fear of it running out, kept my foot pressed down on the petal. Desperately trying to make it in time, my hands shook with every turn of the wheel. Yet to be exactly in time for what, maybe in time to beg him for forgiveness. Or most likely, it was that I had waited so long for him to spill his guts and beg me for forgiveness for all his misery. All this Disney thinking did for me, was get me lost in this fantasy of him crying out and confessing all the love he held for me. That simple love of his, that he kept stored away on a shelf to sit and collect dust. Oh God, it all had me going, my head was pounding, settling deep into my temples. Pulling into the parking lot, I had definitely worked myself into another frenzy, with all my ridiculous, fantasies and pipe dreams. Having the number of his room memorized, while spinning, I knew I had to compose myself and get a grip. "Breathe," I lectured, "Breathe."

After three deep breathes and three exhales, my composure held its ground. But while stepping out of the elevator and walking into room 222, there was no way I was ready for any of this! Oh daddy, his still body was hooked up to an IV with tubes running in and out from everywhere. He was out of it and I wasn't sure if he was even conscious, let alone aware that I was there. After giving him several gentle shakes and calling out his name, it was no use, he wasn't responding. It was ripping me up, and after calling out to him repeatedly, it still didn't bring him around. Tearfully reaching out to him, I began to caress his hair softly with my fingertips. Fearful he was going to die, my body slumped down into a hard plastic chair, just a foot away, facing his bed. Past stressing, there was nothing to do, so as my eyes rested on his motionless body, I sat thinking. Staring at him in his unfamiliar white hospital gown, I drifted back into the years in shivering thoughts. Back to where we once called home, where he only wore army green fatigues and white v-neck t-shirts. Those ragbag white t-shirts he always wore showed off his muscular arms, developed through his drive of exercise. Daddy's wardrobe consisted of two shelves lined with only t-shirts and army fatigue pants, stacked neatly in rows of three. Even his closet sat empty of any life, except for one long sleeved wrinkled shirt and four empty metal hangers. Suddenly I cringed, imagining the walls in his room echoing back at me with his whispers.

Rubbing my throbbing head, no matter where my head drifted to, it returned back to that house. Between scrutinizing our yesterdays and how he called for me today, prayers took over my attention. In all my prayers I was pleading with God, to give daddy a chance to live, so he could make up for all the days he had foolishly thrown away. Inside of a bubble, I was blinded by sorrow and was truly convinced that if God gave him a second chance, all of life would change for us. It was in the midst of my prayers, when the loud sound of clanging, coming from the metal bed that the male nurses were maneuvering into the door, interrupted my prayers. "Damn them, why are they making so much racket?" My mood quickly changed and with all the noise going on, it was the perfect time to leave to go call Eileen.

Riding the elevator down to the cafeteria to find a phone, a hodgepodge of visitors stood out. By now my nerves had gotten the best of me, and seeing the candy machine next to the phone, I bought a chocolate bar for a quick pick me up. Reaching for the receiver, there was foul graffiti written on the wall. Suddenly I felt so very alone and unprotected. After stumbling with a handful of coins, after dialing Eileen, she answered on the second ring. With a quick clearing of my throat, by the time I got out the whole story, she was ticked off and in tears, because she was not notified sooner. Now that she had daddy's room number, she couldn't have blown me off any faster. Walking towards the elevators to go back up to the room, I was arguing with justification for not having called her a lot sooner. The fact that I didn't tell her that he was only calling out for me; eased my guilty conscience. Once I was back in the room, waiting on Eileen, in one split second daddy partially opened his eyes, bringing me abruptly to my feet. He was struggling to see me and as his calloused hand reached out towards me any guilt relating to Eileen drifted away. Promptly she arrived, out of breath and in a state of muddle. Now here laid our father, broken down and still in the weeds, yet we were both competing for his calloused hands and a first place stand next to his hospital bed. Obviously we were sickly driven to gain his acceptance, before he fell away from us. Perhaps ill minded as we both were, we believed if we gave up on him, it was like giving up on ourselves. So we sat and prayed and by some miracle, God surely heard our prayers, for daddy not only pulled through the night, but everyday, he grew stronger. With his girls by his side, it took no time at all for him to slip right back into the good-old daddy we had known. After fantasizing, that if he pulled through, everything would be beautiful now and forever, became more of a let down every day. Even his playtime of calling out degrading nicknames, began to squeeze its way into every corner of the ward. Every doctor, nurse and patient he came in contact with, was labeled and referred to by the ill-fated name, he had created. Now that daddy was meeting so many men in the same condition as himself, his attitude grew more pungent. Even our Witch-like-aunt with her disappearing acts, got the whip from daddy's tongue. Now that Eileen and I were in, she was out and it left us ecstatic that we didn't have to see her face or hear how poisoned we were.

Daddy's hospital stay, fell into months while we lovingly gave him all our blood. But it wasn't our good blood that he wanted! Since he didn't like movies or ping pong and didn't want anything to do with anyone past his own caretakers, he was bored stiff right into crime. Regardless of right, wrong or consequences, as for my part, the excitement of sharing anything with daddy, was far more valuable than getting caught. Standing proud by his side and eating up all his attention, I wasn't about to say no. Besides, I was gutless. There was no way I would allow for him to see the cowardly side of me, knowing he believed, I was his spunky little Beaky-Nose. He began to grumble from day one, my damn purse was too small and the opening was too narrow. Lost in his own high, he'd stuff and squeeze every item he collected, into the mouth of my purse. Hospital-gowns, silverware, salt and don't forget the pepper! Once he had shoved the last of his steal in, he'd grumble for me to bring a bigger purse next time. My eyes rolled, as I exited out of his room, hearing the rumble of his insane laughter following me from behind. Checking out the halls for anyone, a feeling of fear ran through my veins as I dumped the stuff in a deserted corner, praying no one heard the jingle jangle from the silverware. Regardless of the pressure he put on us, with his release now in our view, it left us with a new fear for his return home.

But still when the big day arrived, we were both riding on hope and excitement for his return. Having worked with Eileen to put everything in perfect order, with blindfolds on, we were eager for all our new today's to begin. Well what did we expect? Love, communication, kisses? None of it saw the light of day. Like clockwork, once he fell comfortably back into his surroundings, he became good old hard-core daddy again. Inside one short week, he was back to editing the newspaper with nasty comments, about every neighbor he angrily sat watching from the corner of his world. Past chatting nonstop with Sonny, Dexter Chester, as far as daddy was concerned, was still limping around the house somewhere. Meanwhile, Jessie had to stay clear of the mess, until I could get the word out to daddy that Dexter Chester was no longer among us. Now that all our children had at long last been introduced to the strange man in the chrome chair with wheels, they were bursting at the seams to win over his attention. Forget their names and forget their voices calling out grandpa to his deaf ears, for he remained off limits to them.

His disinterest, only made Eileen and I more determined to win his hard-earned acceptance. But in that one weird moment when he lifted up his head and gazed deeply into my eyes, we somehow connected. As short lives as it was, it fueled me up with more fight to win his love. But while frantically wanting to break the news of Dexter Chester and Jessie, I stood in front of his chair blocking his vision to get his attention. Even after he nearly ran over my feet trying to turn his chair away from my stern face, I wouldn't budge. Putting my foot on the footrest of his chair, awe, he was cornered. Loudly clapping my hands, only inches from his face, I shouted. "Daddy-daddy listen, listen daddy-hey-daddy, I am divorced. Dad-Dad, listen!" Clapping my hands again, until finally he had looked up long enough to mumble, "What?"

It was unbelievable that I had managed to capture his attention; only his attention was short lived. Oh but he was hopeless. Disappointment set in because he wouldn't hear, that as of a week ago, Jessie and I had a date set to be married. Losing my cool, I decided it was just best to bide my time, until another opportunity came along. But as each day passed, it got so; he grumbled and tore apart everything from the moment he opened his angry brown eyes. It was only when his head hit his flattened out pillow, sitting on his mat that still lay on the floor, did it stop. It was all hitting home and a strong resentment began to creep in for everything he stood for. Since he never stood up for any of us, past the hours he spent walking on his parallel bars, I didn't have a leg to stand on, in his never ending arguments. His brutal behavior was never enough to stop either one of us from going back for more, no matter how much he dished out. We were gluttons for his punishment.

But on the day that forbidden word mother, was somehow dropped into the air, his ears perked up taking him into a rage. His arms began to swing, he was out of control and I was stepping away in fear. His voice began echoing off the wall, taking me back in time. "She had holes in her shoes, holes in her underwear, she was nothing but a whore. It was an instant replay and covering my ears I began to scream, "Stop it…Stop…Stop it."

He didn't buy it back in the day and he sure wasn't buying it now. He stopped dead in his tracks, giving me back a hateful stare of betrayal. In his madness, he began to flee, his calloused hands frantically worked the wheels on his chair, into the narrow opening of his bedroom, slamming the door behind him. That was that now it was over! It was finished! Copouts! So no new today and no new tomorrows, we were stuck with the same old yesterdays. Once again we were both shut out, disowned. Seeing Eileen had been out that day with her family, she remained in denial to my dialogue to his outrage and the dreadful outcome. Instead, she ran back to him in hysteria, so sure, he would open his arms to her. Poor broken down Eileen, all her tears and promises couldn't convince him to open that damn door. Now with him hiding again behind closed doors, we left him, to go live life as he had taught us.

Obviously, Eileen and I couldn't let go of our yesterdays and we began falling back into, who was who. Thanks to my big mouth for dropping mother's name into daddy's lap, Eileen now blamed me for her loss. With tension building, it carried into our relationship, putting Jessie right in the spotlight. We weren't holding our tongues, but even as she was all for him, her buts were making my skin crawl. What was she so worried about, but then again, she always had a lot to fear from my bad choices. Well that was before the Jessie days, things were different now and nobody, was going to block my happiness. Being she was so perfect in my head, her questions felt like they were loaded with ammunition. Just the fear that our love was at risk, brought my fists up. Quickly things began to change and all the closeness we shared began to dwindle and soon after, we fell back into a rivalry.

PASSAGE XII

Rags to Riches

Dream lover, you give me love and you give me hope, which allows my heart to continually float. My darling you're my dream lover in everyway, bringing to me the true meaning to our dreams. I love you so; you bring love to spring, creating all the wonderful memories that songs relate our life to be.

Even with Eileen's emotions unsettled, still I was engrossed in making everything perfect for Jessie. Seeing he was still number one, two and three, on my list of dos, I just pushed her moods aside. With our wedding day sitting only months away, I was working hard to strive for perfection. In the midst of all my busy days and happiness, it was quite a shock when mother dropped it in our laps, that she was getting married. She showed up that day with her hair done in a soft upsweep, while her face stood out in a lustrous glow. Who would have thought she could keep a secret like that, tucked up her sleeve? But being love struck and all, when she mentioned the name Wayne; she had stars in her eyes. She didn't have to say another word; her face said it all…she was in love! Looking at her, I was seeing her in a different light, away from all those awful memories, when father had ruled her every move. Wayne, he was a nice looking man, from his southern accent to his cowboy boots and big-rimed hat. Loving music like he did, mother confessed that she had been out on the weekends square dancing with him and learning to…do-si-do. Carefree in her excitement, she was so taken away. Never having seen her like this before, Eileen and I were overwhelmed in delight, yet with things moving so fast, a list of uncertainties sat with us. Now I will be like mother and tell you not to worry, that everything will turn out just fine, her life would be beautiful and joyous and not to worry over her. Regardless of her confidence and our concerns, it didn't take much to get comfortable around Wayne. After a few evenings out and our family picnic, we accepted his happy go lucky personality into our family. Being the wedding was only weeks away, there was still so much to do. But with mother on cloud nine and with her sewing machine, she got right down to business. In her determination, within days, she made her and her Maid of Honor's dresses, the cake and flowers were ordered and the deposit was put on a party room.

With the days falling into one another, before you knew it, their special day had arrived. It was to be an early evening ceremony, followed by a reception, being held in a large carpeted room surrounded by glass, widely displaying nature. The day was filled with sunshine and the evening was clear, while the outside scene of nature set the mood. In addition to mother's creativity, the second she walked in wearing her elegant dress, she was surrounded with compliments. Nearly touching the floor in length, it had ruffles made of soft white lace around three shades of orchid. She stood beautiful with lavender and white flowers woven through her hair, looking as innocent as a new bride. Standing beside her dressed in pink, was my angelic aunt, her Maid of Honor, while Wayne's best friend stood in a tux, as his Best Man. In those next sands of time, they became man and wife. With tears spilling over, and congratulations in order, soon after the party began. Everyone feasted on all the delicious trays of food and we danced until our feet could dance no more. Before you knew it, the cake was cut and mother was throwing her bouquet, with the sounds of laughter in the air. Once the band began to play their requested song, lost in their moment, as Wayne held mother tightly in his arms, they swayed together back and forth, to the end of their magical evening. Eager to fire up their honeymoon, right after everyone joyfully kissed them off, they darted out the door.

So inside of all this perfection of mine, with mother content, we set a goal to remodel the house before our own wedding date. Now that Jessie and I were working towards the same goals, while he was putting in long extensive hours, in addition to working on the house, his personal needs became my first priority. Given that mother was a natural; having been hard-pressed by father, all her knowledge and creative skills was the key to our affordability. Working hard, side-by-side, we knocked out project after project. Once each room was finished, knowing Jessie's eyes would light up with approval, left me filled with a pleasing satisfaction. Since his praise always left me more eager to please, I knocked myself out to finish by our wedding day. Stepping back, with all the dust and clutter now gone, the reality of what we had accomplished was amazing. It was so comfy cozy, while the new addition of thick chocolate brown carpeting, added the final touch of warmth. By then, our wedding day was planned out in perfect detail, from the church to the reception. It would be held at an old stone church, located in the old district of downtown. When mother and Wayne persuaded us to have our reception at their home, it enabled us to afford the two-piece band we loved, boosting our excitement.

With everything in order, the crossed off days were slipping by, while life was looking nowhere but up. Now with Jessie climbing the ladder to his success, his mother was not only proud, but she opened her arms to me with acceptance. Up to now, we were basically strangers; so this gave me a new, but intimidating sense of belonging. But still, she held on to her secret life, never allowing me to get to close. It was true; Jessie admired everything she stood for. Any kind of criticism she gave to me was pushed under the table, along with all my frustration for his lack of ability to perceive it. Certainly the desire and care to be liked rather than tolerated was there, but somehow, I felt in the distance, whenever she was near. Closed-minded to my input, all her carefree efforts, just made Jessie smile for his part to bring us together.

The sun was fading in and out on the day that I was to become Jessie's wife. The lavishness of wild flowers in full bloom, were all around us. Having arrived at the church with mother, we waited off to the side, as she brushed at the wrinkles in my dress, which had accumulated on the drive there. Once the loud organ music began streaming through the church, as I began walking down the aisle, the faces of everyone I loved came into view. When I met Jessie's blue eyes, they were sparkling with an alluring charm. He was so handsome that he looked sinfully forbidden somehow. Surrounded by the fresh scent of flowers around the altar, with love in our hearts, we exchanged our sacred vows. Now pronounced man and wife, as Jessie's warm lips met mine, overwhelmed in the moment, he took in one sharp breath. Suddenly, voices filled the air and as we exited out of the church, white rice was being playfully thrown at us. Unexpected, Jessie pulled me close giving me a passionate kiss, with our guests cheering on. Following a series of posed pictures, we went to mother's house, where friends and family awaited us. The whole time congratulations were being offered; I stood proud next to Jessie, aware of everyone around me. Feeling confident and pretty, all my hard work of striving for perfection paid off. Even my long gown of soft peach and burgundy hung perfectly on my hard driven, trim figure. Looking over the room, when Jessie's mother smiled over at me, at that moment, it felt so right. Suddenly a soft tap on my shoulder brought me face to face with my sister and Sonny. With open arms, she was wishing me the very best of luck with no buts attached. Here, I was so mistaken; she did want me to be happy. Suddenly in a whirl of commotion, her children loudly tore off to hunt down their cousins, taking us into laughter. The ice was broken and we hugged with tears of regret, for having acted out in anger. That Eileen, she looked absolutely stunning in her lime colored dress, bringing life to her hazel green eyes. Right in the heart of all our tears and embracing, mother proudly walked over to us, relieved that her girl's were once again seeing eye-to-eye. In a calm state, her face was radiant; it was such a proud moment, knowing we were all standing in a new era of life together, after our life with daddy. Once again mother had outdone herself and I knew without a doubt, she had worked her fingers to the bone, to make it so. Every table was set with white linen and a scented burning candle, while a large buffet table sat waiting to be filled. Through it all, with the mouth-watering food, the live music and the great company, the evening came to a slow end with me dancing the last song in the arms of my new husband. This time, it was our turn to eagerly dart out the door to fire up our honeymoon in the Florida sun.

In all the amazing weather, every morning we sat enjoying our coffee, staring out at the sunrise. Later in the day we bought seashells and t-shirts out on the strip for the kids. Every evening after we pigged out on seafood by candlelight, we snuggled up on the beach to watch the sun go down. Upon our return home, tanned and feeling good, in the beginning we lived everyday in each other's hearts. By now, all our loved ones had returned back to the hustle and bustle of everyday life. While Jessie's mother's disproval for me, did return, visit to visit. In spite of everything, it carried its benefits, leaving us with little interference in our corner of the world. Going back to the nights when Jessie held me in his arms under the stars, promising to adore me forever, we were living life only through love. In spite that Jessie was gone from morning to night, his off days were marked for catching up on fun and love. When it came time for dinner, his mouth would water the whole time our steaks sizzled on the grill. Once we all got comfortable to watch the sun go down, only the crumbs on our plates, were left. It was always a great ending to a full day. But like always once morning had arrived, it was back to climbing the ladder for Jessie and several days would pass before we played again and soon after even more days.

It was plain to see everyone loved Jessie and as long as he was number one at work, he was on top of the world. With Jessie gone so many hours out of each day, anxiety for his job began to inch its way in, leaving me with a sense of restlessness. With all the inside remolding done, past working, there were still too many hours left in each day. In my boredom, I ventured outdoors, to bring the landscaping up to date. In the heart of digging and working through the rich soil, I realized, the earth touched me and my love for plant life began. Having found a new sense of peace and tranquility, it kept me busy for months filling in the lonely gaps when Jessie would be gone. It was quite by accident, when I learned from a neighbor's realtor that all our hard work had nearly doubled the market price on our home. Bragging in excitement about my accomplishments to get Jessie's attention, did just that, it got his full attention and than some. Putting a brainstorm in his head, only days later he had it all figured out. Wanting to jump on the wagon to make a killing, he was trying his best to get me to sell. In the beginning it seemed unfair, to put my blood into something, just so someone else could enjoy all the pleasure. Except Jessie wouldn't let it go, pointing out we should leave all the stained memories of Dexter behind and have a fresh new start. On that note, he got my attention and I must admit, it was very alluring. Jessie knew darn well he had sparked my interest, pointing out this was our chance to get the dream house we always talked about. It wasn't until he promised we would have lots of trees near and far, that he reeled me in and captured my support. Lost in a new excitement, we sat down together to begin our new dream. Once we got the juicy appraisal on the house, we jumped at the chance to build a home way out in the suburbs. Searching for weeks on end, after a series of disappointments, we stumbled across a subdivision with several wooded lots, close to our budget. Perfect in everyway, we picked out the ranch model with the inviting double front doors. It was only after we began to add in all the extras to the base price, when it went way over the top. Even after excluding the wallpaper and landscaping, the high numbers were still staring us in the face. Wet behind the ears, in our eagerness, we dismissed any concern to the bottom line and attached our names to the contract. For the next few days, we sat on pins and needles up on cloud nine. Neither of us could sleep in our excitement, fearing we would be turned down for the loan. It wasn't until after we received the news that we had been approved and celebrated with champagne, that reality began knocking at our door. Being so inexperienced, we were incomplete and out of our price range. None of our figures were adding up, no mater how much we refigured it. Once coughing up Dexter's share from the divorce agreement, it put a negative outcome on the deal. It looked pretty grim and our voices rose in argument at one another, in criticism. Overwhelmed in defeat, the pressure followed us into the bedroom. Barely brushing his lips on mine, he rolled far over to his side of the bed, keeping his back towards me. Roughly pulling at the blankets and tossing annoyingly, the sound of his breathing told me all my efforts were in vain.

Starting with the late alarm, the day got off on the wrong foot with Jessie rushing out the door, again, barely brushing his lips to mine. By my second cup of coffee, I knew if we didn't come up with a solution, it wouldn't take long for us to sink. With all the kids clinging to my every move, by the time the phone rang, my mood was all over the place. Hearing Dexter's familiar voice didn't help and perhaps it was my tone that tipped him off to my frame of mind. But seeing we were the ones who had bitten off more than we could possibly chew, I couldn't blame him and actually he would be the cleaver one, to get us out of this mess. It was out of the ordinary, that he even called, let alone in our financial time of need. After apologizing for my tone, he made it easy for me to fall right into his line of concern. Unloading on him back in the day was nearly non-existent. It surely was impressive that he was now taking in every word I said so I began to pour out my guts. By the time I laid out all the dilemmas we were facing to build our new home, along with the difficulty to come up with his money, it was hard to call his mood. Suddenly feeling a chill through the phone, I felt like a blubbering fool and clamed up with regret for having opened my big mouth. It was plain to see, he was still carrying around a load of bitter resentment. In those next moments, it was an angry blast from the past. But once he hit on the need for his share, his anger faded and his tone came back with ease. It was then when he suggested that if we listed the house ourselves, we would save a bundle. It was a massive idea…a real brainstorm. Awed, Dexter really knew his stuff when it came to the almighty dollar, even more so, if it was pertaining to his pockets. The fact that he was so helpful and supportive getting me started on all the paperwork put me over the top in excitement. Hanging up the phone with relief, without wasting a minute, I grabbed a pen and paper and got down to work. It took awhile, pushing numbers from here to there, before achieving the same figures Dexter had preached. Hours later sitting proud, Dexter was right on, there would be plenty of cash to pull it off, with a little extra to put a deposit on that bright red blazer Jessie had his eye on. Confident that we would pull it off and sell the house ourselves, a lot of my strength and drive to conquer this challenge, was fueled with the need to ease all of Jessie's frustration and disappointment.

Getting lost in an early victory, after dinner I took the children out for ice cream, followed by a game of putt-putt. By the time they were tucked in for the night, I was planning in my head, a romantic celebration for the evening. You can bet your life, when Jessie walked through the door it all came at him…the excitement, the house, the car; the whole spiel. Grinning from ear to ear, once it sank in and registered, he began to twirl me around in delight, until I begged for him to stop. Once again we were back to being friends and lovers. Laughing in each other's arms, we topped off the evening, with a late dinner of scampi and baked potatoes smothered in chives and sour cream. It was true, these days with us both working with a low budget; we lived like big fish in a little pond. It was something we never thought about and we came to take it for grated. In the days ahead, in all our celebrating, the ad was in the paper and we opened our doors to have our first open house. Yet who would have thought, selling the house would turn out to be a piece of cake. Three hours into the first day our house was sold, getting just a small percentage lower than our asking price. Jessie was ecstatic, we had pulled it off and all Dexter's figures matched ours perfect. It was hats off to Dexter, the brain of money!

In our success, while observing our lovely home that we had worked non-stop to achieve, I was filled with a sudden sense of panic and loss, knowing it was gone. My mood began to sink and I kept my uncertainties to myself the entire time my mind wandered uneasily. By the time we stripped down and climbed into bed, Jessie took notice to my grim mood and drew me close. After trying to pull out of me what was wrong, not responding back, rolling over he hoarsely mumbling under his breath. Having tossed and turned half the night, it felt like I never slept. But by the morning, Jessie was as carefree as ever, so I suggested we take a ride out to the property on his next day off. Only half smiling, his face lacked expression and as I sat drinking my coffee, I wondered if he was also feeling the loss. Pushing everything out of my head, I started putting our plans in order for our next adventure out. It was all decided, first we would tour the model ranch home we had chosen, then we would go and enjoy a wonderful picnic lunch on our very own wooded lot.

On the big day when the alarm went off, we scrambled to get dressed, have breakfast and gather up our things. In the excitement, two hours later, the car was packed and we were on our way with our picnic basket. The sun was shinning and traffic was light, making it a splendid drive. We took turns choosing songs, filling the car with our happy voices, as we sang along. By the time we turned onto the gravel driveway for the model homes, our excitement quickly faded. According to their posted hours, it wouldn't open until later that day. But Jessie blew it off, suggesting we come back, after we finished our lunch. Being the drive was only a few subdivisions away; we waited the extra mile to stretch our legs. Once the car came to a stop, overloaded with excitement, the children jumped out racing to the ravine. Before I even had a chance to yell out to be careful, Jessie grabbed me in his excitement and kissed away my worries.

Setting down our basket, suddenly all I was thinking about was the smell of nature all around me. Though most of the foliage was nothing but a bunch of tall overgrown weeds, it was only the green I saw. Once we were actually walking the dirt property, there were no flowering trees near and far as Jessie had promised. But still, we had a small family of tall oak trees, infested with carpenter ants. One mammoth tree of ours, looked as if most of its trunk had been eaten away. Nevertheless they were my trees, my beautiful wonderful trees with wild foliage surrounding them. Looking past the wild blackberry bushes that were scattered here and there you could hear the sound of water coming from the ravine. Standing over it, I was taken aback, it was simply beautiful. It was several feet down and had a healthy supply of water that was rapidly running over rocks. Oh…letting out a deep breath, it was a picture of perfection and we both stood in awe, as we visualized our dream home sitting right where we stood. It was hard to concentrate on one thing for very long with so much to take in, but then the horrible gut feeling of having to leave my home began to slip away. Softening me even more was the picture of the boys running up and down the ravine with their happy faces spotted in mud. Laughing, Jessie and I exchanged a look, with our love shinning through.

By now we were all plenty hungry and after gathering everyone up, just as we were ready to dig into our picnic lunch, Mae let out a loud scream, pointing to all the ants crawling all over the basket. Judging by the inside of things, the ants were way ahead of us. Noticing the boys were running and swatting away at several angry bees, we packed it up and headed back over to the model homes. By then, the children were squabbling non-stop amongst themselves. Brad turned to me with a mouthful of bubble gum, giving me his mischievous grin, while Mae's lip stuck out pouting. Once young Dex had strict orders to keep an eye on them, his face stood proud to be in charge. Letting go of my irritation, we walked inside through the double doors into the foyer. The wide-open foyer led us into the spacious kitchen, past the ongoing counter tops and off to the left was the living room and a formal dining room. While taking my breath away, all over again, off to the right was the lower level family room with sliding glass doors, which soon would display our family of tall oak trees. The field stone fireplace from ceiling to floor put cozy into the entire room. Just the thought of cuddling up with Jessie and enjoying a romantic fire together was so inviting, it put me in the moment. The talkative sales manager interrupted my image, pointing out that the basement ran the entire length of the house, making it possible to add extra rooms later. Getting antsy to get back to the car, we shook his hand and thanked him kindly for the tour.

Once we got back to the car, all hell had broken loose. With both Mae and Brad crying, young Dex was yelling out how bad they had behaved. It was definitely time to be heading back. It had been a tedious day and with the children complaining they were hungry, when Jessie spotted a little hamburger house, he took a sharp turn in. It gave everyone a quick pick me up and being so close to our dream home, made it exciting. Driving towards home, the sun was going down, next to my mood of suddenly fearing moving so far out to the country. Whatever it was that alienated me, faded away just as Jessie pulled up into our driveway. Home sweet home, yes, that's what it was, home sweet home. Walking and stumbling around on the uneven property with flimsy sandals had done a number on my feet. But still, the first thing I did when we walked in, was hang up our family calendar, so we could share in marking off the days till our dream house stood finished. Looking over at Jessie, he was rubbing his neck with a grim face. Knowing I had passed my temperament to him, I coaxed him out of his mood, by playfully patting his behind. Smiling back at me, with everyone in better spirits, it was bath time then it was off to bed for the kids, while Jessie and I snuggled in with a good movie, munching out on buttered popcorn.

In the many days following, one day I would pinch myself to believe our dream house was real, while the next, the reality of leaving our perfect home behind terrified me. In spite of teetering back and forth, there was still the excitement that always went with me to the property. Eager to know if anything had gone down, we would high tail it out there every night, with a thermos full of coffee and a matching set of charged up flashlights. Everyday was marked off on the calendar and once they broke ground, it finally brought me acceptance. Norma was smiling along with me in those moments of reminiscing, sinking comfortably down into her chair, taken in by my excitement.

It was somewhere in all our love and happiness, when things took a turn for the worst. With Jessie always away at work, it left me to fight, having everything the builders did wrong, fixed. It all began to wear at me and after arguing with Jessie, my mood got the best of him and he gave voice that the house wasn't going anywhere but up. But when the builder's got behind schedule, it hit us where it really hurt, our wallet. It was hard to swallow, having to pay the new owners of our house, more rent than our original payment. It had all taken its toll putting additional pressure on us. Through all these tensions and delays, the days passed one by one, until our calendar was marked with our move in day. Then at long last our dream house was complete and waiting on us to come home. Jessie was on top of things and had a truck and three of his buddies reserved to help with the move. Now with everything in order, the timing was perfect and our big day arrived with sunny skies. Hours later with the truck and two cars filled to the gills, we were merrily on our way. Even with the children squashed together like a can of sardines, the long ride was filled with enthusiasm all the way there. By the time we arrived and got unloaded, it was decided that I would stay behind to unpack the things we needed and organize the rest of the boxes. Once the guys drove to get another load, there were no complaints from me, it gave me time to take it all in. Hours later, past the take out pizza we had for lunch and dinner, everything was unloaded and the guys waved us off, eager to leave. Jessie was bushed and though he looked as if he hadn't shaved for a week, he looked rugged and handsome as hell. He dropped down to the couch and began running his fingers through his hair, before giving me one big ass grin and spouting off, "Yea baby we did it, come here you!"

Once we put our play to rest, Jessie suddenly jumped up and wandered outdoors in the dark, waving me to stay put. Leaving me standing there bewildered, he returned only minutes later with an armload of firewood, wearing his biggest grin ever. Seeing we were going to camp out in the family room on our first night, the boys built the campfire with Jessie, while Mae helped to divide the mound of pillows and blankets with me. Feeling comfy and cozy and with boxes stacked high around us, we all sat talking at once. Occasionally a little argument would break out over who was going to be the first one in the morning to play down in the ravine. Looking over at Jessie and then back to the children, all their faces shined in their own excitement. Somewhere between the fire dying and the bowls of popcorn eaten to its last kernels, everyone was sound asleep. Smiling contentedly, I pulled the covers over my head and drifted off peacefully.

Morning arrived with excitement in the air and after our bellies were full of french toast smothered in maple syrup, we were ready to get down to business. Both Jessie and I had taken off a few days to rest up, finish unpacking and get set up. One of the first things we did as a family was to cut and stack up the hefty load of firewood we had ordered. We laughed and played until the sun went down, while our bellies growled back at us in hunger again. Everyday was like a picnic in our own back yard, but before you knew it, the days were gone and Jessie had to return back to work. It was somewhat of a letdown, being there was so much we didn't get finished, with so much still left to do. Now with the lack of furniture, the bareness of the rooms and the colorless walls were staring back at me in coldness. Everything looked so different than the beautiful decorated model with finished off landscaping, that we had awed for months. In a moment's moment, a flash of our warm and comfy old house sent a chill of longing up my spine. Looking over our property, past the wild foliage and tall-infested oak trees, the land was covered with unleveled layers of clay loaded with a ton of stones. This entire project was going to cost a whole lot more than we had planned and this time; it was all staring me in the face from where I stood. Letting out a defeated breath, now working with such a tight budget, we would surely be living now, like little fish in a big pound.

In the days that followed, a surge of determination hit me to try to conquer the challenge of taking on the house and taming the dirt. After stopping at mother's house, I borrowed all of her books on seeding a new lawn. According to all of my calculations, I had just enough cash and headed right for the nursery. Being it wasn't crowded, gave me a chance to observe all the beautiful shrubs and flowers, cringing at the high prices. When my turn came, with my arms holding a big bag of wild birdseed, I fumbled to read off my list, as the helpful clerk gathered my things. By the time he was finished tallying up all my items into his old fashion handled, adding machine, his glasses were slipping down his nose. Looking up, "Okay lets see, bird food, sprinkler, seed, lawn seeder, fertilizer and four bales of straw." In his next breaths he gave me the total, throwing me for a loop. It wasn't even close to my calculated amount, even after taking off the birdseed. Swallowing in anxiety, after digging in every corner of my purse, I used our credit card, reserved for emergencies. Once everything was loaded into my car, a large bale of straw was sticking out each of the back windows, while the children were stuffed together in the front seat. Once the clerk securely tied down my trunk, he cleared his throat, wishing me a lot of luck with my mission. Wrinkling my nose, as he was wiping his forehead with a handkerchief, I put the car in gear and bit my lip the whole way home.

By the time Jessie walked through the door that evening, I was bursting at the seams to give him the lowdown of the day. Failing to mention it cost a lot more than I had bragged on, not counting the cost of renting a tiller, I easily got it past him. On the morning that I had the rotor-tiller reserved; the forecast wasn't calling for any rain and with all the materials in order, I opened the book to the page marked instructions. Eager to get started, I slipped into tennis shoes. One hour later, past throwing out my shoulder and bruising my rib cage, turns out starting the tiller up was the easy part. Looking grimly behind me, I barely managed to turn over a foot of hard clay. My positive attitude was miles away now, as I plopped down on the dirt, just starring angrily at the tiller. Other than an occasional passing car, past the turnpike over the hill, it was like morgue city. Trying to figure out what the hell to do, it was quite obvious I had rocks in my head, to think I could conquer this alone. It was totally hopeless and while sitting Indian-style on the hard clay, I noticed a yellow industrial tractor slowly coming down the street. As it approached, you could make out that two real cute guys were inside the tractor. When they suddenly stopped in front of our curb, they looked at the tiller and back at me, before they broke out in laughter, asking what the blaze I was trying to do. Near tears, as I tried to explain, they both began to laugh louder. Just when I was about to tell them to go and take a hike, they took their laughter with them as they pulled the tractor up into the yard. In the blink of an eye, without a sweat, they began moving the dirt and loosening all the rocks back and forth, then moved on to the tree lawn. Standing off to the side in a daze, I began to thank God, my angels and every Godly person I could think of for sending me this miracle. With every inch of the front yard roughed up, they cut off the engine, laughing in their own joy. Holding up my finger for them to wait, after running into the house, when I returned, I gave them a six-pack of soda and a worn twenty-dollar bill. Yelling goodbye at me over the loud sound of the tractor, once they were out of sight, I cried.

Grabbing the wide metal rake, hours later, with callused and blistered hands, the sun was already setting. Once the boys got home from school, they worked their tails off, earning fifty cents for every wheel barrel filled with stones they had to lug to the ravine to dump. Covered in dirt from head to toe, with time having gotten away from us, all too soon, Jessie arrived home. Grinning from ear to ear only lasted until I bragged on just how cute the two swell guys on the tractor were. He responded moody, as if he were jealous instead of grateful, putting me on the defensive side. It really angered me, so much so, well the macaroni and cheese dinner, says it all. If he picked up that I was upset, he failed to mention it and that night when the lights went out, his arms never came around me. But by morning Jessie was back to being my sweet Jessie. Seeing it was Saturday, the boys and I went back to raking and hauling away the rocks and stones, from the break of day to completion.

Early the following morning, both mother and the sun arrived right as expected. Proud of all my accomplishments, while we finished the last of the raking, I bragged on the cute guys, bringing a smile to mother's face. Once the spreader was filled with a mixed formula of seed, we all went in for a break. It couldn't have been long; at most it was as timely as it took to share in a pitcher of ice-cold lemonade. Stepping back outside, noticing the winds had briskly picked up, quickly got my attention. Looking up to the east, dark clouds were rapidly moving our way. Knowing if it rained the ground would have to be raked all over again, was enough for me to start yelling out for mother. She came running out of the house, stopping in her tracks when she took notice to the weather. She knew even more than I what we were up against and ignoring my defeat, tore back into the house. Returning only a minute later, while struggling to hold on to a large piece of Saran wrap, she covered the top of the spreader. While looking at the stormy skies above our heads, she shouted over the wind at me, "Run, just run!"

Reaching for the handles, run like a fool I did and as the seeds were spitting out, mother stood on the sidelines, frantically waving her arms, loudly yelling out "Run, run, you can do it!"

In my dash to finish, mother ripped and spread out the bails of straw behind me. By the time the last of the straw was down, it was not a minute too soon…for last came the rain. Dashing into the house out of breath and soaking wet, having beaten the storm, we laughed in our victory. Later that evening when Jessie walked in with that gleam in his eyes, my face proudly beamed back. In the days that followed, mother began to teach me everything daddy had once driven her to learn. It was mother again, who in the first month taught me her skill to measure, glue and hang wallpaper. Room after room of pasting and hanging carried into the many months that came to pass. Season after season garage sales helped to furnish the empty rooms and bring our decorating ideas to life. Jessie was charged up, loving and admiring every change he walked into. Since he was working later and later to achieve his goals, lonely as it was, I got lost in the challenge to get everything done with my greatest flaw, perfection.

Between what mother had taught me and balancing my job, the busy months quickly passed and with blood sweat and tears, five long years had passed. Little by little, our home had come alive with exquisite beauty and warmth. Even the yard was breathtaking in its completion, overflowing with young flowering trees and soft shrubbery. The double wood deck was enclosed with a red brick patio, built brick by brick. In all its perfection, it was beautifully done, surrounding you with flowering bushes and clusters of soft colorful flowers, making you feel like you were in paradise.

By now, being Jessie was doing well for himself; he was on top of the world waiting for the big one, head manager of one of the brand new stores. Whenever a promotion passed over him, while his disappointment took him down, the excitement of the house brought him up. But now even with everything complete, loneliness ate at my contentment. It was all stemming from Jessie's job this and Jessie's job that, leaving me with many empty hours to fill. He surely must have believed by now that he had proved himself, only it wasn't so. For he continued to work nonstop, even with the dent it was putting in our relationship. It got so, in these long spans of time, resentment for his job started to filter in. But just as I was falling into protest, his company would send us an invite to attend one of their favorite nightclubs. It always gave me a quick pick me up and I would push away the feelings of neglect that had been piling up. Being with Jessie swelled me up with pride, knowing that everyone recognized I was the one that belonged by his side. When the music started and he took me in his arms, well, he had all the smooth moves of dancing away my objection, making our love feel brand new. Somewhere along the way, we both became sharp dressers and for the most part, I was feeling the acceptance of fitting in at these gatherings. While we were out laughing it up, my need for perfection doubled and I counted on liquor to help me achieve it. But how short lived was an empty acceptance, if it only gave me a temporary escape from reality. What really came to pass, once I lost the image of a counterfeit glory after stepping out of my sharp clothes, high heels and flaunty jewelry? Past my hazed memories of the expensive champagne that bubbled over the night before, the recollection of the night was uneventful. Reality was, if I wasn't working or getting dolled up to go out with Jessie, all my clothes either hung in the back of the closet or sat squashed in a corner of my room. Truth of the matter was I didn't know how to be sociable or connect with anyone, past being a caregiver. It was always the same, once the music was turned off and the lights were back on, it was back to working in the dirt and connecting with the earth.

In Jessie's high expectations, when the exciting gossip about the new stores and promotions that were coming available, hit the newsstand, he began stealing even more time from home. When he stopped taking his early outs, in our squabbles, it left me feeling like his stardom was at my solitude. It left me hungry for affection and I felt that unsound need, if you can't fight it, just give more. Giving up the battle, I came up with a prime idea of striving to be the perfect wife, better described, the caregiver at full strength. Being eager again to support Jessie's career, every week I made a big platter of golden brown chicken, fried to perfection and hand delivered it myself. When it began to pay off in Jessie's mood, it enticed me further. My idea to invite the entire crew of salesmen for a hearty smorgasbord was a brilliant idea, a complete smash. Even as Jessie was highly envied for having a superb wife who was willing to support his long hours, they were thoroughly convinced he had the world by the tail. This full bloom of attention left him bright eyed and in his exhilaration, he would dance me around in front of everyone, giving me a taste of his acceptance and glory.

Whatever it was that was driving me to carry on, the truth was, it took a lot of energy on my part. It got so that our romantic candle light dinners, that once ended with us tumbling in the sheets, began to dwindle further and further apart. Perhaps that should have been a flashing warning, that our priorities were shifting. Only I never saw it as such, nor did I believe all my energy and hard work was connected in any way to his pride and success. But being friends and lovers, after an evening out together, any doubts in my head as to whether we belonged together, vanished.

It was early evening on the night of the big gathering, when Jessie's boss Rudy showed up with a colorful, bouquet of flowers for me. It's the evening that marks the beginning of great change, awaking my inner child in a new era of life. When Rudy handed me the flowers in appreciation for all the fried chicken and other home cooked meals, it left me flattered. To receive such a lovely gift from a man, who was so respected by everyone, moved me. Mum…they smelled heavenly and I was shining like a star for capturing his attention. Cutting the stems and arranging the flowers in a vase of cool water, from across the room Jessie's heated energy reached me, scorching my mood. Once the last person had walked out the door, Jessie turned on me, accusing me of coming on to Rudy. His jealousy floored me; he was not responding at all like my Jessie. Arguing back that it was merely an act of appreciation didn't put his accusations to rest. It was already set in his mind that I was being engaging, so on that note, I angrily stomped off, leaving behind his mood. Ducking into the bathroom with an armload of my things, I turned the faucet on full blast, to run a nice bubble bath. Filling the tub full, once the candle was lit and a soft tape of music was in the cassette player, my clothes dropped from me to the floor. Climbing in and sliding down, awe, it was wonderful and my mood relaxed in the warm water. Lost in the radiance of the beautiful flowers now sitting in full view, if truth were told the flowers and Rudy's attention; well, I liked it, I liked it a lot. Besides being good-looking, confident, witty and charming, he had achieved everything in his career Jessie would die for. Oh Jessie knew darn well, that every woman thought the sun, moon and stars, rose above Rudy. Being the player that he was, married or not he was still one hell of a successful businessman. Of course in my head I knew darn well, I had responded back captivatingly, lost in his charm. But the fact that Jessie begrudged me the reward of those flowers, when he always got his glory, left me soaking with a bitter taste in my mouth.

It was also during that ball-busting gathering, when Jessie came to realize, dirt or no dirt I was still flower material. Having taken me for granted in all my aloneness; my sudden popularity was a wakeup call for him, and it began to stir up his imagination. In his insecurities, he was getting more unsure, jealous and overprotective of me as each day passed. When he dropped the bomb on me that he wanted me to quit working, it hit me like a ton of bricks. It was then when he angrily commented that my place of work was nothing more, than a meat market for men. Not responding and ignoring his insecure, trumped up comments, only pushed him further into arguing me down. Taking a stand, while concentrating on me, even the value of his job was put on the back burner, until quitting my job, became the center of his attention. Even after pointing out the need for two paychecks to run our home, he wouldn't budge. Through love and war, his temperament and mine, they both remained unwavering. Soon after, we were becoming distant friends and lovers. If it was lonely before, it was now agonizing in the numbered days that we didn't laugh or wrap our arms around one another. Jessie remained stubborn and unreasonable, holding on strong to keep me at home and I couldn't take it. Breaking down and choking on resentment, I gave myself the boot and gave my two-week notice. Crying in despair, in the days that followed, I was left longing for all the laughter and independence I had given up with my coworkers. In broken spirit, I picked myself up by planning to work on a new project, promising to enjoy my freedom. It all sounded promising, only I was quick to discover after paying the bills, basically we were broke for any special, anything. Convinced that when I took it to Jessie, he would be on his knees begging for me to return to work, gave me a lift. Only nothing turned out the way I had it pictured in my head. His mind was set in stone and he stood firm and unbending. Observing him steadily moving forward in his career, one way or another, it left me feeling cheated. It felt like thievery to me, now that my tips, which were my only means to independence, were snatched away. It left me more furious at myself, for having allowed my choices to become his, leaving me, the thief of one self.

While Jessie was busy with business golf outings and dinner meetings, his mind remained distant to my needs. In my protest, he kissed away my tears, kissing away any fight left in me. Poor mother didn't mean to over season my grief, when she called my angelic aunt, so she could tell her daughter my job was up for grabs. When Missy called only days later in high spirits, thanking me endlessly for the awesome job, it placed me into a state of only half listening. Since I hadn't seen her or Joshua, since back in the day of their wedding, it left me feeling unconnected to her. Within minutes of cutting her short, jealousy emerged thinking about her having my job, making my money and laughing it up with all my old coworkers. Oh God, it was now set in stone, my job was gone! It all made me cry harder and that night, I slept as far from Jessie as the bed would allow.

In the days and weeks that followed, with mother tied up with Wayne's sons, it left a wide gap in all the hours we normally spent together. It was lonely without mother and even lonelier without Eileen, being we were at arms length again. In our on going fight to connect, we still struggled to see eye to eye, while nothing really changed from our younger years. This time Eileen insisted, I had pounded our relationship into the ground, with my on again, off again mood swings. It was true and like in the past, I just couldn't come clean with my misery and let her see me fall short, of her on going achievements. So rather than be honest I didn't reach out to her, when she began slipping away as the lonely months slipped by without her and mother. Now with the season changing, the snow was beginning to fly, covering the rooftops and keeping me indoors. With the children at school, the days seemed longer, making it harder to fill the gap of time. Actually it was Dexter, that put all my thoughts to work, when he called catching me off guard, announcing he was getting married. While he was going off and boasting that he bought a one-karat diamond for his future wife, the memory of my flawed diamond began to choke me. My hands were cold and clammy and even now, he was still dexterous at rubbing salt in my wounds. With a profound lump of resentment in my throat, it was hard to swallow his display of generosity. By the time he hung up, my twisted theory to give twice as much to Jessie, than I had to Dexter to keep his love alive, vanished into thin air.

In all my efforts, every morning, once Jessie slipped me a kiss, rushed out the door taking his coffee with him, I was alone again. Being away so many hours, he was essentially out of reach to witness my solitude and irrational behavior. In the long weeks of winter, my negativity brought me nothing but misery. Perhaps, I was more like daddy than I cared to own up to. Now with too much time on my hands and my pockets empty, I sat as isolated and friendless as he. Perhaps daddy felt as useless as me or was it really me who felt as useless as him? My mind ran through all the years of father's cruel insanity, only to be rescued by Dexter, who wanted me to do nothing but work. It all left me remembering how Jessie had promised to love and cherish me forever, only for him now to suddenly want me to be nowhere, nowhere but home safe and sound. Safely away from all the sweet temptations of life or anything else that would prevent me from achieving success outside of our home. It all read control in one-way or another, from every male that I had so blindly loved and eagerly tried to please. It was true, I surrendered everything, in which I stood for and believed in. In my mind it was gone forever and a strong depression like I had never known, began to invade my body and devour up my energy and motivation. Even after conquering the earth and sheltering our home in warmth and beauty, all of my confidence and self-belief swiftly dwindled away. It was all so clear and ridiculous in my head, that my anger and profound laughter, reminded me of daddy's irrational behavior. It was in these silent hours that I found myself listening to the clock, as it bonged its way, through another day. It's sinful to say, that the value of time sat meaningless. Since I had nothing but all this time on my hands, I had lots of time to wonder why, for the first time in my life. To wonder exactly why I was so damn willing to give everything I stood for away in trade, all in the name of love. It's absurd that the importance of choices, still sat unoccupied in me, while the empty hours ticked away. But with the hands of time, a strange and powerful encounter took control of me, leading me into a new era of shame and humiliation.

PASSAGE XIII

The Missing Mystery

In broken spirit I sit humble, with this heavy weight sitting upon my shoulders. It is pulling me, pulling me down, further and further away from reality. My heart, for it is surely suffocating in shame and humiliation, in trade for something so real, that I was determined to hold on to.

Having lacked knowledge to alter any part of my life, or balance out any of my reactions, there was no way I was ready for what was to come. This was the first of my undeniable awakenings and it took no time for this nightmare to begin to eat at me. I do not want to try to make sense out of this illusion, for I cannot. My mind cringes just to tell the story, for the humiliation can still hurt. Mind power some called it, while others held on to their own theory. Yet the shame of being abandoned and left to face its existence alone was unbearable. Even after months of living outside of reality, help remained a far cry away. Who really knew, all the same, a better description sums it up to the winding case, of the missing mystery.

Oh Norma, she had the endurance and understanding of a gifted soul. In my reluctance and discomfort to continue, she waited patiently, offering me a gentle smile of encouragement. My head hung low, trying to start at the very beginning. When Norma's eyes met mine, the awkwardness was enough for me to turn away. While trying to pad myself from shame and embarrassment, that Norma would think I had been despondent and in a state of denial during this ordeal, left me fearful. When I first began to confide in her, she showed genuine concern, she cared she really cared. It gave me the courage to breathe life into those past shameful memories bringing them back to the now.

When tiredness and breast tenderness first set in I realized the calendar was past my cycle. If my tubes weren't tied I would have sworn I was pregnant. In the days that followed, the symptoms intensified while my second cycle passed. Looking in the mirror and observing my bare breasts, they were filling out and had hints of dark discoloration. While wondering what if, I caught a glimpse of my reflection looking back at me with a glow of excitement. In an unproductive state, I scraped up enough loose change and drove straight to the nearest drug store. Looking over the shelf, I picked up a two-hour home pregnancy test and headed back home. After reading the label, the test had to wait for a morning urine sample. Whether it was excitement or fear, in my confused state of mind, somewhere down to the root of my soul, my heart was pounding out of my chest. Sleep that night was next to impossible, but with an early rise, I jumped out of bed and grabbed the test that had been safely tucked away under my bed. Now with the children out the door, my hand trembled as I carefully followed the directions on the package. Once the test was complete and sitting in place, it sat silent doing nothing, making me more nervous. It's amazing how such a small plastic object could hold enough power to shake my world. Of course, even I was aware that any chance for it being positive, stood virtually impossible. Even so, staring at it only took me to pacing, while I returned every few minutes to look for any hint of color. Finally the results appeared and after scrutinizing it, dazed and in a state of shock, it stood *"Positive."*

In disbelief, it was hard to believe my eyes and I began to argue myself down, "But what if, what if I wasn't, but what if I was? Oh God, a little baby Jessie to hold on to. Oh God, but what if I'm not?"

Dazed I dropped down into the chair, covering my face with my hands thanking God for giving me this second chance. It was strange, because somehow it made me feel worthy for the first time, in a long time. But that night my secret stayed with me and not one word passed to Jessie, fearing the worst.

The next afternoon, calling for an appointment, they scheduled me in with my regular physician, the following week. After arriving at the office, as he walked into the room, he was impersonal from the moment his eyes met mine. It became obvious, he remembered me very well; perhaps it was the outcome from the abortion that had left him cold and sour on me. He listened quietly, ordered a pregnancy test and examined me. Afterward his voice came to life, claiming there was just not enough change to warrant a pregnancy. But when he told me the test results came back negative, I argued back repeating myself that my test results had shown positive.

Looking satisfied, he was already dismissing me, only the desperate need I had for him to believe me, gave me a boost of strength. Standing strong to his aloofness and because I would not accept his answers, he reluctantly agreed to retake the test. When the second test came back positive, I began to breath with ease thinking, "See, I'm not crazy after all."

Momentarily observing me, before he turned to walk out, he instructed me to stop off at the desk. With twisted thoughts, as I dressed, his attitude left me uncomfortable. Prior to leaving his office, Gertrude his receptionist set up a follow up appointment and handed me a prescription for prenatal vitamins. Heading home, I pushed the belittling thoughts my doctor had left me with, to the back of my mind. By late afternoon my mood began to climb and the children and I played croquet, grilled hot dogs and laughed over burnt marshmallows. But as late evening began to move in, I began to pace the floor in a restless state, waiting on Jessie to break the news. It was later than usual and still he had not arrived, even that didn't bother me, not tonight, for in my own uncertainty to his reaction, my spirits were high.

Catching the flow of headlights, he was pulling up into the driveway. Oh God my heart was pounding and no sooner had he opened the door, every emotion that had been locked away, came at him in full throttle. Drowning in tears, I owned up to all my misgivings. Looking ecstatic, Jessie dropped his car keys to the floor. His face fell into a big ass grin and he immediately reached over and picked me up off my feet. With a tilt of his head and a twinkle in his eyes, he swung me around in pure delight. In his excitement every fear and doubt that had been building, disappeared into the woodwork and it was a night of celebration with hot dogs and sweet marshmallows. Adding to our celebration, Jessie brought home the exciting news of his over due raise. It couldn't have come at a better time and knowing all it would do for us, we lived in bliss for the next three weeks.

The weeks passed quickly and before you knew it, it was time to return back to the doctor. His attitude in the last three weeks had changed just about as much as his age, so again, we carried on in an awkward silence. Once he finished the exam, stepping back he looked puzzled. Shaking his head, he stated that there was no change in the size or color of my uterus. When he ordered another pregnancy test, a rip of panic flowed through my unprepared gut. In the next long agonizing hour, I sat waiting on the edge of my seat twisting at my fingers. Once the test results arrived back, the receptionist had me take a seat in his office, laying the results across his desk. Of course it entered my head to snoop, but I held back, afraid to take a chance of getting caught. So I just sat quiet, occasionally peeping over to the paper, trying to catch a corner of an upside-down anything. The long wait left me squirming and after an hour he finally walked in and took a seat. He sat silent observing the results for only seconds before leaning towards me. With a slim silver tip pen he circled the results, reading out loud my worst fear, *"Negative."* Even with my jaw shut down in anguish, there wasn't a chance in hell for any further debate. Stopping me in my tracks, he was quick to refresh my memory, reminding me that he had tied my tubes and burned them down. It was obvious that he thought, I just did not want to listen or accept anything that he was saying, but with all these symptoms going on, I was having a melt down. Evidently he was finished and blew it all off to a false pregnancy. Looking me straight in the eyes, his emotions remained detached, pointing to my discredit to bear a child again. Emotionally fried, nothing he was saying was sinking in and I half whispered that I needed to know why the other test came back positive. He briefly stood looking at me, this time, with a hint of pity on his face. Repeating my question to him, he suddenly looked bored and fed up with the whole thing and reaching for the door he mumbled, "Loopholes, just loopholes, nothing is one hundred percent accurate."

Suddenly the door closed behind him, he was gone, and it was clear that he was still holding on to his judgment. It felt degrading, like a slap in my face. But regardless of what emotional damage it left me with, driving home to break the hideous news to Jessie, that his wife had imagined this whole thing, was almost unbearable now. On the ride home, my mind was filled with thoughts of this imaginary pregnancy, my past abortion and the baby that never came to life, it was all so eerie, a chill ran up my spine.

Oh but Jessie was so understanding. Heartbroken as he was, he pushed aside his own tears of disappointment and holding me in his arms wiped away my tears. Between working for stardom, he tried to ease my misery by pointing out my self-worth. Jessie's words were magical, even after having been so emotionally washed out, I hung my tears out to dry and my disappointment began to fad. As a matter of fact, this whole thing began to feel rather ridiculous and I just wanted to get on with life and put this all behind me. In the days that followed, I did in-fact begin to work on my self-worth as Jessie had pointed out, as the thought of returning to work was scrambling around in my head. Only after realizing I had not only skipped another cycle and that my clothes were getting smaller, I axed that idea. Inside myself I was an emotional wreck and with my doctor's cutting judgment still so fresh in my mind, the thought of seeing another doctor, remained a far cry away. Determined to beat this beast that I believed was a curse, left me morally unsettled. It's amazing how close we can get to God, when the unknown is knocking at our door. It took me to praying for a miracle that it would just disappear. Only it didn't and got progressively worse as each week passed and a silent hysteria was living and breathing in me. Even Jessie's career, for me, fell to the bottom of the ladder. It was good he was still to busy reaching for the stars, to notice the change in my body, I was struggling to cover up. But a secret such as mine couldn't hide forever; turns out Jessie caught me off guard while my secret was bulging out. It was in the heat of the night when he lustfully pulled up my baggy nightshirt and he let out a shriek in disbelief. Instantly losing his desire, he accusingly demanded to know why, I had kept his baby a secret from him. Oh God, he still didn't get it "Baby, what baby, there was no baby. There is no baby!"

Sobbing out my defense, as to why I still looked pregnant, I stuttered between lame excuses, having no answer. Staring back at me in disbelief, Jessie clamed up and rolled over as far as the bed would allow. In spite of everything that I should have felt, I slept better than I had in weeks. It was as if unveiling my secret had cleansed and nourished my soul. Apparently on the other side of the bed, Jessie didn't get much sleep, because by early morning, he was sitting voiceless on the edge, starring down at me. It was a real surprise to see him home and even better that we got to share in our morning coffee hour together. It was then, when he dropped it on me that he had arranged to take some time off. With all Jessie's concern taking control, it not only felt good it felt safe. But he wasn't taking no for an answer when he firmly said I was going to see another doctor.

Doctor after doctor test after test, being diagnosed with one condition after another, the end result was always the same and I was dismissed with another sociological evaluation. Nobody could have thought that I was crazier than myself and every visit ended in frustrated tears. Except it was only a matter of opinion, when Jessie swayed towards their notion that perhaps a shrink was the answer of all answers. Oh God, maybe he was right, but now with him on their side I felt completely unaided. Once he had their theory in his head, he wasn't helping me with any of his off the wall suggestions; instead, he was putting up a wall of tension between us.

With no solution in sight, Jessie was frustrated trying to deal with his embarrassment and returned back to his long working hours, leaving me to deal with all the inquisitive faces and questions. No doubt, it was hard for anyone to understand, including mother and Eileen. In my own isolation of loneliness it was more than difficult not to need them, let alone avoid them. But it was even harder, knowing that their frustration and grief was caused, I believed, by me. Sure they wanted to believe me and they were always shedding a tear, begging me to stop this nonsense. "Stop, Stop," I would cry back at them, "It won't stop I tell you, it won't!"

It got so bad I couldn't hold my head up and even began to avoid my neighbors at any cost. In my head, they were spying on my every move and whispering amongst them selves. Dodging became my logo, "Out of sight, out of mind." Days turned into weeks and all that changed for me, were the hands of time, along side of my growing gut. It was after a visit for a teacher's conference, when it became obvious that the children had been quizzed and it left them squeamish to talk about it. It was the last straw giving me the courage and strength to wave the white flag and call on a therapist, whom I had found in the yellow pages. After explaining my circumstances, to my surprise they had plenty of openings and scheduled me for a session only a few days later. No sooner had I hung up, a strong sense of peace flowed through me. Maybe just maybe, there was some hope and I would be saved. Just the mere thought of being normal again, carried me through the next few days in a more relaxed state of mind.

On the ride over, a million thoughts ran through my head and I was ready to surrender anything that it would take, to make this invisible thing growing in me disappear. As I was turning into the lot, a car was backing out, giving me a prime parking space. Once I got to the glass doors, a gentleman stepped out and opened the door for me with a warm smile. While riding up the elevator to the eleventh floor, I wondered if all this goodness was a sign that things were finally looking up. Only as I walked into the office, the place was decorated too rich for my taste, bringing me back down in spirit. Subsequent to signing in and sitting in one of his expensive chairs, in a moment of fear, all the past insults I had endured began to ransack my brain. Suddenly worrying this doctor would turn on me, imagining the worst, the fear to confide in him took me miles away. When the receptionist called my name, interrupting my train of thought, I was brought back to the now. She carried a carefree light stance in spite of her heavy size, hungrily chewing and snapping on some gum. She smiled wide, partially revealing the contents in her mouth and guided me into the office, closing the door behind her. Wishing I could have her confidence, went out the door with her, for when the Doctor walked in he was so darn good looking, I nearly swallowed my tongue. But his sun-streaked hair, his blue eyes, meant absolutely nothing, once his low voice displayed his remote attitude. Highly intimidated, I began to crumble and turned into a blubbering idiot. Every fear and insult thrown at me over the last several months that brought me here came pouring out of my mouth. Without taking any breathing space, I begged him to somehow make this fake baby disappear. His eyes briefly looked at my bulging belly, then appearing confused, he responded, "Slow down, just slow down and start at the very beginning."

In the midst of my detailed explanation, noticing he looked somewhat amused began to distract me. Just as I was imagining here it comes, he began to give me some lecture on his own theory of false pregnancies. His wire-rimed glasses began to slip down to the tip of his nose as he spoke. "Well my dear, look, in my profession I believe if a women truly believes she is experiencing what is known as a false pregnancy, well, chances are that's not the case, understand?"

Mumbling, "I guess so"

"Well in most cases, a false pregnancy is triggered by someone with a strong yearning to bear a child and they are absolutely convinced they are pregnant and remain in a state of denial."

Interrupting him, "But-but listen what if I fooled my body into believing I am pregnant and got my mind to believe I am not?"

After having ridiculously challenged his logic, it was obvious I ruffled his feathers and he immediately lost his professional cool, "That is highly ridiculous, you are not being rational about this whole thing and I highly recommend you see a specialist for this problem."

Choking on my frustration I whimpered out, "I have, lots of them and they couldn't find anything wrong and suggested I see a therapist."

Rubbing his forehead, "Well, I truly do believe this is something for a medical physician. Well, I honestly feel I cannot help you and would only be taking your money, well then I would definitely try a different doctor, or try a clinic."

Just like that the session was over and as I got up on my feet, he exited the room, leaving me following from behind. Having left his office with nothing but a bunch of wells, as I was walking back to my so-called, lucky parking spot, sarcastic digs were amuck in my head. "Well-well to you, you Mr. Handsome Psychologist, so much for the yellow pages, that will be the last time I let my fingers do the walking."

Heading for home, my thoughts ran over his gibberish and it left me skeptical, that maybe he never dealt with a case like mine and didn't know what the hell he was talking about. Wondering if my mind could actually be so powerful, that it could create such an illusion, left me soul searching for an answer. "Was I punishing myself for turning to an abortion, or was God giving me the burden to carry this out full term? Or, did I feel lonely, ignored and in need of attention, or was I just crazy and out to prove a point to the whole damn world?" Or...or...or, nothing made sense and I was more than willing to except any answer, any answer at all, just to feel like a normal person again. God knows any desire or longing to have a baby was long gone, right along with my sanity.

In spite of reaching another dead end, after passing up a grocery store on the way home, it reminded me that regardless of my state of mind, everyone still needed to eat. Pulling into the next plaza, judging by the numerous open spaces, it didn't appear busy. That was just perfect for me. In and out was my newest logo these days. After throwing a little of this and a little of that into the cart, I headed straight for the checkout line. Oh no, it couldn't be. Oh God, there was nowhere to hide and it was too late to turn around and pretend I hadn't seen Eileen! It had been quite some time since I had seen her and after she looked down at my belly in shock, she gasped, remarking how very pregnant I looked. Quite aware that I had been avoiding her and all of her past suggestions, she began referring to the imaginary baby I was carrying around. Seeing her lovely face in the bright fluorescent light with disproval written all over it, was enough to make my skin crawl. My face stood out red in shame the whole time the cashier was totaling up my items and bagging them up. I knew sure as hell she heard everything because when she glanced over at my belly, the amused look on her face said it all. In my mortified state, as I handed her some crumpled up bills, resentment took over my mood. Cringing I could hear Eileen lecturing under her breath, something like it was time to knock it off. My head was lost in twilight and instead of hanging around to hear her next words of criticism, I started to run out of the store with a waddle. She was loudly calling out my name, pleading for me to wait. But it was too late; I was silently screaming and began throwing my bags of groceries into the trunk. Reacting like a crazy maniac, the sound of my screeching tires drove me home. Crying and laughing in hysteria, again, I recognized it as daddy's insane laughter. Tearing into the house I left the groceries behind and crawled into bed, covering my head and sobbing loud enough for the whole damn world to hear, "Why…God why- why- why?"

The phone, it was ringing and it sounded miles away. My sobs stopped long enough to poke my head out from under the blanket and I sourly wondered if it was that Eileen, unless, she ran and opened her mouth to mother about my outburst. Believing they were teaming up, I laid my head back down ignoring the ongoing ringing, not wanting to have to answer to my uncontrolled frightful behavior. Covering my head back up with self-pity, I continued to wonder why no one could help me. Emotionally beaten down, somewhere in my desperation, prayer took over, being that it often gave me the strength to help relieve some of the stress during the day. But by nightfall the burden of this demon would return, stealing back all the strength I had managed to gain.

Day after day, life remained going around in a vicious circle, until one day our world was turned upside down. It started around three am; the pressure in my abdomen was so intense it woke me out of a deep sleep. It was the sounds of moans that woke Jessie, while it was his persistence that got me to the emergency room. Once he called on mother, no sooner had she arrived, we were on our way. While Jessie's face displayed fear, my heart was hammering to my own kind of fear, the fear of here we go again. In fact, here we go again took no time at all, for once we arrived, they took one look at me and assumed I was in labor and were about to wheel me to labor and delivery. Staring awkwardly at Jessie and silently begging him to say something and tell them, he didn't, instead he stood quiet looking like he was beyond himself. Tripping over my tongue in defense, it took no time for them to look back at me in disbelief and less time to feel like a nutcase again. Following a series of their whispers, they took me into one of the rooms, had me change into a gown and after a head full of questions I was laying back and waiting on the doctor. Left alone in a restless state, it was taking a long time and my body felt chilled in the cool air. Seeing that Jessie had to wait outside the closed curtain until the doctor came in to examine me, left me feeling more afraid than ever. Now that the intense pain in my abdomen was gone, it left me feeling stupid for being there at all. But when the doctor walked in, he had a tender smile with a crease of concern crossing over his brow. Judging by his inquisitive nature someone had to have clued him in and he appeared cautious not to ruffle me. Once the exam was complete, he stepped back and told me to sit up and relax, while he then stuck his head out of the curtain to have Jessie step in. Jessie immediately stepped towards me and grabbed hold of my hand, giving it a gentle squeeze. It was obvious, that the doctor wanted us both to hear what he had to say. While tensely waiting on edge, before either of us could let out another labored breath, he grinned and dropped the news, "Okay, you are definitely pregnant and I would calculate you are due in approximately four weeks."

Looking over at Jessie, he looked so pale, like he was ready to fall over in shock. In a state of my own panic I began to wave my hands in protest, "No-no please, you don't understand, I'm telling you there is no baby."

It went back and forth, with the doctor accusing me of being in a state of denial, offering me the name of a therapist. Once Jessie stepped up to back me, the debate came to an abrupt end and he momentarily excused himself. During his absence, Jessie began whispering words of comfort to me, trying to ease my tension. In the still atmosphere I felt so washed out, wishing I were back home safe and sound in my bed. Interrupting the soft humming sound coming from the florescent lights, the doctor walked in. Not only did he bring in another doctor, but he was also carrying a heart monitor in his hand. No one could have been more patient and it helped me relax while he put the monitor on my abdomen, making the comment, "Okay, ready, this will tell the story."

So as we were all listening to the rapid sounds, both of their faces stood out confident, then the doctor who performed the exam spoke up. "Well there you have it, that's definitely a baby's heartbeat, we all heard it and it should certainly clear up any doubts you might have had."

But somehow, trusting to count on this monitor for accuracy, left me nothing but skeptical. Especially with my (x) gynecologist's professional opinion still engraved in my head, "Loopholes, just loopholes, nothing is one hundred percent accurate."

Besides being only two opinions out of a baker's dozen, it would take a lot more to convince and guarantee me that I wouldn't end up back at the beginning. Except I have to admit they had my heart pumping with hope. But with both of their expertise, the truth was it was something, it made some perfect sense to my unexplained ongoing torment. Somewhere in my heart, I ultimately broke and began to trust in them. Hell, two of the same answers out of a baker's dozen, was more progress than either of us had since day one. Right before we left, as the nurse gave us a list of do's and don'ts, she informed us to expect a call later that afternoon, to schedule an ultrasound. We both looked down at the instruction sheet at the same time chuckling, as if to say, better late than never.

On the drive home, the morning sun was shining brightly through the windshield, putting a strain on our tired sensitive eyes. It was a long night and we both had been emotionally put through the mill, but Jessie was in his own world and wore blinders to the fear of this backfiring in our faces. By now having put his dark shades on, his carefree spirit told me he still wasn't listening to any of my words of warning that they might be wrong. Feeling my tenseness, he reached over giving my hand a little squeeze. It was as if he had lost the weight of the world, off his shoulders. Obviously he had released an enormous amount of stress and was as relaxed as a kitten, lovingly putting my worries to rest.

By the time we were pulling into the driveway, while catching Jessie's yawn, a wave of relief went through me that we were home. Hopeful that once we gave mother the low down and got the kids off to school we could sneak back into bed, didn't quite work out. Seeing as the moment we walked in through the door, without even detaching from his jacket, Jessie headed straight for the phone. Realizing he was dialing his mother's number, a wave of panic ran up my spine. He ignored my whispers to hush until we knew for sure. He wasn't listening, even my waving arms did absolutely nothing but get a work out. By then, it was too late. He had already disclosed everything down to the last detail. His face was beaming with pride, his eyes twinkling in sheer delight. It left me wondering if maybe he truly needed to prove to his family, that I wasn't so crazy after all. That thought was hard to swallow, seeing when it came to his mother, she intimidated me even more these days.

The second he hung up he smiled broadly, announcing that she would be over in one hour. Instantaneously my perfection mania moved in. My face must have showed my panic and seeing that mother had already heard the entire scenario, while Jessie was on the phone spilling the beans, she gave me a faint smile and waved me off. As mother made a polite exit, she had a look of pure relief on her face and again I feared, what if they were wrong. A twinge of guilt was pulling at me for not asking her to stay, but with so much skepticism floating above my head, I wanted to keep a lid on things for a while and asked her to do so. But now with Jessie's mother on the way and with the children hustling to catch their bus, no matter how washed-out my overall senses felt, changing into something fresh and dabbing on some mascara were the necessities to my profound perfection. Surely his mother would arrive looking nothing less than perfect, carrying the same stance of profound perfection as I.

Dressed and waiting with every strand of hair in place, it was already ticking way past the hour. Letting out a restless sigh of energy, a knock on the door interrupted my thoughts. Jessie rushed to the door whistling a tune of Dixie. It was she and I could hear their happy voices trailing over to me. Bringing me to my feet, this time, her perfection was accompanied by an armload of diapers, toys and a smile across her face. Looking lovely as usual, without a hair or a pound out of place she wrapped her arms tightly around my slumped shoulders. Displaying tears of happiness, she nearly bowled me over, after catching a genuine glimpse of care and interest in her eyes that I had never seen before. When she opened her arms out to me with acceptance, I put my guard down for the very first time. Pumped up, Jessie took the floor in excitement. In honor of our baby celebration, he offered a toast of wine for them and with a chuckle, a toast of milk for me. We sat around the table, talking back and forth, about the baby this and the baby that. When they laughed out loud at how silly this nightmare turned out, my response was a fading smile. Wanting to lay my cards out on the table and prepare her in the event the doctors were wrong, I shyly began to confide in her my inner fears. She and Jessie were both talking at once, weighing out the odds, while they both sat in agreement to the improbability, of both doctors picking up a heartbeat. On the other hand my gut was saying, if it turns out there is no baby, it'll be chopped liver for me. The mere thought of the consequences, was enough to send a streak of fear up my spine But in reality, just watching all the love on their faces and feeling such a genuine acceptance from his mother for the first time, sucked me in. Pushing my worries away, with this new acceptance, how could I bring myself to jeopardize the progress we were making? Adding to the excitement, our conversation was interrupted by the hospital calling, to set up a time for the ultra sound later that afternoon. It made everything seem more definite and solid. By now Jessie's mother was moving her chair out and ready to call it a day. With an exchange of hugs and kisses, we agreed to meet later in the week with the rest of the family, to share our amazing news. It was such a content feeling of acceptance with the air standing so clear between us. Yet in spite of the excitement Jessie and I were worn down and after sharing a bowl of cereal and toast smeared in jam, we decided to crawl back into bed for an hour. Once we were in our positions, I snuggled in as close to Jessie as my belly would allow, secretly frightful for my next tomorrows.

Just hours later, up and running, Jessie returned to work and it was time for the ultra sound. Tears of relief ran down my checks. Thank God the misery was over, Oh God it was really over! The sun, it was shinning brilliantly; it couldn't have been a more perfect day. Later I promised myself I would call on Eileen and mother, being ready to share the excitement and joy with them. In the midst of this cleansing, my hand touched my swollen belly, while my heart cried, "Oh my precious little baby, your head still soft of newborn, so delicate, yet you will be born into this world in perfect form.

Arriving right on time, when I signed in for my appointment, my face was glowing in pride. Being treated like a normal person, felt far different from what was, leaving my spirits high. Seeing the ultra-sound hadn't been around long it was exciting to learn that it would determine whether the baby would be a little Jessie, or a baby girl. Once my turn came up, I slipped on the flowered gown and followed the technician into the room. We chatted back and forth while she rubbed the gel all over my belly. She continued to chat evenly, running the wand back and forth, until suddenly her chatty spirit went silent on me. Something wasn't right and I couldn't put my finger on her sudden change of mood. It put a chill in the room making me quite nervous and uncomfortable and instead of answering my questions; she said she wasn't authorized to give out results. Only a few minutes went by before she excused herself, leaving me with a million frightful thoughts. She returned back shortly with a doctor and once again, she ran the wand over my gelled up belly as he now viewed the screen. Seconds later, he abruptly shut off the monitor and left the room. When the attendant told me to get dressed and that my doctor would get in contact with me, my gut told me something was dreadfully wrong. After getting dressed and not wanting to bring any attention to myself, without a word I exited down the steps and out the door. Walking to my car, I held nothing in hand past my car keys, not even a clue to whether I was having a boy or girl, or if my baby was even alive. Maybe that was it, maybe my baby was dead and that's why no one was talking. It was so wishy-washy, that those short-lived hours of tranquility were gone. Once I got home as I sat staring at the empty walls waiting for a call from the doctor, I began to fear that I lost what I had gained and would wind up back at the beginning. With time ticking away, the doctor still hadn't called and by the time the children got home from their friends, I composed myself enough to fake being trouble free. The night dragged and Jessie was late. By the time he finally stepped through the door he shot me a list of questions and with no answers, I gave him my mood of misery instead. Gulping down his dinner with attitude, he retired to the family room, getting lost in the news and dozed off.

The sound of the alarm sounded off to early, still leaving me exhausted, after a night of tossing and turning. In a restless state of mind, I waited on the doctor to call with the results. Just as I started to sound off under my breath, the phone rang. It was the doctor and his voice came through uneasy, leaving me to dread his next words. He was quick and to the point, and he begun to utter in a nervous state, that there had been a terrible, terrible mistake. With a sincere apology from everyone, who had put me through this ordeal, he revealed that the ultrasound showed no fetus of any size. Oh Dear God, I was losing it…my tongue sat thick and frozen, while the sound of sobs escaped from my mouth. Following another apology, before I even had a chance to think, the dial tone took us to disconnection. Knowing I was right back to the beginning again, my mind was twisted like a pretzel. For which it stood, both my baby and my sanity were gone and I was back in the maze.

This time when the children walked in, there was no hiding my tear stained face. Offering them a bowl of cookies got their attention off me. The rest of the day for me held tears of disbelief and anger. Someone just had to give me some kind of answer; how in the world could I break it to Jessie's mother, not to mention, Eileen? Just that fear, drove me to pick up the phone to call the hospital and speak with the doctor on duty that night. Right from the get-go they switched me from one department to another, until they finally transferred me over to someone who was willing to look up my chart. Putting me on hold, it took a long time before they returned. "Okay, let's see, yes, you saw Doctor so and so and it says here that you came in with lower abdominal pain.

Interrupting her in my defense, "Wait, what about the baby, what about the heartbeat?"

"I'm sorry, there doesn't seem to be any record concerning any baby or heartbeat. It only shows that you were admitted with pain in the abdomen, diagnosed with a false pregnancy and discharged the same day."

Something wasn't adding up and my voice rose in hysteria, insisting to speak to the doctor who was on duty that night. Right after she put me back on hold, after a long wait, all that came back was a dial tone. Calling back was useless. No one could find any evidence to prove anything about any baby. One big storm of anger ran through me, wondering what kind of conspiracy was going on.

Frustrated I looked down at my big ridiculous belly and began sobbing. It was all too much and after the kids were in bed, I cried until Jessie walked through the door. There was no denying that he had to be told, only when I dropped it on him, this time, it was him who was sitting in disbelief and denial. He had reached his limit and wasn't taking any of this well. Shaking his head in anguish he began to hammer at me for answers. Not having any, it only made me cry harder and instead of reaching out to him with comfort, only callous words reached his heart. His eyes watered, suddenly he looked so worn down and all the stress was wearing on his face. His tears made me sorry that I had lashed out and hurt him. Only it was too late to reach out, for he drew back, as if my hands had scorched him. He retired to the bedroom, leaving behind his leftover casserole, in the oven. Following from behind, he was awake, but he rolled over giving my touch his cold shoulder. Just imagining, how it would wound his pride when he had to tell everyone the gory details, moved me away from him.

It didn't take long when I could tell from the rhythm of his breathing, he was asleep and at that moment I felt more alone than I had ever felt in my life. Convinced I was cursed, with no way out, it felt as if society had kicked me to the curb, like a bag of garbage. It had all taken its toll and that night I cried my last tear. I became so numb that I began to shrivel up inside myself, wanting the world to leave me the hell alone. This curse or whatever it was finally did me in. Now I was just a stone's throw away to believing, I was just meant to die and dwindle away. But even those dying emotions could not be laid to rest, for fate has a way of showing up, just when you think there's no where left to turn. Sometimes it shows up to give you an ounce of strength, or an ounce of miracle, in my despair it was both. Who knew the end result was sitting in my mailbox, having reached me all the way from the unknown.

It was a simple white envelope, hand written in ink and addressed to me. It was strange and it immediately got my attention. Looking it over, it had no name or return address on it. Eagerly ripping it open, something tumbled to the floor. Looking down, I struggled to bend over to grab hold of it. Here it was a small green scapula with the Scared Heart of Christ. Looking back to the letter, my heart began to swell because somebody out there cared and a mass was being held for me. Holding on tight to the scapula, I placed it around my neck and attached myself to it.

It was only hours later, when I was soaking my weary body in the tub. It was a pregnant looking body that I no longer wanted to claim as mine. While meditating to music, a feeling of wholeness seemed to wash over me. Because it steadily felt as if one hundred pounds of bricks were being lifted off my chest. After getting out of the tub and drying off, I was breathing easier and I didn't have a clue to what I had just experience. I figured I was better off keeping my mouth zipped. It somehow left me with a strong sense of freedom, perhaps like one might feel after they had finished serving their penance. Well as far as keeping this to myself, there was no way of covering this up, because after carrying nothing but misery for months, it ended as abruptly as it began. Unbelievable as it may sound, miraculously, thirty inches fell off of me and my body returned to its normal size in only weeks.

Perhaps it sounds way too ridiculous and unbelievable to happen. In all probability, most everyone would claim they would never allow this kind of insanity to swallow them up in such a sick obsession. But as for me, this was not an illusion, but a reality that was living and breathing inside me. Not a day went by that I didn't swear I wouldn't allow myself to live like a nutcase and I fought back with every ounce of energy squirreled away in me. Still left with no answers today. What was it? Was it the power of God? Because it's near impossible, to believe that after months of opinions, accusations and judgment, this mystery still stands a mystery. Past pointing to insanity, everyone was left with his or her own theory. But then I was left to wonder, was it guilt? Remorse? But once it was all over and past me, I could only be grateful to God. While today, my own theory still sits unidentified, somewhere between the destruction of a life, to the wrenching pain of an empty birth.

PASSAGE XIV

The Secrets We Keep

When your knees tremble and your heart begins to pound, you know you're in for another round. And just when you think their out that door, they turn around and give you more. There is no right or wrong you see, they just want bad company. It goes on and on all through the night, it becomes one frightful sight. But the end does come down, at the first sight of the break of dawn.

Since the day of reckoning, our life never did return to where we were before we got caught up in the drama of an empty birth. In the weeks that followed, there was no way of going back to the empty days of misery, to sit and watch that everlasting clock. Truth of the matter was I only wanted to put this shame behind me and to just get on with my life. This whole nightmare had left me looking forward to change and I just wanted to live life at its fullest. Having been filled with grief, because my children had to carry their own burden of fear, left me trying to mend the damage. Only it didn't take any time at all to realize, life had continued on for everyone else and a great deal of change had taken place. It was like waking up out of a coma, finding out my children had grown independent and no longer depended on me with the same neediness. Being Jessie was still number one in my life, I took my insecurities and worries over to him. Past his expression of appreciation that he held for me, he remained voiceless. It seemed to satisfy him that he did his part. Only it still left me feeling unsatisfied and undernourished. It was then when I came to realize that even our relationship had suffered. Except I began to take in, since I rarely ventured out, he was confident in his comfort zone to my whereabouts. In essence, since he didn't need to worry about me, he was tied up even tighter in his job, skipping over his early outs once again. These days it left me wondering just how many more years his job would take first priority over our lives. Resentment was steadily building for all the hours he was away and I realized that in those long months while I was missing somewhere in lulu-land, I had lost a lot more than precious time. It all stirred a heaping teaspoonful of self-hatred into my life, taking me back to the past, where my unbalanced emotions laid dormant. It was then when change began to manifest and my way of thinking began to change, while returning to work became my secret desire. Besides that, with the doctor bills facing us, it gave me the perfect reason and opportunity to take it to Jessie. Just the inspiring thought of having extra cash and independence pumped me up with strength. It became my first priority and I began to work hard, once again, at building my self-worth and self-esteem, the very same self-worth, Jessie had pointed out to me in my hours of need.

With my plans all in order my determination grew solid, giving me the courage to finally hit Jessie up for approval. No sooner had he walked in that evening and picked up his dinner plate my argument greeted him in. Immediately my defense went into action, never letting up the whole time he downed his pasta, occasionally dipping his warm roll into the rich spaghetti sauce. Eager to continue, he seemed to be taking it all in, while no signs of argument crossed his face. It fed me the confidence I needed to continue justifying, just how good it would do me, to get out of the house and socialize again. Proudly waiting on his response, had I misunderstood something, because Jessie's face stood out confused as if I were speaking in some foreign language? When I started up again, he stopped me dead in my tracts, responding back mad and bullheaded. He stood strong, fighting me tooth and nail to keep me at home, while his handsome face remained firm until he won his triumph. After arguing back that no wife of his was going to be out working around liquored up men, I argued back standing strong, to everything he was throwing at my game plan. Only, all the determination instilled in me to win, turned to jelly, ending with me sobbing in tears. It must have hit him below the belt, because his face softened and he took me in his arms and kissed away my tears. By the time he whispered that he would take care of me forever, my fight for independence and self-worth lost, dwindling down to nothing. Instead of standing up for myself, I allowed his dazzling eyes and the sweetness of his touch, to win me over for now. Disappointed as I was in myself, for not standing strong, would be nothing compared to the regrets and brutal consequences I would later face, written in my own blood.

So as the world turns, the only thing that returned back to normal was

Jessie's persistence to keep me home, safe and sound, away from the outside world. It went hand in hand with my theory of becoming chopped liver once the ultra sound took the baby out of the picture. One way or another it was adding tension to our relationship, stirring the air around us. In the weeks that followed, while Jessie continued working long hours to achieve his dream, resentment began to replace the excitement I once lived for. It left me feeling cheated and with a lot of anger building, I returned to feeling useless. Sure, I can admit it, I didn't feel pretty, confidant or even interesting. Then it happened, there was absolutely no excuse, no excuse at all, for falling under his spell! "The Woodsman," that's what I'll call him.

We first met, after we noticed one of our tall oak trees was totally eaten out by carpenter ants, with its trunk oozing sap. Loose piles of sawdust had replaced its once strong trunk, weakening our tree to survive another strong wind. In fear another storm would take it down, we let our fingers do the walking, only it was in the want ads this time. Hoping to make it more affordable, we called on several contractors for estimates. Becoming discouraged, tree removal was more expensive than we had imagined and after several high estimates, we came across the ad for the Woodsman on the last missed column. Once he arrived, with confidence, he immediately took it upon himself to walk the yard. Observing him closely, as he was looking high up to the treetop, than back down to the trunk, scrutinizing it from every angle, he definitely looked like a man who knew what he was doing. He had me convinced, he was the man of all trees. Let's just say I was impressed! Once he finished penciling in his notes, he said he would get back in touch with us in a few days.

It was unexpected, when only hours later he called and wanted to shoot back over, to go over his estimates. Eager to please me and determined to get the job, he then offered to beat our lowest estimate. After giving Jessie the bottom line, we eagerly agreed and he said he would be right over with a contract. When he finally showed up, he was an hour late, leaving me irritated with his lack of respect. Shaking our hands without extending an apology, since he was giving us such a good deal, we buttoned our lips. Looking him over with a bit of attitude, this man was a strange kind of guy but yet; he was definitely different in a luring kind of way. He might have been short on height, but his stocky frame was entirely built with muscles, obviously from climbing trees and running his chain saw. He definitely carried a certain roughness about him and while closely observing him it was hard to tell for sure, if he portrayed coarseness or just arrogance. His dark short hair matched his dark eyes that had an air of mystery about them. Once we signed his hand written contract, it was decided that he would start early morning in two days. Past being late, he appeared to be business all the way and Jessie was comfortable to let me handle it from there.

The next time he arrived, he was not only prompt, but he was also extremely pleasant. Working our way to the backyard where our tall oak trees stood, out from nowhere the dark clouds brought down one heck of a downpour. Laughing, we started running and took cover inside the garage. Soaking wet, from head to toe seemed to warm things up between us. While pushing my wet hair away from my face, I invited him in for a hot cup of coffee until the downpour let up. Giggling at how we were dripping wet, any thoughts about inviting a stranger in never crossed my mind. But to me, he wasn't a stranger he was just the Woodsman. He was more than quick to accept my invitation and we sat down directly across from one another at the table. As we sipped our coffee, we talked casually for nearly an hour about the close calls he encountered while taking down some of his biggest trees. This attention he was giving me, felt like a blast from the past and for the first time, in a long time, I found myself laughing and feeling attractive. It had been a very long time since anyone thought of me as witty and interesting. Having been living in a maze for so long, it didn't take much to fill the lonely gaps my illness had left behind. This charming Woodsman, not only thought I was charming, but he let it be known that past my face and hair being beautiful, I was downright striking. It was simple really, as he was putting on the charm I fell right into it. Even with the downpour letting up, showers were left behind for the rest of the day, delaying the job. Now that our coffee time came to an end, as he playfully waved himself off, I found myself mischievously smiling back. In-spite of the fact he left the impression he was nothing less than a nice guy, once he was out of my sight, a wave of guilt washed over me for being so taken in.

Before you knew it, two days had passed and he arrived right on time with his truck loaded up. Looking intensely into the bed of his truck, he had a pile of heavy braided rope, a couple of chain saws wedged under a red rusty wheelbarrow, along with some brooms and rakes thrown on top of the pile. Noticing he was watching me scrutinizing his stuff with a half-assed grin, seemed to make him uneasy. After giving me back a bothered smile, he pointed out in defense, that he hadn't gotten his business off the ground yet, so his new truck was still on hold. It wasn't until after he dropped it on me that he was staying with a friend, when I realized that we had never asked for references, or the length of time he had been residing here. In my head, it was too late, so, I let it go. But one thing for sure, in the days ahead, no one could have argued that the Woodsman didn't know his stuff. Like clockwork, every morning he and his worker showed up right on time and past stopping in for bathroom breaks and water breaks they worked nonstop. Perhaps it was his confidence that made him shine in the sunlight, perhaps! Bringing out ice-cold pitchers of lemonade and cookies to them drew me into more conversation with him every time. In those brief days, as special and desirable as he made me feel, it held the power to brighten up my attitude. It was refreshing, a real pick me up. It was just what I needed to start rebuilding my broken spirit and bring my confidence back up to pare. Even Jessie was receiving a little extra tender loving care, from my uplifted spirits. Then just like that, his work was finished and it was over. Right after I paid him in cash, with a twinkle in his eye, he stepped back and proudly looked over the job one last time. He was taking his time about it, as if he were waiting on me to say something. Only this time, he left me self-conscious and following an awkward thank you, silence filled my lungs. Walking back into the house, as the sound of his loud muffler disappeared into the distance, I was left feeling stupid and let down. Stupid for getting caught up in the drama of his charm and let down, because it appeared as if I was the only one who cared, it was time for him to pack it up. It was a vicious circle, having felt stupid and feeling let down and after a few days, my disappointment and his face both began to fade into thin air.

Catching me off guard, when the phone rang a few weeks later and the charming voice of the Woodsman came sailing through, I was sucked right back in. He was calling to see how my trees were doing. Letting out a giggle of surprise, it felt like he had never been gone and we continued talking exactly where we left off. When his phone calls began coming in regularly, before you knew it, I found myself looking forward to his calls that were boosting my ego. Guilt began to inch its way in, as I argued back with myself that this wasn't adultery. Winning my battle wasn't difficult, having convinced myself, that I wasn't doing anything more than Jessie, when he put on the charm for his female customers. I know I was reaching below the belt, but that simple logic was enough to keep me accepting his calls. It was only a matter of time when I felt at ease enough to express my deep love for Jessie and our beautiful home. But that expression of love, didn't keep me from mentioning that it felt like Jessie had swept my needs under the title of his job.

Shocked, surprised, for a split second when he asked me to go out for a simple cup of coffee, it took my breath away. Kidding myself to what was really taking place; I declined on the first few invitations anyway. Because it was only a short time later, when I was swayed and accepted his offer. It was to be nothing but an innocent cup of coffee, with no strings attached. Once we set up the day and time, we began working on a safe place to meet. Since he was staying with friends and their house was far out on a country road; it appeared to be the perfect place, considering, all this deception was taking place behind Jessie's back. Ignoring the inner voice warning me, I was playing with fire, I brushed it away. Seeing as from his place, we were going over to his favorite coffee shop right down the street. The day of, I must admit my excitement had my heart racing and I dressed with a little extra zing and perfection. It wasn't until I was well on my way, when my conscience began to eat at me. After arguing myself down that I surely deserved some fun, the insight of hurting Jessie made me cringe. For a second I felt stupid and the thought of turning around passed over my head. But with my thoughts cluttered up with guilt and whatever other temptations that were going on in my head, obviously, I wasn't guilty enough or smart enough, because my foot stayed glued to the pedal, as I continued to cruise forward.

Whatever emotions it was that drove me there, suddenly I found myself pulling up into the long cinder driveway. The small badly dressed house, sat further back from the road, while all the other houses in the area were isolated from one another. It was definitely scenic and with acres of trees, it set me right at ease. Stepping out of my car, you could have thought it was deserted, if it were not for the light flickering in the window and the scattered blooming flowers. Walking up the walkway towards the house, I passed a dried up waterfall surrounded by dirty sand, reminding me of a house loved in earlier years. Not seeing his rusted out truck around, left me uneasy to his whereabouts and it wasn't until after a series of knocks, when his voice could be heard through the open window, "Hey, honey come on in, hey, the doors open, I'm not quite ready, I just need a few."

The moment I reached for the handle, a wave of hesitation shot through me, stopping me from walking in. Stepping away from the door, I yelled back at the window that I would rather just wait out on the steps. His voice traveled out to me laughing it up, "What do you think I'm going to do to you, kill you or something, my-my you are such a little sissy."

After throwing out a number of lame excuses, he wouldn't hear of it and continued to tease me, while I just stood there worrying, feeling like a moron. His humor definitely left me feeling ridiculous, enough so, that I began arguing again with myself. "For crying out loud, it's a stupid coffee date, its not like you're going to get jumped for God sakes, go on in."

Bearing in mind my background and behavior patterns, as far as I was concerned, nothing was really out of order and I ignored my inner warning and the waving red flag. Stepping cautiously inside, letting out a sigh of relief, everything looked normal. But taken aback, he walked in from the other room, wearing a very clingy, black silk wrap around. Noticing right away how much it revealed his masculinity, a wave of desire shot through me. Letting out a wind of hot air, my embarrassment quickly rose to my face, while regret for having come, brought me to my senses. In a moment of hesitation, Jessie's face flashed before me, bringing to light, exactly what I was doing. Undeniable, to simply leave might have been the answer to, exactly what I had gotten myself into, but that wasn't my smarts at the time. Shame may have been pulling at me to leave but desire and lust were pulling me back into my own tug of war.

When the Woodsman looked over at me, giving me a charming wink, he put on a soft tune of romantic music, offering me a drink. Declining on the cocktail he began to shake up, being so early in the day, didn't keep him from pouring himself one, in a chilled long-steamed martini glass. Fearing he had planned on settling in instead of going out as we planned was ultimately being spelled out for me. Sinking down on the multicolored couch, I made a loud comment that we better get going, hoping he got it. Ignoring my suggestion, he walked over with his drink, set it down and plopped down real close to me. With his arm stretched out around me, as he pulled me in even closer, he was breathing way too close, way too everything. Reality hit home, things were not just out of hand; they were out of control. As I tried to squirm out of his tight clutches, he started to whisper hoarsely in my ear, how excited he was that I was there in the flesh. Oh God, suddenly this man's face looked strange and I wanted to get out of there and this time, lust was not pulling me back in. Knowing I was so foolishly outwitted and so far out in the sticks, it was obvious I was in deep trouble. It was when his fingers eagerly began to caress my lips and then my face, that I put the brakes on to him. Only instead of backing off me, his mouth came hungrily down on mine. In a panic, I began to struggle to push his heavy face off mine, crying out, between gulping for air for him to stop. Instead of stopping, he held on even tighter to my face, struggling himself to keep his lips locked on mine. Breathing heavy from his lungs, he backed off, as he whispered in a moan, "Come on honey, don't do this, chill out already, don't be such a prude, huh."

Prude did he just say prude? Out from the past a flash of Dexter's face appeared and his familiar words of accusation began going off in my head, "Prude-prude."

Instant fury took hold of all my fear and brought me right up on my feet shrieking out, "Stop it…please, can you just stop?"

With a stormy look of fury in his dark eyes, it brought attention to his fuming hostile anger. My knees instantly started to quiver, I could feel my heart pounding in my head as I began to inch my way towards the door, babbling with self-blame, "Please, please I'm sorry, it's me, it's not you, it's my fault, I made a terrible mistake and I can't do this to Jessie. I'm sorry, maybe I better go."

He just sat staring, without blinking so much as an eye. Careful not to make him any angrier than he was, I continued to blame myself, praying for his mood to bend. Just enough anyway, that I could inch my way right the hell out of there. When and how it was that I learned that the price of consequences would be less brutal, when you were the one willing to own the fault, was back in the day. Not so, not this time. It didn't lighten his anger, instead he transformed into a vicious animal, growling profanities. "Shut the *^up, you stupid little *^.$%. If you know what's good for you, you'll just shut your *^* high-class *^* mouth."

Tripping over his words in wrath, he was up off the couch and I was backing up. His face held disgust as he rambled on under his breath that I was nothing, but a *^*^cheap, teasing bitch, claiming he would teach me a thing or two. As soon as my mouth opened in defense, his hand swung out slapping me across the face. His gaudy ring caught my check, generating instant pain. My lip was throbbing hot and after touching my check, my fingers revealed traces of blood, instantly silencing me. It was obvious, I wasn't up against my good old daddy, Dexter-Chester or Jessie who was living and breathing for his stardom. Truth was I didn't know what I was dealing with or how to escape out from this madness.

There was that moment when he turned his back and I saw the first opportunity to run and I went for it. Evidently, he was smarter and faster, because within only a few steps, he was in reach, grabbing me by the hair and roughly pulling me down to the floor. Only it was his attack of verbal threats, which held the greatest power over me. Trembling from head to foot, I sat huddled in the corner listening to his sworn promises that he was going to tell every one! He was going to tell if it were the last thing he did, starting with my Jessie. He snickered out angrily that after he told, I would lose everything I owned and everyone I loved. He had control and I felt like a sitting duck without water. He wasn't letting up, letting me feel his power, by continuing to reinforce his threats. Fearing whether or not I would make it out alive, I began plotting irrationally how to escape from there, without anyone knowing I came in the first place. Because I was certain my rejection was what set him off, it wasn't difficult to determine his motive and the secret formula to my escape. If I do whatever he says and lay down for him, he'll keep quiet, but if I keep quiet and give in to all his sexual demands, no one will ever know my sinful secret. My two choices of escape, obviously, were one and the same.

The agonizing thought that he would take this to Jessie, kept my mind crazed. But even if he was on a power trip and just bluffing, who knew for sure what he was capable of. Oh God, I just wanted to get back home where I felt safe. Oh God, my body hurt from the bruises, my senses weak from defeat. One way or another, I knew I needed to do whatever it was to escape out from the hands of this hard course man. No, it was not force that raped me; but it was the fear of his threats that took me. Worn-down, after agreeing to the terms I knew he wanted to hear, dazed, my trembling fingers undid one button at a time, until my dainty blouse and bra slipped off my shoulders. After struggling with my zipper, I unzipped my jeans and stepped out of them. As he eyeballed my panties, a solid, silent nod from him, informed me to remove them.

Standing completely nude with no argument, I surrendered lying down on the multicolored couch. Dropping his black silk wrap to the floor, he boldly stood over me, displaying his sexual desire in full view. Staring out in space, illness filled my gut, wishing that the world would just swallow me up. He was feeling his power over me and his heated face was lost in his own world of excitement. As his body came down heavy on mind, he roughly pushed in and began pumping, spitting out words of disgust the whole time, that I was. He kept me there long enough, thrusting forward, until he reached satisfaction, leaving a trail of sperm. Suddenly his tune changed and with a hint of nervous energy surfacing, he began to claim his innocents. "Hey listen you. I didn't do nothing wrong. You know damn well you agreed to this and don't you go getting any stupid ideas about making any trouble for me and telling anyone I forced you, you hear?"

His voice sounded a million miles away, yet it still held enough volume to instill the fear of God in me. Looking past my tears, he exhaled adding more insult, "Hey don't tell me, you didn't like every bit of what I gave you. You make trouble for me, I swear that fancy husband of yours will find out what a tease you really are and just how bad you wanted it."

Turning his face away he mumbled, "Go on now, get your self out of here, go on and get out!"

In turn for his cruelty, all I could feel was relief that he was letting me go. Careful not to alter his mood or give him a reason to change his mind, I slowly began reaching for my clothes one at a time. After buttoning and zipping myself back together, my eyes spotted my purse and car keys only a few feet from me. Just as I grabbed on to them, I was waiting for him to stop me, only he didn't and I flew out the door like a bat out of hell. Not daring to look back for fear it would slow me down, believing he might come after me, kept my legs racing forward. By the time I got into my car and securely locked the doors, fear was eating me up.

During the long emotional ride home my mind was fogged up with flashing memories of his degrading and intimidating words of warning. A blurred vision of his twisted vicious actions left me thinking that maybe I brought this on myself for lying and meeting him in an isolated area in the first place. Oh God I was so deeply ashamed and I promised myself that no one must ever know. By the time my car was turning into the driveway, I could only pray my children were not home from school yet. Glancing in my rearview mirror, my face was in a shambles, between my smeared makeup and red blotches from crying. But it would have to be some kind of miracle to get the rest of my messed up face past anyone, unnoticed. Grabbing on to a sweater from the backseat, I slipped it on to cover all the unsightly bruises on my arms, just in case someone was around. With a twist of the key, I yelled out and with no voices coming back at me, I immediately dashed into the bathroom and locked the door behind me. Striping off my clothes and dramatically kicking them to the corner, I stepped into the shower and turned the water on as hot as my body would allow. The water ran long and hot with the frantic urge to scrub every inch of me over and over, trying to get the pungent scent of his cologne and the awful smell of his body off me. Turning off the faucet, my tears and what little respect I managed to hold on to in my life, was being washed down the drain with the filthy water from the Woodsman's touch. Stepping out of the shower, I patted myself dry and slipped on the white terry cloth robe, which was hanging on a hook behind the door. While it hurt to comb my wet hair back away from my face, it brought the sickening painful image of the Woodsman back into my head. Hearing the children shattered my dazed flash backs and brought me back to earth. After yelling out to them, I placed a plateful of cookies and a carton of milk with glasses on the table, yelling out once more, for them to come and get their snack. Gathering up an armload of all the soiled clothes that came off my body, I angrily shoved them down deep, into an empty black garbage bag, never wanting to lay eyes on them again.

Digging out a fresh pair of jeans and long sleeve t-shirt to cover the unsightly bruises on my arms, only left me having to explain my swollen lip and the small gash on my bruised cheek. Painting on a normal face for the children, I started a simple dinner of eggs and french toast, while the whole time all his feared threats and brutal actions were being played out in my head, over and over again. Getting this past the children was one thing, but Jessie was another and with him due home, I could only pray he wouldn't be able to read into my rehearsed lies or see the shame in my eyes. No sooner had he walked in, he took notice to my face and his bright smile broke into alarm. With a thin smile and a wave of my hand, once he heard that I was clumsy, with the excuse of walking into the half open garage door, his face fell into a relaxed state. Jessie, he was quick to wrap his loving arms around me with compassion. Quickly moving from his gentle touch, his sympathy felt uncomfortable, believing that my lies had put them there. My painted smile got him past my face and I began to prepare the same simple dinner for him as the children, eggs and french toast. The quiet air and the lack of interest in his day were blamed on my throbbing headache. But later that night, once the lights were off and the rhythm of his breathing told me he had drifted off, I sobbed in a way like never before, praying that the air inside me, would just evaporate.

In the days that followed, lying to everyone was the only way to get past this and lick my wounds alone. Poor Eileen, avoiding her, was the only way to keep this disgrace from her and to brush my failure once again under the carpet. Giving her one excuse after another to keep her face away from mine, pushed her into swearing, she knew my lies. That Eileen, what she didn't even know was that she was way smarter than she could imagine. So while avoiding everyone, I stayed covered up for days until I could stop hiding under long sleeves. But when the bruises started to fad; I believed it was time to put this behind me. Only regardless of how much I scrubbed, it never washed away any of the shame and guilt for my part. So it was stored in the back of my mind to sit and stew, until later!

Oh, but the lies we tell and the secrets we keep for one taunting reason or another. While holding on painfully to my own shameful secret, it was life changing. For the second time in my life, the promise to make up for all my evil ways and be the best wife any man could ever want became my own personal penance. In the many months that came to pass I worked hard without complaint to stay focused and to live out my promise. Now that Jessie did not have to be concerned with any of my needs, it made life easy for him to continue to climb his ladder of success, worry free. The Woodsman definitely left his black mark upon me, so after that; I did what I did for as long as I did. That is, until all of life took a sharp turn when two faces from way back when, came into our life.

Maybe all of life would have turned out differently if it weren't for that sunny afternoon, when I ran right smack into Missy at the five and dime outlet. Yes, perhaps we would all, have all, been spared all, the anguish and shattering consequences we had endured from our on going drive to succeed and all of our reckless choices. Bringing both of their images to Norma's office that particular day, she was not surprised, for she already knew their names, Missy and Joshua.

Considering it had been years since any one of us had seen each other, I almost didn't recognize Missy. She was the one that had taken my serving position, after Jessie insisted I give it up. She was also the small child in which my brave angelic aunt and uncle had once brought over, to our unruly house. She remembered me very well, considering all the times mother had sent me to her house to escape the taste of daddy's violence. There she stood sweet, her long soft brown hair hanging loosely down to her shoulders. Occasionally her bangs would flop down over one eye, reflecting memories back to her youth. She looked shapelier than I had remembered her in earlier years. Her soft blue eyes held the same shyness, exposing an earthy smile at the mere sight of me. We chattered on for nearly an hour both talking at once and never did I realize she had looked up to me as children. Being a few years younger than me, according to her, I was her long-lost hero. All at once she laughed, reminiscing back to her memories of the spooky stories, I would makeup halfway through the night. Her eyes stayed lit as she reminisced on, with her most cherished moments, making her seem like the Missy I knew. Somewhere throughout our laughter, her mood shifted and she began to confide in me that her and Joshua had separated. Wanting to set her mind at ease, I made a joke about good old married life. Joking back, we got lost in chatter again, when she made a remark about time slipping. With her having brought it to my attention, I looked down at my watch, getting uptight over how late it was. Missy let out a giggle, displaying her calm composure. Yes, cool and collected, that was patient Missy all right, the opposite of me. Giving her another grin we hugged goodbye, swapped phone numbers and promised to stay in touch.

Before you knew it, two long years slipped by and we never did get in touch with each other as we had promised. This time when I ran into her, it was a spring day and everything about her was different, starting with the baby girl in her arms, that she called Haley. No sooner had I reached out my hand, her brown eyes hit the ground, reflecting Missy's shyness. She was around seven-months and her chubby little legs were sitting up on Missy's big round, belly full of baby! She was quick to explain that she and Joshua had gotten back together and the next thing she knew, after number one number two was on the way. She uttered that they were trying to see eye-to-eye. One goofy grin crossed my face and after the remark I knew exactly what she meant, we laughed and relaxed into conversation. Once Haley, her baby started fussing, Missy apologized, expressing she needed to get her down for her nap. Looking at her watch again, after she made the comment that she still had to pick up groceries before Joshua got home, she was ready to head off. Only this time as we hugged goodbye, we set a day and time to get together at my house the following weekend.

Before you knew it, one week later, there they were, standing outside our door. Joshua was holding Haley, while Missy was holding a bag of chips and a six-pack of root beer. At the moment Joshua's eyes met mine, something weird, passed between us. Throwing me briefly off balance, by his disoriented and confused reaction, he must have felt it too. It surely was neither interest nor appeal! In essence, being attracted to another man was the farthest thing on my mind. For reason in itself, the Woodsman and his brutal abuse, still lived fresh in my mind. But in those eerie seconds, it left me spooked enough to wonder, what in the hell, yes, it was strange all right, but definitely ridiculous and I shook my head to gather my thoughts.

Getting past that, as everyone gathered into the house, my children were anxiously waiting to meet Haley, having heard all about her. It didn't take, but five minutes for her to steal their hearts and start them bickering over whose turn it was to hold her. Over the loud commotion, the sound of the telephone could still be heard. It was Jessie calling to say he was going to be late. Disappointment set in, as he pleaded with me not to be angry and to please hold the fort together, until he got there. With our company's laughter in the air, keeping me company, I felt content inside myself and reminded him, everyone was waiting on him. Hanging up, my attention turned to Joshua. It had been a long time since I had seen him and he still carried the same slim frame as his younger years. His thick curly hair still had that reddish highlight thing going on, while it was obvious that Haley had received his dark brown eyes.

He appeared as if he had tamed down over the years; something was different, perhaps, it was his eyes when he spoke, so sure, so confidant and so book smart. The air he carried was way different from anyone I've ever known or met. It would eventually surface that he was the sinner and the saint…the courteous and the reckless and a self-taught man of all trades. Turning my attention back to Missy, who was chatting away at me from across the table, we got up and began putting out munchies. Here they brought the chips we had the dip, they brought the root beer, we had the ice cream, it was as if we were just meant to be. So we sat around the table like one big happy family, sipping on our root beer floats, while waiting on Jessie's arrival. Just as we were noisily sipping down to the bottom of our floats, he walked in, stirring up the air. Before long, he was holding on to his own root-beer float and had no trouble joining in the conversation, laughing between mouthfuls of his chicken casserole and sipping on his float. It was almost ironic to discover that Jessie and Missy, not only had blue eyes, but also both carried the same personalities and characters. But it was mind-boggling when Joshua and I discovered that we shared so much of the same background and had the same disposition, that we could have been pored out of the same mold. It was his grandmother who tried to shield him from his alcoholic father, while the subject of his mother who fled, was off limits, period. Being that we both suffered violent childhoods, we both understood the term lockup, whether it meant inside a locked closet for him, or kept behind closed doors and covered windows for me.

But that first evening, we all had the best time ever, sitting at the table playing board games and munching on unhealthy goodies. Jessie and I found ourselves laughing more than we had in a long-long time. Even the children were having the time of their life, grabbing a handful of popcorn from the bowl, as they ran in and out of our laughter. It felt good, it all felt good and I knew Jessie thought so too. Being so drawn to one another, we had the time of our lives and our laughter carried over into the night. By the time we put the game boards away and brewed a pot of coffee, the guys got lost in a serious discussion. They talked for hours in detail about Joshua's construction company to Jessie's career. But our dream to add two bedrooms and a bath, down in our unfinished basement, took first priority in their conversation. By the time they were pulling their chairs back to call it a night; the guys had everything figured out on paper. Being a general contractor and finish carpenter, Joshua, agreed to do the work for a small profit, in exchange, that we helped at their house. The extra hands were what they lacked and Joshua's skills were what we needed. It was the perfect opportunity to add on those two bedrooms and a full bathroom, that we were only able to dream about. With time having gotten away from us, we were just wrapping it up, when we could hear the birds chirping out the window. Having gathered up Haley, as we opened the door and saw the first signs of light, we humorously raised our eyes as we hugged goodbye. Waving them off, I felt like we had known each other forever. Stepping back into the house, sometime through the night, the children had drifted off on the pit group in the family room. They looked so snuggled in, we decided to just let them be and try to get a few hours of shuteye ourselves. Once we crawled into bed, Jessie held me tight in his arms, caressing me softly. His touch was needy, pushing his moist lips against my ear whispering how much he loved me. Things between us felt so fresh, so very much like when we first fell in love, yes, Joshua and Missy were definitely good for us.

But who in the world, would have believed it could be so easy to get a loan, to cover the expense of the materials and Joshua's pay. It was even harder to believe, that after two short weeks had passed, the construction was well under way. Working together hand in hand, our friendship grew stronger day by day. In the beginning we spent every weekend together, then before you knew it we were spending every other evening together. Soon after that, we bunked up together for days on end, before we took a breather. If we weren't cooking outdoors, watching the stars, or playing all our favorite games, we were out doing business. With Jessie high on hope to receive his promotion soon, he was on top of the world and these days, he was even taking his early outs. Oh life was grand and I had never felt such fulfillment in my life. No more watching the clock for me. Even Missy genuinely appeared fulfilled and often expressed that her days of loneliness were over. On the day we decided to color her hair ash blond and style it to fall softly around her face, with a boost of confidence, she went out and purchased a pink maternity outfit to match her mood.

Unexpected and only hours later, after an evening of monopoly, she got her first contraction, then second, moving right into labor. With everyone scrambling about, Joshua got Missy to the hospital on time and hours later, she gave birth to a baby girl, naming her Charity. She was so finicky and colic quickly set in. It had been pretty much the same story when Brad was born; and it just felt natural to help with the feedings. Being she was my best friend, or rather, my only friend, my co-dependency kicked right in. Even my children became active, pitching in to care for the babies, loving all the amusement they brought to our family. Family, yes we were now a family. Because it was only a short time later, when not only was our competitive board games getting more serious, but we were now living as one. Now that we were literally taking turns camping out at each other's house, we were swiftly moving ahead in progress and all our hard work was paying off. Once getting their place done and our downstairs finished, everything looked magnificent. Our dream had finally come true. The boys, in all their excitement, packed it up and moved all their stuff down to their rooms. That Joshua, when it came to finish carpentry, his style and perfection could have labeled him as the great one. But regardless, he still wouldn't bend over to accept any praise, having had his own undeserving issues. He would much rather put his brain to work, whenever we got lost in the bottomless conversations, we regularly shared in. While the guys would discuss success and security, Missy and I would share our deepest secrets and our wildest dreams. During those months when we were living in utter fulfillment, the guys also shared their tears and their dreams. They laughed and they fought and what Jessie didn't do Joshua did, while what Missy wouldn't dare dream of doing, I did for her.

Having been overly protected as a child not only was Missy naïve and uncomplaining, but when it came to taking chances, she closed herself up, exposing her insecurities. Basically she had been raised wrapped in cotton wool. While I was trying to teach her to stand up for herself, some of her patience began to rub off on me. It got so that we were spending so much time and energy, within the walls of our own two families, there was no time left for anyone else, that included Eileen. Poor Eileen, again, she was left behind in the dust and demanded to know, what the hell was going on between us. Her anger and accusations, displayed rejection and jealousy causing another battle between us. From her standpoint and her comments, she was reading into our close ties, as being unnatural and a train wreck waiting to happen. She had stepped up in judgment right along side of the outside world that was looking in, adding in their critical theory that we were playing with dynamite. With my on-again, off-again, neediness, that Eileen always had to endure, guilt was ripping at me. In the months that followed, it got to the point that I began to feed her whatever she needed in order to keep all our involvement and projects away from her. Part of me wanted to reach out to her, because she was the one who grew up with me, we shared the same sealed off windows and listened to the same unhappy mumbles from behind daddy's closed door. Yes, yes dear God its true, she was my blood sister! Except, the insecure and unbalanced part of me, held on to this enormous fear of losing what I had gained. It was only a matter of time when I started fighting back with more lies and more secrecy. We failed to believe there was anything resembling unhealthy or abnormal in our relationship and we began to let Eileen and society stew in the distance. So while we lived far off from everyone's pointing fingers and harsh judgment, we all continued to carry on as a family. In the early days of our relationship, I had the passing thought, that maybe daddy had the right idea after all. Was I living a lie, or just living life as daddy?

The truth was, the ongoing concern from everyone outside our family, stayed out of our minds. Besides, we were way too busy weighting out our possibilities for a brighter future. We searched for days on end for the perfect, affordable, business we could share in. Only with one failure after another, we found ourselves back to the drawing board in disappointment. It was during those trying times when Joshua and I would bump heads and it didn't take long to realize, somehow, we were able to communicate without words. It was that same eerie feeling like before. Ever since that first eerie encounter, we became an open book to one another. Perhaps we should have run like hell, only we didn't. Instead, it only brought us obsessively closer together.

But with time and hard work, the lucky stars were with us and not only did we come across the perfect little business, but the owner was willing to do everything in his power to see that we got it. After we got as much as all our borrowing power would allow, we were proudly holding on to the keys to a corner beverage store in one of the west suburbs. In the hours of our excitement we believed it was a deal made in heaven. From day one, the hours were long, seven days a week and we worked hard and endless from morning till night. In all Jessie's excitement, he would stop in on his lunch hour to help set up the new displays. Once we had things up and running to our expectations, it was everything we had dreamed. But day-by-day things began to crumble and the newness of the store began to wear away. When all of the grocery stores went to war competing to remain open the latest, our sales rapidly dropped in half. After that, when gas stations received liquor licenses, our numbers fell even lower. And even lower once the city put their barricades up and down the road in front of our store. We knew we were in big trouble, once we found out it would take years to complete the project. Until then our customers would have to drive through a congested single lane, just to get their beverages. We were a sinking ship, but our desperate need to hold on, kept us struggling to stay above water. What a horrible mess we got ourselves into, this lemon had gone sour, turning our hard earned dollars into blood money. It began to make total sense why the owner was so obliging to get this deal off the ground. When Eileen started calling daily in her anger, after stating she was being treated down right shabby, it left me convince she was just snooping to see if we had drowned yet in our failure. When she downright accused me of behaving irrationally, she was right on and I started to avoid her, period.

Inside of this mess I began hiding our finances from Jessie, he couldn't have handled any more of the truth. Seeing he had just received a small promotion, he began to experience some difficulty with some of the guys under him. Even with all the problems over our heads, once we became aware of his mood change, we began to point out his greatest assets to him. But none of it held any value and he started to lose his motivation and his depression began to climb. If I believed for a minute that he was running out on us, I would have been running right behind him. It got to the point, it was hard to concentrate on anything past his mood and seeing his birthday was right around the corner, we began to focus on throwing him a big surprise party. We saw it as the perfect plan to lift him out of his slump, so we went ahead and sent out invitations to all the stores in the city. Almost everyone accepted and when word got out, even some of the big wigs were seeing their way clear to dropping in. Wanting to make everything perfect, we dipped into our emergency funds and decided to put a closed sign up on the door, on the day of his party.

By eight pm, when everybody yelled, "Happy Birthday" Jessie stood looking shocked and prouder than ever. His eyes danced as he greeted his guests one by one, high on excitement. Everyone loved everything, from the house, to the ins and outs of the entire party. It was all worth it, the bar was fully stocked, while the tables were lined with several delicious and colorful dishes. We had everything from shrimp to lasagna and for desert, rich chocolate torte and everything in between. In the other room, a game of darts and a pool game were going on, with the sounds of loud outbursts, coming from a won victory. Joshua had arranged for a belly dancer to put on a show, making Jessie the guest star. When this sensuous dancer began wrapping her scarf around Jessie and shaking on him, while observing his delight, jealousy ripped at me, carrying over to his cute secretary, who was hanging on his every word. In spite of the laughter going on around me, I just could not get my mind off the store and the chains that held us to it. By the time everyone left, my head was heavy, just knowing by morning, we had to wake up and face the music again.

The party blew everyone away and in the days that followed, Jessie had gained what he needed to carry on again. But the beverage store continued to drain the life out of us. Time, that simple thing called time, no longer would I take it for granted waiting for the hour to pass. During all these unrewarding hours of maintaining the store, without precious time, my life became totally unorganized and disrupted. Having extended our hours past midnight, we were working around the clock. Still there wasn't enough cash to go around and tension was building. It left us all in a state of panic, without any hope for our tomorrows.

PASSAGE XV

No Turning Back

Fantasies...
>*Shattered dreams...*
Peace of mind...
>*Crying through time...*
Damnation... Surrender...Sweet Salvation...

Ambition, fate, perhaps as we continued on our journey, we truly believed that we could achieve all of our hopes and dreams. At the same time, according to everyone that crossed our path, they continued to believe our goals were impossible and irrational. In our struggle, as time passed, it seemed as if our good times were dwindling away. Just when we were ready to throw our arms up in defeat, a streak of good fortune came whistling its way in. It was right in the middle of the day, when, a well-dressed gentleman, with a set of pearly whites walked in. He was looking to purchase several cases of a particular vintage of champagne, which no one was able to find. Seeing he was willing to pay top buck, Joshua was eagerly scribbling notes on his pad. As the gentleman casually opened his royal blue sport coat, he flashed Joshua a stack of crisp one hundred dollar bills. He pealed off a few, handing them to him and asked if he could see himself clear to get right on it. Joshua's eyes lit up, promising it would be a done deal by the end of the week. Once the gentleman gave Joshua his number and walked out, Joshua ignored all my negativity about locating the rare bottles of champagne. Instead he looked past me as he stretched his neck to watch the gentleman climb into his red, flashy sports car and drive off. Immediately Joshua got down to business and after several discouraging hours of phone calls, he put all of life on the back burner and dug deeper. Knowing the effect this could have on our finances, Joshua was driven to find these bottles and remained on the phone, long distance, for hours. Finally after locating a dozen bottles out of one state and the rest of the cases from another, he laughed out loud in his victory. Without wasting a minute, he had arranged for overnight shipping and then called the gentleman to give him the news. When he nonchalantly dropped the remaining high balance on him, once Joshua winked at me, I knew it was a go. From the rest of their conversation, he was picking up the order on the following afternoon. Joshua pulled it off, just as he had said. But the following evening, when dinnertime came and went, the order still sat in the isle blocking our clear path. Nagging Joshua to keep calling, only wore his patience thin, taking us into silence. Seeing we were both on edge, even our silence remained strained. The thought of this deal going sour, with all the wasted money sitting inside those boxes, was going around and around in my head, like a runaway carousel. Hours later, just as we were on the verge of losing it, suddenly the bell on the door jingled and the gentleman walked in, clicking his fingers to the tune playing in the air. Seeing his pearly whites coming into our vision, with a breath of relief, our energy came back to life. As he looked over the cases of bottles, a smile of satisfaction crossed over his lips. Reaching into his sport coat pocket, he pulled out a wad of crisp bills, handing the balance and then some, to Joshua. Once Joshua got the sports car loaded up, the gentleman got in and zoomed off, with his radio blasting to the oldies. Grinning from ear to ear, we made enough money on this deal, to ride the waves smooth sailing for the next few months. No sooner had Jessie and Missy got word that it was a done deal, they rejoiced in their own relief and planned a celebration of warm blueberry muffins and campfire coffee when we got home.

It was less than an hour later, when Dwaine one of our favorite regulars walked in and invited us to a party at his place. It was obvious that we were both starving for any kind of fun, besides working long unrewarding hours, for days on end. It had been months since we had been out and just the thought of having a little taste of excitement pumped me up. Joshua looked over at me shrugging his shoulders, with a mischievous grin for his answer. Rolling my eyes with a silly giggle, gave him back my answer. It was all settled and without a word, we were going. Seeing Dwaine was a great guy, we failed to see any harm in going to his party. Now all we had to do was pull off closing early and get Jessie and Missy to give us their blessing. To justify my guilt for wanting to go so badly, my mind cruised over to Jessie's secretary who had hung on to his every word. It was enough to give me the courage to call and after promising it was just for an hour, hesitant he agreed. But he kept a stiff upper lip, repeating, one hour. Joshua on the other hand, blew through it before I even realized he had hung up. Bothered, I wanted to know what the hell was going on and when I called him on it, he said nothing! That was it, nothing. With only one short hour to kick up our heels, as I waved off his flimsy response we jumped into his brown van and took off with his radio blaring out to his favorite country songs. Pulling into the dirt driveway surrounded by wild foliage, we were thrown from side to side all the way up the driveway. Laughing in amusement, after we walked up the uneven sidewalk together, and up to the old three-story house, Joshua banged the rusty doorknocker loudly. Without a delay the door opened and Dwaine stood there buzzed with a drink in his hand and a lit cigarette dangling out of the corner of his mouth. "Hey, come on in you guys, you're missing all the fun. Hey go grab a drink, the bartender's expecting you guys."

He was wearing something resembling a black smoking jacket, with a wild tie dangling down loosely over his bare hairless chest. His cool-hip mannerism was almost comical putting me right at ease. Once we stepped in, the house carried a strong scent of earthy incense. Ready to kick up our heels, the next thing you knew, we were sipping drinks. Off in the corner of the room, two couples were passing a joint from right to left. It was simply amazing; somehow we managed to fit right in with them, without even knowing anyone. The first drink left me feeling free and confident, then we had another, then, two hours passed over the first hour that we were due home. When someone passed us another drink, we were feeling no pain and seeing nothing bothered us, not even the time, we didn't say no.

At some point I lost Joshua in the crowd. After looking from one end of the room to the other, someone else had moved into his place, handing me another drink. By then my brain was burnt toast, how and just when I ended up in one of the bedrooms is a mystery. There are no memories past the sounds of echoes playing off in my head and the quick flashes of responding in and out in desire. It felt like time stood still in a strange twilight and then somehow morning had arrived. The sheets were twisted around me in knots and the sun was streaming in through the windows displaying the dirty cobwebs in the corners of the panes. It made the place look like a run down motel **5.** Unfaithful, it was obvious, pure disgust for myself ran through my veins. But it was nothing compared to the guilt and fear that began to penetrate into the crevices of my brain. Looking around, my clothes were scattered here and there across the floor, jarring flashes of memory. In a state of panic, I gathered them up and while dressing, I was trying to smooth out the wrinkles and pick off the lint. Softly closing the door behind me, I began frantically searching for Joshua. In another room, he was asleep with a blanket only half covering him. Judging by the looks of things, it left no question about what had gone on. For a moment, the passing thought of Joshua making love to someone else left me squeamish. But with time so critical and ticking by, I relentlessly shook him, yelling loud enough to wake up the whole damn house, "Get up, get up Joshua, its morning, oh God, we did it this time."

Joshua opened his eyes looking sheepish and confused. When he sat up, his curly hair was bushed out and he mumbled out to me for the time. Once it registered that it was morning, he attentively wrapped the blanket tight around him and hoarsely said he needed a minute. That was his cue for me to leave and only minutes later he opened the door and blew out of there. Dwaine saw us heading out and with a large mug of coffee in his hand he called out after us "Hey how did you guy's like that buzz we fixed you up with?"

The morning sun was shinning and now with the clock staring back at me, getting home to enjoy our warm muffins and campfire coffee was a day too late. Scrambling to get home, we didn't talk; even with that weird thing with our eyes still going on, talking or not we both knew we screwed up. But while looking intensely at him, he had both hands casually on the steering wheel, paying me no mind. He didn't seem bothered one little bit, unlike me, that he had been with someone else; instead, his eyes remained locked on the road, detached. Getting lost in my thoughts, there was only one excuse that would fit this picture, the truth. But even if I had managed to come up with some scheme to get out of this mess, it was too late; Jessie was standing at the door to meet me face to face. Instantly as he was looking me over, his eyes were eyeing my smudged mascara and falling back down to my wrinkled clothes. Having been in such a state of panic to get home, without a fix up, I knew it looked just like it was. With a look of disgust, he stared straight into my eyes, waiting for an explanation. Too ashamed to lie; I remained silent. It would only hurt him, oh God I hated lying, but I just couldn't give voice to the truth. There was nothing to gain and everything to lose. But what was going on with Joshua and Missy, I couldn't put my finger on what the hell was up with them again. At that moment there was no truth lying among any of us. But by the looks of the kitchen table, it was obvious that Jessie and Missy had been up all night doing their own kind of speculating. Staring at the table, it was covered with muffin crumbs and a dozen empty sugar packets, thrown sloppily over the spilled, dried up coffee drips. By now his face was looking at me, flushed red, displaying his unfamiliar fury, making him more of a stranger, than my Jessie. In his next effort to search for some hidden answer in me, his mistrusting eyes were staring through me again.

Norma, awe yes, while struggling to get passed that liquored up night with excuse, she was showing signs of her prime and proper side. But in spite of how that made me feel, I jumped forward to when it was Jessie's anger that held the wall up between us. In my heart I knew how deceitful I had been and kept my mouth shut, doing anything it took to help moisten his scorched heart. Despite all of my efforts, it took weeks for the air to absorb all the hurt and anger, standing between us. As for my reckless and sleazy actions, Jessie eventually put them off to a thoughtless night of getting trashed. His logic was a pure case of relief on my end and without blinking an eye in defense; I took ownership for the entire fault. Once the air cleared, life went on as before, but seeing past dark, due to the torn up roads, with hardly anyone venturing in, we cut back our hours. So as far as our great gain, well, nothing last's forever and it got eaten up, just as fast as every other extra dollar Joshua and Jessie managed to earn. With our pockets on empty, even a good steak was getting harder to come by these days. So our dream that we believed was made for us in heaven, turned out to be nothing, but a green, eating machine, straight up from hell.

Throwing a monkey wrench into our complicated lives, Eileen called to inform me daddy was ill. Even while we were at arm's length, she never once hinted that she was seeing him and no longer disowned. Pushing all my problems to the bottom of the list, without losing a moment in time, I high tailed it right over there. When I arrived, the big picture window was staring back at me, with no sign of his shinny chrome wheel chair, off to the side of the drapes. Slowly turning the knob on the front door, it was open. Following a soft knock I let myself in and a weird stillness met me. His beat up wooden desk that was still hanging around from the past and the faded cream-colored couch that once furnished the beauty shop, was all that was left of the living room. My heart began to flutter at the bare sight and I fearfully called out to him. "Daddy, daddy, are you here?"

Spotting him, he was in the dining room, with his wheel chair pushed up snug to the table. His head was tucked down into his folded muscular arms. Slowly picking up his head, his flushed face gave reason, for all of Eileen's concern. Never questioning why I was there, he responded back, as if he had forgotten that he had disowned me. Looking frantic, he threw himself into pleading for me to take over doing his laundry, cleaning and grocery shopping. When he eagerly mentioned that the state would pay me well, knowing how much the cash could do for us, it felt like a gift from God. Suddenly in all my gratitude, my mood shifted sarcastically, over to my Witch-like-aunt, "Hum, perhaps she was the one that got her-self, disowned this time."

That thought was tickling, since it put me back to being number one on his list. His offer was too good to be true and it didn't have to be thought out twice. There wasn't even time to run this by the others. He wanted a yes or no, right here and now. Nodding my head, it was a yes, yes, yes. He mumbled out my duties, repeating himself a couple of different times, before he moved away from me in spirit. In a seen opportunity to speak, I began to question where all his electronics and furniture had gone. Instead of cutting me off like always, he silently began working the wheels on his chair towards his room. Closing his bedroom door behind him, he was gone. Sitting with only a night-light shinning, as the sun went down, an eerie karma was bouncing off the shadowed walls, giving me the willies. In the silence surrounding me, the worry of trying to fit in all his needs, was pushed to somehow, someway, we just would. Satisfied with my own theory, I grabbed my purse to leave and locked the door behind me. On the drive home, Eileen's face drifted into my vision and left me with the fear, once she got wind that I was taking care of daddy; it would shake things up again. Pushing her face out from my mind, I pressed down on the gas pedal, anxious to get home, to break the news. Only trying to convince everyone to look past daddy's unruly disposition, my work would be cut out for me. Past all the begging to finally have this chance to make things right with him, it was the extra cash we needed that sold them and by nightfall, they were all in favor.

Seven days later, there I was right back at daddy's, doing his laundry, cleaning his house, changing his sheets and listening and listening. If I wasn't at his house listening, my ear was stuck on the phone hearing him rambling, all over again. In a few weeks, he was definitely feeling better and back to being good old daddy again. Nothing had changed in my years of absence. He was busy laughing out cruel demeaning remarks to all the neighbors. He began cornering me with his wheel chair, at every turn I took. Between his grumbling and constant distasteful laughter, he was wearing me thin. Weeks into it, my nerves couldn't take his constant jibber jabbering and I invested in a pair of headphones with the radio built in. Unaware that he was zoned out, his mouth was moving to every beat of the music, while sealing in the peaceful melody. If I though for a moment of walking away from him, past the need to love him and the guilt pulling at me, the extra cash kept me there under his thumb. Still, even with the extra money coming in, the store was devouring it faster than it took to clear the check. Nothing was getting better. Everyday was another loss, until we were forced to weight out our options. Regardless of all our efforts, it became a long drawn out emotional and financial mess, as we fought to hold on to what was left. Being hammered down to the ground, left defeated and worn out, after we lost our battle, it was Morgan our attorney, who helped us put our lives into perspective. Being he was a Mennonite, he was in favor of our close ties and suggested we stand together and go for a chapter thirteen. Once it was all said and done and put into action, we were able to start to clear ourselves financially and emotionally begin to heal.

It was a new morning of rise and shine to the alarm beeping at seven am. The aroma of fresh brewed coffee and bacon and eggs had traveled to where I laid my head. Hearing the sound of bacon spattering, mum...I was home sweet home once again. With a sigh of relief, that I didn't have to be at that forsaken store, jumping out of bed, putting on a pair of army shorts and a black tank top, I joined the others. Joshua and Jessie were preparing breakfast and whistling a tune. Missy flashed me a smile raising her eyes in amusement. It was more of a feast, between the yummy food and the kid's happy faces that showed their excitement that we were home. Now without the store hanging over our heads everyday and robbing us of a life, daddy got to meet everybody. No way was I prepared for him to cling to Jessie and Joshua like white on rice. In disbelief he was talking this, talking that, about things that I didn't even know he knew anything about. They looked over at me with a look on their faces, as if to say, my stories were larger-than-life. He was in his glory and with his arms wide open with acceptance I let the guys handle him. Seeing he still never stopped talking long enough to take notice to any of the children, they remained invisible in his eyes. Regardless of the hurt feelings of rejection it left, his acceptance of the guys, gave us some hope for a brighter future. Having bought him a new grill and some lawn chairs, somehow Jessie and Joshua, as unbelievable as it sounds, had maneuvered him into going out on his deserted patio for a cook out. In spite of all his grumbling, referring to the salty hot dogs and the weeds we missed while cutting the grass, my face shinned in delight.

Daddy had everything, with us at his beck and call and we would have done anything in this world to bring him happiness. It was around the time when he began to complain that the apples weren't red enough and his sheets were too stiff, when things began to run down hill. It was just about the same time, when he dropped it on me that Eileen had been coming over to see him, from time to time. It was too early in his game, to realize he was working up to no-good. He was smart and somehow managed to maneuver things so that Eileen and I would bump into each other at the house. Now that he had both his girls back home and under his thumb, he began a war taking it to the limit. Oh but daddy was in his glory doing what he lived and breathed for, combat and war. He began instigating one argument after another between us. Somewhere between our anger and all of our unforgivable accusations, sadly, we reached the point of no return. Now, after having dished out many years of my on again, off again, attention to Eileen, all her understanding and devotion was destroyed, by whom, me, so I cried and did nothing! That father of ours, minus the wire hangers, he had become a real, "Daddy Dearest."

Now with Eileen out of my life and huddled in her own devastation, a strong inner anger was building up towards daddy. There was absolutely no getting through to him. It was as if he had this obsession to keep any affection between us at a distance. Even in my on and off again moments of compassion, while reaching out, it was no use he was untouchable. But I should have known that it would only be a matter of time, until it was the highway for me.

On and on it went. A day without troubles, was a day of rest, yet, our destiny never seemed to sleep. In my heart with all the hurtful stuff going on around me, I knew something had to give. But there was no way I was ready for what tragically marked our lives forever! In a world of readiness, we carried on; each of us eagerly bought a one-way ticket headed straight for Hell!

Hours before Jessie was due to arrive home from work, it was a real shocker when he walked in early. He had a wide smile spread clear across his face. But I never even had a chance to ask, before his excitement began spilling over. It was the big one! The big promotion he had been drooling over and had been waiting for, for years, finally had arrived. In a breath of excitement, before he even had his leather jacket off his back, we could hear the thrill in his voice as he yelled, "Big bucks, company privileges and its mine, all mine!"

Gathering around to join in Jessie's excitement, his face was flushed in exhilaration. This was a dream come true, for him, for me, for all of us. It wasn't until the cork on the champagne bottle hit the ceiling fan and a roar of laughter left our lips, when things began to quiet down. But it wasn't until after the toast, when Jessie casually clued us in that his new store was several hours away. Being he was nonchalantly, rattling on about selling the house, it appeared to me as if he already had planned it out in his head. My face instantly fell. As I set my champagne flute down, before I even had a chance to compose myself, Joshua jumped in, pumping him up even more. He began reassuring him, it was the opportunity of a lifetime; a fresh start for everyone and it was just what we needed. They were going at it back and forth, their voices talking way too loud over me. Completely intimidated, it was impossible to even try to talk over their enthusiasm and all their pumped up excitement. Sick at heart, the fear of losing our dream house silenced me and instead of voicing any argument, I broke into tears. Before anyone could say a word to me, I ran into the bedroom, slamming the door behind me.

Throwing myself into bed, after pulling the blankets over my head, I barely could hear the knocks on the door. Peeking out from the corner of the blanket, Missy opened the door and stuck in her head, gently calling my name. With the guy's voices, still laughing it up in the background, my tears started all over again. Missy bent over backward to make me feel better, swearing, she would stand by me no mater what. Through thick or thin she repeated, until I calmed down. Like always, calm Missy managed to put things in a different light. She was sure that once the boys had time to think without the champagne clouding up their heads, they would come to their senses. She had a good point, so I dried my tears and we returned to the guys, who were still going at it. By this time, Jessie had promised Joshua, that he could get him in with the contractors, building the new stores. Now with Joshua's head filled with his own hopes and dreams, the wheels were turning and together they began to plan a weekend getaway, to check out the area. When Jessie wrapped his arms around me later that evening, there was no moving me.

As the hours went by, the pressure of leaving our home and moving to a strange city sat heavy on my shoulders, while Jessie was lost somewhere in his dreams. Stressing to the guys that even if we did stand together, we still needed time to financially mend was completely voted off the ballot. Jessie, he wanted this so bad; he argued back, that this is what he had been working for, all these years. Being it was decided we would go together; Joshua became Jessie's first hand supporter. Even behind our bedroom door, Jessie remained closed-minded. My home or Jessie, only one of them was sure to win. His mind was set firm and after shedding the last of my fallen tears, I gave in. After giving him my answer that he had been anxiously waiting on, he let out a breath of relief, promising, life would be nothing but grand. He couldn't wait and in all his excitement; he picked up the phone eager to give the big wigs his stamp of approval, it was a go. Just as he proudly accepted the position, one tear escaped my eye and retired down into the crease of my lips.

So as we packed for our little getaway to see this township, it was Missy who took over, while I felt the need and fed on her inner strength. This new air of confidence she had gained was growing strong and was slowly replacing her shy personality. Being this was the first time we had the chance to get away from the kids, since mother agreed to look after them, we were on our way. Only it was Missy and I who rode in the back seat on the long ride, while I was doing my own kind of thinking. Wanting to please Jessie, I was determined to put all my fears and my dream house out of my mind and just enjoy this carefree adventure. After checking out a five-mile radius of shopping plazas and available housing, we drove past several public schools. Afterward we headed over to Jessie's new store to check it out and it was nothing but incredible. The royal blue designer carpeting enhanced the wide variety of appliances and electronics laid out in class. Impressed to the max, everything was awesome and it carried me away from reality. By now every eye was on Jessie and he was shinning proud, knowing everyone observing him, knew just who he was. Once all the introductions were finished, we headed across the street to a famous steak house with a few of the big honchos that were there to meet up with Jessie. The conversation involving Jessie seemed to go on forever, he needed to do this and he needed to do that. By then, the newness of everything was beginning to wear off and the tender cut of prime rib was lying heavy against my rib cage. Suddenly reality had caught up with me. Getting through the rest of the night in this lit up strange city, knowing this would soon be our home, left me sleepless throughout the night.

Once we were back and pulling into our driveway, it was home sweet home, but unfortunately, it was not for long. Upon returning, once word got out that Jessie was in; things began to move fast. When the unexpected phone call came in, in his excitement, he blurted out that his company was putting him up in an all expenses paid hotel room for the next few months. Jessie rambled on to us with no mention of me going with him. Instead he dropped it on us that there was a sudden change in plans and we would have to stay behind until he settled in. Now that he was scheduled to leave in the morning, all my enthusiasm flew out the door. As he packed his new dress shirts and ties, he threw in his best casual outfits and practically broke the suitcase trying to get it closed. Eyeing him, he was shinning like a star and I was in a dim place, feeling left out. When he pulled out two pairs of his dress shoes and asked me to choose one, without waiting for an answer, he stuffed both pairs into his duffel bag. Crawling into bed, in spite of my mood, feeling needy inside and out, I snuggled in as close as my body would allow.

Morning arrived with the sound of the birds and a strong aroma of coffee brewing in the air. Across the room Jessie was already up wide-eyed, showered, shaved and dressed to perfection. Walking towards the bed, he lowered his face to me and sweetly locked his lips on mine. Before my feet even had a chance to swing around and hit the floor, my heart was tattered in two, today was the day. Looking over at the clock in dread, in one short hour, he would be gone. My heart began toying around with my emotions and I tried with all my might to carry on with dignity. It took all my strength to hold on to my tongue, in fear I would beg him not to go. He kissed my face, my lips in-between promising he'd be back home every other weekend. Even in my numb state of mind, only a fool wouldn't have noticed he was too caught up in his own excitement, to feel my despair. After Jessie hugged Missy goodbye and gave Joshua his normal bear hug, they helped him load up the trunk. Jessie was high on energy and looked so handsome sitting behind the wheel of his bright red blazer. Noticing a lock of his wavy hair had fallen down over his forehead, only added more good looks to his charm. Waving him off, if only I knew than what I know now, if only, if only, that day would never have come to life.

The remainder of the day, I walked around like a zombie. If it weren't for Missy moving up to the plate and taking charge, we never would have eaten. By evening, it had been hours since Jessie had left and with no word back from him yet, my concern was high on the rise. Insisting to Joshua that something had to have happened, instead of triggering any concern, he shot off at me irritated. He began to sound like a broken record with his sermons, to just relax and let Jessie take care of business. Taken aback by his harsh tone and lack of sensitivity, I turned away from his Mr. Know It All attitude. His remark about taking care of business left me sizzling and by the time Jessie called hours later, letting us know he got there safe, I took my mood over to him. Instead of trying to mend my worry, he blew it off, not hiding the fact, he was on his way out to have a drink with a few of the guys. His honesty only left me feeling let down, left out and jealous as hell. Just as he began to inch his way off the phone, his priorities turned and he began giving me the low down, with a sense of self-importance in his voice. Turns out, his company was not only going to put him up in a hotel, until we found a place to relocate, but were going to pay our house payment, until our house sold. It wasn't until after he had mentioned they were also going to pick up the bill to furnish our place once we found one, when he unexpectedly invited us out for the weekend to start looking for a place. In his excitement, the simple warning I gave him to get it in writing, seemed to simply fly over his head. Once we hung up, I was humming in delight; Joshua even received my blessing of forgiveness. It was definitely a shot in the arm and just knowing we would be together soon, gave me an emotional rest.

Stimulated to no end, after mother agreed to keep an eye on the children again, my spirits were high, but the dread to tell daddy of the changes that were about to take place in his life was growing. If I was nervous, it was with good reason, because once he heard we were moving hours away, he never let me finish, when his face twisted back at me in anger. He went off ranting, raving, "Damn it, whose gonna take care of me and whose gonna do all my shopping and cleaning?"

His tantrum led me to believe he couldn't bear to lose me. Oh, but he had emotionally pushed me right where he wanted me and I wasted no time before I cried out to him. "Oh but daddy I would never, never leave you, I promise to come back every week and do everything for you."

Obviously I was out of my mind with my ridiculous notions, because as he lost control, he shook his fist and violently threatened to give me some knuckle soup, then bellowed out. "Don't bother, get out, get out...you're just like your fu^**kin, no good mother."

In the midst of his rage, just like that, he disowned me and then, his eyes fell off me. But I swear as I was closing the door behind me, I heard him whispering under his breath, that he was going to call on Eileen. All the way home, tears of madness ran down my face and the same old stance crept its way back in. Of coarse I should have known better. Except daddy had this magical way of reeling you in and then, he'd chew you up in criticism and spit you out in pieces. Like always it left you feeling small, less than whole, disoriented somehow. Daddy's rejection had definitely left its mark on me and that night I slept so stiff that when morning arrived I had deep pillow creases, set in my face. But like every other encounter with daddy, his image and cruelty slowly began to fad away further and further into the distance.

But with daddy's brutality behind me, it was a new day and I was determined to move forward. Joshua met my new attitude with a grin of approval, coming from his deep brown eyes. Smiling back at him with satisfaction, I went right to work until my list of dos was checked off, putting us ahead of schedule to meet up with Jessie. Once we were on our way, between listening to tunes, we chatted about all the things we hoped for, planning far into the future. We knew just what we wanted and our price range was set. By the time we met up with Jessie, he was so excited to see us; he insisted after we checked out his hotel room, we all go out to dinner. As we walked down the hall, hand in hand, all my troubles seemed to disappear. Following a mouthful of compliments, to how cool his room was, we freshened up and were on our way. Everything was just perfect from our steaks, to the jazz playing in the background. Jessie seemed to know his way around like the back of his hand and it left me to wonder!

Interrupting those uneasy thoughts, our server was holding out a tray filled with coffee and deserts. The dinner, the music, it was just what we all needed to relax and wind down. Later that night, with only a sheet hanging between us, the sound of our breath's breathing in and breathing out put me into a deep undisturbed sleep.

We were all up before the alarm had a chance to do its job. Our day called for a lot of serious work, there would be no time for play. Besides finding a place to live, we needed to check out the school systems. By the time we had burned through two pots of coffee and a box of donuts, we had our entire day sketched out to perfection. Gathering up our things, we piled in the car and headed out to the first place on our list. It was a beautiful scenic ride, everything we liked, we couldn't afford and nothing compared to our dream house. It all came down to our budget, so when Jessie pulled into a new gorgeous development, I assumed he was turning around. Instead he pulled straight up into the driveway in front of the models. Grinning from ear to ear, he was sitting sideways and looked like a mischievous naughty little boy. Suddenly he winked over to Joshua and they both slipped out of the truck at once and began walking towards the model. Chuckling back at them, Missy and I decided to take a look, so we ran, catching up to them. Past being beautiful, it was really an outstanding condominium and once Jessie saw it, he found what he wanted. Beautiful didn't mean practical, since it's size was neither practical nor affordable to us. Besides the manmade lake that surrounded several groups of trees, all it really had going for us, was that it was a side-by-side unit. It was perfect and in line with our way of living as one. Meaning, we would be only a hop skip away from each other's place. The model Jessie was eyeing, had a well-equipped kitchen that led out through a set of sliding glass doors, onto a gorgeous red-cedar wood deck. It held great potential for a single couple, having only two bedrooms, each with their own bath. The living room and dining room were relatively small, while the lower level had a laundry room, which was off one large room. Jessie was quick to jump on the idea the room was large enough for Joshua to divide into two small bedrooms. Pulling at his sleeve, having had enough of this wild dream, Joshua's wheels were turning in the opposite direction. But Jessie was already walking towards the office at the end of the models. Just as I was ready to go in and drag him out, I spotted Joshua and Missy walking up the cinder path towards me. Following a half-assed comment to where Jessie was, speak of the devil he was walking towards us, with his hands full of papers and a bad boy smile smeared across his face. In those next seconds, as he walked over to us, he looked so healthy; his face flushed with color, his shoulders solid. He was smiling as he held out a handful of pamphlets with information about the schools and two lease applications. Looking dumbfounded over at Missy and Joshua, they were looking back at me in disbelief and I knew darn well they were thinking he needed a reality check. But Jessie wouldn't take no for an answer, he was high on excitement; justifying every negative aspect we threw at him. Adding in a little reassurance, he began reminding Joshua of the excellent position he was hooking him up with. Once Jessie got Joshua to agree it was possible for him to turn the open room on the lower level, into two bedrooms, that was it. Before you knew it, we were back in the model, sitting at the table filling out applications. Handing them to the realtor, the fear that our credit scores might interfere, kept my tongue still. Now all we needed to do was kill a couple hours until the credit department got back to them. So after a tedious ride of chatting about our what if's, we stopped at a diner to wait it out. By the time we were seated in a red vinyl booth, with a basket of fries and a pitcher of cherry soda in front of us, Joshua pushing his soda back in restlessness, stood up. Straightening out his baseball cap, he pulled out a pocketful of change and mumbled he was going to go hunt down a phone. Only minutes later, his head shot out from around the corner all keyed up. "Come on guys, this is it."

He sure was appealing in his rough kind of way. If it weren't for the concern of getting approved, I would have laughed out loud. When it came to Joshua, no one knew him the way we did, no one saw past his serious side that consistently strived for success. Nor did anyone see the stormy side of his self-hatred, whenever failure came back at him. Within minutes his restless energy had us up on our feet and we headed right back to the office. No sooner had we walked in, when the realtor greeted us with his congratulations and the leases that were ready to be finalized. The realtor began talking too fast without even pausing; something about a year, while the whole time he was rambling on, my brain began to fog up with second thoughts. Observing everyone's faces, I left my doubts tucked silent under my tongue. By the time my signature was starring back at me, I was never so unsure of anything in my life. Reaching his hand out, the realtor was eagerly trying to shake our hands, before the ink was even dry. It should have been an evening of celebration, but perhaps I wasn't alone with my uncertainty, for no argument came back at me, for wanting to return back early to the hotel. It was on our ride back, when the question popped up to whether or not Jessie had gotten the agreement in writing. Looking stung, it hurt him where it hurt most, his great pride. Heated, he came right back at me in defense, pointing to all the hours he had to put in, just to take care of business.

Having heard that somewhere before, past annoyance, guilt set in for wounding his self-esteem. Instead of emphasizing any more concern, my woes trailed off. By evening, he was sweetly kissing away my worries, promising, he would take care of everything. Saying goodbye and leaving him, was no easier this time than when he had left. But he reminded me; that soon our condominiums would be waiting on us and we would be together again. We were only looking at weeks now, in which to sell our homes, our unwanted items and pack up our households. Knowing all this work had a short cut off date, as Jessie kissed me off, he promised to return home the following weekend to help. But with the winds picking up, my worries moved to the weather. It was already drizzling and a storm looked to be moving in, so we waved off Jessie and headed straight for home. During all the flashes across the sky and loud rumbles of thunder, as the heavy rain splattered against the windshield, my thoughts drifted in and out to the sound of the wipers moving back and forth in rhythm, afraid for our tomorrows. Once we were pulling into our driveway, somewhere along the way we had left the wind and rain behind us. It had been a long draining day and my mind quickly gave way to sleep.

Bright and early the following morning we got right down to business. The first thing we did was put both of our houses on the market ourselves. Now that we were moving into much smaller places we had too much of everything. With so much to do we lost no time and began sorting through things, nagging the children to put their unwanted items in piles. For the next few weeks, we worked side-by-side packing and preparing for our sale. At first everything was falling into perfect order, until reaching Jessie started to become a problem. It was happening two many times lately and it appeared as if he was living the fast life worry-free, while we were left sweating it out. Jessie was quick to defend all his late nights out, pointing to discussions about work and taking care of business, promising he'd be home by the end of the week. Melting at all his sweetness, I became putty in his hands. But as I looked over at Joshua's stern face, his dark eyes were staring back at me in disbelief for being so easily swayed. Annoyed with me for giving in so easily to his flimsy excuses, he began to criticize

Jessie for his lack of communication and the nights he was out partying. Paying his irritation no mind, he simply didn't understand that everything just had to be perfect for Jessie.

Now with the basement sale under way and Jessie on his way home, I was able to catch my breath and get dolled up. By the time his red truck pulled into the driveway, I had butterflies. Giving myself a quick once over, looking back at myself, I felt pretty darn good. When he stepped out of his truck, he looked magnificent; he even had a tan going on bringing a sparkle to his teeth. The very second he approached me, he pressed his lips down hard on mine, taking my breath away. He was as carefree as the wind, stepping over to give Joshua a rough bear hug and Missy a hug of warmth. We chatted our way to the back yard and as Jessie began to toss a ball to the kids, we started up the grill. Knowing ahead of time that Jessie was on his way home, we planned on strip steaks smothered in sautéed mushrooms in celebration. It was a real feast, although, all through dinner as my eyes rested on him, he appeared over confident. Something about him was different and I wasn't sure if his hat was too small, or maybe his head had grown too big for his own good. Seeing he was so self-absorbed in his success and somewhere on cloud nine, he was unreachable. Past a night of games, after tumbling in the sheets, he immediately rolled over and fell into sleep. Lying next to him, after weeks of loneliness I felt stung and ignored. Speculating, like I frequently did, I wondered when it was, that he lost the desire to watch me sleep. But by early morning, once his eyes opened, he was back to being loving Jessie, so my issues never had a chance to bloom into debate. Having been the day of our basement sale, we all scrambled about to keep up with all the sales. Our things were flying out the door so fast; I didn't even have time to think twice about what items I might miss. The sale was a huge success; it cleared out our houses and filled up our pockets with an over abundance of cash. It was more than we could have hoped for and with a celebration in order, Joshua ran out to pick up a bottle of champagne. Once we made a toast, clinking our glasses together, we sat making plans to go out to buy furniture for our new homes. We also made a list of everything we needed to accomplish. Once our lives were outlined in detail, we called it a night.

An early up, a pot of coffee and then we were dressed and out the door, hitting every store from one end of town to the other. Having found the deal of a lifetime, beautiful and rich solid oak is the only way to describe the formal dining room set and matching double hutches. The rich quality of wood matched the triple bedroom dressers and king size waterbed for our bedroom. The potbelly lamps warmed up the living room, blending in with the earth tone couch and the window treatments. Once the salesman tallied everything up, the bill was sent out to Jessie's company. Even Joshua and Missy got a few great deals, including a white bedroom set for their girls. It was definitely lollipops, cotton candy and girly-girly. Seeing Jessie agreed that he could arrange his work schedule around the delivery, we set up the date just a few weeks away. Heading back, after stopping off for some dinner, with Jessie having to pack and head back in the morning, we called it a night. In spite of turning in early, being overly exhausted, morning arrived too soon, shadowed by gray clouds. Jessie was already up and the coffee was brewed. Noticing that his duffle bag was packed and sitting by the door, brought down my mood. It would have been senseless to beg him to stay, he was kissing me goodbye and then he was gone. With time running out, we were hustling to get everything done and still not one decent bite came in on the house. It was truly a lifesaver that Jessie's company agreed to pay the rent on our condo until our house sold. Just the mere thought of having double payments was enough to make me squirm. It went hand in hand with my wild insecure imagination, imaging the worst while he was out so many nights, partying, as I saw it!

In my frustration, by the time Jessie finally got the utilities on, I was nagged out and knee deep in argument. Spinning in circles, things were moving faster than we could keep up with and all the things we had over-looked began popping up. It was around the time Jessie moved his stuff to the condo and when our furniture had been delivered, when suddenly he appeared miles away in spirit. Pointing out his stress, he argued all our concern off, insisting he was fine. So I was taken aback when he called out of the blue and dropped it on me that he was leaving for home. It didn't make any sense; he wasn't even due to arrive for days yet. But in my head, it was an amazing surprise and I kept watch for his red truck. It took hours longer than usual for him to arrive and our worry began to build. We never heard his truck pull in or heard the sound of his key turn in the lock. But out from the night, there he was standing in the foyer, looking relieved he was home. He looked drained and wrung out. But as the night wore on, I realized that somehow he seemed misplaced and unsettled. Several times he hinted that he was tired and wanted to crash. But being it was crucial we talked, he slumped back into the chair with his burgundy cap still in place. Dropping it on him that we had no bites on the house yet and we thought it was time to list it with a realtor, brought him down further. He remained preoccupied and appeared deep in thought, even after the lights went off and the blankets were wrapped snug around us. Gently stroking his hair, his eyes closed and his black eyelashes finally rested peacefully. Once his breathing became steady, my mind couldn't sleep, fearing the unknown.

With the morning sunrise, Jessie's spirits never lifted. Trying to pull it out of him was worse than pulling teeth and he clamed up, leaving us with no answers and an overkill of concerns. Only a few hours into our day, once the realtor had our signatures on the agreement, reality hit home. In my despair, there was no time to cry, because Jessie suddenly stood up and stated he had to leave. With his truck heavily loaded down with boxes, he waved us off, heading back in the direction of the condo. Once he was gone, we all sat in disbelief for hours, trying to figure out what the hell was going on. Following Jessie's eccentric mood, Joshua was filled with his own stressful thoughts, but he wasn't talking. With his emotions out of control, he buried himself behind closed doors in the stock market listings. At a time like this, with so much staring back at us, why was he acting as extreme and temperamental as Jessie? It was days, until his mood finally returned to normal and in turn introduced us to the names of the penny stocks we now owned. Paying them no mind, in my irritation we all worked nonstop, trying to make up for the lost time. Jessie began calling home everyday after that, maintaining he was doing super, just great! Perhaps he had been, just tired as he claimed, but he mentioned he stopped going out and was busy unpacking and setting up. Sounding trouble-free he waved off our concern to whatever it was that had been weighing on him. There was no going back now, all of our things were packed up and labeled in black marker. After weeks of hard work, our moving day finally arrived; everything sat perfect and neatly organized, waiting to be loaded onto the truck. Once Joshua and his friends loaded up all their belongings, they headed over to our place and started loading us up. Hours later, we all sat exhausted and the rooms sat vacant, except for the empty pop bottles and pizza boxes stacked neatly up on the floor.

Everything was going perfect, but it was getting harder and harder to meet all of Jessie's expectations, without any self-allowances to achieve any of my own fulfillments. Undeniably, his expectations were high; he wanted a flawless love, which was rich in loyalty and devotion. It was a sad and miserable choice on my part, because as Jessie climbed the ladder, he had a personal broom and dustpan, me! No matter what got into the way of his success, I would sweep the core of his problems under the rug. Seeing I was the one who foolishly took ownership of our consequences, it left me constantly striving to achieve this so called thing called perfection. Love, that's what I called it, love, sweet love! Norma looked intensely at me in a moment of my rousing memories of regret; my hands covered my face soaked in tears. My sorrow lingered on for years, for having done so much damage, by wanting to fix so much. Being the fixer of all did no one any good, no one at all. Instead it left all the heart wrenching emotions and deadly consequences, embedded in our heads for a lifetime.

PASSAGE XVI

Misery of a Broken Man

Three months sitting along the bay...one month fell off and gone was May...

Two months sitting along the bay, one fell off...and June was lost.

Only one month left sitting along the bay. Best change those ways, or left are no days.

Leaving our dream house was simply unbearable. Locking up the basement windows, the eight ball still sat off to the corner of the pool table that was left behind. A sentimental smile walked up the steps with me and just as I turned the corner, I began eyeing our beautiful fireplace that had given so many comfy romantic fires. Taking a quick breath in of emotion, left me with a strong sense of loss. The truth was, it seemed as if we were taking ten steps back, instead of moving forward. But it was too late to turn back; it was too late for a lot of things. Closing the door and locking it behind me, I sat down on the hot cement steps on the front porch, eyeing the blooming trees and landscape, feeling as vacant inside, as the house. But now with the large truck holding all our belongings and with our cars gassed up and loaded down, it was time to go. Everyone was calling out for me to hurry up. Joshua was sitting in the driver's seat of the truck, playfully honking the horn to entertain the boys who were riding with him. So off we drove, leaving behind our beautiful dream house, right along with daddy dearest, once again.

It was bump idée bump all the way, stopping for only two snack stops and three potty breaks. The ride was much longer than we had anticipated and with the weight of the truck slowing us down, it doubled our planned out gas budget. By the time we were pulling our cars into the driveways,

Joshua was parking the large truck in front of our condos. Within seconds we were out of our vehicles, restlessly stretching out our legs, when all the kids started acting up. But while catching sight of Jessie walking towards us with the four guys he had arranged to help us unload, the kids arguing got pushed aside. Counting all of us, we figured we could knock this thing out in less than half the time it took us to load up. Smiling to myself in a moment of appreciation, I caught a glimpse of Jessie out from the corner of my eye, appearing uptight, leaving me wonder. But as the day carried on and everyone working their tails off, both cars and the truck were emptied out right on schedule. Once we gave the guys their pay, they took off and we all stretched out on our new living room couch, among all the stacks of scattered boxes, too whipped to do any more. Relaxing in the moment, my eyes rested on our new dinning room table that was filled with cartons of our favorite Chinese food. Being our first shared dinner together in our new home, we began joyfully reminiscing over our hard struggle to get where we were. Seeing Joshua and Missy had their own mess of boxes to deal with, we called it a night. Now all they had to do was step out the door and they were home. Walking out of the sliding glass doors onto the deck, we chatted up to the moment they closed their door. Hearing the sound of the lock turning, with the newness of a door separating us, a deep sense of emptiness came flowing over me.

Exhausted and eager to cuddle up with Jessie in our waterbed, I pushed those uncomfortable thoughts away. Once all the children found a comfy place to crash, Jessie and I walked up the stairs arm in arm. It was only a matter of walking into our room, when my contentment turned into shock. There on the floor, sat all the boxes still packed that Jessie had brought back with him on his trips home. In spite of some of the dresser drawers being left open, past a few items, they sat empty. Disappointment shot through me, wondering about his lack of truth. It was hard to feel at ease, when all I could worry about was where all his countless hours had gone. With our words getting lost in a war of accusations and defense, it left me imagining the worst once again, about those nights he was out. With the room heated up, Jessie coolly reacted back and rolled over to the far side of the bed, pulling away from my touch. By morning it was a fresh day, and when it began to rain for the next five days, is when the air cleared and when water began to seep in through the carpeting on the lower level. All the concern for the unpacked boxes we argued over, now rested on the mattresses and children's items, now sitting, on the water logged carpeting where the boys slept. The smell of mildew already began to work its way up through the condo, bringing us to war. Our fight with the development company was a losing battle. Having overlooked getting renters insurance in our perfect plan, added up to our own negligence and loss. Since they blamed it on busted pipes, they only covered their end, apologizing for the inconvenience. It didn't soften the loss, seeing the boys had to camp out in sleeping bags until we aired out the smelly carpeting and tossed out boxes of their damaged items. By the time we got past the fight and the kids were all registered in school, one day had slipped into many. Nothing much was getting done and after a few weeks, the boxes still sat packed, and it was obvious that we had lost more than our get up and go. It was more that Jessie's uneven moods were changing with the hands of time. Reaching out, he would no longer try to communicate, claiming he was fine. Even though his troubled eyes were flashing me a warning, when the lights went off and his arms found me, I pushed his distant moods off to a simple case of adjustment.

With Joshua getting over anxious to return to work, he grabbed two beers before he cornered Jessie for a starting date. Jessie set down his beer and with his eyes drifting off he began to stumble over his words, with everything coming to a head. By the time he got it out that they were flooded with contractors, his face stood out bone white. Falling to pieces, he became an open book. Everything that we had been trying to read from his moods was being spelled out for us. He was near tears, confessing he had kept it to himself, that his company had been coming down on him for his low numbers and were royally trying to screw us. In his next attempt to spill his guts, he left the room and returned back, handing me a bunch of opened bills. He began to cave in as he broke it to me, that the company reneged on paying for our rent and new furniture. In the rays of sunlight streaming in bright through the window, Jessie's face appeared strangely unfastened. Even as he still left every morning for work, with everything now in the open he began to take more steps backwards.

Now with all these extra bills facing us, we were falling further behind and joined forces to job-hunt, taking us to one dead end after another. In a moment of falling into the past, all the contented memories of living in our dream house brought me a strong urge, to just run back home. But home sweet home was a long way off from reality. By now only several weeks had passed since we arrived with our plans to conquer the world. It was obvious; we had been incomplete in our plans and had bitten off more than we could chew. It was all staring me in the face bringing me down further, so I stuck all the bills in one of the empty drawers of our dresser, giving it a purpose. It's crazy, it seemed when things were at there worst; I was performing my best. Better said, I wouldn't dare allow myself to buckle under, not now, not with Jessie needing me. By now, I learned when it rains it can pour. It can pour at any moment, at any time. Sure enough, it began to pour like never before. The sound of the phone, it was ringing. It brought a cloud of darkness in from the day's sunshine that would brew over our heads forever. It was Jessie! It was something in his voice that made my heart begin to hammer and I began to plead for him to tell me what was wrong. Instead he sobbed he was coming home, then, a dial tone took us to disconnection. Gazing into space, I waited on him, as a million thoughts ran threw my head. Suddenly looking up, there he stood, he looked misplaced and the moment his eyes met mine, something about him scared me.

Lighting a cigarette, he let out a long exhale while his fingers trembled the whole time he pored and downed a significant glass of red wine. From there, he turned his back, walked up the steps to our room and with the blinds shut into darkness; he escaped under the covers for hours. The tray of food that was brought up to him was left untouched to dry out on the nightstand. The only activity in the room was the full ashtray needing to be emptied from time to time. In all of those agonizing hours of trying to rationalize with him, in his state of mind, Jessie wasn't Jessie. He didn't laugh, he didn't cry and then, he didn't return back to work! In the days that followed, waiting for him to get out of that chair, to call or return to work, only left all my pleading in vain. Emotionally wrecked, he refused their calls and after making one lame excuse after another for him, his bosses grew tired of talking with me, until their patience ran its course. If Jessie had one shot at making it right, he blew it. He lost his chance when he refused to put aside his pride and step up to the phone and lay his cards on the table. That was the last time they called on Jessie, refusing all my calls. By then my anger moved in and I began to push all the blame over to them, for having reneged on their word. After that, everyday, we tried to pull Jessie out from his dark mood by trying to shine some light on our lives. Only nothing gave him any strength to stand up for what he once stood for, instead he grew weaker. Our constant drilling only pushed him closer to the edge and Joshua's patience began to dwindle and his moods were becoming more like Dr. Jeckel and Mr. Hide every day. Even with

Joshua falling out of line and having his own meltdown, Jessie remained distant. One heavy dread set in, as I picked up the phone and called the only person that I thought could reach him, his mother! Shame washed over me the second I heard her voice, while the anxiety that she would learn about all of our failures, kept me pumped. Getting lost in a muddle of tears, with the words of warning she once preached, that he would run if the going got tough kept playing in my head. She listened patiently at first, but then, she cut me off briskly, promising she would call me back shortly. Placing the receiver back, suddenly I caught sight of Mae, having been eavesdropping, sneaking back up the stairs. It was no secret, we all stood guilty for subjecting our children to all this misery going on around us.

Waiting restlessly on her call, hours later when the phone rang, with Jessie rocking in a weird state, I was relieved it was his mother. With a change of attitude, she hoarsely insisted on speaking with Jessie. Walking the phone over to him, he rested it against his ear and sat quietly, only occasionally responding back. Something she said must have pampered his mood, for he stood up and cradled me in his arms, half whispering that he was going to catch a shower. Waiting on him, it was taking quite some time for him to return and it made me wonder what comforting words she had offered that seemed to bring him around. Whatever she said, it was enough that when he returned, he was standing over me with a blue duffel bag over his shoulder. Setting it down on the floor, when he sat down on the edge of the couch, the scent of his cologne lingered in the air, bringing the Jessie I knew back into my thoughts. But when he began to mumble, his blue eyes revealed no signs of the motivation and excitement they had once held. Without another reason, he got back to his feet, picked up his bag and muttered he had to go. Turning hysterically on him, even after begging him not to leave me in this forsaken place, didn't get him to put down his bag. All of my crying didn't get him to stay, because he wasn't thinking about anything except leaving and getting the hell out of there. Before I could throw myself at him again and beg him not to leave, he was gone. Gone like the wind! Dazed, watching him from the window, I kept praying he would turn around and come back to me. Only he didn't and I felt like I was going to die.

Oh God, I was falling apart and with our dream house ready to go into foreclosure, it felt like I was abandoned by Jessie. In a panic with my head spinning and my face soaking in tears, reality hit home and my gut began to churn. Running into the bathroom, my stomach began to jerk with dry heaves. Depleted to the bone, after pressing a cool washcloth against my face, I gargled away the taste of illness that lingered in my throat. Falling onto the couch, with my tears falling alongside a song playing in the distance, I wondered when my life became so complicated and miserable. Looking into myself, it was a blast from the past; here I was, crying to the same song I had cried too several years ago. "Oh you are so pitiful" I yelled out. "Pitiful, pitiful." The sounds of all my insane laughter filled the room and it was all bouncing off the walls and back at me. Chocking on my insanity, I tore over to Missy's house. In the midst of madness, by the time she got it out of me, that Jessie had taken off and was really gone, she squeaked out from the pit of her throat. "What are we going to do?"

We both plopped down on the wooden steps and after Missy handed me her pack of smokes and lighter, we put our heads together to come up with a plan. Smoking one after another, unsuccessful, our ideas sat as empty as the pack. With the ashtray full of butts, as Missy got up to break the news to Joshua, hearing the phone, I dashed to grab it, praying it was Jessie calling to come home. Disappointment ran through me the second I heard his mother's voice. Right from the moment she started in, her firm persistence not to be interrupted, left me feeling more like a naughty child, than Jessie's wife. By now she knew the depth of his depression and had been informed that we were up to our knees in debt. Quick to defend her accusations, my words were left trailing off, as she spoke loudly over me. It was a definite; she was indeed blaming me! Being her opulent home in the suburbs had several bedrooms, which overlooked acres of forest, she insisted it was the perfect place for Jessie to get his head back on. She met every argument I gave her head on and I was no match. Her last comment, that his spirits were already lifted and most likely he would be back home with me in no time, won the final debate. Suddenly a taste of bittersweet resentment filled my head, wishing she would just butt out. But knowing that it was me, who had called her in the first place and opened the can of worms, I held my tongue. Perhaps, she was the only one that would be able to pull him out of the quicksand before he went under. Only once she hung up my resentment was inching its way back in again and it left me real sorry I called her at all.

The days were slipping by and not one day would go by, that we all didn't try to get Jessie to return home. With everything slipping away, we were grabbing at straws just to survive. Our realtors phone call came after breakfast; claiming it took several calls to reach us. Knowing our dream house was ready to go into foreclosure, he knew we were sandwiched in and didn't waste a minute to give me the offer. It was our last chance and also, way below our asking price, but regardless, as soon as I cleared our breakfast plates, picking up the phone I called Jessie. When he answered, I cried more than talked and this time his mother never came to the phone. Truth be told, he still didn't sound together, but still, this couldn't wait and so we set it up to meet later the following afternoon. By the time we said goodbye, just the thought of seeing him warmed my blood. It felt like a lifetime since we had been together and a lifetime of loneliness. Eager to get an early start, again leaving Missy to tend to the children, allowed me to take care of business. It was a long ride and with so much empty time on my hands, my mind began to wander imagining the worst. By the time I arrived, Jessie opened the door before I even had time to put in my key. Right behind me, the realtor was pulling his shinny black Cadillac up into the driveway. Out of the blue, Jessie gently brushed his lips, softly to mine and as his smile relaxed, his eyes gave way to his haggard face.

Once we were seated at the table we had cherished, but left behind, the realtor set the papers down in front of us. Jessie and I briefly gazed at one another after staring at the ridiculous offer. It felt like everything we had worked for with blood sweat and tears was slipping through our fingers. Their offer was barely enough to pay the balance on our mortgage and would be no help to us. Once the realtor gave his spiel on the offer, he was looking over at us with a hint of pity in his eyes. It was enough to make me want to get up and run to the nearest bathroom. Jessie grabbed for my hand under the table, tightly squeezing, as if he were pleading with me to make the decision. Choices, choices, oh but it seemed that every choice we made had only taken us deeper into dept. By now, insanely funny, even our bankruptcy was on its way to going bankrupt. It was inevitable; we had to let go of our dream house. Looking over at Jessie, his eyes were reflecting back at me his misery, as he picked up the pen scribbling his name, before passing it to me. Once my signature sat below his, it was a done deal. As we were heading out, while glancing back, it felt like years had slipped off our life since we left here, instead of a passing season. But the realtor was still talking a mile a minute as we headed out and I zoned him out, anxious to talk Jessie, into returning back with me. Before the agent even backed his black Cadillac out of the driveway, Jessie grabbed on to me and held me tight in his arms, whispering words of longing. Neither of us could break away from one another and the strong desire to hang on, led us across town to a budget motel. Hoping to stay until late evening, after calling Missy, it went over effortlessly and I relaxed inside of myself. Somehow in spite of Jessie's anguish and his troubled mind, when his lips found mine, in the hours that came to pass, he became a different man. Slipping out of the sheets his ruffled hair, took me back to our days of love and bliss. But then suddenly he was sitting on the edge of the bed smoking a cigarette, looking as if he was a million miles away. Running my hand through his dark wavy hair, only brought him back to me long enough for him to repeat, he was going to return back to his mothers. Hurt and filled with rejection, it was taking way too long for him to get it together and come back home to me. In our last minutes together, I stared into his eyes, looking for a glimpse of the determined Jessie who had once sought after his dream, but his eyes sat vacant, silently starring back at me. With my head full, after making a mental note to call Mike, our long time agent and cancel the insurance on what was once our dream house, it was time to go. On the ride home, it was late and with my arms still empty of Jessie, my mind switched over to autopilot. By the time I pulled into the driveway, at that moment, even this miserable place looked good enough to be called home. Exhausted, I just wanted to peel off my clothes and climb into bed and stay there forever. Walking into the house, Missy obviously sensed my stress and let me off the hook, by not drilling me. Between counting sheep and reliving the past bliss we once shared together in our dream house, the sandman never came.

If things could go from bad to worse, it did just that! It took no time at all for Joshua to get the word that Jessie still wasn't coming back. With everything getting the best of us, Joshua wasn't the ace, he may have seemed. It was just that he was never in the spotlight, not as long as Jessie had the center stage. His self-esteem and defeated attitude had finally hit bottom, and now it was his turn to go off the deep end. After two days of burying his misery in a bottle of 151, he filled an army duffle bag to the max and stormed out, mumbling nasty words under his breath that he was done. Yelling insanely at Missy. "He's done? Really, really he's done, he is really done, what the hell, what the hell is wrong with him." While he was backing out of the drive in his own fury, Missy's pale face said it all, or was it my own stricken face that was reflecting back at me in the window. But truth, we didn't really know if he would be gone for a day or if he would even return at all. First Jessie walked, now Joshua and it left us both shaking in fear from the unknown. With both guys gone, during the empty hours of the days and nights, Missy and I spent hours together whispering and sharing our fears. It was during one of our long nights of restlessness, when Missy came clean about the mystery with her and Joshua. It wasn't the time, my head was filled with sawdust, but it was enough to keep me tossing after we had turned in for the night. When morning rolled around, it was still filtering in and out of my head. But still it wasn't the time to try to talk any sense into her to reconsider because now that we were all alone we needed the time to find a way to fend for ourselves.

If only, if only we hadn't overheard those two women in the grocery store talking about all the break-ins in our neighborhood, if only we hadn't acted upon it, only we did. Living in constant fear, we stayed together in one suite and once darkness approached, we got all worked up and our imaginations got carried away with this burglar thing. One of us got the bright idea that we should buy a gun and just shoot whoever broke in. Being that neither one of us had ever held a gun, we figured we would go to the nearest flea market to purchase one and pick up a few tips on firing. Once the weekend rolled around, there we were in our search, walking the graveled grounds. Where we found a small, two shot Derringer? Was in the last row of stands. Once this county man with a strong southern accent, heard that we were looking to buy a gun; he stepped into his small trailer off to the side and moments later, waved for us to come closer. As he unwrapped the black cloth, he named his price of fifty bucks and a handful of bullets, my size. Noticing that we were green, he offered us a quick lesson. He showed us how to unlock the chamber, load and hold it by the handle. It felt smooth to the touch, like silver and it fit perfect in the palm of our hands. Being over anxious to blow this pop stand as he called it, we handed him a handful of crumpled bills and walked away with the gun tucked in the bottom of Missy's purse. With our mission accomplished, we gave each other a wide smile and a big high five. It went down simple enough that we thought we were pretty smart, yea, pretty damn smart all right. Only now, any chance to change the hands of time, to undo buying that deadly piece, passed.

On our way home, as we expressed second thoughts for having bought the gun, I kiddingly suggested that we use a baseball bat instead. Missy laughed-out-loud and as we cruised along with the windows open and our hair-blowing in the wind, for a little while, we forgot our troubles. But the minute we returned back to the condo, reality hit home and our depressed mood of worry returned. In our foolish naive idea to hurry and hide the gun, we walked upstairs and put it in a dresser drawer, under a shirt Jessie had left behind. We hid the handful of bullets on the top shelf of the closet in a tin box. Relieved to get it away from us, as far as we were concerned, we just flushed fifty bucks down the toilet. But if only we hadn't gotten ourselves so worked up over those anonymous break-ins, we might have realized, the man who came out from nowhere, wasn't who, we thought he was! Oh God, thinking back, yes, by the time this man Simon stepped into our lives, we were already ten times over the limit of insanity. But still, we found it in our hearts to open ourselves up, only to be exploited, never knowing, he would drive us off in the night. It was sometime when we were in our comfort zone, that his wheels must have begun to turn and he wanted more than our open arms of acceptance. After having taken all of his understanding and pity, then turning away from him, once he wanted more, he abruptly turned on us.

The weather already began to turn towards the chilly side. With hooded sweatshirts on to keep us warm, Missy and I were sitting by the man-made lake, while the girls were throwing pebbles into the water. Past the girl's giggling, it was a quiet time and a perfect time for privacy for us to talk and whisper. It was then when a man with dark brown hair surrounding a handsome face, approached us. Introducing himself as Simon, we looked past him to his yellow compact car he had parked against the curb. He was pointing over to the available condominiums, mentioning he was looking to rent. He was doing most of the talking, but hey, no one invited him to sit down and join us, but he did. Looking over at Missy, she raised her eyes, giving him only half of her sweet smile. Wishing he would just go away, his hair stood straight up on edge from the wind, bringing a grin to my lips. He chatted on with confidence and surprisingly before long; we found ourselves taken in by him and enjoying his company. He was very comical and we laughed at every joke he tossed our way. But as blind and unobserving as we surely were, we failed to notice he never did share any information about himself. We were so busy enjoying his humor, that we invited him to share Missy's prepared peanut butter and jelly sandwiches with us. The evening shadows began to set the mood, making it feel safe, so we stayed out with him to watch the sun go down. When and how we began to confide in him was when the question came up, of where our guys were. We were both talking to much and now that he knew our life story, his face lit up, offering his help if we needed anything. So with her face shining, Missy borrowed his pen and scribbled down our phone numbers, eagerly handing them to him. It was later that night when Missy joined me holding two cups of coffee and a pack of cigarettes. Grateful for her kind gesture, we were sipping on our hot coffee, when Simon's name came up. Being suspicious since the Woodsman, for reasons well known, I felt a need to warn her to be on her guard. Instead of taking it for what it was, she referred back to Joshua, reminding me that they had come to their own terms, in regards to their commitment and that was that. But after that night we watched the sun go down, it wasn't the only thing going down. For everyday for the next three days, we became the center of Simon's attention and there was always some reason he was knocking at our door. Once we felt the creepiness coming off him and we put on the brakes to his bothersome visits, it began to backfire. He went off on Missy first, scaring the living hell out of her. She came tearing into the house like a bat out of hell, crying out that Simon flipped and was swearing he was going to get even with us. "Oh God, now what are we going to do?" she cried, looking more like a scared kid than I'd ever seen her look.

Giving her attitude that he was a jerk and just blowing smoke up her chimney fed her just enough reassurance to calm her. In spite of my own padded theory, just the thought of Simon behaving like the woodsman, put the fear of God in me. Only fear was only half of it, because it was well into the night when he called and started in, "Listen you two bitches, you can't just toss me aside because you say so, I gave you my life."

His evil tone, his chilling threats shook our whole world and we took two steps back. Looking over at Missy in alarm, as we hid away from the windows, we knew we were in big trouble! By morning we barely slept a wink and instead of sharing in breakfast with the kids, we started brewing another pot of coffee. But with the sun streaming in, it felt safer somehow, like maybe, it was over and he disappeared with the night. Looking out of the window, there was no sign of his yellow car anywhere and breathing a sigh of relief, Missy and I both decided to stay camped out, in one condo. Seeing we still carried this undying faith, that Jessie and Joshua would spring back and soon return, kept us going and by lunch, we put Simon's threats behind us. Just enough so that Missy had enough confidence to run over to her place to pick up a few items. But it was taking her way to long and just as I picked up the phone, she came tearing in and was gasping for breath. Between her tears of hysteria, she was insisting that she saw his face and he was still out there somewhere watching us. Not a minute went by when the phone rang, cutting off our voices. It was as if we thought he could hear us whispering, so in our paranoid state, we just stared at the phone. We sat trembling, listening to the loud ring, one ring after another, until I picked it up and the second that I let out a faint hello, he came back at me. "Boo…hi ladies…talking about me are you?"

"Leave us alone or we'll call the police on you."

"Yah-yah-yah go on an do it, do it now and someone will get hurt, hey listen, I'm not playing."

He snarled out even more cutting words, before he hung up. In the next several calls we received, any efforts to smooth over his anger was useless and still, we couldn't figure out what it was, he wanted from us. In one of our brave moments, after stepping outside to search for any sign of him or his car, only worked us up more. Believing we brought this on ourselves, by inviting him into our lives, kept us from dialing the police. Even calling on Joshua and stirring him up seemed way out of our reach. Even if we did reach him, who knew what he was doing, or if he was still drinking 151, by the time he got to us, we could all be dead. Meanwhile, somehow we kept it together enough to keep the girls occupied and out of sight, while Missy and I did lots of whispering. Allowing the boys to stay home from school and play all their video games was enough to satisfy their curious interrogation.

So living by what Simon says, surrounded our world with terror! Now with vengeance sitting among us, without any sleep or food for thought for three whole days, we were slowly inching towards insanity. We couldn't take any more and we figured the only way to get rid of Simon and save ourselves was to shoot him, not thinking about afterward. We knew what we had to do and we whispered for hours, planning and plotting. The gun, it was still hidden in the dresser drawer, under Jessie's shirt and the bullets were still in the tin box up high on the closet shelf. When we were sure everyone was sleeping, we tiptoed up the stairs to retrieve the gun and the bullets. With our fingers trembling, we unlocked the chamber and loaded it with two small bullets, just as the county man had shown us. So we sat whispering and just waited! We watched the clock aware of every deadly second that ticked by, getting up every little bit in the dark, to look out the window. A heavy fog was moving in, setting the stage of fright even more.

Our high dose of adrenaline running through our veins was the only thing that kept us going. In a restless and jumpy state, as it was nearing four am, it was time to go. Both dressed in black from head to toe; we slipped out quietly turning the bolt behind us. But somehow the loaded gun ended up in my hands, with Missy as my cheerleader. Cautiously checking out the area, we no sooner turned the corner, when we spotted his parked car. Hiding behind a cluster of bushes, it appeared as if Simon was inside. The streetlight made it possible to make out some form that was moving, but maybe it was just a shadow or maybe our eyes were playing tricks on us. It was pretty foggy, making it impossible to know for sure. Whispering, we figured even if we just hit his car, it would drive him off. Pointing the gun towards his car, while trying to steady it, I pulled back on the trigger thing. Looking over at Missy, even in the stirring shadows, her trembling lips could be clearly read. "Do it... Just do it!"

Something about her face in the dark shadows shook me hard enough that it brought me right back down to earth. With my hand trembling, I lowered the gun, hoarsely whispering. "I cant, I can't."

Not giving her time to answer or waiting on her, as I turned and ran for my life, I could hear her calling after me, as she was high tailing it to catch up. She never asked why, maybe she felt it too and came to her senses. Because once we both tore into the house, we bolted the door and began to throw anything and everything we might need in bushels, because we were getting the hell out of there! We figured with the heavy fog, he might not know we took off. We woke the boys first and in all their grumbling, our reasons were not up for debate. If they sensed something was wrong, it was enough to keep them quiet and kept them moving. Keeping the lights low, as the boys gathered their things, we gathered all the girls and packed everybody into the van. With the van full and Missy in the drivers seat and me as the look out, we were off.

Looking out the windows, the heavy fog kept you from seeing past a few feet ahead on the road. Still, we stayed on our guard, knowing at any moment he could come barreling up from behind. Driving on the side roads, the feeling of blindness left a weird sense of eeriness in the air. Every so often an acorn would fall from a tree hitting the hood of the car, jarring our nerves. But we kept driving on, keeping our conversation to a whisper, careful not to wake the girls. Once we hit the highway, as slow going as it was, we seemed to relax back into our seats. With the fog that never let up, the ride seemed long and endless. Staring out the window to nothing but a haze put me in my own fog and my mind began to cross back to Simon and what a deadly mess our lives had become, mumbling under my breath. Missy looked back at me, her face drained, like my gibbering had spooked her, having sounded like it was the end of the road for all of us. By now, the sun was rising, the fog was lifting and we felt as if we had been washed out, put through the ringer and hung out to dry. Simon or no Simon, we stopped at a fast food chain in the rest area and let the kids fill up on sausage and pancakes. Once we were back on the road, we just kept driving, until we hit a small town on the outskirts of the city. Missy and I thought it best, if we stopped off at the next eatery we saw. When we spotted a rusty metal sign swaying on a crooked pole that read pay phone, Missy pulled into the narrow gravel lot. When she realized it had a small diner, she flashed me a look of relief. Anxious, the kids got out of the car and walked towards a wooden picnic table next to an unoccupied swing set, left of the diner. Grabbing my purse, Missy stayed behind the wheel to keep an eye out. From the second I walked in, every eye moved on me. It was a strange place. It couldn't have seated more than ten people at most, not counting the couple of red swivel stools in front of the counter. Looking past the inquisitive eyes, I spotted the pay phone on the wall and tried squeezing past a very large man, uttering, excuse me three times, before he lifted up his chair to move, eyeballing my bothersome interruption. Dropping in one dime after another, my coins were dwindling and any luck of reaching Joshua or Jessie sat on empty. Down to the last of our coins, I turned to the bills, realizing the cost of gas and food had cut us way short on cash. Suddenly ticked off because Jessie and Joshua had left us, slamming down the phone hard only drew more attention to me. Noticing everyone was curiously staring over at me, my walls of defense went up and I wanted to say something mean, only instead, I began to cry in front of them all! Someone was leaning down, asking me if I was okay. Right when I was ready to let him have it, he said his name was Chip. Looking up he had a gentle face, framed with a crew cut and wire rimmed glasses. By then I was bawling that we were scared, hungry and broke with nowhere left to turn. His face softened, offering his home for as long as needed. He was talking loud enough for everyone to hear, proud like. Once the kids came running in with Missy following from behind, as he appeared to be doing a head count, he never stuttered once. Instead he eagerly suggested we follow him right down the street to his place, where we could also get some chow. Call me crazy, but there was something genuine about this man and Missy, she sensed it too, so we cried in relief and said yes! Perfect timing? Desperation? What? Besides, how dangerous could it be, when the whole town would get wind in an hour that we were staying at his place? But then what did I really know, so far, every pick for me, was no bull's eye. But while following his black pickup truck, Missy and I were in agreement; it was just until we could reach Joshua.

Chip had acres of property. It was the real thing, cows and horses, even a big wide-open barn. Walking into what he called the big room, he offered the room to us, bringing in an over abundance of blankets and pillows. Struggling to keep our eyes open to be on the watch for him, we ended up going out like a light and sleeping for quite some time. We awoke, to the smell of fried baloney with the children gathered around the table, talking a mile a minute with Chip. If he had any questions to what we were up to, he let it ride. In the hours we were there, we got rested up enough, to clear our minds and deal with Joshua's madness, when finally we reached him. Having come home to find us gone, he was frantic, but still we said as little as possible, claiming that we got spooked, that's it, spooked. We held on tight to our tongues, giving Joshua nothing past the hour we should arrive home. Thanks to Chip's big heart, with our tummies and gas tank filled, we were heading back to where we had left Simon. With the radio blaring on the ride back, we kept skipping over words to keep the kids uninterested, while we figured out that we could never admit to getting involved with Simon. Dreading to face Joshua might have been hanging over our heads, but we believed it was his fault for leaving in the first place. Being we had been enlightened, the only thing we were sure of, was Chip had to be an angel in disguise.

Turning into our development, we began to look for any signs of Simon or his yellow car. Taking a deep breath, we took our pasted story in with us and the familiarity of being home gave us strength. The children had their own plans, scuffling off one by one. Having caught the smell of brewed coffee, we grabbed a cup to take with us, to go and face the music. Joshua, his face sat sober, as he listened to our unfastened story of being spooked. Of coarse he never heard about the gun, but his eyes trailed over to Missy and then back to me and I knew darn well he was searching for truth. While his eyes lingered on mine I turned away, but not before I read it in his eyes that he wasn't buying into our bull-tweedy story. Our lips remained sealed and even Joshua couldn't pry them open. Just sitting and refusing to say more, Joshua gave us a look of dissatisfaction and got up to refill his coffee. When he returned back into the room, the subject was closed. His attention had transferred over to the list of alternatives he came up with while he was away. Now with Joshua in charge, we put Simon out of our thoughts and settled back to listen to what he had to say. Only, someone was knocking annoyingly on the doorknocker.

Squirming in my skin, you could see the same fear as mine in Missy's face, what if Simon came back to get us? With no one responding, Joshua got up to answer, calling back strangely for me to come. Nearly chocking on my tongue, the man behind the door, turns out, wasn't Simon. Instead a sheriff handed me a letter in trade for a signature. Closing the door behind him, as I ripped open the envelope, it appeared to be a summons to appear in court. Oh God, I suddenly realized, we were both being evicted from our condos. By the look on Joshua's face, I knew this blew his list of alternatives right out the door. It was no shock when the following day, Missy ran over holding the same letter with the same court date. With both money and time running out, we were facing the possibility of becoming homeless. So the very first thing I did, I tried to contact Jessie. Calling and leaving message after message with his mother, brought back no word from him. Everyday that passed was one day closer to our hearing and still with no word from him; it was in the heat of the moment, when all my anger boiled over to his mother. It was a big mistake…Big.

On the morning of our court date, I was still in a state of denial, waiting restlessly for his arrival. But then, it was time to go and still he didn't show. Once our turns came to stand in front of the judge, there was no fight in us and we admitted our fault. It was quite simple and with no sympathy back, the rulings went against us. We had thirty days before the order to padlock our doors would be carried out, but still they put the large yellow evicted stickers across our doors, adding to our humiliation. With no word back from Jessie, everybody was on the edge and it was just a matter of who was going down first. Personally I had reached my end and all my strength was gone. Crawling into bed, with my body under the covers, weeping for our dream house and weeping for the now, our lives were torn in shreds. Once my tears subsided and the after-sobs quieted, my mind moved into a numb state. After crawling out of bed and pressing a washcloth to my face, the person looking back at me in the mirror drove me to pick up my purse and walk out the door. Missy caught a glimpse of me and headed outside after me, after mumbling words about wanting to die, she ran in front of me, spreading out her arms to stop me. "Stop, stop, where are you going? Don't go, please, come on, come on, we'll get through this, I promise."

Pushing past her I yelled back at the top of my lungs, "God Missy you just don't get it, do you, it's too late, it's too late, it's too damn late."

Before she could get out another word, I walked off into the direction of the dark clouds that were swiftly moving in. The winds briskly picked up, vigorously shaking up the trees and blowing a tumbling trail of leaves up the curbs. When the cool raindrops began to fall over my face, I wished to God that the skies would just suck me up and end it all. It was crazy, because instead of the normal fear I had of storms, I felt fearless. Slightly wet and chilled, it was still drizzling when I spotted a group of condos under construction. Running for cover, the only way to get up into the shell was to shimmy up on the bits and pieces of wood left behind. It was wide open, where the sliding glass doors would be, giving me a full vision of the angry skies. Plopping down to the plywood floor, I bitterly kicked the boards that were lying in my way. Looking out, occasionally the winds would whip around, blowing in a light mist of rain. Empting out my purse, some loose change tumbled out, along with a partial pack of cigarettes and an open book of matches. After fumbling to pull out a cigarette from the crinkled pack, I placed it between my lips. Unsteadily striking at the match, I gazed at the match cover, realizing, it was the name of the budget motel where Jessie and I had made love, right after we had signed away our dream house. Bittersweet resentment filled my lungs, whereas my first cigarette, took me through what was left of the pack and by then, it began to pour. Believing we had lost everything, with thunder roaring through the skies, I took my bolt of anger to God. Only little did I imagine, the word everything, was only a far cry away. Rocking back and forth in anxiety, I wept hard, praying and pleading for a long time for him to just let me die. In those next breaths of life, feeling immobilized, the fear of dying suddenly took my voice. This was definitely more than I had ever bargained for. Tingling inside and out, it felt as if something took me outside of myself. It was like nothing I had ever felt, something was lifting me up in spirit and brought an enormous amount of peace to my soul. Sudden glimpses of my own life were going around and around in my head, leaving me with a strong sense of inner strength, bringing me up to my feet. Determined to tell the others of this strange power that had taken control and calmed all of me, I began running for home. Even the pouring rain didn't slow me down, or wash away any of my new given strength. Rushing into the house, Missy's relieved face met mine, after apologizing for scaring her; all she heard about was this gift of inner strength I had felt. But in my mumbo-jumbo, it was just about as unexplainable as it was unbelievable. But in my enthusiasm to begin to put our tattered lives back together, Joshua came walking into the room, eavesdropping on all the commotion. Carrying on with this spiritual purpose, he looked at me with his eyes filled with his usual thoughts about my spiritual hocus pocus and just how far he thought, that could take us. But something was different between us this time, besides the laughter seeping out from the corners of his lips. Brushing the tingle away, he felt it too; I saw it in his eyes. But Jessie, I was going back for him, determined to bring him home with me. Somewhere in the middle of this tranquil miracle, daddy's face flashed before me. It was only a flute of hope, but it was all we had. Holding on to my nerve, I couldn't get out of there fast enough to go back to where home once was and find Jessie and to pay a visit to my daddy dearest.

It turns out finding Jessie was right at my fingertips. He was sitting on his mother's deck and it took next to nothing before he went in, grabbed some of his clothes and got into the car. We talked for a long time before we headed over to my father's. Leaving Jessie in the car, being disowned and all, I walked up the walk alone, taking quick notice to his shinny chrome chair off to the side of the drapes. With hesitation as I turned the door knob and found it wasn't locked, I pushed open the door calling out, "Daddy, daddy, it's me, Beaky-nose." His voice came back at me gruff, "Huh."

That was my cue so I stepped in. Shuffling my feet I knew why I came and tried not to appear desperate. Pacing he wouldn't stop talking long enough for me to get a word in. Determined to reach him, my voice grew along side of his, refusing for him to override me, while I pitifully begged for help. In the next moments, his face softened and I silenced my mouth when he began to talk so unlike him. "She's gone you know. She moved out of state, you should call, she's your sister you know."

Of course mother had filled me in and not wanting to cause a tidal wave and rock the boat, I was careful not to mention the word Mother. When he wheeled himself over to his wooden desk and pulled open the drawer, the sound of the handle falling back down, took me back in time. Suddenly realizing he was writing out a check, tears of relief ran down my face. Staring uneasily at his swollen, worn calloused hands; guilt filled my gut for taking from his low income. In all my promises to pay him back, he wasn't listening and after kissing the top of his head, I don't think he ever noticed that I slipped out the door. Sliding back into the car, I knew basically Daddy's money was merely the aid of a band-aid, to get us out of the condo and into another place. It surely couldn't fix Jessie; it couldn't do a lot of things, but it would prevent our family from going down in size and keep us from becoming homeless. Showing Jessie the check, relief was written all over his face and after his lips met mine, he agreed on the spot to come home with me. Tears of relief took over when he went home to get his car, and he passed on calling his mother. In those cherished moments, Jessie's spirits were amazingly high. And on our arrival home, between the money and the sound of chatter, it felt like old times, almost like Jessie had never fallen. Enjoying a late night pizza, we stayed up searching most of the night for the best way to put our lives back together.

In those short hours, we had our game plan to go out and search for a new home, sketched out. Eager to take everyone, Joshua held up his hand in protest, there could be no fallbacks, no delays. For whatever reason, it would be me that went with Joshua to find our next destination. By early morning my backpack was stuffed with a spare set of clothes and once we iced our sandwiches and sodas down in the cooler, we were off. After hours of driving and getting nowhere, our patience was sitting on empty. We had driven from one town to another, down one street through every block. We saw it all, from fishing lines leaning empty against a brick wall, to bald tires thrown on several run down and forgotten properties. Looking for something big enough for all of us with the amount of cash in Joshua's pocket was looking mighty grim. The first night, exhausted, we crashed in his truck. Blocking out Joshua's negative attitude and his comment about my hocus pocus, I prayed for all we needed. By the first sounds of morning, we were back on the road with dry mouths and the need to shower. Having found a small gas station half buried in the woods, we stopped off. It was a quick freshen up and after putting a comb to my hair, my tired reflection starred back at me. Picking up a couple cups of coffee and some directions to the next populated areas, we headed outside of the winding hills and cattle farms. We drove searching high and low, only stopping off when we got sidetracked with the greatness of the countryside and awesome views looking straight down for miles, from high mammoth rocks. If all of its beauty had softened my mood, once we were back in the truck feeling the pressure, we were back to bickering. By nightfall, parked off to the side of the road, the lighting bugs lit up the sky in the hundreds, leaving me to wonder where I had been all my life. But trying to cuddle up against the door, cramped my style, trying to ignore Joshua who grunted in his sleep. If the first night was uncomfortable, then the second night was unbearable. Since Joshua always loved a challenge, he took my complaints as whining. Observing him, he looked comfortable and had adapted well, ignoring my comments. Before the birds were even chirping, I awoke with my mind set on going home empty handed. Believing we had failed, in my mind, it was useless. In my strong rigid argument to Joshua, we began to head back and it felt like we had been driving for hours, when Joshua finally owned up poorly, to being lost. Pulling off to the side of a narrow lane is where we saw this big old house, being emptied out by a moving company. It caught our full attention and Joshua was already out of the truck and walking towards the back of the house, with me trailing behind him. Knocking several times on the back door, a rosy-faced lady, came cautiously up to the door. "Yes, can I help you?"

She patiently waited for an answer, while her eyes remained cautious, observing Joshua while he spoke. Being this was a small town and we were obviously strangers, left me feeling anxious. Only Joshua stepped up and by the time he finished his sad spiel of needing a place to live, she was eating out of his hand and opened the sliding glass door with a wide smile, "Well yes, as a matter of fact it will be available soon, I just haven't had time to put it in the paper."

Offering us a tour, she led us up an old winding stairway to four bedrooms and a full bath that had a porcelain bathtub with a tiny dressed window. Across the hall was the door to an old empty dusty attic that left me with a case of the willies. On the main floor, there were two living rooms, a kitchen, dining room and another large bedroom and full bath, with an attached laundry room. With lots of trees surrounding the house, being late fall the trees were beginning to shed the last of their colored leaves. We had seen enough; we were sold. She got right to the point that she required the first month's rent and a security deposit. When she told us the price of the rent she wanted, it was beyond perfect, it was incredible. Joshua began digging in his pockets and as he pulled out a wad of bills, he told her we would take it. Holding my breath, it wasn't until she took both sets of keys off the wooden hook and handed them over to Joshua, that I began to breath with ease. Wanting to give this lady a hug, the thought of her picking up on my desperation, drew me back. But as she rambled on about all the past memories of her deceased husband, I was lost in my own thoughts of how weird it was, that this house met all our needs, including the price. Looking around in disbelief, it was too good to be true and it left me to wonder, if this was a joke, or indeed a gift from God. So with the keys in our hands and a move in date, as we headed out, Joshua winked at me with confidence. Once we were in the truck, we looked for a payphone to call home and report in that we found a great place and that we would arrive home, later that evening.

In our relief and curiosity, we decided to check out the entire area where we would be living. Our new place sat in front of a single lane road, directly across the street from the only shopping plaza within fifty-miles. There were only eight stores in the plaza, with only two fast food chains in town. Ten miles going up one hill and down another, the dirt roads had miles of farmland with only a peek of civilization between the ongoing rows of corn. Laughing it up with Joshua, the whole time his truck was riding rough and wild on the dirt roads, "Our little Amish land," is what we named it. By then, it was getting late. In all our playtime, we had for-gotten to eat, while both food chains in town were closed. By then the long hours of our hard work had caught up with us and we knew we were too tired to make the ride home. Spotting a dingy motel on the edge of town we agreed, after all our hard hours of searching, we deserved to sleep in a little comfort. It was only a six-room motel at most and yet they had six vacancies, so we had our choice of rooms. Peeling off a few bucks from Joshua's small stack of bills, we took the key and headed to the room. It was a small room and while eyeing only one bed, I caught a glimpse of Joshua eyeing my response. Pushing the bed off to the back of my head, feeling dirty, tired and hungry, I jumped in the shower first, while Joshua went to hunt for food. Oh~~ but the steaming hot water felt so wonderful running over my achy body. Not wanting to use all the hot water, I quickly scrubbed up and rinsed off and after wrapping a towel around me and stepping out, I came face to face with Joshua. Awkwardly, clearing his throat, he was holding on to an armload of snacks and sodas he had managed to retrieve. Setting them down, he gave me a crooked smile and grabbed a towel. Moving out of his way, I let out a heated breath. These heated moments, seemed to be happening more and more these days. By the time I slipped on a simple change of clothes, he returned back from the shower with a towel wrapped loosely around his waist. It was a moment, just one moment in time of being alone after years of our passion building, his mouth, his arms, his warm wet body, it was all swallowing me up. Tearing off any clothing that was standing between us, our bodies blended into perfect harmony. No Joshua, I wanted to cry out, no, but it was too late, for it had been done. It felt like I had finally climbed all the way to the top of the highest mountain and found myself in him. It was bound to happen sooner or later. But none of that mattered now. Through the dark night, we never let go of each other long enough for either of us to call home and report in. Instead I was breathing in every ounce of affection he showed.

It was the morning sun that brought Joshua up to his feet and out of my arms. By the time he dressed, he returned to the normal unbending Joshua. On the long scenic ride home, instead of clinging to me, he kept both his body and mind at a distance. Just as we were pulling into the drive, Jessie came into my view, taking me back in time, to when we had messed up at Dwaine's party. It was the same story. Jessie was angrily eyeing me and waiting on my excuse. Except that there could be no lying or faking the truth, for this time, Jessie read it in my face. He saw the truth in my eyes and after I read the misery and shock in his eyes, he was gone, vanished! This time it was my fault and from that day forth, Jessie was all over the place. Raising my eyes, suddenly Norma appeared to be struggling to hold on to her emotions, with some control. She was showing signs of having moved out of her comfort zone, as she brushed away a tear from her eye.

PASSAGE XVII

Town Without Pity

They said insane is a frame of mind never to find what really lies way deep down inside. No one sees inside the soul, forgotten are yesterday's goals, never to capture the simple bloom of a rose. Free thy mind to free thy soul, so once again there is control.

At this point one way or another we were all living in our own world of insanity. Little did I know then, that once it became known that Joshua and I had bankrupted our trust, we would be forever judged, until the last shovel full of dirt was thrown down upon our remains! It doesn't sound pretty. But now that Jessie was gone and my secret was out, Norma knows somewhere along the way, I had fallen in love with Joshua. It was a deep love, a love mainly connected with our souls. All my guilt and excuses for my weak actions were spun into a web of justification. It's something I could never put into words, it would sound like I was just trying to wiggle my way out of lust, instead of the strong bonds that tied us together. It was mystical and fatal. Motivating and crippling, but it was a thief, robbing us both of the lives we may have had. There, I finally said it! Perhaps in the end, in spite of the forgiveness in Missy's understanding blue eyes, it was hard to admit that I had no control of anything in my life, not even myself. Self-hate for having been so weak in the heat of the moment lingered on in my head, yet like paper to glue, it bonded us even tighter together. So after years of hiding behind a wall of deceit, too ashamed to claim and take ownership of what was, finally, it stands free. Yet we, Missy, Joshua and I continued to stay together, through thick and thin, love and war, struggling to survive, with no idea that our lives were already out there, somewhere, smoldering in the coals.

Feeling lost without Jessie, the only peace or consolation I felt was the miracle of having found this old house. Yes, the perfection of it all came in the nick of time. In many ways, this small town was the answer to our prayers. It was a place to heal, to regroup and perhaps it would bring Jessie back around with forgiveness in his heart. Once the children got word we were moving to a small town, their acceptance was upon us, except for Brad, who argued down all our reasoning with his mouth full of bazooka. Convincing him this was our stepping-stone back home, put his debate to rest. With time ticking against us, after securing a rental truck, stacks of cardboard boxes sat waiting to be put together. With our work cut out for us, we got right down to business and began packing the things we needed least. The ongoing chatter of the children and the sound of their music streaming through the air, made it feel like we were more of the family, we once were. That evening, we cooked a big bowl of pasta with garlic toast and for the first time, since we received our eviction notices, my appetite stirred. In the days that passed, by the time we got through most of our houses, I started on Jessie's dresser drawers. Reaching under his shirt and sliding my hand around for the gun, my heart stopped. It was gone, it was freaking gone! Running to the closet, in my panic the tin box on the top shelf came tumbling down. Lying on its side, it sat empty! Dear God! Simons face flashed before me and a hot streak of fear ran up my spine. Tearing down the stairs in search of Missy, the moment my eyes met hers, I whispered out in alarm. "It's gone, the gun, Simon must have taken it, oh my God, what should we do?"

She didn't answer; her face was frozen with fear, hoarsely whispering that maybe somebody else took it. Her comment kept my heart racing and my mind speculating. There was no way we could tell Joshua about the gun, hell, he was still in the dark as far as Simon was concerned. So we had no choice but to come painfully clean about buying the gun, failing to mention Simon. Once we knew neither Joshua nor the kids took it, I called around for Jessie. With my nerves knotted up in a ball, it took three days before he got back to me, swearing on his life, he never saw any gun. But his spirits seemed higher, claiming he was coming home to help us pack up and make amends. By the time we hung up, it all made sense that it had to be that creep Simon who took it, after we fled in the fog that night. After whispering back and forth to Missy, about Simon most likely having taken the gun, we figured in less than a week we would be gone and he would be out of our lives forever.

Again, Jessie never showed his face or stayed true to his word. Not having heard or seen, neither hide nor tail of him, the worry and let down of it all, drove me to calling all over town for him. With the truck sitting and waiting to be loaded, we carried one box out at a time, while Joshua stacked them neat and high. By noon, still with no sign of Jessie, we took off with the first load without him, having taken on a hired hand to help with the furniture. As we pulled up into the dirt driveway, Joshua already had the truck parked alongside of the house and was walking towards us. The newness of the countryside surrounding us brought on so much excitement amongst the kids, that we had to keep reminding the boys to keep moving. We kept trucking away until the truck sat empty; then we were back on the road to load up again. Getting down to less than twenty-four hours meant no sleep for us. When the boys began to argue us down to work through the night, in our desperate need to finish we didn't say no. Sometime halfway into the night, as Mae was curled up in the corner, I brushed her blond strands of hair from her face, silently promising her everything will get better now. By the time the birds were chirping, the boys were crashed out, but we figured we still had hours left. It was around noon, when I spotted a black van, looking as if maybe someone was trying to catch our address. It wasn't until the van made a u-turn and parked right across from our condo, when I panicked and began yelling out for Joshua. "Their here. They are here to put the padlocks on, they'll wait won't they, won't they?"

Joshua replied back sternly, "Just keep moving and don't even look at them."

His tone came off so firm, he was scaring me! Peeking out the corner of the window, a man wearing his pants too high and a hefty woman were coming up the walk. Keeping my eyes glued on them, when they pounded on the door, even though I knew they were there, I nearly jumped out of my skin. Joshua half opened the door and still I would not show my face, instead I moved closer in to listen. Stepping in uninvited, I quickly moved back putting space between us. Gazing around, according to them it was time, but for whatever reason, they gave Joshua an extra thirty minutes to finish up. But who was counting the hours, in my head, a day was a day, but it wasn't the time they were looking for, it was the date and today was that day. The hefty one stood anxious with her arms crossed, showing her authority, making a comment here and there. Thirty minutes goes awfully fast when you still have a room filled with mounds of boxes. Pleading got us nowhere; they just wouldn't go the extra time. In an angry moment I snickered under my breath to Missy, "God, her mouth is almost as big as her butt, but, if you ask me, she's becoming a real ass."

Missy started laughing, just as Joshua yelled. "Come on guys, give it up, let's just get out of here."

Walking towards him, I started to protest, but he interrupted me with a pained look, pushing us along. "Come on damn it, come on, the hell with them just let it go."

The sound of a loud click and it was over and they were now putting the padlocks on over at Missy's. After they left, only a fool wouldn't have run back to try to get back inside and I was no fool. But it was hopeless; the padlock was locked tight in place. Shaking it vigorously, determined to get it to fall off, didn't happen. The lock was strong and all this wasted energy was irritating Joshua enough, that we could hear his attitude loud and clear, right from where we stood. Giving him back some of my own attitude, in spite of his wisdom, he didn't seem to show any intelligence to sensitivity. In my irritation, I told him so and he looked at me amused and with my words falling under my breath, I thought, "Oh Joshua, Joshua, whatever."

"Give it up," Joshua yelled over to us from the front seat of the truck. It was time to go and after waving a flag of surrender, we got in our cars to follow him from behind. Once we got out of the busy section of town, in spite of the weight of the truck, he was sailing way ahead of us, up one winding hill and down another. By the time we were miles away, Simons face began to fad into the distance, while a sense of freedom came over us, no longer feeling chained to him in fear. With Joshua leading the way and not taking any time to stop, we got past the outskirts of cattle farms and oil wells and got into the heart of the small town, faster than we imagined. By the time we were pulling in, Joshua was already out of the truck and lifting up the door of the truck. The breeze in the air felt so refreshing after the long stagnant ride, I took in one long breath of air. In a relaxed state, the comforting feeling of home sweet home, momentary passed through me. Grabbing several cans of root beer out from the cooler, after we drank in thirst, we were eager to get right to work and start unloading. It took no time for Bee, the little girl with red curly hair from next door to come running over to play with Haley and Charity. When her mother, with a brighter shade of red hair, stuck her head out of the window calling out for

Bee, is when we met her. Dolly was her name and her fancy cowboy boots and southern accent, made her come across like a real country gal. After chatting with her with ease, our conversation felt effortless. Offering her a chilled root beer, she just drank in wonder, watching and looking intrigued at our ways and all the activity going on amongst us.

By the time we unloaded the truck, being there was nowhere to move anywhere on the first floor, she left, saying she'd catch us later. Exhausted by now, we had built up quite an appetite. Everyone perked up at the idea of walking across the street to the Plaza, to get something to eat. Walking into one of the two fast food restaurants in town, it only took minutes to realize, it would be hard to go unnoticed here. It was obvious we were not just city folk to them, but new strangers to their town. With every eye on us, we stood out like prunes in a raisin box. Every now and then, someone would look our way and nod their head hello, in a curious gesture. By the time we arrived back to the house, we were nodded out and unsure of our new whereabouts. Rolling my eyes in disbelief at Missy, she appeared just as up in the air about our chances, for any acceptance. Not like Dolly, who welcomed our city ways with open arms and her on going chatter. But the one thing no one could deny, there was peace here, here nature ruled the land. Between all of the peaceful forested areas and running streams, that surrounded us, it took my soul to comfort. But after a long hard day, the kids grabbed a blanket and pillow and claimed their favorite chosen spots to crash. With peace and quiet finally filtering in the air, we relaxed in the moment, before going to our separate sleeping quarters. In the darkness of the night, the harmonized sound of crickets, took me into a deep twilight of sleep.

Bright and early the following morning, we were anxious to get down to serious work, so we spent the day unpacking, arranging and rearranging rooms of furniture. After a late evening dinner of grilled burgers, the place looked more like home, than we could have hoped for, while everyone appeared more relaxed and on a happier note. Now with the beds set up, as the kids slept upstairs in their rooms, we settled in for a movie, munching out on their left over popcorn and snacks. As tired as the day had left us, it wasn't until I crawled into bed and pulled the covers over my head, when Jessie's face began to filter in and out of my uneasy thoughts, stirring my sleep. After a night of tossing, the strong image of him stayed glued to my mind, right up to when the mailman knocked on the door with a certified letter. Having put in a change of address, after signing for it, he handed me a handful of forwarded bills, giving me a crocked smile. Feeling my body heat rise up to my face, once he walked off, I inquisitively peeked out the door, noticing a red truck identical to Jessie's. It was sitting out of place at the end of the plaza and the sound of my heart hammering, was telling me it was he. It had me running in circles for as long as it took to hunt down a jacket, only by the time I got out the door, it was gone. Running to Missy, after swearing that it just had to be him, she responded by breaking down in a flood of tears. Having been through thick and thin and mud and water, the love and care she felt for him, emotionally had done her in.

The red truck returned everyday for the next three days, but it always vanished before I could show my face. It had me going and the next time it appeared, I tore out of the house, like a bat out of hell. Briskly walking towards the plaza, once I got closer to the truck, as the tinted window slid down, suddenly we were face to face. He looked tired and the dark circles under his eyes stood out like shadows. Reaching out, as I gently caressed his face, guilt washed over me, for having spent that lustful night with Joshua, which drove him off. He responded back, by patting the seat next to him and so I walked around the back of the truck and slid in. Silence gripped us! Putting the car in gear, he headed out to look for someplace more private. Spotting an old run down bridge, he pulled off and cut off the engine. Staring silently out to a trail of drying up patches of water a fluttering dragonfly took my attention. Lost in the sound of a bird in the air, Jessie's cracked voice suddenly broke our silence. "Oh baby, I really do love you and I'm so sorry, but I wasn't okay. I have been going crazy searching everywhere for you, I finally got this address from a postman. Honey please, I want to come back, I swear, I'll be stronger."

In spite of having been burnt by his no shows, in relief, my tears let loose, silently crying out his name. "Oh Jessie, Jessie." Just as I turned my face to cover my tears, he came at me energized. "Look baby; look in the back seat I even got myself a job."

As I turned my head and looked back to the rear of his truck, noticing his seats were down, there were two vacuums and a filled cardboard box of attachments. His face beamed back at me with pride, waiting for my response. In disbelief that he would leave the job of his dreams for that, the disappointment he read on my face, left him even more anxious to win my approval. Grabbing a brown briefcase from behind my seat, before he could pull out what he needed and close it, I already saw them. It was too late now to hide the truth, having gotten caught red handed, with a dozen or more scattered condoms in his briefcase. Moving as close to the door as my seat would allow me, feeling stung, his flushed face looked back at me with guilt. Here, after countless times of hiding my own deceit, the shoe was suddenly on the other foot. Melting into his defense. He swore he just bought them to hurt me back. His reckoning softened the blow just enough anyway, to get me to buy into his reasoning faster than he could have sold me a vacuum. His eyes were filled with relief as he shyly cradled me in his arms, whispering sweet and loving promises for the rest of our tomorrows. On the drive back to town, jittery as heck, I talked nonstop, until he came to a stop and silenced me passionately with his lips. Once his mouth left mine, he hoarsely promised to call in a few hours; with a time he would return. Jumping out of his truck like a schoolgirl with her first crush, I ran carefree up the steps. Before I could even get the door open, having been eavesdropping, Missy already had her head out the door, watching as he sped out of sight. The instant she got word he was coming back, she let out a sound of relief. Time ticked, hours passed, sadly mistaken and misled, he never did call nor show his face as he promised, well, what did I expect! In my efforts to reach him, he was unreachable again. But one thing we couldn't put off any longer was finding work. We were taken by surprise, that being the city girls we were; gave us enough leverage to move up to the top of the waiting list, leaving the country girls behind. With next to nothing in this town, guilt gnawed at our joy, when we both landed jobs, not only at the country club in town, but also at the hotel resort. It offered elegant as well as casual dinning, with a fireplace in both dining areas. The locks on the river were the tourist attraction in this town, while the little shops surrounding the hotel, were done up from the nineteen hundreds. While Joshua did a little of this and that to generate cash flow, even the boys landed part-time jobs at both of the fast food joints. It appeared as if any real opportunity to get ahead in this town was locked up, being money was the key. In spite of the children's acceptance among their classmates at school, still we remained friendless. Other than Dolly of course, who stopped in daily to drop off the latest news, traveling around town about us! It was clear from her tidbits of gossip that we were still unaccepted by the town folk and they weren't budging any time soon.

Shortly after our move, Halloween came and passed, before you knew it we were gathered around the table on Thanksgiving, passing around a platter of sliced turkey and all the fixings. In mid December, we cut down a fresh tree in a pine forest and while the lightly covered snow laid on the eve of Christmas, all of the bright lights sparkling in the night, gave us the spirit of Christmas. Once we lived out the holidays, in spite of the cold winter being at its peak, we couldn't help but settle in cozy. With a warm crackling fire, burning most of the winter, we just ignored the town folk's gossip. This big old house definitely held plenty of positive energy to help us heal, but the strange occurrences in-between, surely raised the hairs on our arms. But while you slept in a deep-rooted sleep, you dreamt and when you woke, you would awake with the true reality of where you were in life.

It was also in the peak of winter, when Joshua learned his penny stocks had taken off and it looked as if the tables were turning. Seeing that they had grown, everything in life began to change, starting with Jessie, having mailed him some cash. Trying to pull himself together, by now, he was staying with one of his old friends. It was a number of things that had lifted his spirits; starting with this guy he met who had just started his own limo service. Jessie went on about him and all the opportunity that this guy had offered him, defining him as kick-ass remarkable. Once he told me he invested in his company, he ignored my suspicious comments, angrily hanging up. No word came back from him and in anger, I arranged for a few days off to go and find him. With Missy naturally on my side and just enough cash in my bag for the road trip, I was on my way to where my heart still lived. If the thought of seeing him heated up my blood, the anger pumping through me, kept my heart from fluttering.

The closer I got to what was once home, the more regretful I became for driving so far unexpectedly in such a suspicious state, just to track him down. Walking up the walk, one thing or another began to look familiar from our visits, back in the day. Breathing with anxiety, I knocked on the door, not once, but several times and still no one answered. After facing it that he just wasn't there, I headed back to my car, parked on the street, slid in and just waited. With time, I needed to use a bathroom, so I left and stopped off at a coffee shop and afterwards, I bought a black coffee and picked up a love story magazine off the rack. Engrossed in a story about a wife who nurtured her ill husband back to health, after reading through the book for another hour, I scanned through the rest of the happy endings, wondering why I read such crap. Putting the book to rest back on the shelf, I returned back, parking in the same spot. By then it was getting late and the house sat dark, but I knocked anyway. Still with no answer, as I sat waiting in my car, a steady stream of chunky white snowflakes began to fall, covering the branches and rooftops, shimmering in the moonlight. Even with my car pumping out heat, my feet felt cold and it felt spooky sitting alone, with only the moon and the eerie shadows of the night to keep me company. Well after dark, I dozed off and awoke to the same sun rising that was just going down when I arrived. Looking up the driveway, still there was no sign of his truck and I began to wonder what he was up to and if he told me the truth about where he was staying. Before my mind had a chance to wander any further out of control, his truck appeared out from nowhere and was sitting parallel to me. When his tinted window went down, his eyes revealed his shock at my unannounced visit. He held his hand up for me to hold on, then pulled his truck up into the driveway. As he walked back down the smooth surfaced drive towards me, he was wearing a different look from his face down to the way he carried himself. Noticing he was wearing a nice jersey under his open black leather jacket, with a sharp scarf loosely hanging, zapped me with jealousy. Opening my door, as he reached for me with this cool, carefree manner thing going on, after a miserable night stuck inside the car, my inflamed attitude took his smile down. Staring at one another without any passion in our hearts, he came back at me in defense claiming, he couldn't possibly have known I was coming, since I showed without so much as dropping a dime.

"Damn it Jessie, call, you expect me to call, you never answer any of my calls!"

His face fell deeper into anger and we argued all the way into the house, before we both went for the throat. After throwing one insult after another at each another, it came to an abrupt end, with us crying in each other's arms. In those next spills of tears, deserving or not, Jessie offered his forgiveness, for the night I spent with Joshua. But instead of feeling relief, it left me cringing with guilt, knowing soul-to-soul Joshua and I were still strongly connected. Pushing the guilt away, we needed to make sense out of the mess we had made of our lives. We needed to figure out a way to piece it back together, before it was too late. Putting on a pot of coffee, Jessie walked over to the cupboard and took out two white mugs. Black, we drank it black, yet, he sat stirring his coffee with a teaspoon, around and around. Watching him, he was miles away and it was obvious something heavy was weighting on him. Noticing I was monitoring him, he grabbed on to my hand and began to lure me towards the door. "Come on baby, come with me, I want to show you something. It's fantastic, wait until you see, you'll be so proud."

He was pulling me outside towards the garage, reminding me to keep my eyes closed until he gave me the okay. The sound of the garage door opened and before Jessie could say the word, my eyes were already staring at an older model silver corvette. Looking from Jessie's twinkling eyes, then at the corvette convertible I got chocked up "Is it yours?" Sensing my shock and disproval, he was quick to step up to the plate defending his grounds. "It's an investment, can't you see that? I'll damn near double my money in just a few months. Besides, it's nearly paid for and the balance, well it's a family thing, okay?"

Stuttering, "But, but why?"

He didn't answer, but he didn't have to, not with the money tied up. Obviously he went ahead with his plans and of course it never entered my mind, that he might have any. Not even after he had spelled it out that he invested some cash, with this so called remarkable guy he mentioned. It all left me so unsettled that my mind began to scramble from one feeling to another. Running my fingers through my hair, with my emotions tangled up in frustration and anger, I snapped out, "I can't take anymore, no more, no more, no more!"

That's all it took for his finger to come back at me with blame, throwing Joshua back in my face. Squirming in our discomfort, we gave each other nothing, but a handful of bull excuses. Shaking my head in defeat, things were going nowhere and nothing we said at this point made a difference and we were silenced. Once Jessie walked me to my car, he only held me long enough to pacify me. Once he broke from me, I kept my lips sealed to avoid quizzing him for a time he would return home. With words so lost between us, after he gave me a faint smile, he turned and walked away. It was a bad emotional place to be left, a bad place on a long lonely ride back home with too much time to realize, that Jessie appeared to be doing great without me and no longer needed me. Believing in my heart, without need, he wouldn't love me, left me disoriented. It was a care-giving trap that I undeniably was chained too. By the time the bright headlights were coming up from behind, I was back in the heart of town. Barely getting up the steps, Missy stuck her head out the door whispering that Morgan was waiting on the phone. Taking my attorney's call, past a hello, he got right to the point. Having had a consultation with Jessie, he voiced his concerns to the damage his reckless actions could do to our chapter thirteen, that we had somehow managed to keep in tact. He emphasized the need for me to get him home, before disaster met up with him. It didn't seem possible that he was talking about the same carefree Jessie, I saw only hours ago. Frankly to me, it sounded like a bunch of malarkey. In spite of his chilling warning, I pushed it to the back of my mind and anger for that silver corvette ate away at me. Blaming his corvette instead of Jessie made me resent every other sports car I had ever laid eyes on, as I sat dwelling on the porch.

Now that the last of the snow had fallen, we got through another season in one piece, moving past the snowstorms and icy roads. While living in this old house surrounded by its comfort, it was doing its job of nurturing us emotionally back to health. Ever since the warmer weather began to push its way in, with spring in the air and Jessie's calls coming in less frequent, he caught me off guard when he called to say he was on his way over. He was all keyed up and in a hurry to get off the phone. Determined to get his attention, after hunting for my prettier blouse, when Missy saw it she gave a goofy whistle, as if to say it looked good. Carefully putting on the finishing touches to look my best, the mirror was reflecting the added pounds all the hours of worry, had added to my figure. Dressed ahead of plan, during the hour we were to meet, being as perfect of a day as it was, I sat waiting on the porch for his arrival. Lost in my own world, while watching the activity at the plaza, a silver corvette with the top down came speeding down the street, coming to a long screeching halt. Grabbing my attention, it was definitely Jessie's silver corvette; only he wasn't in the driver's seat. Instead a well-dressed guy got out of the driver's side, wearing a snazzy black silk shirt. Casually holding on to the top of the car door, as he stretched out his long legs, his fingers flashed a series of sparkles from his diamond rings. It was hard not to notice that he was good looking, confident and with out a doubt, was full of himself. Vacant of a smile, he intimidated me on the spot. His eyes soberly glared my way, as if I were a misfit, instead of Jessie's wife. Noticing Jessie as he got out of the car, he had on the same black leather jacket and silk scarf around his neck, as the last time I saw him. Standing tall with a luring aura, he looked fabulous and with all his confidence shinning through, next to him I felt plain and simple. As this guy got back into the car to wait, Jessie chatted briefly, wanting to meet with me over at the fast food joint. No sooner did he put his lips on mine, the sound of the horn took his attention back over to the guy, who by now was pointing to his watch. Jessie quickly reacted, taking it as a cue to get a move on. Zooming away in the two-seater, as I walked across the street to meet with them, I was trying to figure out who the hell this creep was and why he was the one driving Jessie's corvette.

Walking towards them, they got out of the car at the same time and seconds later, they both grabbed for the restaurant door. With both of them seated next to a window, I slid in across from this guy, giving him a bland smile. Attempting to get serious, they had to struggle to stop their laughter and making stupid jokes, while my painful irritation was bleeding through. It was somewhere in between their corny jokes and laughter, when Jessie introduced this guy. The second he told me his name, I half opened up my mouth without a voice, feeling swindled. "Oh, so this was that kick-ass remarkable guy, that got Jessie to invest in his limo business."

His name was Santana and again placing the blame on him, it appeared as if he had already corrupted Jessie. Their gestures were identical; it was almost as if Jessie had gone out and gotten himself cloned as this kick-ass remarkable guy. Our attorney's warning came to mind and I could only shudder. "So this is where Jessie's new face and happy-go-lucky attitude came from."

Checking him out, you could tell he had heard some hearsay about me, obviously from somewhere. It left me thinking plenty hard as I eyed them, just watching and listening, trying to catch what they were up to. Ignoring my presence, Santana's eyes stood out as he began to toy with the town. "Hey wow, this is some exciting moo town. It's exciting as hell, don't you think Jessie?"

I was uninterested in what he had to say; quite frankly I was board stiff. Ignoring him back with attitude, he seemed higher on himself than drugs. But with my opinion of him on the x rated chart, I stared him down cold, dropping the temperature of air sitting between us. Seeing that Santana had convinced Jessie, our losses could bring us more tax dollars, he had a fancy ink pen and the papers ready for me to sign. Trying to talk to Jessie, without Santana butting in and coaching him along, only got me up in arms enough to scribble my name on the form and walk out. Jessie came running out after me, claiming, all his efforts were for us. It would have softened me up, if Santana didn't give me a mean dagger as he walked past and got back into the driver's seat. Staring at Jessie in disbelief, he made his own statement, after he worked his way over to his car and got in. Looking over at me with a plea in his eyes not to make a scene, I declined. In spite of the extra pair of ears in the driver's seat, I let out my dislike for Santana, "What the hell are you doing with this control freak, he's got you by the balls Jessie, lose him, he's nothing but a gold digger."

"Honey, come on, we're in business together."

Pulling away, he only fought my resistance off for less than a minute, before letting go of my arms. Having been sitting there all ears, Santana didn't waist a minute, before he tore off leaving a trail of burning rubber behind. Gazing down the street at nothing but a cloud of smoke floating up midair, I could only pray this wouldn't hit the town news. Crying on Missy's shoulder, after she classified Santana as nothing but a real ass-wipe, she left the room, returning with a box of Kleenex and two cups of steaming coco. Desperately needing a friend, once again, the indebtedness of her friendship moved me. It wasn't until the lights were off, when my frustration and anger came to life and I got lost in a one-man pity party. All that silenced my sobs was the fluffy bed pillow that was pushed up in my face. Five am came and went and with six am and the sound of the birds I knew sure as hell I would be worthless for the remainder of the day. Hating everything that Jessie stood for at that moment, this time Santana received the blame for the second time.

Memorial Day weekend was approaching; it was hard to believe that only three seasons had passed since we moved out from our dream house. Somehow Joshua had managed to get his hands on tickets for a Memorial Day, baseball game. When he held them out to the kids with a gleam in his eye, just the idea of driving back home to where friends and family lived, had everyone jabbering. Gathered around the table, we planned out the day in excitement, down to the last hour we would be there. Everyday for the next two weeks we lived on cloud nine. On the morning of the game it didn't matter that it was cloudy or that it was drizzling, all that mattered was that we would soon be on our way to visit familiar and loved territory. Anxious to get an early start, by midmorning we planned on making our breakfast, an early lunch instead. Planning to take our packed up meal, to eat on the drive, we all pitched in, making cheeseburgers and a batch of fries. While Joshua got out the cooler and iced it down for the drinks and condiments for the burgers, the boys kept an eye on the grill. While Mae insisted on frying up the fries that were sizzling in a pan of grease on the stovetop, after lecturing her to be careful, she did good, beaming proud. By the time the pans and cooking utensils were rinsed and stacked in the sink, waiting for our return to be washed, Joshua grabbed the cooler and we were off. Just as we stepped out the door, I realized I forgot to take the whole chicken out of the freezer. With everyone running ahead, I stepped back in and pulled the chicken out, placing it on the counter to thaw for tomorrow's dinner. Turning the bolt on the lock, once we began to pile into Joshua's truck, the boys claimed the seats in the back of the truck. Halfway to the stadium, the sun came out with the temperature sitting near perfect. With traffic moving consistently in our favor, we had time before the game, to stop and view the lake from up on the fishing pier. Our seats were great, our team celebrated their victory and with our bellies full from dogs and cracker jacks, we exited out of the park and dropped my children off one by one at their friends. With both of our families less than a mile away, we headed over to pay them a quick visit. The time went way too fast and before you knew it, we were picking up my children. With Haley and Charity asleep, we kept our finger to our lips at every stop, as one by one the children climbed back into the truck.

On the ride back to town, everyone was tired and other than the sound of passing cars, you could have heard a pin drop. Lost in thought, it was at mother's house where I had no luck reaching Jessie. Having heard he was down again, kept my mind preoccupied for most of the ride home. Once we pulled back into town my thoughts cleared when Joshua said he needed cigarettes; suddenly I was aware he had stopped off at a corner deli. In the short time he was gone, a van filled with a number of kids, pulled up along side of us, yelling out loud enough to get our attention. We all looked over at the same time to see what the uproar was all about. While Brad was the first one to say "Hey," young Dex only half waved. Assuming both of the boys knew them, took my interest off of them. But just as Joshua came walking out from the store, all the kids began laughing and yelling over one another out the window at him, "Excuse me sir, sir, excuse me, have you been at home yet." Joshua gave them back a weird annoying look, answering, "No, why?"

Backing up their van, they busted out in more laughter, "Oh you'll find out!"

Joshua started to react; only Missy spoke up in annoyance over him, "So what's up with your idiot friends; do they always act like such jerks?" Brad shrugged his shoulders, "Hey, they aren't my friends." Young Dex was quick to jump in. "Hey, I don't know them kids either, so don't blame me."

Blowing them off to being just the town's kids, Joshua backed up and headed for home, cutting in and out of the side streets. It took less than five minute to get there, but it took less time to smell the heavy smoke in the air. As we got closer to our house and the plaza, two fire trucks with their lights flashing bright came into our view. It didn't take but a moment for it to sink in, that dear God, they were at our house! Having realized it was our house that could be on fire, our loud outbursts woke the girls from their sleep. We couldn't get out of the truck fast enough, yelling back to the boys to stay put. But they didn't listen and followed us from behind, as we ran for the house. Two firemen stood in our path blocking us with their arms out, "Woo now, take it easy, its okay, the fire is out."

Looking past them, up past the tall trees that shaded the second floor, some of the windows had been blown out and sections of the old shingle siding looked scorched black. Missy stared voiceless, leaning back against one of the trees, sobbing. When the fireman told us it looked as if it had started on the stovetop, Mae began to cry in hysterics, insisting it was her fault. Soothing her at that moment brought her no comfort, while the boys stood in quiet shock. The Police Chief and some lady representing the Red Cross were the first ones to approach us. While several neighbors were already gathered around, they watched inquisitively, as we pleaded to go in to see the damage. Knowing our emergency cash was secretly stashed in the cupboard, no matter how much we begged to go back in to get our valuables, the Fire Marshal refused and wouldn't budge. After claiming with no electricity, it would be dangerous with all the debris and broken glass lying around, he stood firm to his decision. Looking over to Joshua to argue him down, I never saw him so slumped over and immobilized to protect our family. Numbness replaced my strength and the voices in the air now sounded miles away, but the sound of the clap of thunder in the distance and the bright flashes of lightning was enough to put the fear of God in me. With a storm brewing in the air, the Chief assured us that they would immediately board the windows to guard against theft and water damage. Once they carried the stove top out for inspection, the assistant from the Red Cross handed Joshua one hundred dollars for every family member and several packets of food vouchers to get us through. On her last note, she gave us the name and the address of the motel where they were putting us up for a number of weeks. If only one more thing could have added to my misery, it was the six-room motel we were assigned to. It was unbelievable; just unreal, here, it was the same motel where Joshua and I had fallen and tumbled in the sheets. It was also the same day, when we were on top of the world, after having found the wonderful old house. Driving to the end of town, who ever would have thought in our despair, it would bring us right back here to square one. Expecting us, we only had to sign our names, while the old desk clerk rambled on, never taking any notice to Joshua or me.

In spite of the hard times we had been through, in fear of the unknown abundance of our loss, we were left staggering on our feet and emotionally crippled. When we began to speculate about our options, after going back and forth in argument, it got laid to rest when we refused to talk to one another. Scrambling to get settled in, with one bed in every room, Joshua bunked with the boys, Missy with her girls and me with Mae. Poor child, she emotionally exhausted herself and after stroking her hair for a spell, she went out like a light. Not wanting to wake her, I slipped out of bed, stripped down and got in the shower. Even the hot running water couldn't generate any warmth or comfort to wash away the fear ripping at me. Instead, flashing memories of that heated night with Joshua lingered in my head, for as long as I let it. Once I stepped out from the shower and dried off, I slipped into the same clothes and sank down into the chair, next to the red heavy draped window. The memories of the lustful night in this motel, was only adding another ration of guilt to my plate, bringing to mind Jessie's pained face and how it ran him off. The thunder was back and this time it was loud enough to shake the sky. When the rains came, it was a downpour. The sound of the rain hitting hard against the window, left me praying that they had boarded up the windows by now, fearing the worst if they hadn't. Sometime in the night I drifted off where I sat. The following morning the rain was still pouring down. Planning to work at the house bright and early, with everyone hungry, we first went into town to catch the early bird special. It was crowded and we were eyed the second we all gathered in. Getting into our seats, the town breakfast crowd kept looking our way, yet no one spoke a word, at least not to us. Once we finished, we began to move back our chairs from the table, making enough noise to let everyone know we were leaving.

Once we got to the house, the Fire Marshal and a pickup truck sitting with several sheets of plywood was there. Shocked, all the windows still sat open; nothing had been boarded up. Sick at the thought of all that rain pouring in all night, as I turned to Joshua, he gave me a dazed stare and said nothing! Being we had to wait before we were allowed back in, until they could determined how the fire started, left us worrying about leaving our valuables in the open house. Feeling as if we had no say or control over our lives, we headed back to the motel. It was later in the day when Missy and I called work to request some time off, only to hear, not only was the word out, but our shifts were already covered too. It wasn't until evening, when we could finally drive to the plaza to pick up some items with the money from the Red Cross. When we were finished, in spite of only getting the bare essentials and several 99-cent bushel baskets for our belongings, the register tape read well over our allotted amount. Day by day as our cash was dwindling down, our stress was mounting up. After arguing Joshua down to his limit, in his anger, he didn't want to talk about it; he didn't want to talk about anything. In my unstable frame of mind, as I stomped out, I threatened to take myself out. Heading to a small diner near the motel, it took less time than it took the server to pour my coffee, to realize, that every eye in the place was on my tear stained face. Staring angrily, getting up I threw a dollar on the table and gave silent daggers to every eye I met on my way out. Heading for the woods, the breeze quickly began to cool my scorched mood. Sliding down against a rock, paying no mind to the patches of damp moss, the sound of nature was tweaking in and out of the silence all around me. When Jessie's vision came into my head, still not being able to reach him, this time in my anger it was him that I blamed and I cursed him loud enough, for my voice to travel on for miles.

Getting up to my feet, having mellowed, I brushed off the dried foliage and started walking. From further away, I could make out Joshua's image, sitting down under a tree, smoking a cigarette. As his face slowly came into focus, his faint smile had relief written all over it. For a moment I felt myself falling into him and quickly pulled back, as if I were stung. Joshua yes Joshua, he still held the power to move all of me and it took a couple of days to shake him off my mind. But it took seven scorching, record-breaking days, for word to come in, that the wiring in the stovetop was faulty and we were allowed to return back into the house. When we first arrived, Dolly came running over and after delivering the latest news; she offered to let the girls come and play with Bee while we went in. Opening the sliding glass door, it was like a hotbox and the horrible smell of heavy smoke hit us in the face. Starting to step in, Joshua told us to wait, as he ran out to his truck, returning back with a spotlight, running the cord back from Dolly's place. From where we were standing, we didn't need light to see the horror of it all! Stepping in over shattered glass, on the counter, the whole chicken we left to thaw, sat with hundreds of maggots feasting on its remains. All of our stashed cash from our stocks, which was hidden far back in the cupboard, was still there. A strong wave of relief set in, having discussed how much that money would help us to save ourselves. Joshua reached into the tin can and stuffed the wad of bills down into his pockets, mumbling under his breath, "Thank God."

Staring over at all our beautiful, destroyed, oak dining room and living room furniture, my children ran ahead with their flashlights, in spite of our warning. Soggy pictures, smelly bedding and toasted electronics, nothing much made it through; everything was coated in smoke or covered in wet black soot. It was the same story on the second floor, where the children stood in shock, with their flashlight's dangling from their fingers. Between the hoses that were dragged in and the windows that never got boarded up, the clothes still hanging in the closet or sitting in the drawers reeked from smoke and mildew. Having seen enough, we were sick at heart and just had to get out of there. Grabbing Joshua's coin collection and our jewelry, we headed back to the dreary motel. With Jessie having taken up my brain space, I was a fool again, for having failed to call Mike our agent to get insurance, pretty much sums it up. Being Joshua took out his own small policy; the adjuster came back at him after walking through, offering next to nothing, without receipts. It was all adding up to more misery and more loss. Nothing made any sense and after begging, than threatening for just one more week at the motel, getting nowhere, we had to turn it over to an adjuster. Weeks, they said it could be weeks, even months. Just the cost of the removal and clean up was so far out of our reach; we had no choice but to do the clean up ourselves. We rented a thirty-foot dumpster and pulled it as close to the house as it would allow. Jumping over the waterlogged grass, past the singed shrubbery growing against the house, it showed its own loss. In the depressed hours ahead, we all worked sorting, tossing and crying, occasionally stopping to blow the black soot out from our noses.

Covered in black from head to toe by the end of the day with soot having settled into all our crevasses, we scrubbed our skin until it was pink again. It wasn't courage that gave us the strength to go on, it was either keep going or lie down and die. With the dumpster just about full with all of our belongings, we gave up trying to save the impossible. Seeing some of the town folks looking on, was one thing, but trying to return to work was useless, so we picked up our last checks as they became available. With our time up at the motel and the house cleaned out, we had nothing left here in this town. Looking around one last time, with everything out, the house was literally gutted. Along side of our belongings and our cherished possessions, gone were the peaceful feelings that had nurtured us back to health. Out of time, out of everything, it was over! And in our despair, we were convinced; this time, we were surely doomed! Here we were more injured now, than when we had arrived at the old house. Since this sleepy town didn't want anything to do with us, except to bring us into their conversation, we didn't even have to be rich or famous, to discover who are friends were. There were no casseroles delivered to the motel in our time of need. Beyond stares and pointing fingers, no kind words ever did come our way. Their on going cruel remarks made us believe, that getting burned out to them, meant that we would be driven away and our jobs would be back up for grabs. In this small town, white wasn't white and black wasn't black and nothing was as it seemed. This town was closed-minded to change period. If anyone cared, it was lost in resentment that we were there in the first place. What was once important and crucial to our wellbeing was unsalvageable. It was more sad than heartless, because as we drove off with our bushel baskets and as little as we managed to salvage, we never looked back.

PASSAGE XVIII

I'll Cry Tomorrow

When the clock stops and the seconds begin and you feel the earth move within…you're now on your way for what's to begin. It was too late the second you didn't hesitate. All within my heart and soul I felt out of control…to all of me to all I shall be.

Headed back to where we once called home is the direction we set out for. Once we were back on familiar ground, it was another motel for us, then another. Only being on our own, our funds were dwindling down fast. With record-breaking temperatures soaring, the out door pool and nearby playground, kept the sanity and temperaments cool amongst the children. But it was next to impossible to keep our moods in tack, when we didn't know where any of our tomorrows would be lived out. The fire had done its destruction, having charred Joshua's pride for not being able to fend for his shared family. Now with his emotions all over the place, he was like a walking time bomb, set to go off. Seeing that both Joshua and I carried a very potent energy, whether it was in strength or in our meltdowns, with both of our fuses ready to blow, we were at each other's throat in one way or another. In the hours we had our heads together, no matter how hard we tried to come up with a solution, money, money and more was the main ingredient missing, leaving us with the fear of homelessness. Gone were those days of sitting around a table laughing with confidence, planning out our lives to perfection. Gone were a lot of things. We truly believed that everything in our life was gone or had been destroyed. Yet little did we know that the word everything, was only a far cry away. But time doesn't wait for anyone and our time to stay on at this motel finally ran its course. With our pockets nearly empty, we checked out in the heat of the day, not knowing where we would lay our heads that night.

Riding around was one thing we did a lot of that day, searching and praying for something, anything to spring up and save us from going down the rest of the way. It was less than a mile from where our dream house stood, with its family of oak trees still standing, when everyone's bellies began to growl. In all my anguish I didn't know if I hated the idea of being so near to something so far, or whether or not it brought me comfort, to be so close to something I had loved and lost. When Joshua stopped off at the fast food chain I had often gone to during our busy dream house moments, I was the one nominated to go in. With my attitude being as such, I was walking like a zombie, not watching where I was going, when I ran right smack into David. It was a shocker, you remember Georgette, his ex? In spite of all the nudie cutie pictures of me he had carried around for years, his face immediately lifted me up. Wow, I hadn't seen him since Dexter and I had called it quits. Overwhelmed at seeing one another, we were anxious to chat and moved away from the hungry line of traffic. In spite of not having seen each other for ages, we hugged like it was yesterday. It was so very good to see someone who cared, after the town folk and I told him so. In delight, we were both talking at the same time and in a quick summery, a lot of things had apparently changed for both of us. Even as he still lived in the same house with the same tree, with oodles of its fallen buckeyes, his hair was no longer spiked up way cool. Instead it laid flat against his head, with straight bangs, outlining his plastic, black glasses. But he was still tugging at his belt, bringing a genuine smile too my lips. In those brief moments, it felt so good and safe to be back on familiar territory. When he heard about the fire and our losses, he would hear no more, we were going to stay with him for as long as needed. Refusing to hear another word, that was that. By the time we hugged goodbye, as I ordered the food, there was such an overpowering relief in me that I could have dropped to my knees to thank God, right there in front of everyone. Instead I dashed outside to where everyone was waiting on the food and me. Opening the door, if Joshua was thinking about crabbing, for taking so long, something stopped him, because the moment he took notice to my tears, his irritation melted into pure compassion. Before anyone even had a chance to start complaining of starving, David, the buckeye tree, a place to regroup, came barreling out of my mouth, without a breather. Somewhere in my relief and my tears of gratitude, Missy's tears let go, expressing her appreciation. But even as Joshua said nothing, I would have sworn that he wiped his eyes, as he turned his face away. It would be a long day, having to kill the rest of the afternoon and early evening, since we had to wait to meet up with David, until the end of his factory shift. In a calm state, the rest of the day for us was amazing. We took in everything that nature had to offer, from the lake that cooled us, to the campfire where we roasted hot dogs and marshmallows. It was also amazing how mellow we got with one another; just knowing we had a place to lay our heads. With a breeze and feeling the vibration from the planes above my head, I stood there with my hair-flying wild, feeling as free as a bird. It just seemed as if one good thing after another, was falling effortlessly into our laps. When Dex and Brad left the park for a time, they came back with the news that they could stay with their grandparents, to help take the load off of David's invitation.

Hours later, beat from the sun, we packed it up and were on our way to David's. Pulling into his driveway, the big old buckeye tree, with lots of loved memories that had grown with it, instantly caught my eye. Other than his place being run down, with chipping paint and overgrown foliage, it looked the same. Walking up the cement walk, memories walked with me to the same door that Georgette, back in the day, had angrily slammed behind me. It was a Dexter moment, remembering how they had rolled in the hay together with lust. Knocking on the wooden door, within minutes, the white lacy curtain on the beveled glass moved and David's smiling face came into vision. Straightening his glasses, he unlatched and opened the door wide enough, for us all to gather in with our bushel baskets. After a small lecture for the boys to behave for their grandparents, once they drove off, David began showing Missy and Joshua around. It had been so long since I had been at David's; I had forgotten his house only had two small bedrooms upstairs. Past David's room, we gave the girls the other bedroom. We would be sharing the living room, alternating sleeping on his red and black couch. It was definitely going to be a lot less space to breathe in, with a lot less privacy. Even in my relief, having gone from living in the roomy old house, down to the dingy six-room motel, it was obvious we were going nowhere but downhill, in size and comfort. It was hard to brush off that hollow feeling gnawing at me, as I watched David carry out a tray of pop for the kids and cocktails for us. Good old David was so giving and good, asking us for nothing back.

Joining him for another drink, we all took another cocktail and freshly cut lime from his tray, while he reassured us that we were welcome to stay as long as we needed. Having opened his home to us, it was plain to see that he was truly living in a man's world, with no sign of a woman's touch anywhere. Noticing I was observing his place, David was quick to defend the stacked up dishes and his lack of vacuuming. He didn't have to say another word, by the time we finished our cocktails it was decided. Besides insisting that we would take care of his laundry and do all of the cooking, we maintained that we would take care of everything for him and be his personal maids. This time it was us, who would not take no for an answer and that was that. His face filled up with self-importance and in celebration of his new family and laughable maid-service; with the tray empty, as he got up to go fix another cocktail, he looked back, offering us another. Declining on the next few offers, it was late. It had been a long day and with the girls already down for the night, we were just waiting on David to call it a night so that we could crash. That first night, with the lights out and the sound of us breathing in and out, I let out a breath of relief. A great relief flowed through me, that we were out of the motel and back on homeland, to begin to rebuild what was left of our tattered life. In the cramped days ahead, the simple freedom to turn in at your leisure or use the bathroom in a timely manner was everything we'd once taken for granted. Everything! Everything, it's a powerful word, a word that holds no end and no beginning, yet, it means everything and still we had not lost what the true meaning of everything, meant to us.

One day led into another, then, we were all working, doing a little of everything, saving every penny for our stepping stone out of David's and into our own place. Staying true to our word, we did all that we promised, and not a day would go by, when David's face didn't shine in celebration, enjoying his cocktails every evening, along with all the attention we gave him. It was hard not to notice, he stopped off more nights than not, for a few, but still he remained the respectful friend he was, sometimes slipping into a silent trance. It was one afternoon when we were down stairs doing his laundry, when we saw it. Off in the far corner of the basement, Missy moseyed over, to check out a big refrigerator box overflowing with toys. There were tons of awesome toys for little tots. Near the box, a Christmas tree sat with strands of shiny tinsel, left dangling on the branches. There was plenty of evidence to know that there was some weird mystery to this story and we began to dig into the box. Standing off to the right of Missy, she was rapidly going through the box like there was no tomorrow, tossing everything she checked out on top of my sorted pile. It didn't take long for her curiosity to get the best of her. "Why do you think these were left down here, in a box like this, but why would David leave all these new toys in a damp mildewed basement?"

Wow, I don't know Missy, but look at all these neat toys, look trucks, cars, a spinning top and look at these beautiful baby dolls, man your not kidding, its unbelievable that anyone would just leave them down here like this."

Our curiosity eventually got the best of both of us and we spent the rest of the afternoon, as we starched and pressed David's shirts, whispering among ourselves. By the time we could come up with a hundred and one explanations, we had the unexplained bunk beds up where the girls slept, included in on our list of concerns. That evening, because she beat me to the punch, it was Missy who confronted David when he came in late, having stopped off for cocktails. She was staring at him and waiting on his answer, as if she had just asked him for nothing more than the time. He was definitely feeling no pain, at least not before Missy opened her mouth and let it all out, the box of toys, the bunk beds, what she forgot to point out in question, I covered. If we could have thrown him for a loop, I guess we did just that by being so darn nosey. He was not prepared for that and he began to tear up. Nudging Missy, I gave her an eye rolling for making David cry. Opening her mouth, I knew she was giving me back her look of "Well, what did I do," before she turned her attention back to him. He was still wiping at his eyes, when he identified his tears with the toys and his three-year-old twins, a boy and girl he had lost sight of, after their mother fled out of the state. In a lost moment of emotion, after he cried out that he had searched for them for a few years and finally gave up; he shook his head back and forth in defeat. He rambled on in tears and whether it was the liquor he needed, or the numbness to help him let go of the pain, he raised himself out of the chair to pour a drink, squeeze a lime and began to stir it with his finger asking, "Want one?"

Shaking my head no, suddenly my mood crashed, because it all seemed so heartless and unfair. Suddenly I understood why David buried himself in cocktails and why his home, never really seemed like a home to him. Home, where his buckeye tree stood as the entrance up the driveway to his palace. God, I wanted to cry my eyes out for him, really I did, only, there was nowhere to bawl in private, except for the bathroom and Mae was bathing. Needing some air, I walked outside going over to the buckeye tree and slid down against the trunk, gazing up past the sky out to the stars, feeling the void in David's heart for the loss of his children.

It took nearly a month before I could get Jessie's mother to clue me in to Jessie's whereabouts and to track him down. Here, he was searching for me when he saw the full dumpster, just as it was being hauled off with a lifetime of all our belongings. Having felt the impact of our loss, he began to fear the worst, having been left with the unknown to our disappearance. By the time we met up, past our tears and sorrow for our losses, Jessie was back to earth, Santana was out and his silver corvette never cruised into our conversation. Jessie expressed his love and relief that I was on home ground, leaving us still hopeful for a future together. Adding to our hope, Jessie just started a new job as a salesman and appeared to be adapting. His face shined with pride, as he handed me the number to the store, in case I needed to reach him. In spite of knowing everyone had labeled all of our hopes and pipe dreams as pure lunacy, well? Okay maybe they were right to over see and judge, but what if they were wrong! But it wouldn't do any good for us to cry over spilled milk or for the loss of our dream house, which in reality was just that, a dream that turned into a real living nightmare. During the times when Jessie was up, we had purpose, when he was down, we wouldn't talk for days. In spite of having no space to move and constantly breathing down one another's throats, I don't think we had a minute to forget what we were up against. Just the thought of snuggling into our own beds, with our very own blankets, made our hearts grow with determination. We hit garage sales every chance we had, setting our finds, right next to the big box of toys, downstairs in the basement. A mysterious box it was and I couldn't tell you what it was about that big box of toys; that held our interest or why it pulled us in. But one day, it will symbolize the great importance of, "The power of one!"

But we continued to work hard towards our stepping-stone to get our own place, then months after our arrival, it finally happened. Basically, it was in the same way in which we found the big old house, just driving around past the cattle farms and winding hills. Driving all over the city this time, it was a moving truck again, that tipped us off. In one way, it was another small town. Only it was really only a small section of town, which was located inside of the big city. It would have to be nothing short of a miracle, to find something to accommodate all of us; with the limited cash we had saved. That it was, a miracle! It was a true gift from God that we didn't have to come up with any rehearsed answers to get approved with a move in date. Saying goodbye to David, after he helped to carry the last of all the garage sale boxes up from his basement, was a tearjerker for us all. After promising we would stay in touch and pay him back for all his hospitality, once the adjuster came through, we were off to our new place. Only a year and a half had passed since this journey began, but it felt like a lifetime in our lessons learned.

Pulling up to the narrow driveway, it was a small rundown double house, which was quite the opposite of the big calming house, we had adapted to. This place, only had two small bedrooms and one bathroom, but it would give us more space to breathe. Yet, there was excitement in the air as we washed and put away our garage sale dishes, eager to have a nice family dinner at our long folding table. Having given the children the bedrooms to divide-up, we were still confined to one room, so again we took turns sleeping on our new comfy couch. It was closeouts and more closeouts all the way and the place was feeling as homey as one could expect. Although, there were those times, when sleeping on the hard floor and pounding on the bathroom door to get in, left me to wondering, if we were ever going to climb out of this slump. Friends, we had no friends past David, so we didn't need to worry about pride or shame, for being stuffed in together like a can of sardines. If anything the household upstairs, filled with numerous people, running above our heads and shaking our ceilings, set us at ease. With no one around talking about us and judging our every move, we had no worries about where we laid our heads.

The very first time we saw the young adults and all the children from upstairs, is when they were laughing and piling into their rusted van and backing out on four bald tires. Soon enough we learned in their struggle to survive, they grouped together to provide for their children. It was sad for as much as their struggle became our inspiration, their way of life for us, was a constant reminder to keep working, to escape from poverty. If we were judgmental, like we were, it was just that they were living examples, of what I feared the most. "That we would give up on ourselves."

With everyone working, life was moving at ease and when the adjuster called to inform us, it was time to settle with the insurance company, life took a positive turn for us. It wasn't the world in which we received. But we figured after we sent David a check in the mail and paid Daddy back, we would have enough to scrape up a small down on a house and get those beds we had been dreaming about. Between all of us working we began to search for a house by driving up one street and down the next. Again, we spotted a big moving truck. It was almost comical, just the way everything fell into our laps in the same way. It was a two family home, in our price range and everything about it from the rooftop to the garage, needed a makeover. Reminding us of his contracting skills, Joshua made it sound so simple and affordable, that he sold us on the idea of this fix me up deal. It would definitely be a challenge and while we had to wait with crossed fingers, we did just that, praying for this break. It only added to all our good fortune, when the call came in that I had landed a job bartending. Just the fact that I would be starting in a few days left me rejoicing for all the positive changes that were coming our way.

Once we sent David his check, he was nothing but grateful, but daddy's letter was returned twice unopened. It was enough to get me thinking and I was all over it and on my way in no time. On the ride there, my nerves were doing its damage to my gut, it had been quite a while since I had stopped over to beg him for the money. It was the same routine there, up the long driveway, past the picture window searching, for some sign of his chrome wheelchair off to the side of the drapes. Nothing changed and as his doorknob turned open, I stepped in and called out to him. "Daddy, Daddy, are you here?"

Not even three steps in, I never heard the sound of his normal gruff; instead, he started right in on this one, that one and lastly, mother, which told me, he was on the warpath. Ignoring his outrage, I proudly slipped the cash on his lap, when he suddenly stopped ranting and let it slip off to the floor. Yelling he didn't want it, he was on his muscle and in a foul mood, I should have left, but didn't. Even after begging for him to take it, he began to swat at my hand, bellowing to get out and take my lousy money with me. For him, it was all about mother, dear sweet mother, who he was still on the warpath with in his own head. For me, it could have been one of many things that had left me emotionally injured, but one thing for sure; my tolerance was not up to taking any more crap from him. It pushed me hard enough to explode right in his face, yelling loud above his voice, with insult on top of insult. Wide eyed, his face twisted in rage and he said it all, throwing good old Eileen in my face. With our faces one of the same, I stormed out slamming the door hard behind me, and mumbling under my breath, kind of like him "Man you're such a jerk, God I hate you!"

On the ride home, even as it was my first time to have lashed out at father, I refused to give way to tears and figured with his high expenses he could damn well call me when he needed the money. Oh but the thought of Eileen and the fact we were still not on speaking terms, drained what energy I had left in me. When it rains it pours and no sooner had I arrived home, the phone rang and Jessie's voice came through nervous, informing me, Morgan our attorney, needed to see us both in his office right away. It sounded serious coming from Jessie and not two days later, I dressed to perfection and put on two dabs of the perfume, I knew he loved. By the time we met up, my heart was racing in fear as to why Morgan wanted to see us so badly. Watching me in an odd fashion from time to time, it was hard to know where Jessie's head was and I kept my fears to myself. As awkward as it felt, it was plain to see, in spite of everything; we still had our own love thing going on. Once we arrived, Jessie opened the door for me and after coming face to face with Morgan, he told us to have a seat in his office. Minutes later he walked in talking as if he was in a hurry to just get to the point. Having been up on everything going on in our lives, he started by mentioning Jessie's reckless behavior. None of what he was saying made any sense. He was suggesting we file for divorce, to separate the financial mess we made of things, to protect ourselves from a lawsuit. Looking inquisitively at Jessie, I couldn't help but to speculate what kind of added financial trouble he might have gotten us into.

On a casual note, Morgan suggested that we do a quick no fault divorce to keep it simple and keep what was left of our credit, out of harms way. While he caught sight of our fallen faces, he padded our troubled reaction, with the objective that once this was behind us; we could remarry and have a fresh start. With our emotions stirred up, between the shock and confusion of it all, we signed our names. It was official, we had just filed for divorce and yet, we still didn't get it. Pushing his desk chair back, as Morgan got up to shake our hands, he made note that we would receive our hearing notice in the mail and he would see us then. Walking out of the office with Morgan following us, as Jessie stepped into the restroom, Morgan leaned forward, whispering firmly "Just, get him home."

Once we were back on the road, Jessie pulled up to a well-known drive through window and ordered two cups of coffee. With our emotions in a knot, when he then suggested we stop off to talk, my head nodded in agreement. Having parked with a view of the lake, with the high waves splashing up over the rocks, it was the perfect private place. Snowflakes were already in the air and the dread of winter moving in so early, affected my mood also. We started out on a calm note, but as our voices rose, so did our frustration and accusations, taking us to livid tears. We cried for all our losses, for what was and what was to come. When I mentioned we had a chance of getting approved on the double house, it brought a smile of hope to Jessie's lips. Just the fact that it was big enough for all of us to reunite back together, at that moment we saw it as the answer to all of our problems. With this hope of sunshine peeking through the stormy clouds over our heads, it felt as if our hard times might soon be a thing of the past. One long passionate kiss lingered on, before we parted.

In the days ahead, my attorney's heavy words to get him back home, stayed glued in my head. It haunted me right up to when our court date arrived in the mail, taking my troubled mind elsewhere. Just as Morgan said, it was scheduled for only weeks away; only Jessie was nowhere to be found. It left me crazed, wondering how he could just disappear at a time like this. With the holidays having come and gone, December would soon be here and already I had the Christmas blues. Seeing it wasn't the jolliest time to get a divorce, Missy lightened my anguish, by pointing out, maybe that was all it was with Jessie, the blues. Instead of allowing me to dwell on the divorce, two days later, she came home with a basketful of apples, suggesting we should bake our troubles away. Pleased with herself, she said they were the last pick of the liter, laughing, because she meant to say it was the last pick of the season. So, we baked five homemade apple pies, until they were golden brown. Mum they smelled delicious and filled the house with their wonderful aroma. Having gone totally overboard, we were overwhelmed in pies and decided to walk two of them upstairs to the people, we still didn't know. Climbing the stairs, we were giggling at how out of breath we were and on the third knock, just when we were ready to hike back down, the door opened and a lovely girl with a baby boy on her right hip, stood staring at us. Realizing the pies were for her, her face lit up and she shyly invited us to step in. Just as she finished setting them down on the counter, three toddlers with their mouths smudged with traces of jelly, came tearing in. Turning shy the instant they saw us, they began to hide their faces behind her frilly long skirt.

Making small talk with all of the children crying in the background, we chatted about the snowflakes arriving early, which took us to asking her when she would be putting up her tree. Her face fell; it was hard to tell if it was devastation or embarrassment as she spoke. "With two sick children, we are fortunate if we can put food on the table, there is no extra money for things like trees or presents, we make our own presents from noodles and paints."

Laughing in the background the children were tearing through the house in play, which explains all the footsteps above our heads and the shaky ceilings. Guilty of having been judgmental, I had failed to see the burden of hardship, they carried with such strength and sacrifice. By the time we walked back down the steps, we were both on the same page and knew just what we had to do. We waited until late that evening before we put in a call to David, just in case he stopped off for cocktails. His heart made it easy and we didn't have to ask twice. He expressed his relief for them to do some good, since the toys only sat useless, offering for us to take the Christmas tree as well. In his pain it was all about the power of one! One giving man would make Christmas for all those little toddlers. Here that big box of toys, that had drawn us in time and again, carried its own purpose and had a mind of its own.

Lost in the excitement of giving, we put our own worries to rest and got right down to business. Before you knew it, the toys were wrapped in red Santa paper and stacked in cardboard boxes, ready to go. On the day we were planning to take the tree and boxes of presents upstairs, snow lightly covered the grass, adding to our spirit. By noon, we headed up the stairs with the over filled boxes, dragging the tree from behind, creating such a ruckus, the door flew open just as we got to the landing. When her wide eyes fell on the tree and the boxes filled with wrapped presents, she began to weep in joy. By then all the little tots were squealing and tearing around in excitement. Her face shined while she sorted through the colorful gifts, expressing how excited she was to get out the decorations the children had made and to put them on the new tree. It was enough to melt us down into tears and for the rest of the day, we felt trouble free and we knew, we did good!

Having put my depression and concerns to Jessie's whereabouts on the back burner, it was back to the old grind, being it was only days from our hearing. Still there was no word from him. According to his mother, no one knew anything about his disappearance or his whereabouts. It was one story, then another while nothing added up. Worrying that he would not show his face in court, reality set in, raising my anger up another notch. On top of my anger, a million fearful thoughts were running through my head. It left me wishy-washy; Jessie had certainly proved he was no angel, having seen the condoms. It left the possibility of another woman floating in and out of my jealous thoughts. Something wasn't right. This time he really did it and this time, Missy couldn't smooth things over for him with excuses. It was down to the last day and just when I was ready to call and postpone the hearing, the phone rang and it was Jessie. His voice flowed through the receiver, as if he did not have a worrisome thought. Steaming in his calmness, I snapped. "So where the hell have you been, you had me sick with worry, so tell me, where have you been the last few weeks? And please tell me, you didn't mention the divorce to your mother."

He told me exactly what I asked for him to say, that she didn't know jack about nothing. Once he set my mind to rest, I let out a moan of relief. Past that, utter silence filled the line, that's it nothing was his answer to his whereabouts, so I started in again. After ignoring my interrogation, he moved my anger over to where we should meet in the morning and cut it short. Holding the receiver with nothing but the sound of buzzing going on, felt like a slap in the face. By early morning with my emotions still scorched, my gut churned with the dread of the day. Getting ready, after having been living in a state of denial, it was hard to believe that this day was even real. By the time I arrived at the restaurant, Jessie was waiting outside, looking more handsome than ever. Still in search for some answer to his whereabouts, studying him, he stood with the same face and same smile. Yet staring into his eyes, his blue unreadable eyes gazing back were those of a stranger. While we were waiting for a table, in a restless state, Jessie excused himself twice to use the phone. Once we were seated, seeing neither of us had an appetite, we only ordered coffee, while Jessie added in several packets of sugar. Maybe having switched back to sugar, is what made him seem so antsy, but when I asked him again where he had vanished to and whom he had called, he quickly changed the subject. His secrecy to his whereabouts wasn't helping any; it was only giving me more reason to keep drilling. By then it was time to go and we drove all the way to the courthouse in silence.

Once we arrived, Morgan was there and we waited outside the carved wooden doors, restlessly sitting and occasionally standing, until someone stepped out and loudly announced our names. His voice silenced the hall and it was sensitive to my jumpy nerves; it added more tremble to my fingers. Standing in front of the judge, it was simple and quick, while our voices were barley needed past a yes or no. It was over just like that; even Morgan, past standing there, skated on that one. Once we were informed that the divorce wouldn't be final for three days, we walked out together. Waiting on the elevator, it was obvious we were both rattled and Morgan took that note on which to exit, saying he would stay tuned. This ordeal had taken its toll on our emotions and we sat out on a bench and shared a cigarette, just people watching. Once we were back on the sidewalk, Jessie was back to being the Jessie I knew and we began to cling to one another for dear life. It was a moment back in time and I wanted it to live on forever and it was obvious, we felt one of the same. With love in the air, it didn't take much to talk our selves into grabbing a bite to eat. Stopping at a place in the busy section of downtown, like the old days, we had salad with the same dressing, shared a shrimp cocktail, taking turns dipping one into the spicy sauce. Once the server picked up our plates, we were sitting over a cup of coffee lost in serious talk. In a heated moment as our moods began to change, a look of stiffness covered his face. Evidently, he didn't want to say where, or whom he had been with in the last few weeks and he began to stumble over his words, trying to satisfy me with an answer. Something wasn't right; he was too incomplete and mysterious and it was plenty obvious he was covering something. Of course I knew he was lying through his teeth. But when he came back at me with that boyish grin of his, it blew my suspicion of him being with someone else, out of the picture. Falling right into his charm, while pushing the unevenness of his story out of my mind, after battle and war, we were back in a love mode.

By the time we had left the restaurant, we decided to make a day of it and Christmas shopped for hours, we shopped till we were ready to drop. Jessie picked out a special present for each of the kids, along with a few shaving items, he mentioned he needed. Our bags were full, snowflakes were falling and when he lovingly brushed the strands of hair from my face, his warm eyes twinkled, melting me like a snowman in the heat of summer. Oh Jessie, with his mood uplifted, he appeared so together; just like times past. Now a tinted mirage was all that I saw, a pretense of what my hungry heart had been yearning for. Walking thought the snow, the bright sparkling glow of lights and all of the decorated trees displayed on the square, brought us to a standstill. In a moment of being swept away, we held on tight to one another's hands, promising that today, would mark our new beginning. The evening frigid air broke our trance and we found our way to a warmer place, settling in to have dinner. Reminiscing over the memories of when we first met, we shared a seafood fondue and it was somewhere in the heart of the strawberry pie, when reality hit us right between the eyes.

It took no time, no time at all, for our conversation to become as uncomfortable as the fondue that already settled hard in the pit of my ribs. Joshua, all the condoms in Jessie's briefcase, along with everything else we had lost in our struggle, hit the fan. Accusations and more flew, until we were emotionally exhausted and laid down our arms in defeat. It was the hot coco that Jessie insisted we get, that chocolate covered our mood, and shortly after, we talked of our future with the high hope, the house loan would be approved and he would return home. Loading up my car with the packages and the children's cherished presents, by the time his lips left mine, I was sure that all of our promises for our tomorrows would come to life. With my last promise being, I would call him the following day, just as he stepped into his truck, he sent me a contented smile of leisure. Pleased that our day had been filled with so many possibilities, I returned his smile with a contented smile of my own. Again in my mirage, he appeared nothing less than together and everything felt next to perfect. Only in all of my perfection and denial, I was wrong, our attorney was wrong, and the whole damn world, was wrong, wrong, wrong!

The following day, it was clear skies and frigid cold and my mood was somewhere up on cloud nine. No sooner did I get out of work, just as I promised, I put in a call to Jessie. By late evening, still with no answer, after having spent a day in love and bliss, my heart sank to my knees. Convinced his mother may have gotten wind of something, I was betting she was trying to put the brakes on to anything, surrounding my name. When another twenty-four hours came to pass, still with no word from him, I was crazed by the time I picked up the phone and called the number he had given me to his new place of employment. When a male answered announcing his name, I asked to speak with Jessie. Seconds of silence passed before he began to speak again. "Who, who's calling, please?"

Not taking our divorce to heart and anxious to get past him and over to Jessie, I answered with no second thoughts. "His wife."

He never once stumbled on his words, instead, he responded as if he were reporting on the weather, "Oh I'm sorry, but he expired sometime yesterday."

What! His damn choice of words was ridiculous and I figured he was just like everyone else who thought I had injured Jessie. Not waiting for him, I responded first, "Oh, okay I see, expired, as in dead, please, would you just let me speak to him."

Just as I started to repeat myself, the volume of his voice was so soft, I had to strain my ears too make out what he was trying to say. "Yes, I'm so sorry, he killed himself yesterday, he shot himself, I'm so sorry."

No longer hearing his voice, the phone tumbled out from my fingers to the floor, right as my knees gave way. The receiver was left lying on its side, with a faint hello calling out to me. It took moments longer for the sound of my outburst of sobs to catch up to my moving lips. "Oh my God, he shot himself, why, oh why, God why? The gun, oh God the gun, the gun, he must have taken it, oh God, he's dead, he's dead."

My hysterical cries and screams filled the room and traveled out of the open window getting Joshua and Missy out of their chairs and up on their feet. In a panic they both came tearing in, yelling, "What, what happened, what's wrong, are you okay?"

Screaming, no one could understand one hysterical word I was trying to get out. "The gun, he's dead, oh God, he's dead."

Frantic, Joshua began to lose his cool at the same time that he was trying to shake me out of hysteria. "Please damn it talk to me, who's dead, come on, please, will you just talk to me."

Crying out in a low hollow voice that I didn't recognize as my own, the words finally escaped from deep inside me. "Jessie, he's dead, he's dead, oh God, he shot himself, I think he took the gun, why, why dear God would he do this?"

Breaking, Joshua yelled out looking at Missy, " What gun, what gun is she talking about, the gun you guys said disappeared?"

Without acknowledging him, she broke, sobbing with her face buried in her hands. Joshua stood hunched over with silent tears and later that evening, he disappeared for many-hours. Running I suppose, from him self, from guilt, perhaps he was running from everything that we had portrayed as a family and had failed at. My children and I clung together in devastation and when we could sob no more, a fog of emptiness hung above our heads.

Once I reached Jessie's brother, it was true, oh dear God it was true, Jessie was dead. Even while he was pointing the finger of blame at me, he broke down sobbing; he had shot himself at his mother's. As he described the unexplained gun with the finest of details, there was no doubt in my mind. It was the same missing gun we thought Simon took, the same gun

Jessie swore on his life he never saw. Sobbing to his brother, the second I brought up Jessie's wedding ring and begged to have it, he cut me off, not waiting for my reply before hanging up. Hours later, when he finally called back, his voice came back at me dead cold; claiming it disappeared. In spite of knowing in my heart, his brother wasn't going to allow me to have it, the shame of it all, left me feeling undeserving and I couldn't argue it. He cut off every word I tried to get in about the loving time we had shared, avoiding the word divorce. No longer allowing me to connect with or share in his broken emotions, he wasn't interested and turned the conversation to his mother. It was worse, than what the worst of the worst, could be expected. She held no mercy and as far as she was concerned, final or not, we were divorced. During which time he expressed how it would just kill her if I dared to show my face. My mind drifted, wondering how she got wind of our hearing. But! She was willing to grant me one hour after she left. It would be after everyone had the chance to pay their last respects before the casket would be closed. Again without my face in her sight, at their wishes, he would be cremated the following day. Without any concern for me, I was forbidden to share in the loss of Jessie or allowed any closure to his suicide. It was a brutal punishment! It was excruciating torture and I couldn't get past the shame and I couldn't get past the hate in their voices as they pointed out, "It was my hand and my hand alone that pulled the trigger on the gun!"

Oh God, in all their blame, my sorrow and shame was filtering in and out of a great silent anger. Having been stripped down like a criminal, I waved my rights, nothing mattered, Jessie was dead, he was dead and over and over I sobbed out "Oh God why-why-why? Their aloofness froze me stiff and she would have her way. Reacting back like a spineless, beaten down animal, shamed me then. But it shames me even more today that I stepped to the back. If only, if only…but then again, what if!

On that day, after the sun had gone down, the time had arrived for me to leave. It was near freezing when Missy and I headed out, while Joshua stayed behind in broken spirit, refusing to accept an allotted time with all their fingers pointing in judgment. Looking out through the car window, the last of some fallen leaves, blew wild through the wind, slowly winding down and sticking to the snow. Pulling in the parking lot, there were still several cars there, while I heard myself praying, I could get through this. After walking through the exquisite doors, there was a small number of people left scattered, quietly talking. Catching quick sight of me, without delay, Jessie's brother walked over to us. While never making eye contact, he mumbled out that I was early and luckily missed his mother. Nodding towards where Jessie laid, he said, "Well go ahead."

Before we had the chance to approach the casket, a woman dressed in business attire approached me. She introduced herself as the head director, before openly stating. "You're not welcome here by the family members, so please, you have exactly thirty minutes."

Thirty short minutes, was only half the time I had been allotted by his mother. Something deep inside me, longed to scratch out her judgmental eyes, but her strong intimidating tone kept me still. With the last of the people standing around watching, I walked over to where Jessie's body lay without any life, silently crying out to him. "Oh God Jessie, please Jessie, please, don't leave me."

Oh God, this couldn't be happening, but it was...and he was dead! Staring down at him, my eyes rested on his chest, praying that he would breathe and that his chest would rise just once and then he would come back to life, come back to me. Only he lay lifeless with his head resting on a satin pillow. Staring down at Jessie's set face, lacking any expression, breaking my heart I cried out in anguish, for everyone to hear "Oh Jessie, I love you, I love you, I will always love you!"

Kneeling down in front of the casket, my heart was locked into begging him, begging God, begging and begging for forgiveness. But he couldn't hear me, but if he could in spirit, I wondered if he would cast me away, as the horrible undeserving person everyone believed that I was. Inside of my head, their crucifying words of blame were going off. "It was my hand and my hand alone that pulled the trigger. Dear god was it, was it my fault?' Someone was motioning to me, pulling me away from my self-conviction and destructive thoughts. It was the heartless director who refused to hear a word I tried to cry out to her. Having been standing guard to keep an eye on me, she was looking at her watch, motioning it was time to leave. Deep shame set in and if insulting and humiliating me in front of the people still there, was what she was trying to do, she had succeeded endlessly. But the faces staring at me, were pointing, blaming and driving me further into guilt. In the hours that came to pass, I had been stoned with blame and accusations and marked, as some sort of a demon. With all their silent daggers, it would have been less heartbreaking, if they just stuck a stake through my heart. In my despair the deliberation of dying with him, walked out with me. Having been kicked out to the curb in such disgrace and contempt, the outcome would forever carry on.

Tears filled the room, I noticed Norma was sniffling and wiping at a tear as she excused herself and got up to give me a time out. This time when she poured a cool glass of water from her iced pitcher, she poured two and after a few swallows, she appeared to compose herself. Moving back into my session with more self-control, Norma relaxed back into her seat.

Two days later, having had to return to work, was one of the hardest things I ever had to emotionally hold up to. A painted smile didn't hide every emotion I harbored. At the end of my shift, my manager was waiting on me in his office, leaving me with the hope he had a change of heart, and would offer me the time off I had requested. Only he didn't, instead, he fired me for having heavy baggage. On the ride home, humiliation took me over to bitterness for everything society and all their self-seeking rules stood for. Emotionally broken, a couch, a blanket, was all I needed to bury myself from the whole damn world. Now my battle and the anxiety over Jessie's wellbeing were out of my hands. It all left me powerless to fight off the heavy depression in me. Seeing Jessie had been cremated and his ashes were put in a mausoleum up in the top vault, taking him even further from my reach. The devastation and loss inside my soul were taking me so far down to a place of darkness, that I couldn't see to find my way back.

After emotionally exhausting myself, my mind would shut down, with time of nothingness. In the hours that my mind would run wild, Morgan's words to get Jessie home left me with the regret, if only, if only I hadn't brushed off his warning. The haunting what ifs and all of the unexplained questions sat unanswered like a puzzle with pieces missing. Everything surrounding Jessie's death was left a mystery, with any answers out of my reach. His family's accusation that it was my hand and my hand alone, that pulled the trigger, began to trigger nightmares of gunshots going off in my head. While my nightmares woke me in a cold sweat, past getting up to relieve myself or feed my belly that churned from the build up of acid, I remained on the couch for days. It was a few days before the eve of Christmas, when the gifts Jessie had chosen with love, was my strength that got me off the couch. But my own thoughts of dying got up with me and walked every step of the way with me. When Missy saw me up off the couch, relief ran across her face whispering. "Thank God, Oh thank God."

It was only days after the holiday's had passed, when the news came in that we had been approved and could take ownership of the house. Even with all its needed repairs, finally it was somewhere for us to call home. When our big day finally arrived, having had no closure, there could be no forgiveness, no healing and no moving on, only, moving in. In spite of fighting off guilt, it became apparent that all of our fault and blame for our part followed us from behind and moved right in with us. Everything, that taunting word, everything! In our heads, it finally had its day of victory; wiping us clean of a life we had fought so hard for. All of our emotions remained sickly twisted for everything we did and everything we didn't. But when the lights went out each night and only the sound of the creeks from the unfamiliar house could be heard, I crawled into bed and slept with the softness of the blankets tucked in tight all around me. No more sleeping on the floor and no more sharing one couch in such a small space. The fresh sent of linens and its comfort was something I had once taken for granted and oh, but it felt so good, so wonderful and safe. Only it didn't matter, nothing now mattered, not today, not tomorrow, because yesterday will never live again! "Oh God, Jessie why aren't you here!"

...Butterflies Fly Free...

*Oh precious china doll upon my shelf I bought you for only
myself...so now I could see, the child within I missed of me...This
gift of a doll has helped me to recall, some of my bad falls...to
help me stand tall...to see I deserved all the rights to reserve the
giving to myself and to change these cards of feelings, in-which
they were dealt*

Day after day falling into many, many months, guilt continued to eat
away at everything we stood for and the life we had together was slowly
deteriorating. It was all preventing us from moving ahead. In his own state
of turmoil, Joshua was ridden with fault over Jessie's death. Recklessly
and selfishly he began to play out all of his emotions, until he gave way to
exhaustion. Then, he was back home again, loving and giving, until his
temperament exploded again in another storm of fury, leaving behind hot
callous words, to simmer in our hearts. But Joshua, with his eyes dark and
stormy, was off to escape the bad sin of our forbidden love, which could
never receive the nourishment to live. It left a great energy of fear that he
was slipping further and further away each time he was off and running. It
almost made me hate him, during the times of his fury and selfish reckless
actions. Suddenly, Joshua was someone I used to know. It was ripping me
apart and I realized that I didn't like how I felt inside when I was with
him. This was the same Joshua, who had once shared a strong and lasting
bond with me, now we were becoming disconnected, leaving me feeling
lonely in his company. It was driving me to the brink; I couldn't sleep, I
couldn't think and I sank deeper down inside myself. And I didn't rise up
to fight back, as some might expect. But I too, began to run in an angry
and reckless state, blaming Jessie and Joshua for all of my anguish and for
leaving me alone in this damn world of misery.

Only my misery was interrupted by the heartbreak of having heard,
David had lost his life to liver disease. Perhaps his broken heart robbed

him of his fight for life. Still it all seemed so unfair, that David, who gave so much, still had so much taken from him. But his death touched us all, it seemed as if everyone we touched in one way or another was dying and it was all dancing in my head, adding more misery on top of misery. Trying to escape from it all, there was no place to run and no place to hide. It felt as if death was the only way out, keeping the thought close to my heart. Driving for miles, living in a song and running from both life and death, it was all following me in my rearview mirror. All of the emotional chains from my past that were never released still kept me a prisoner. Anti-social, hell, that's what I was! It was another one of daddy's crippling traits that eventually caught up with me. Undeniably, I had pushed and drove off everyone in life, living in a bubble of pretense, believing I had created my own little world of peace. Only it had all crashed down around us, while running harder, only left me out of breath ending up on another dead-end street. It was never a leap forward; instead, it always took me back to the days of my yesterdays, with time slipping deeper into each day. It was all eating at me, turning my emotions into uncontrolled anger. Eventually, with all of this anger and misery going on and taking up my brain-space, I would sit pondering, whether I was worthy enough to live or contemptible enough to die. For two grave years, I began living unoccupied in myself, while my irrational behavior, was slowly pushing me over the edge to self-destruct. Still with no place to run and no place to hide, a glass of wine held the power that took me out of my shell and kept me smiling, for as long as I fed it and fed it I did.

It was a drizzly and cloudy afternoon and the forecast was calling for severe thunderstorms. In a small corner bar, it was white zinfandel I was drinking and the second glass had just come my way. It was then when I saw her for the first time. Sabrina was her name. Her big round blue eyes brushed with a soft lavender shadow stood out against the strands of blond hair, falling short around her chubby face. Her bright wide smile brought attention to her painted colored lips and big white teeth. Her smile was the first thing that attracted me and instantly set me at ease. Being she was one of only a few people there, she struggled as she slid over to the seat next to me, making way to small conversation. Making the comment that there was something about me that drew her to me, she had some silly notion there was some spiritual reason we were supposed to meet. Suggesting that we move to a table, without waiting for my answer, she grabbed her green and brown colorful cane and began carefully getting up to her feet. Thinking to myself, "Okay, what the hell," I picked up my glass of wine and cocktail napkin and joined her at the small corner table for two. Her face flashed with pain, as she struggled to get seated and get comfortable in her chair, bringing me an instant wave of compassion for her. She was easy to talk to and it was even easier, after a loud crack took us into darkness, silencing the blaring jukebox. With only the candlelight flickering between us, she began to chuckle at the dark reflection of my eyes, nicknaming me on the spot, the brown-eyed baby. Relaxing into my seat, we began to compare notes about our lives and before long; she had me spilling out my guts to her. At some point she reached over and placed her dainty hands over mine and began to pray in tongue for me. It didn't seem silly, in fact, this unknown mystifying lady in the candlelight, smiling as if she was talking to God, brought me so much comfort, it left me with a desire to soak up more of her healing energy.

When Sabrina began to confide in me details about her life, even in the candlelight, when her tears began to give way, they stood out like glitter in the night. But when she began to reveal her horrifying secrets, it was such a horrifying visual image; it took me instantly to tears. She had been raped from the very young age of five, recalling the first time, only wearing little white ankle socks. It continued up until her early teen years, when the rapes abruptly stopped and when her brutal beatings began. Emotionally and physically scarred from abuse, she ran off and married at fifteen, failing with every abusive man she married after that. Her last attempt at another failed marriage is what led up to her becoming his hostage at knifepoint, for many horrifying days and dark nights. Sabrina had been repeatedly raped and beaten, until this imposter that she had married, was led away in handcuffs. In the end, left shamed and homeless, in her struggle to find her way back from poverty, she became the mother on the street for all the prostitutes and beaten down girls. Her delicate hands trembled as she revealed that he swore revenge, when he got out. It was clear she lived her life in fear of that day, when his jail sentence was finished. By then soaked in tears, suddenly with a flash, the lights came on and the jukebox began blasting, breaking the intensity of our intimacy. But it was one thing or another she had shared with me that hit home and made a great impact. It shook me hard enough to realize it was me that I was running from, me! For whatever reasons, somehow my life felt workable. Hugging Sabrina I squeezed her scribbled out number tightly in my hand, promising to call as I darted out.

No sooner did I walk out of the dim bar and into the fresh sunlight; I headed straight for the place that gave me the most healing energy, the lake. Plopping down onto the sand, the sound of the tide slipping in and slipping out put me into a trance of thought. Memories of Jessie and the life we had, was flashing in my head, bringing Joshua's forbidden love to my mind. The hate that had been building, because Joshua was running from himself, was on the rise. The power he was holding over me, was the power in which I gave. It was the power to make me laugh or cry and the power to bring me up or lay me down. It was enough to make me cringe inside of myself for giving away, the power that should only belong to me. Words of wisdom began dancing in my head, "Do not hate, it does not become you, do not love unhealthy, for it will dissolve you." Staring out to the water and beyond, its miles and miles of beauty took me to a spiritual plain. Loud echoes of the water were like music to my ears, calming my scattered thoughts that were running wild in my head. "Butterflies fly free, oh God please let me breathe again without this pain and remorse."

The waves were picking up and rapidly rolling in, slapping against the break wall, as the cool water ran back down over my feet, soothing my troubled mind. This was life and with the full view of the skies and the powerful roar of the water, it displayed its fortune of beauty. All this was our gift to help us endure life at its hardest moments and I wanted to stay locked into this peaceful tranquility forever. Oh how badly, I needed some kind of help to get me out from under these rocks that were binding me, and the quicksand that was pulling me down further. Suddenly the love I felt for God and his universe got me to my feet with the strength and courage to reach out for help, without the remorse that had been crippling me against taking steps forward.

If it were not for that day of recognition and only days later to accept Norma's hand that was held out to me in my unbalance state of mind, dear Lord, if it were not for that day. If I had not allowed Norma to guide me back from those horrifying roads of no return, this story in all probability would have had a different ending, perhaps more tragic. Yes, Norma was her simple name, yet she carried the strength to guide me to places, few of us would dare return, a place where our deepest secrets, lies and fears are met with the truth and forgiveness that awaits us. In our struggle to heal and grow, we, Joshua, Missy and I still struggle with many of our own un-dealt with emotions, in order to bring forth self-forgiveness. Still everyday is an ongoing struggle to make the right choice, falling back at times, in spite of knowing all the choices we make today, are what can bring forth great change and better tomorrows.

On that day when the loud ring of the telephone sounded, it was she, delivering the gruesome news. It was our cruel Witch-like-aunt. Oh God, she said, he said, but it was too late now! It was too late to say how sorry I was, remembering our last visit together and the big explosion of hateful words that had passed between us. It was daddy, oh dear God; he was cold and buried. Now with his flesh falling from the bone, she only now called us! Weeks had passed, weeks and in her own malice defense, she was casting accusations at us, Eileen and me. Yes, we were robbed of paying our last respects, blindly robbed of Father's inheritance and left with the torment, for the second time in my life, of having no closure! Her sneaky devious intentions of having held on to one of many, of father's wills, left her the soul beneficiary of all the $$$$, we never knew he had. Clean out and clean up. Afterward, she had the state lay him to rest, where his stone lays flat, covered with overgrown weeds. In our distortion of what had been cruelly done to us, Eileen and I came together shattered over the outcome of what our Witch-like-aunt had indulgingly dished out to us. Here, Daddy was gone and yet, we were still struggling over who was who and what was what and why he had left everything to turn out the way it did.

Daddy in all his bitterness and anger died an unhappy and lonely man. Seeing father had been emotionally crippled from all his hate, in my heart I knew I had longed for his love. It's almost ironic, here I have waited a lifetime for his simple words of love, that were now buried deep down under the dirt with him. But perhaps, as he has risen above his crippled mind and the vengeance that he had left for his children to bear, maybe in his penance, he will bring about a great change through some spiritual form, perhaps, somehow, someway!

It was exactly one year to the day of daddy's death when she passed. My Witch-like-aunt that is and my heart held no mercy. In my mind, I cursed her loud, again and again, hoping she would rot in her cruelness and greed, having buried the whereabouts to father's money with her. It took a long time to realize, that all of the heavy build up of hate and bitterness that I had been carrying, just the weight of all these emotions, drained me day to day. Realizing along side of Norma, that my anger was keeping me a prisoner for as long as I let my hate rule, was a big break through for me. Once I truly got it and began to connect the dots to these empty emotions, it was strange. In as much as I gained an inner strength like I had never known and the strong desire to live, it ate away my desire to die. It was as if a light had been switched on and I could see past the darkness of my eyes the true definition of life and mortality.

Little did I know that the action of forgiving, gave me the freedom to move on to polish the tarnish that lay heavy on my bones. Slowly I began to learn to pick up the pieces of my life with this overwhelming feeling of deserving, guilt free, for the very first time in my life. It was somewhat of a miracle that I found, that the gift of acceptance was as great as the gift of feeling deserving. If only we would give the same unconditional love and care to ourselves, that we so generously are willing to give to others, just imagine, the rewards are glorious! Knowing we cannot fix or alter anyone other than our selves, it doesn't matter if it takes a lifetime to achieve self-respect and self-worth. If only I could have identified the difference of giving kindness and compassion, instead of needing to take on all of the rescuing to the degree that it was controlling me, if only.

Now after years of having gone down one terrifying road after another with Norma by my side, no longer wondering what it was, that made her think she could help me, we hugged as we said our goodbyes. It felt like a lifetime of gifted help that she had left me with and yet, I knew there was still a lot of work for me ahead. But! How does one ever say thank you to someone, for all of their care and patience? It was a second chance at life for me and as long as there is life there is hope. If you are breathing, you are a survivor! But the strange ability of writing that came about from nowhere and the eeriness of it all, just might make you wonder, it did me. In the early stages of my writing, in my denial and disbelief, the words wore me down, until I began to listen and better yet, hear. With the help of my spirit guides protecting and guiding me on this journey, it was faith wrapped around trust and belief, that had walked with me; with not one, but two sets of footprints.

The new growth of ones soul is nourished from within...let your own light shine for all the stimulation of new growth...let all the tears fall cleansing and bringing great change. Let us flower as spring...bringing on the brilliant radiance of colors to be shone upon our faces...with the greatest of desire of living through life throughout our souls...from our greatest consumptions... to the greatness of our goals.... Amen.

26559787R00179

Made in the USA
Charleston, SC
11 February 2014